THE HISTORY OF QUAKERISM

THE HISTORY OF QUAKERISM

By

Elbert Russell

DEAN EMERITUS OF THE DIVINITY SCHOOL
AND PROFESSOR OF BIBLICAL INTERPRETATION
DUKE UNIVERSITY

RICHMOND
INDIANA

Library of Congress 79-53169
I.S.B.N. 0-913408-52-2

1979

Printed by
PRINIT PRESS
Dublin, IN

To My Son

PREFACE

A SURVEY of Quaker historical literature reveals the lack of a relatively brief history giving a balanced treatment of all phases, periods and divisions of Quakerism with scholarly impartiality and scholarly method. The existing histories are either too long or confined to particular periods or phases of Quakerism. Brayshaw's *The Quakers: Their Story and Message* most nearly meets the need of a one-volume history, but it ignores later American Quakerism almost wholly, and in style and purpose it confessedly departs from a historical treatment. Elizabeth B. Emmott's *A Short History of Quakerism* stops with the year 1725.

Since none of our competent historians has such a history in hand or in prospect, I have undertaken the task of writing one. My purpose is to provide primarily a history of the Quaker movement as a whole, treating it as a segment of modern church history, relating it to its historic roots and to its environment, and in each period paying attention to the elements which are most important, such as the outstanding persons, the discipline, the conservative or progressive tendencies, or influential outside forces. I hope to give a balanced picture, unobscured by too much detail, of the Quaker movement, embracing all its periods and sections, including its chief phases and the significant activities, both personal and official, to which it gave rise.

The "Rowntree Series" of Quaker histories was planned by John Wilhelm Rowntree and edited and completed by Rufus M. Jones in collaboration with William Charles Braithwaite, Isaac Sharpless and Amelia M. Gummere. These volumes give with great detail and careful scholarship the basic material for any subsequent history of Friends down to 1900 A.D. My studies have deepened my appreciation of the painstaking and scholarly work of their editor and authors, and I acknowledge my great obligation to them both for materials and for frequent quotations, especially from passages of particularly apt expression or historical insight. For the quotations and particular information I have acknowledged my indebtedness in the footnotes.

The present work, however, is more than a one-volume abridgement of the Rowntree series. Since the publication of the latter, substantial additions have been made to our knowledge of Quaker history and to our historical literature; and in the last forty years many significant movements, changes and events have taken place. I have made use of this later literature and acknowledged my dependence on it in the footnotes. I have examined the original sources wherever possible in the preparation of the present work. In some cases I have referred to citations made in the Rowntree volumes or other modern works rather than to the original sources which are not easily accessible even to students.

I am under special obligation to the Duke University Library for assistance in securing needed books and periodicals; and to the Duke Research Council for financial assistance. I wish to acknowledge the many courtesies shown me by John L. Nickalls and Muriel Hicks of the Friends Library, Friends House, London; by Thomas E. Drake, Anna B. Hewitt and Amy L. Post of the Haverford College Library; by Virginia Walker and the late William I. Hull of the Swarthmore College Friends Historical Library and by Katherine C. Ricks of the Guilford College Library.

I was able to attend the Oxford and Edinburgh conferences in 1937 and the Utrecht conference in 1938 through the assistance and encouragement of Duke University and a group of American Friends, in connection with which trips I was able to make extensive use of indispensable material in the Friends Library in London. Among the Friends who made this possible were Walter C. Woodward, Editor of the *American Friend,* Alvin T. Coate of Indianapolis, J. Passmore Elkinton of Moylan, Pa., and Alfred C. Garrett of Philadelphia. I received helpful criticism of the prospectus and outline of my proposed history from A. Neave Brayshaw and Edward Grubb; and of the manuscript from Hubert W. Peet, Editor of *The Friend* (London) and John L. Nickalls, librarian of Friends Library. Thanks are due to the following American Friends who have read the manuscript and given helpful criticisms: Walter C. Woodward, Editor of the *American Friend* who also read the proofs, Harlow Lindley, Secretary of the Ohio State Archaeological and Historical Society, Thomas E. Drake, Assistant Professor of American History, Haverford College, Henry J. Cadbury, Professor of Divinity, Harvard Divinity School, and to my son, Josiah C. Russell, Associate Professor of History, the University of North Carolina. Valuable aid by many other friends in supplying materials and information is gratefully acknowledged.

Permission to reprint quotations from the following books is gratefully acknowledged:

Graham, *Conscription and Conscience,* courtesy of Thomas Nelson and Sons, Ltd.

Kelsey, *Friends and the Indians,* courtesy of Jonathan M. Steere.

Klain, *Quaker Contributions to Education in North Carolina,* courtesy of the author.

Thomas, *History of Friends in America,* courtesy of the Book Committee of Philadelphia Yearly Meeting.

Trevelyan, *England under the Stuarts,* courtesy of G. P. Putnam's Sons and Methuen and Co., Ltd.

Wright, *The Literary Life of the Early Friends,* courtesy of Columbia University Press.

I wish to acknowledge the assistance of my secretary, Margaret Smith, in preparing the manuscript of the book; of Asmond L. Maxwell in the checking of references and in the preparation of the bibliography, and of LaFon Vereen in preparing the index.

ELBERT RUSSELL

Duke University,
Durham, N. C.

CONTENTS

II. The Age of Quietism, 1691–1827

Period I. *The Aftermath of Toleration, 1691–1737*

Period II. *The Peculiar People, 1737–1784*

Period III. *Philanthropy and the Transition to Evangelicalism, 1784–1827*

III. The Modern Revival and Reconstruction, 1827–1941

Period I. *Separations, 1827–1861*

Period II. *Reconstruction, 1861–1914*

INTRODUCTION

1. The Method of Quaker History

Quaker history involved many elements, each of which may conceivably be given the primary emphasis. The biographical interest is naturally prominent. Quaker history is the creation of its great leaders. A religion of the spirit expresses itself primarily through the personalities of men and women. Its method is the method of incarnation. The Quaker organization has been relatively unimportant except to serve as a nursery of sensitive and adventurous souls, and to carry on and perpetuate their concerns and principles. A large part, almost a preponderating part, of the Quaker historian's source materials is found in journals, memoirs and correspondence. The early histories, especially Sewel's and Bowden's, were largely extracts from the biographies of the founders. The biographical element must always be prominent in any true presentation of Quaker history.

Another element that bulks large in all Christian history is church organization. With some religious bodies it is the prominent element—the organization dominating, using and eclipsing to a large extent the personal interests. Such is not the case with Friends; yet the Society as an organization has a history, embracing its constitution, its rules of discipline, its separations and its official activities. The minutes of yearly, quarterly and monthly meetings are a rich mine of source material for the history of organized Quakerism.

The history of a religious denomination may also be

viewed as a phase or division of Christian history in the large. It is interesting that two of our most widely used histories were originally written as sections of a series of publications on church history: Harvey's *The Rise of the Quakers* and Thomas' *History of the Society of Friends in America*. Remote as Quakerism may have seemed at times from the world about it, it has always been a part of Christian history, influenced and conditioned by the life, faith and actions of the contemporary religious world. This has been brought out with especial force in Jones' *Later Periods of Quakerism*. A striking evidence of this is the fact which Amelia M. Gummere has demonstrated, that in spite of Friends' desire to avoid following the vain and changing fashions of the world, most of the Quaker styles originated in Paris.[1]

2. Divisions of Modern Church History

Before examining the periods into which the history of Quakerism naturally divides, it is well to have in mind an outline of modern church history for the sake of comparison. It is usually divided into three divisions somewhat as follows:

1. *The Reformation Period* (1517–1648). It extends from the posting of Luther's theses at Wittenberg to the Peace of Westphalia, which closed the Thirty Years War. In this period the Protestant Reformation spread throughout western Europe; it obtained a permanent hold in the northern countries, chiefly in the form of national churches, and settled its doctrines and polity. It was finally turned back by the Catholic reaction in Spain, Italy, Austria, and parts of Germany. It became involved in political struggles and civil wars in Germany, Switzerland, France and Holland. The Thirty Years War marked the end of the growth of Protestantism on the Continent.

---

[1] *The Quaker: A Study in Costume*, p. 190.

2. *The Period of Critical Individualism* (1648–1789). It extends from the Peace of Westphalia to the outbreak of the French Revolution. In this period the whole system of Protestant beliefs and practices, especially its inheritance from medieval Catholicism, was subjected to critical examination in the light of individual reason. It began with a period of religious exhaustion and indifference which was followed by the rise of various forms of rationalism and by the religious revivals of continental Pietism and of English Wesleyanism and Evangelicalism. The doctrines of the supremacy of the individual reason in religion and of the "rights of man" in politics culminated in the overthrow of autocratic authority in church and state in the French Revolution. In this period the latent individualism of Protestantism worked itself out to its logical negative results.

3. *The Period of Revival and Reconstruction* (1789–1941). It extends from the outbreak of the French Revolution to the present time, although the actual reconstruction hardly began until Napoleon's overthrow (1815). In this period occurred the beginnings of the positive social expression of Protestantism and the reorganization of church and society on a voluntary and democratic basis. It was characterized by organized Bible study, foreign missions, evangelical revivals, theological reconstruction, individual coöperation in organized philanthropy and social reforms across denominational lines and finally by interdenominational coöperation and federation.

This survey shows that Quakerism arose after the close of the Reformation movement on the Continent and raises the question whether it was a belated wave of the Reformation or a forerunner of the individualistic developments of the succeeding period. The English Reformation, of which the Quaker movement was a part, was really twofold: its first phase was mainly political, being initiated by the king, and the second, religious, being forced by the Puritans. The French Revolution did not produce such an immediate effect in England as on the Continent. The real beginning of the modern period in England was marked by the repeal of the Test and Corporation Acts in 1828 and the passage of the Reform Bill of 1832. The periods of the English Reformation are therefore more nearly as follows:

1. *The Governmental Reformation* (1509–1558), from the accession of Henry VIII to the death of Mary Tudor. The Oxford reformers, Tyndale's Bible, and Henry's divorce of Catherine led to the break with the Pope (1531); but the church, with the king as its head, was still Catholic in doctrine and ritual, although slowly driven toward Protestant positions. Under Mary came the Catholic reaction when many of the most conscientious Protestants were driven to the Continent where they came under Calvin's influence.

2. *The Puritan Reformation* (1558–1689). With Elizabeth's accession the exiles came home determined to purify the church of all remnants of "popery." The Bible was translated in 1611 under the patronage of King James. The Puritans put conscience with an emphasis on personal and social righteousness into the English religion. A new phase began with their control of the Long Parliament, and after the Civil War and the execution of King Charles I, they ruled England under Cromwell. After the reaction of the Restoration the government was made permanently Protestant under William and Mary, and a measure of relief was secured for Nonconformists in the Toleration Act of 1689.

The Period of Critical Individualism in England extended from the Toleration Act to the repeal of the Test and Corporation Act (1828) which removed the political disabilities of Catholics and Dissenters. It was characterized by religious apathy, the influence of Deism and the Wesleyan and Evangelical revivals with their social, educational and missionary "programs."

The Period of Modern Reconstruction in England was

practically the same as in Europe and America. Of special importance were the disestablishment of the Irish Church, the Tractarian movement, the Great Disruption in the Church of Scotland and the final reunion of the Scottish churches, the relief of the Nonconformists from church rates, and the reconstruction of theology in the light of the natural sciences, Darwinism and Biblical criticism.

3. The Place of Quaker History in Modern Church History

The foregoing outline shows that the rise of the Society of Friends coincides with the last part of the second division of the Reformation in England. George Fox began his Seeker wanderings in 1643, the year after the outbreak of the Civil War; he began to preach in 1647 and he died in 1691, shortly after the Revolution of 1688 and the Toleration Act. The formative period of the Quaker movement was thus coincident with the fiercest struggles and the moral victory of Puritanism. If, therefore, Quakerism was organically related to contemporary history, it should be by its chronological position the final development of the English reformation, the most protestant phase of Protestantism.

This suggestion is confirmed by an examination of the geographical distribution of Quakerism. Throughout most of its history, it has remained almost altogether within the English-speaking world. The territory in which it got a foothold during its formative period, and beyond which it did not extend until the latter half of the nineteenth century, included England and Wales, Protestant Ireland, the Rhineland in Europe, and the English colonies in America. Hallowell asserts that "All Puritans were not Quakers, but all Quakers were Puritans." [2] This is true in

[2] *The Quaker Invasion of Massachusetts*, p. 125.

the sense that it was from among the English Puritans, Independents, Baptists, Seekers and other Nonconformists that the Society was chiefly recruited. Catholic France and Lutheran Germany remained practically untouched by the Quaker movement, except where the Albigenses in the south of France and the German and Dutch mystical brotherhoods along the Rhine (and in a few other places) had prepared the way for a religion of the Spirit. The "Publishers of Truth" made practically no converts directly from Catholicism and few from the state churches which represented the first stages of the Reformation, such as the Lutheran in Germany, the Reformed in Holland and Switzerland, and the Presbyterian in Scotland. The leap was too great from these faiths, which denied man's spiritual capacity and relied on the outward authority of church and state, to the Quaker reliance on the Inward Light. In Ireland it was only among the sectaries of Cromwell's troops and the Protestant "plantations" that Quakerism got a foothold. The Catholics of French and Spanish America proved as unresponsive to the Quaker missionaries as their co-religionists of Europe. The sects which fled from persecution in England and on the Continent and colonists who had lost contact with organized religion in the New World (as in Virginia and the Carolinas) formed the seed plot of American Quakerism.The geographical distribution of the Society of Friends indicates therefore that it constituted a third stage at least in the Reformation process.

This is indicated also by the relation of Quakerism to the Protestant principle of religious authority. The first Protestant leaders claimed the right to follow their own sense of truth and right as the ultimate authority. Luther asserted that "it is never safe for a man to go against his own conscience;" and Calvin claimed the right to interpret the Scriptures for himself under the leading of the Holy Spirit. But they refused to allow other Christians the same right; they were afraid to trust the Inward Light in other men as an adequate basis for church and society. Consequently Protestantism in its earlier stages felt compelled to rely on the state to supply an outward authority to safeguard the faith, preserve morality and enforce ecclesiastical discipline. It came to limit severely the rights of reason in the determination of religious truth and of conscience in the determination of duty; and it put the outward authority of state, church and Bible between the individual soul and God. On account of this inward contradiction between principle and practice Protestantism has never been at peace with itself. This contradiction the Quakers escaped by their doctrine of the sufficiency of the Inward Light. They are not unique in claiming for themselves the right to follow the Inward Guide, but in trusting it in all men as a sufficient basis for the reconstruction of the whole of life. It is in this sense true that, as the Discipline of the Five Years Meeting of Friends in America states it, the Quaker movement was "the logical conclusion of the Protestant Reformation and the culmination of the development of doctrine which had been advancing by irregular stages for more than a century." [3]

4. Divisions of Quaker History

The history of Quakerism falls naturally into three divisions as follows: [4]

I. *The Rise of the Society* (1647–1691), from George Fox's great experience until his death.
II. *Age of Quietism* (1691–1827), from George Fox's death until the separation of 1827 in America.
III. *The Revival and Reorganization of Quakerism* (1827–1941), from the separation of 1827 until the present time.

---

[3] *Uniform Discipline,* Introduction. Cf. Rowntree, J. S. *Quakerism Past and Present,* p. 165.

[4] See the table of contents for the subdivisions.

The first division naturally begins with Fox's decisive experience of the Inward Christ, although some would date its beginning from 1652, when he had his vision on Pendle Hill of a gathered people and began forming groups of followers among the Seekers of the North. Fox's death marks the close of the formative period.[5]

For nearly half a century afterward the Society remained in all important respects as it was in 1691. It had entered the territory which it was to occupy. Its organization had been outlined and the principal features put into operation. Barclay had given its doctrines classical form and Penn had founded Pennsylvania. The Toleration Act had relieved the Society of most of the persecutions and disabilities that so rigorously conditioned its early efforts and had given it at last a legal place among English Nonconformists. Most of the active leaders in the founding of the Society were dead. The three leaders, Margaret Fell Fox, William Penn and George Whitehead, who survived Fox, added nothing creative to the Society after 1691. From this point its history was determined by the second generation to whom Quakerism was chiefly an inheritance to be preserved.[6]

The second division, which has been called "the Middle Ages of Quakerism," [7] comes properly to an end with the "Hicksite" separations in America in 1827–1828, which had repercussions in English Quakerism in 1835–1836, and in large measure dominated the Society's history until 1861. Friends shared to a large degree in the general apathy

---

[5] Some would put it at various later dates, such as, about 1700 (which is an abritrary date, better for America than England) or at 1718 when Penn died; or as late as 1722 when a satisfactory Affirmation Act was passed (so apparently Braithwaite); or at 1725 (so Jones and Emmott, apparently for the sake of a round number). Harvey on the other hand closes his account of the rise of the Society at 1675.

[6] Rowntree, J. Stephenson, *Quakerism Past and Present,* p. 68.

[7] See Rowntree, J. S., *op. cit.*, p. 67, and Thistlewaite, W., *Lectures on the Rise and Progress of Friends,* London, 1865, pp. 76–111.

toward religious matters which prevailed in England after the Puritan struggles. In America the Society continued to grow in numbers within the territory where it was already established, but without important changes in customs or organization. After the establishment of North Carolina Yearly Meeting in 1698, no new yearly meeting came into existence until 1812. This division was marked off into three periods by developments in the discipline and organization.

A revival of religious interest in England occurred about the end of the first third of the eighteenth century. Its most noteworthy manifestation was the Wesleyan movement. Among Friends it took the form of further development and stricter application of the discipline to maintain the separation of the Society from the world as "a peculiar people." It began with the minute of 1737 which established birthright membership, and ended with the establishment of the women's yearly meeting in England. In America Friends withdrew from the Pennsylvania Assembly in 1756 and within the next few years the disciplines were put in manuscript [8] and there was a general revision of the membership. The last period was characterized by the dominance of Quietism in the Society and the flowering of philanthropy. Evangelical tendencies made themselves felt toward the close of the period, which came to an end with the separations of 1827–1828 in America and with the repeal of the Test and Corporation Acts in England.

The third division was dominated by the Evangelical theology and program. It was characterized by frequent separations and the growth of both liberal and evangelical tendencies. The period was divided by the Civil War in America and by changes of policy in England and Amer-

[8] There was a manuscript discipline in Philadelphia Yearly Meeting as early as 1704 which was enlarged in 1719 and in 1762.

ica, which led to the abandonment of many of the old "testimonies," the discontinuance of disownment for "marrying out" and produced significant changes in organization. After 1860 there began a general approximation to the life and methods of the surrounding Protestantism, especially in the "Pastoral" meetings in America, and a marked growth in coöperation with other Christian organizations. In the latter half of the period there was a great expansion of the Society as a result of revival, missionary and post-war relief work, and important steps were taken toward unity between the various divisions of Friends.

The history of the Quaker movement, which this work is to recount, covers a period of almost three centuries and has a living interest today. The Quakers are one of the few indigenous Nonconformist sects of the Cromwellian period of English history which have survived to this day. The English Baptists and Congregationalists, the most notable of the other survivors, have increased greatly in numbers, while there are but few more Quakers in the world today than there were in 1700. After a long period of decline in the eighteenth century, however, the Society of Friends has shown itself capable of renewed life and influence as well as of great changes in its outward forms.

On the other hand the Society has exercised an influence on the thought, religious practices and social ethics of the English speaking world out of all proportion to its numbers. Many of its once radical beliefs and practices are now generally accepted in English and American Protestantism; but while many of Fox's contentions have been conceded, there remains of the original Quaker heritage "yet much land to be possessed." The Society has still a "testimony" to elements of the Christian gospel not yet fully acknowledged by even Protestant Christendom, such as simplicity in manner of living, complete spiritual democracy in the church, the ministry of women, inward spiritual authority, personal religious guidance, sincerity and truthfulness in speech, freedom of conscience and worship, simple mystical public worship, a classless Christian Society, reliance on spiritual forces only to overcome evil, international peace and the brotherhood of man regardless of sex, class, nation or race. There is still an urgent need also for its ministry of impartial love in a divided, war-torn world.

I

The Rise of the Society
1647-1691

Period 1

Quakerism under the Commonwealth, 1647-1660

Chapter 1

THE ENGLAND OF GEORGE FOX

The life of George Fox covers that part of Stuart England which was most distinctly Puritan, the period in which the fundamental institutions of modern England were fashioned and its distinctive principles established.

He was born in 1624, the year before the accession of Charles I and his death occurred in 1691, closely following the Toleration Act (1689) which brought relief to the Nonconformists. Within his youth occurred the accession of Charles I, his marriage to a French Catholic princess, the Petition of Right, the personal rule of the king, Archbishop Laud's high church and Strafford's "Thorough" policies, the inequities of the Star Chamber and High Commission, the Puritan emigration to America and the assembling of the Long Parliament. His public career included the Civil Wars, the Scottish Covenant, the defeat and execution of the king, the Westminster Assembly, the rise of the sects and Nonconformity, and the Puritan Commonwealth under Cromwell, including the Protector's attempts at religious toleration, his parliaments, and government by major-generals, his Scottish, Irish and foreign wars, and his death. Fox saw the Restoration, with its immoralities, excesses and persecutions: the uprising of the Fifth Monarchy men, the Acts of Uniformity and Supremacy, the Conventicle and Quaker Acts, the Plagues and Great Fire in London, the Dutch War, Monmouth's Rebellion, the Acts of Indulgence, the pro-Catholic policies of the Stuarts, Charles II as pensioner of the court of France, the accession of James II, the attempted Catholic reaction, the Rye House Plot, the birth of an heir to James, the Bill of Rights, and the "Glorious" Revolution of 1688, which established William and Mary on the throne, brought toleration for the Nonconformists and established the Protestant succession.

The England of George Fox was in many respects so different from modern England that it requires an effort of the imagination to realize it. The population was relatively sparse and unevenly distributed. At the middle of the century the population was about four and a half millions, the great bulk of it south of the Humber. The northern shires contained sparsely settled moorlands, with villages scattered through the dales, connected with the outer world by narrow trails over which merchants' pack-trains carried wool, cloth and cheese to the ports and towns of the South or the cavalcade of the king's justices travelled the circuit to hold the Quarterly Assizes. The border wars with the Scotch had ceased with the accession of James I, but were revived during the Civil Wars and Commonwealth. Cattle thieves, called moss-troopers, were still common in the northern counties.[1] In the Midlands and the South the enclosure of the common lands had begun, but much of the country was open plough-land and undrained bogs. During the Civil Wars, Rupert's and Cromwell's cavalry manoeuvred with ease across a country not yet broken up by hedge-rows and dykes.[2] Small landowners

---

[1] Cf. *Camb. Jour.* I, 125.

[2] Trevelyan, *England Under the Stuarts,* p. 37.

still formed a sturdy and influential part of the population. The hired farm-laborer was, on the whole, well fed and well cared for.[3]

The largest city was London with probably a half million population; next were Bristol and Norwich with about 30,000 each, and York with 10,000. The roads were in poor condition; the old Roman roads were not kept up and the frequent rains made the roads almost impassable at times. Vehicles were rare and most of the travel was on horseback. The large cities were all accessible by river and sea, which was essential both for trade and for supplies of food and fuel.[4]

London was spread out with gardens interspersed, and the city proper occupied but a small part of the modern metropolitan area, which contained many hamlets or suburbs (such as Hammersmith, Hampstead and Westminster) clustering around churches or palaces or residences of nobles, interspersed with barren or open stretches. Westminster was quite isolated so that members of Parliament dared not go into the city alone after night sittings. The streets of the city proper were mostly narrow and unlighted and the water supply poor, derived chiefly from wells unprotected from ground water. The sewage ran down the middle of the streets or was carried off in open ditches, inviting the plague, which devastated the city in 1647 and again in 1665. Conditions were somewhat improved when the city was rebuilt after the Great Fire in 1666. Vehicles were comparatively rare even in the city. Sedan chairs were used by those who could afford them for protection from mud, weather or curiosity. Much of the travel in and about the city was by boats on the Thames. The city apprentices easily formed the nucleus of a mob; they thronged to see a hanging at Tyburn, crowded the pits of the theatres, or

---

[3] Trevelyan, *op. cit.*, pp. 37–39.

[4] For much of this and the next paragraph I am indebted to Macaulay, *Hist. of Eng.*, chap. III.

gathered in vacant lots for wrestling bouts or fights. The London militia often turned the day in the political struggles of the century, as did the wealth of London merchants.

Most of English manufacture went for home consumption, except in the case of the cloth trade. Manufacturing was still done under the domestic system. Master and apprentices and workmen lived together, the master's house usually serving as residence, factory, warehouse and shop. In the country villages each workman had his loom or bench in his own cottage. The cloth industry had spread from East Anglia into the villages of the northern dales of Yorkshire and Westmorland and southward into the downs of Devon and Somerset. Iron manufacture was beginning to use up the forests of Kent, Sussex and the Midlands for its smelting furnaces.

Foreign trade was largely in the hands of chartered monopoly companies of which the East India Company was destined to become the most important. But there were many adventurous "interlopers" who scoured the seas for a share of the world's trade, and often made common cause against the chartered companies or joined forces as Protestants against the Catholic traders, whether French, Spanish or Portuguese. These conflicts were an important factor in molding the Protestant prejudices of the sea merchant cities. As English commerce grew, it also brought them into contact, friendly and hostile, with the Dutch, who were destined to exercise a powerful influence upon English ideals.[5]

The courts were held by the king's justices who were mostly the local squires. They were largely illiterate with strong prejudices, without training in the weighing of evidence and dependent upon their clerks for knowledge of the law. Accused persons were arrested, taken before a local magistrate and committed to jail in default of bail until

---

[5] Trevelyan, *op. cit.*, pp. 44–50.

the Quarter Sessions. The laws were severe, and even savage, especially where they concerned religion or property; and the justices had large personal authority and discretion. Punishments were largely corporal or "bloody" punishments—whipping, the pillory and stocks, mutilation and hanging; fines were frequent, and transportation beyond the seas not unknown. The number of capital offenses is shocking. The prisons were chiefly intended as places of detention while awaiting trial. Many of them were dark and filthy and they were often crowded. The jailer was under obligation to furnish bread and water to the prisoners and straw to lie on; but he expected to make money by selling food and drink to prisoners able to pay or by fees from the prisoners' friends for favorable treatment. He had it in his power to be inhuman with prisoners lacking in-influence or wealth or popular sympathy.[6]

It was a brutal age, although it is probably true that the English were less brutal than other peoples. Crowds flocked to a hanging. At the court of Charles II, parties of men and women were made up to go down to the Bridewell to see women stripped to the waist and publicly whipped. The victims in the pillory and stocks were objects of public scorn and abuse. Fights were common diversions of idle crowds. There were no rules; the spectators enjoyed it the more when a nose was bitten off or an eye gouged out.[7] Yet there was a strong sense of justice among the people; their sympathy was easily aroused by the sight of undeserved suffering. They naturally took the side of the under dog. Torture was no longer used to secure confessions or evidence. Witches were hanged rather than burned as on the Continent and the last execution for heresy was in 1613.

The Poor Laws required each parish to care for its own

---

[6] See Burrough, *Works:* "Epistle to the Reader"; Fox, *Bicent. Jour.,* I. 282, 532, 533. Whitehead, *Christian Progress,* pp. 83–91.

[7] Macaulay, *History of England,* chap. III (p. 140 Bowley Ed.).

poor. These dated from the suppression of the monasteries by Henry VIII (1538), when the paupers who had been fed by them, reinforced by unemployed due to the rapidly increasing population, turned into marauding bands, terrifying and plundering the country.[8] A generation later, when much plowland was converted into pasture, many able-bodied farm laborers also were driven to the roads for a living. The Elizabethan laws dealt with the evil by requiring each parish to care for its own poor. Vagrancy was made a crime in order to protect the parishes from the burden of caring for outside paupers and beggars. Economic interest insured the careful and often savage enforcement of the law. In 1657 the laws were extended to cover all persons wandering about without sufficient cause although not taken begging.[9]

It is difficult to separate the religious and political history of the period and for the purpose of the present work it is unnecessary. The Puritan movement aimed at religious control of the state and at political liberty. The period was dominated, on the one hand, by fear of the Catholics and, on the other, by the religious and political struggle of the Puritans against the king and the bishops of the Establishment. Involved in it was the struggle between Episcopalians and Presbyterians for control of the state church and the struggle of the Nonconformist sects against religious dictation by both church and state.

The fear of Catholicism was strong throughout the period. The savage laws of Elizabeth against "popish recusants" were prompted by the memory of "Bloody" Mary's persecutions, the French religious Civil Wars and the threat of the Spanish Armada. The Thirty Years War raged on the Continent until 1648 with the advantage mostly on the Catholic side. The Stuart dynasty began with

---

[8] Trevelyan, *op. cit.*, pp. 23, 28, 29.

[9] FPT, p. 347. For explanation of symbols see page 550.

the terror of the Gunpowder Plot and ended with that of the Rye House Plot, both plots for the supposed purpose of restoring the Catholics to power. It was believed that they were responsible for the Great Fire in London. The western and northern counties were still largely Catholic in their sympathies. Both Charles I and Charles II had Catholic wives; the latter was secretly a Catholic, and died in the faith; and James II worked openly to tolerate and restore the Catholic faith. The easy way to discredit or down an enemy was to call him a Papist, just as it is today to call him a Communist.

Puritanism began in England when the exiles under Mary returned from Geneva under Elizabeth with the Geneva Bible, Calvin's theology and a determination to "purify" the half-Catholic church of England of its "popish idolatry." They inclined to the presbyterian polity in the church and to limited monarchy in the state. They wished to impose the law of God on the king. They feared God but no other king. They studied the Geneva Bible with its Calvinistic marginal commentaries and found in the Old Testament authority for a theocracy. They made England the people of one book for several generations.[10] They brought conscience and deep conviction into the English Reformation for the first time. Sin was a terrible reality to them and hell the common destiny of man, only to be escaped by the free but rare grace of God. They feared the devil, hanged witches[11] and combatted heresy in high places and low, while fleeing themselves from the City of Destruction. It is easy to caricature the seriousness of the Puritans by taking a few extremists as typical of all. Nevertheless in the seventeenth century the English people did become divided into two classes differing in religious and political faith and manner of life.

---

10 See Bunyan, *Grace Abounding* (*Works,* 1872, I, 7, 8).

11 It is estimated that 70,000 witches were put to death in England between 1604 and 1680. Cf. Traill, *Social England,* IV, 86.

Over against the Puritans, or the "Roundheads" as they were called after 1640, were the "Cavaliers," the party of the king, nobles and bishops. They represented the feudal and Tudor tradition of privileged power. They believed in the divine right of kings and of the Anglican bishops, and were mildly Arminian in theology. They practiced artificial courtesies in speech and manners and were much given to recreations and amusements. They insisted on the plural address, the doffing of the hat, and "bowing and scraping," as the acknowledgement of their superior place and authority, and punished, as far as they were able, any neglect of these from Puritan or Quaker.[12] They wore long hair or wigs and extravagant clothes. During the reign of Charles I, there was a movement of the provincial nobility to London to take part in the gayeties of the court; the accumulated wealth of the counties was squandered to fit out the young people as courtiers[13] as it was after the Restoration to maintain the Stuart mistresses and favorites. It was the Cavaliers who were the patrons of art and the theatre, of music and literature, and of social life and who indulged in the recreations of hunting and horse-racing and kept up the games and diversions that survived from Tudor England, the maypole dances, bell-ringing, markets and fairs.[14]

Two contemporary descriptions show the opposition on religious and social grounds which these extravagances provoked.

They must be in the fashion of the world, else they are not in esteem; else they shall not be respected, if they have not gold or silver upon their backs, or if the hair be not powdered. But if he have store of ribands hanging about his waist, and at his knees, and in his hat, of divers colours, red, white, black,

---

[12] Ellwood, *Life*, p. 48. *Camb. Jour.*, I, 211, 341. Brayshaw, *Personality*, pp. 116–118.

[13] Lossing, B. F., *A History of England* &c., pp. 449–453.

[14] *Bicent. Jour.*, I, 39, 40.

or yellow, and his hair be powdered, then he is a brave man; then he is accepted, he is no Quaker. . . .

Likewise the women having their gold, their patches on their faces, noses, cheeks, foreheads; having their rings on their fingers, wearing gold, having their cuffs double, under and above, like unto a butcher with his white sleeves; having their ribands tied about their hands, and three or four gold laces about their clothes; this is no Quaker, say they. . . .

Now, are not these, that have got their ribands hanging about their arms, hands, back, waists, knees, hats, like unto fiddlers' boys? This shows that you are got into the basest and most contemptible life, who are in the fashion of the fiddlers' boys and stage players, quite out of the paths and steps of solid men; and in the very steps and paths of the wild heads, who give themselves up to every invention and vanity of the world that appears, and are inventing how to get it upon their backs, heads, feet, and legs, and say, if it be out of the fashion, it is nothing worth. Are not these the spoilers of the creation, who have the fat the best of it, and waste and destroy it? . . .

And further, if one get a pair of trousers like a coat, and hang them about with points, and up almost to the middle, a pair of double cuffs upon his hands, and a feather in his cap, here is a gentleman; bow before him, put off your hats, get a company of fiddlers, a set of music, and women to dance. This is a brave fellow. . . .

And to see such as are before described, as are in the fashions of the world before mentioned, a company of them playing at bowls, or at tables, or at shuffle-board; or each taking his horse, that has bunches of ribands on his head, as the rider has on his own (who, perhaps, has a ring in his ear, too) and so go to horse-racing, to spoil the creatures; O these are gentlemen indeed, these are bred-up gentlemen, these are brave fellows, and they must take their recreation; for pleasures are lawful.[15]

And Taylor the "Water Poet" protests on social and moral grounds against the folly of those

> Who wear a farm in shoe strings edged with gold,
> And spangled garters worth a copy-hold;

---

15 *Bicent Jour.*, I, 220–221.

A hose and doublet which a lordship cost
And gaudy cloak three manors' price almost;
A beaver band and feather for the head,
Prized at the church's tithes, the poor man's bread.[16]

The Puritans, on the other hand, had abandoned and condemned these "vanities" for the most part; partly because of a fear of Catholic art, partly from the Old Testament fear of idolatry, partly from a confusion of values, which recognized only truth of fact and ignored truth of imagination and beauty. They were more serious in manner and simpler in dress. They believed in the popular rights; and exalted the power of parliament against the king. Many of them preferred the presbyterian to the episcopal form of church government, while others became Independents and would separate church and state altogether.

The popular study of the Bible and the Puritan pulpit stimulated the intellect and led to the discussion of religious, constitutional and political subjects during the Civil Wars and the Commonwealth and produced an unprecedented religious and political literature. During the Commonwealth there were published about 30,000 pamphlets and tracts.[17] Milton, writing in London in 1644, thus described the intellectual ferment:

> Behold now this vast city; a city of refuge, the mansionhouse of liberty, encompassed and surrounded with his protection; the shop of war hath not there more anvils and hammers working, to fashion out the plates and instruments of armed justice in defense of beleaguered truth, than there be pens and heads there, sitting by their studious lamps, musing, searching, revolving new notions and ideas wherewith to present, as with their homage and their fealty, the approaching reformation; others as fast reading, trying all things, according to the force of reason and convincement.[18]

---

16 Cited in Lossing, *op. cit.*, p. 450.

17 Trevelyan, *op. cit.*, p. 200.

18 *The Prose Works of John Milton; with a Life of the Author*. Symmons Ed., London, 1806, I, 321–322.

Authorities generally agree that the English pulpit was at a low ebb during this period. Generally speaking, Puritan England was fond of going to church. The Anglican clergy made little of the sermon, the service consisting chiefly of the liturgy. Calvinism appealed, however, to the intellect rather than to the emotions and shifted the center of the service from the altar to the pulpit. The Anglican preachers in turn were driven to preaching to meet the competition of Presbyterian and Puritan preachers and to hold "lecture" services. They were often quite ignorant, with few books and little knowledge of the world. Many fell back on sermon helps or plagiarized from the many published sermons. At best they rehashed theology or took sides in current politics.[19] Under the Commonwealth some 2,000 Anglican priests were displaced and many Independents and even Baptists got their parishes. After the regular minister's hour was up (by the hour glass) others had a legal right to speak. At the Restoration about 2,000 again were ejected because they would not conform to the restored Episcopal Prayer Book. The great mass of the ministers, however, during the many changes of the long-drawn-out English Reformation kept their parishes, the people being content amid changes of government and ecclesiastical names to keep their accustomed priests, churches and ritual for their prayers, marriages, and burials. Naturally these priests had little depth of conviction and little more than a professional interest in their work. They fell low in the social scale[20] and got a bad name as mercenary and incompetent. On this Baxter, Milton and George Fox were heartily agreed:[21]—these ministers, supported by tithes, benefices and livings were the "hirelings" of their invectives.

About the middle of the seventeenth century there was

---

[19] Richardson, *English Preachers and Preaching,* 1640–1670, chaps. II and III. Trevelyan, *op. cit.,* pp. 63–64.

[20] Macaulay, *op. cit.,* chap. III, pp. 44-54. (Bowley Ed.).

[21] Brayshaw, *Quakerism,* pp. 24–31.

a reaction from the national preoccupation with politics and theology. Men turned to the study of nature; and a new era began in the development of the natural sciences. Newton and Harvey made their epochal discoveries; the Oxford and Royal Societies were established for the promotion of the natural sciences;[22] chemistry and physics became the avocation of many clergymen as well as of statesmen and scholars;[23] and the influence of the new ideas affected even the common people.[24]

The period of the Long Parliament and the Commonwealth (1640–1660) saw the rise of the multitude of religious sects. Edwards lists 199 "errours, heresies, blasphe-

---

[22] This is illustrated by the following description by John Wallis of the business of the Oxford Society:

"Our business was, precluding matters of theology and State affairs, to discourse and consider of philosophical inquiries and such as related thereunto, as Physick, Anatomy, Geometry, Astronomy, Navigation, Statics, Magnetics, Chymics, Mechanicks, and Natural Experiments: with the state of these studies, as then cultivated at home and abroad. We then discoursed of the circulation of the blood, the valves in the *venae lacteae*, the lymphatic vessels, the Copernican hypothesis, the nature of comets and new stars, the satellites of Jupiter, the oval shape of Saturn, the spots on the sun and its turning on its own axis, the inequalities and selenography of the moon, the several phases of Venus and Mercury, the improvements of telescopes, the grinding of glasses for that purpose, the weight of air, the possibility or impossibility of vacuities, and Nature's abhorrence thereof, the Torricellian experiment in quicksilver, the descent of heavy bodies, and the degree of acceleration therein, and diverse other things of like nature." (Quoted in Green, *A Short History of the English People,* III, 293–294.)

[23] Richardson, *op. cit.,* p. 492.

[24] This is shown by the entry in Fox's *Journal* for 1648:

"After this I returned and went into the Vale of Beaver. As I went I preached repentance to the people, and there were many convinced in the Vale of Beaver, in many towns; for I stayed some weeks amongst them. One morning as I was sitting by the fire, a great cloud came over me and a temptation beset me; but I sat still. And it was said, 'All things come by nature'; and the elements and stars came over me, so that I was in a manner quite clouded with it. . . . And as I sat still under it, and let it alone, a living hope arose in me, and a true voice which said, There is a living God which made all things. And immediately the cloud and temptation vanished away and life arose over it all; my heart was glad and I praised the living God."

mies and pernicious practices of the sectaries" in England.[25] Cromwell's army was a veritable debating society of the champions of all kinds of religious and political opinions. His tolerance gave the sects which sprang up in this period opportunity to organize and spread their doctrines.[26]

Some of the sects were continental movements carried to England, usually by refugees from persecution. Such were the Anabaptists, Familists or Family of Love, the Behmenists, followers of Jacob Boehme the Saxon mystic, and the Mennonites. The Seekers and Ranters also had continental backgrounds.

Practically all of these sects shared with the Puritans the desire to simplify life and to "purify" the church, but most of them would go further in these directions. The Mennonites especially stressed plainness of dress. The Baptists believed in the separation of church and state and in religious liberty as well as the Independents. Naturally they were opposed to church tithes. The sects who attempted to make over Christianity after the New Testament pattern were opposed to infant baptism, capital punishment, war and oaths. They were generally "low church" in their ideas of worship and church authority and had no creedal basis of church membership. They believed public worship could be held in unconsecrated buildings, and insisted that the church was the body of believers, not a "steeplehouse." The Baptists and Seekers had a lay ministry, often itinerant, of which John Bunyan was an outstanding example, and the "she-preachers" of Baptists, Brownists and some Independent congregations were notorious. Many besides

---

25 *Gangraena,* 1646. A single sect of course usually held to more than one of these "errours." On these sects and their influence on the Quaker movement consult: Jones, *George Fox: An Autobiography.* Intro. pp. 18–23. Barclay, *The Inner Life of the Religious Societies of the Commonwealth.* Tallack, *George Fox, the Friends, and the Early Baptists.* Chap. III. On the general subject see Jones, *Studies in Mystical Religion* and *Spiritual Reformers in the 16th and 17th Centuries.*

26 Brailsford, *A Quaker from Cromwell's Army; James Nayler.* pp. 12–16.

the Baptists and Familists opposed an educational qualification for the ministry.

There was a strong mystical element in most of the sectaries, especially the Seekers, Ranters, Familists and Behmenists. Most of them had free congregational worship, laid stress on personal spiritual guidance and on a religion of experience. The Seekers, like the Collegianten and the Schwenkfelder on the continent, had discontinued the historic forms of worship and sacraments, waiting until God should reveal to them the true way.

Most of these sects formed brotherhood groups for mutual help in things temporal as well as spiritual. The Seekers had regular meetings to provide for the work and welfare of their local groups, and to care for the poor and persecuted. The Baptists supervised the marriages of their members, and discontinued the use of the "pagan" names of the months and days of the week, as the Quakers did later.[27]

The sects which influenced Quakerism most were the Baptists, Seekers and Ranters. The General Baptists, (who are to be distinguished from the later Particular or Calvinistic Baptists) represented an Anabaptist, particularly a Mennonite, influence in England. They furnished many converts to Quakerism. George Fox had an uncle who belonged to them and he associated with some rather unstable groups in the Midlands in his early ministry. The Seekers also had an Anabaptist background.[28] They formed the original nucleus of the Society of Friends in the northern counties of England. The Ranters were an English development of a continental pantheistic sect, *The Brethren of the Free Spirit.* They identified religious guidance with strong feeling. A large part of them "ran out" into bizarre and even immoral practices. A large part of the sect was absorbed

---

[27] Tallack, *op. cit.*, pp. 78, 79, 83.
[28] Sippel, *Werdendes Quäkertum.*

into Quakerism, to which they contributed a highly emotional, individualistic and anarchistic element.[29]

After the Restoration there was a violent reaction on the part of the upper classes from the strictness of Puritanism and the radicalism of the sectaries, which found literary expression in the satires of "Hudibras;" and bore fruit in the corruption of theatre and court. There was a similar reaction against the degree of religious tolerance which Cromwell tried to maintain. The Puritans, however, retained a measure of power over the sovereign, partly from the nation's remembrance of the despotism of Charles I, Laud and Strafford, partly from fear of the Catholic leanings of Charles II and James II, and partly from the king's remembrance of the fate of his father and his advisers. In the end, the lessons of the Puritan period were not lost—toleration, parliamentary government and the Protestant succession were secured through the revolution of 1688 which established William and Mary on the throne.

The notable impression which George Fox made on the English people was not due to lack of other interests to attract their attention; he was merely one of thousands who was preaching new ideas in his day. England did not listen to him for lack of great men or distracting events. In philosophy there were John Locke, Hobbes and Lord Herbert. In the literary world there were Milton, Dryden, and Bunyan; in politics Pym, Hampden, and Elliott; in war Fairfax, Cromwell and Monk; there were Newton and Harvey in science; and in religion, Baxter, Taylor, Ussher and Chillingworth. Fox appeared among them without learning, without sword, without official position, and by force of character and the great spiritual truths of his message made a notable contribution to English life and thought.

---

29 *Camb. Jour.*, II, 498.

CHAPTER 2

THE FOUNDER OF QUAKERISM

GEORGE FOX, the founder of Quakerism, was born in 1624 in Fenny Drayton, a Midland English village in Leicestershire. His mother, Mary Lago, came of a good family, "of the stock of the martyrs," and was an upright woman. His father, Christopher Fox, called by the neighbors "Righteous Christer," was a weaver, a substantial citizen and church warden of the parish church. His nickname shows both his Puritan environment and his character. Fox was a serious and delicate child, little given to play. He "knew pureness and righteousness" after a preadolescent religious experience at eleven; and was scrupulous, truthful in his speech, and abstemious in his way of living. His parents thought at first of educating him for the ministry; but he was finally apprenticed to a shoemaker who was also a grazier and wool-dealer. During part of his apprenticeship he was a keeper of sheep, which occupation left an indelible stamp upon his thought and speech.[1] Probably aided by his outdoor life, he grew into robust physical manhood, which later enabled him to withstand the hardships of travel and imprisonment.

He was firm and scrupulously honest in his dealings as an apprentice; men learned that when he said "verily," he could not be moved. He had little or no schooling; but his keen and open mind acquired, largely by his own efforts, an extensive education. He attended the parish

---

[1] See *Bicent. Jour.*, Pref. I, xliv. Brayshaw, *Personality*, pp. 8–13.

church regularly with his parents until he was nineteen years of age, when to his parents' grief, his spiritual unrest led him to quit. From his fourteenth year until 1642 he sat under the ministry of Nathaniel Stephens, an Oxford graduate, a Presbyterian who took the Covenant in 1642 and a noted doctrinal preacher and writer. The impressionable youth thus received a thorough exposition of the Calvinistic theology.[2] He heard the Bible read and quoted from childhood, in home and church, and after he gave up attending church he spent much time in the open studying it. He knew his Bible almost by heart[3] and in his early ministry he carried one with him. He knew several versions of the English Bible although he used the Authorized and Geneva versions chiefly.[4] His writings and speech were saturated with Biblical thought and imagery. He had relatives and associates among the Baptists. After he left home at nineteen, he consulted various priests of the Established Church and many Dissenters who had a reputation for unusual religious beliefs or experience. In this way he acquired a practical knowledge of the history, beliefs and practices of the English Protestant sects. He brought to his work at the outset of his preaching a better knowledge of theology, church history, and the Bible than many a theological student today. In after life he showed a keen interest in natural phenomena and languages—in fact in "everything useful and civil in the creation."[5] At his death he had accumulated an extensive library for one in his circumstances, a good proportion of the books dealing with other than Quaker or even with religious subjects.[6] He had a passionate faith in the power of truth, which

---

2 Cf. Bunyan, *Collected Works,* I, 10.

3 Croese, *General History of the Quakers,* p. 14.

4 Cf. Cadbury, "George Fox and Sixteenth Century Bibles," JFHS, XXI, 1.

5 Brayshaw, *Personality,* p. 114.

6 Nickalls, "George Fox's Library," JFHS, XXVIII. Cadbury, "George Fox's Library Again," JFHS, XXX. About 730 titles are known.

was to him a manifestation of the Divine. This is perhaps best expressed in the following epistle, written in 1670 at the height of the persecution of the Quakers.

My Dear Friends:

The Seed is above all. In it walk; in which ye all have life.

Be not amazed at the weather; for always the just suffered by the unjust, but the just had the dominion.

All along ye may see, by faith the mountains were subdued; and the rage of the wicked, with his fiery darts, was quenched. Though the waves and storms be high, yet your faith will keep you, so as to swim above them; for they are but for a time, and the truth is without time. Therefore keep on the mountain of holiness, ye who are led to it by the Light.

Do not think that anything will outlast the Truth. For the Truth standeth sure; and is over that which is out of the Truth. For the good will overcome the evil; the light, darkness; the life, death; virtue, vice; and righteousness, unrighteousness. The false prophet will overcome the true; but the true prophet, Christ, will overcome the false.

So be faithful, and live in that which doth not think the time long.

G. F.[7]

At the age of nineteen George Fox began a four years' wandering as a seeker.[8] He was at that time under a great spiritual depression. This was not due, as was the case with so many of his Puritan contemporaries, to a sense of personal sin. Among the causes of his spiritual *malaise,* which are revealed in his *Journal,* was the disparity between the professions of his Puritan neighbors and their daily lives.[9] His wanderings were precipitated, as religious crises often are, by things relatively trifling in themselves, by some

---

7 Quoted from *Bicent. Jour.,* II, 134.

8 Parallels to Fox's experiences may be found in Howgill's *Works,* pp. 39 ff. and in the experiences of John Bunyan described at the beginning of *Grace Abounding* and in those of the pilgrim at the outset of his career in *Pilgrim's Progress.*

9 Fogelklou, *James Nayler: The Rebel Saint,* pp. 45, 46.

"professors" who challenged him to a drinking bout, the one who gave out first to pay the whole reckoning. The frivolous, mercenary and persecuting spirit of the clergy troubled him especially, and the way in which they "pleaded for sin and imperfection for term of life." [10] He thought religion should make people good.

A second cause of Fox's spiritual depression was doubtless the civil war between Parliament and King Charles I, which had been in progress for a year. It was difficult to reconcile the king's claim to divine right and the professed religious aims and zeal of the Puritans with the brutalities and passions of warfare. One of the first effects of Fox's great experience was the obliteration from his nature of everything warlike.

A third cause was a profound sense of the sufferings of humanity, unusual in one so inexperienced. He became convinced later that his sufferings had for their purpose that he should bear the spiritual burden of all conditions of men so that he could sympathize with their needs.[11] In after years he had a keen sense of the needless and unjust sufferings of the poor and afflicted, of the all-too-frequent victims of capital punishment, of slaves, of underpaid servants and laborers, and of those who suffered for conscience' sake.

Fourthly, he was suffering from the pessimism of Calvinism. He had been steeped in its doctrines of human depravity, predestination, reprobation and eternal punishment. In its popular forms it made much of reprobation and little of election; so that in effect it consigned the great mass of humanity to eternal torment. Popular Puritanism believed theoretically in God's omnipotence; but in practice, as the writings of Milton, Cromwell and John Bunyan show, it believed more seriously in the devil, in hell and in sin. To Fox's sensitive soul this was a gospel of despair. The

---

[10] Trevelyan, *England Under the Stuarts,* pp. 280, 311, 315. Brayshaw, *The Quakers,* pp. 25, 32.

[11] *Bicent. Jour.,* I, 19.

best it could do was to present a legal fiction by which the elect might be accounted righteous before God, but it knew no way by which in this life even the elect, with their heritage of sinful dispositions and half-pagan society, could be made righteous. From this ocean of darkness of Calvinistic pessimism Fox was seeking a way of escape.

On the positive side he was seeking, with the mystic's thirst, for direct access to God. He was restless with that restlessness which can only be quieted when the soul finds rest in God; and a fifth cause of his spiritual gloom was his inability to find him. The priests with whom he came in contact or whom he sought out knew the symptoms of physical and social illness but knew neither the signs nor the cure of the hunger for God. They offered him "carnal physic for a sick soul."[12] At best they only offered him substitutes for the knowledge of God; theological "notions" about God instead of a vital faith;[13] the mediation of a church whose rites and orders were established centuries before by a Christ who once lived on earth but was no longer accessible to men; and the Bible which told of men to whom the Spirit once spoke inwardly, but now spoke so no more.[14] Like the accredited ministers of the Established Church, the sectaries also failed him although they professed to have found a secret hidden from the clergy. Fox's quest resulted at first in despair and left him in his own slough of despond.

It was only after he had abandoned all these "miserable comforters" that his great release and transformation came —a circumstance that convinced him beyond question that ecclesiastical rites and doctrines were not necessary conditions of access to God. "But as I had forsaken the priests so I left the separate preachers also, and those esteemed the most experienced people; for I saw there was none among

12 Bunyan, *The Pilgrim's Progress. Collected Works,* London, 1847, I, 2.
13 Like Bunyan's "Talkative." *Ibid.,* pp. 85–94.
14 Jones, *A Dynamic Faith,* pp. 64–66.

them that could speak to my condition. When all my hopes in them and in all men were gone, so that I had nothing outwardly to help me, nor could I tell what to do, then, I heard a voice which said, 'There is one, even Christ Jesus, that can speak to thy condition'; and when I heard it, my heart did leap for joy. Then the Lord let me see why there was none upon the earth that could speak to my condition, namely, that I might give him all the glory. For all are concluded under sin, and shut up in unbelief, as I had been; that Jesus Christ might have the preëminence, who enlightens, and gives grace, and faith, and power. And when he doth work, who shall hinder it and this I knew experimentally."[15]

Gradually the results of his study, his thinking, his inquiries and the travail of his spirit began to crystallize out in clear convictions, in "openings" of truth, such as that "all Christians are believers and are born of God"; that a university education does not make one a true minister of Christ; that God does not dwell exclusively in temples made with hands; that every man is enlightened by the divine light of Christ; that God ministers directly and inwardly to human needs quite apart from ecclesiastical agencies; that there is an ocean of infinite life and love that can overflow and swallow up the ocean of human sinfulness, misery and despair; that it is possible to be delivered from the power of sin in this life—to "come into the state that Adam was in before his fall," as he phrased it.

These convictions came to him as distillations from his transforming experience; "the whole earth had a new smell" for him and he "came up through the flaming sword into the paradise of God." These truths he knew experimentally and not as mere speculative doctrines and these experiences gave him a positive, optimistic, overcoming faith. To the Puritan faith in God's omnipotence, he joined

[15] *Bicent. Jour.*, I, 11.

the faith that God is love and truth; he lived henceforth in the conviction that Truth and Love are over all, that God is "a-top" of all evil and of the devil himself, that those who open their lives fully to God may continue to live in that power "that is over all." He believed that such religious possibilities are in all men, and this grace is for all of every race, class, nation and clime.[16] Fox's experiences in 1647 changed him from a wandering seeker into the joyous possessor, and the preacher of a joyous gospel.[17] They improved his physical condition, and his mental and spiritual life became more unified and vigorous.

Fox started out at once to live according to this new experience and to bring all of life and its relations into harmony with these new ideas. He had no idea of founding a new sect, but only of revealing to other men and sharing with them this uncovered secret of righteous and joyous living.[18] The forms in which his experience expressed itself were not new in contemporary society. Just as practically all of Jesus' ideas can be found in the teachings of contemporary Judaism, so George Fox originated no new practices. We have already seen that they had all been tried in the sects of contemporary England. He furnished an organizing personality around which they crystallized and provided a principle that served as a basis of selection among them.[19] He was inevitably, although unconsciously, affected by the Puritan bias of his upbringing and environment, such as his lack of appreciation of art, music and drama; but the forms in which, according to the guidance of the Inward Light, he attempted to realize the new life, were, to his mind and that of his co-religionists, the expression of vital principles.

It is remarkable with what unanimity Fox's followers

---

16 *Camb. Jour.*, I, 34, GTD, p. 660.

17 See Cromwell's words to his daughter, quoted in *Camb. Jour.*, I, 456.

18 Fogelklou, *op. cit.*, p. 51.

19 Trevelyan, *op. cit.*, pp. 312, 313.

agreed with him as to the forms which the new life should take. Even when we make allowance for Fox's personal influence, the common Puritan environment and the elements inherited from the mystical and other sects, the method of following the Inward Light proved itself marvelously adapted to serve as the basis of a religious society with a common life.

Fox and his followers set themselves the revolutionary and complex task of revising the whole life of a half-pagan society in conformity with the mind and power of Christ as revealed within—a task vastly more radical than the purifying of the ecclesiastical and moral life proposed by the Puritans. This made Fox a pioneer in a great number of reforms and new religious and social movements.[20] The clearness of his moral and spiritual vision is astonishing. He had a soul rarely sensitive to the wrongs, injustices and needs of his fellow men, and a rare faith in immanent spiritual powers to right wrongs and to redeem and develop men. Rarer still perhaps is the promptness and courage with which he attempted to live up to his sense of truth and right.[21] To see a wrong with him was to intervene to set it right.[22] Among the reforms and social movements in which he pioneered were care for the poor and aged, prison reform, just treatment of the American Indians, provision for the insane,[23] opposition to drunkenness, capital punishment, and slavery. He insisted on honesty and truthfulness in all affairs, renounced oaths, believed in the one-price system in trade and just wages for working people. He was opposed to all kinds of war and refused any participation in it. He taught that governments exist for the benefit of the people as a whole and are bound by the moral law. He believed in a religious democracy in the church based on

---

20 *Bicent. Jour.*, I, 38–41.
21 *Ibid.*, II, 134.
22 Fogelklou, *op. cit.*, pp. 64, 65.
23 *Epistles*, p. 287.

the equality of all, both men and women, before God; and championed the right of women to preach. He refused to conform to customs which gave one class honor, power or wealth at the expense of others. His insistence upon simple dress, upon the singular pronouns in addressing all classes, in refusing to doff the hat to (so-called) social and political superiors sprang from the same spirit of Christian democracy. Many of these things were trivial in themselves but had become symbols of oppressive power or privilege to which the possessors attached prime importance.[24] He was a Nonconformist; he believed in the separation of church and state, and in universal religious toleration. In his *History of Modern Missions* Robinson credits Fox with being among the first Protestants to grasp the idea of foreign missions.[25] When John Wesley took the whole world for his parish he had been anticipated by Fox, a century earlier, who wrote letters to the Pope, the Great Turk, Prester John, the people of Cathay and printed an appeal "to all nations under heaven." [26]

Fox was the creative personality in the Quaker movement. He supplied its type of experience and its fundamental ideas, and was himself its chief preacher and evangelist in Great Britain and America. He contributed a noteworthy part of its literature, outlined and set up its organization and bore the brunt of the persecutions which the movement provoked. His vigorous body withstood the hardships of travels, imprisonments and abuse by mobs and provided him with an impressive presence and a powerful voice. He was imprisoned eight times for an aggregate of six years,[27] including a brief confinement at Nottingham, a year in Derby jail, nine months in the foul

---

[24] BBQ, 152.

[25] *History of Modern Missions,* p. 45.

[26] GTD, 31, 171–211, 603, 954. See *Camb. Jour.,* II, 336, 337 for list of Friends who went beyond the seas and the collections for them.

[27] Brayshaw, *Personality,* p. 59.

dungeon of Launceston jail, nearly three years together in Lancaster and Scarborough castles, in quarters which exposed him to cold and rain, and fourteen months in Worcester during which time his mother died. After his Scarborough imprisonment he was so weak and his legs so swollen that he could hardly stay on a horse. Yet after that he recovered and travelled over most of England, and in 1671–1673 he made a visit to America where he traversed the wilderness twice from Carolina to New England, enduring almost incredible hardships.

He was temperate in his habits, knew how to take care of his body and was careful of his health.[28] Penn testifies that he was "civil beyond all forms of breeding in his behavior; very temperate, eating little and sleeping less, though a bulky person."[29] He had the magnetic character of a great leader and the sympathetic winsomeness of a warm friend. Men could not be indifferent to him; they were either strongly for him or vehemently hostile. Fox was the natural leader of the Quaker movement by his initiative and courage and by the winning power of his personality. He gave no orders but he was quick to see and point out opportunities and needs which his co-workers recognized, and to make plans which they gladly carried out. His judgment was usually so patently right that he found willing coöperation in his projects. Friends were accustomed to write to him or consult him personally about their problems and prospects. Men offered to lie in prison that he and other leaders might be free. The few who later opposed his scheme of organization for the society were mostly jealous of his prestige or victims of an inadequate conception of the Inward Light. They afforded the only instances of defection from his following; but their opposi-

[28] *Ibid.*, pp. 32, 33. Cf. Fogelklou, *op. cit.*, pp. 105, 106, 160 for the contrast with Nayler in this respect. Among his books is listed a work on popular medicine, *The English Physician Enlarged* (Brayshaw, *op. cit.*, p. 37).

[29] *Bicent. Jour.*, I, 1.

tion made little headway against the moral authority of his leadership. He was fervent and reverent in prayer and a powerful and convincing preacher. Men stood for hours in orchards or in the open fields to hear him preach. He could win and hold cultured men and women, such as Isaac Penington, William Penn, Robert Barclay and other scholars among the early leaders, in spite of his lack of breeding and education.[30] Whitehead says of his style, "The simplicity and plainness of the author's style is not to be despised, he being more in life and substance than wisdom of words or eloquence of speech."[31] His style was rugged and homely, abounding in Scriptural phraseology and in illustrations from common life. Penn says of him, "He was a discerner of other men's spirits and very much master of his own; above all he excelled in prayer; . . . The most awful reverent frame I ever felt or heard was his in prayer."[32]

There was an inward confidence and assurance in Fox which sustained him in difficulties. His faith in the supreme power of God gave him courage. He derived from these a spiritual authority in his relations with both followers and opponents. William Penn expresses thus his impression of him:

> And truly, I must say, that though God had visibly clothed him with a divine preference and authority, and indeed his very presence expressed a religious majesty, yet he never abused it; but held his place in the church of God with great meekness, and a most engaging humility and moderation. For upon all occasions like his blessed Master, he was servant to all; holding and exercising his eldership, in the invisible power that had gathered them, with reverence to the Head and care over the body; and was received only in that spirit and power of Christ as the first and chief elder of this age; who, as he was therefore worthy of double honor, so for the same reason

---

30 Brayshaw, *op. cit.*, p. 154.
31 Fox's *Epistles*, "Pref. by Whitehead," p. 1.
32 *Bicent. Jour.*, I, xlvi, xlvii.

it was given by the faithful of this day; because his authority was inward and not outward, and that he got it and kept it by the love of God, and power of an endless life. I write by knowledge and not report, and my witness is true, having been with him for weeks and months together on divers occasions, and those of the nearest and most pressing nature, and that by night and by day, by sea and by land, in this and in foreign countries; and I can say I never saw him out of his place, or not a match for every service or occasion. For in all things he acquitted himself like a man, yea, a strong man, a new and heavenly-minded man; a divine and a naturalist, and all of God Almighty's making.

He was of an innocent life, no busybody nor self-seeker, neither touchy nor critical; what fell from him was very inoffensive if not very edifying. So meek, contented, modest, easy, steady, tender, it was a pleasure to be in his company. He exercised no authority but over evil, and that everywhere and in all; but with love, compassion, and long suffering. A most merciful man, as ready to forgive, as unapt to take offence. Thousands can truly say, he was of an excellent spirit and savour among them, and because thereof, the most excellent spirits loved him with an unfeigned and unfading love.[33]

Since this is a history of Quakerism rather than a biography of its founder there is no need to dwell on those personal characteristics, limitations and defects which did not contribute to the permanent pattern of Quakerism: his psychopathic states and illnesses, his visions, reputed healings, his *dilettante* interest in languages,[34] his denunciations of his enemies, his strange "leadings" (as at Lichfield) and his superstitious belief in providential judgments on the persecutors of Friends.[35] They add rugged lines to his portrait, afford the subject of interesting psychological studies, and shed interesting light on his age but add little to an understanding of Quaker history.

---

[33] *Bicent. Jour.*, I, xlviii–ix.

[34] BBQ, 302.

[35] See Brayshaw, *op. cit.*, p. 61n. *Bicent. Jour.*, I, 197.

Chapter 3

THE BEGINNINGS OF THE QUAKER MOVEMENT

After his decisive experiences in 1647 George Fox began to declare his new beliefs and to point people to the Lord's teaching in their inward parts.[1] During the next three years he found receptive persons among the scattered Baptists,[2] Independents, Ranters and other sects in Nottinghamshire, Leicestershire and Derbyshire, especially about Mansfield. Among these, were formed the first groups of converts who were at first called "Children of Light" but afterwards "Friends" and "Friends in the Truth."[3] Probably the first such community was the one near Mansfield (1648) where Elizabeth Hooten became the first woman preacher among Friends.[4] At this period Fox frequently interrupted church services or spoke after the preacher had finished, for which he was often mobbed or imprisoned or both.[5] He suffered a brief imprisonment at Nottingham in 1649 and later spent a year in Derby jail, at first on a charge of blasphemy and later because he would not enlist in the parliamentary army for the Second Civil War. On this

1 *Bicent. Jour.*, I, 34–36.

2 BBQ, 44.

3 BBQ, 24, 73, 132.

4 Fox says "The Truth first sprang up in Leicestershire in 1644," evidently considering his return home as the beginning of the Society. *Epistles*, p. 2. BBQ, 42.

5 The interruption was contrary to law but others than the regular minister had a legal right under the Commonwealth to speak after the preacher's hour was up. BBQ, 52.

occasion he gave his first pronouncement against war: he told the soldiers and officers that he "lived in the virtue of that life and power that took away the occasion of all wars." [6] It was during one of the hearings in connection with this imprisonment that the name Quaker was given to him by Justice Bennett, because Fox bade the court to tremble at the word of the Lord.[7] After his release he began his itinerant ministry in earnest and from this time on his life and work are merged in the growth of the Society.

The development of the Quaker movement consisted of a series of more or less definite campaigns, covering ever widening circles. From 1651 to 1654 Fox travelled chiefly in the northern counties of England—Yorkshire, Westmorland, Lancashire, Durham and Northumberland. In the next two years there was an extension of the work by Fox and his northern assistants to the south of England, especially to London and Bristol. After that the message was carried to Wales, Ireland, America and the Continent.

Fox's first northern journey was the most fruitful of his whole career. In the dales of Yorkshire, Westmorland and Lancashire, he found groups of Seekers who were "a prepared people" and who were gathered almost *en masse* into the Quaker movement within two years. Climbing over Pendle Hill in eastern Lancashire in 1652 he had a "vision of the places where the Lord had a great people to be gathered"; and the night following he saw a great people by a riverside coming to the Lord. These Seekers were groups who had become alienated from the church, largely under Baptist and Familist influences,[8] but who had not yet found any satisfactory form of worship. It was especially

[6] *Camb. Jour.*, I, 11, 12.

[7] *Bicent. Jour.*, I, 58. The word "Quaker" had been used in connection with another sect as early as 1657. Barclay says that "the name came from the trembling of Friends under the powerful working of the Holy Ghost," BBQ, 57. The name appears first in the parliamentary records in 1654.

[8] Sippel, Theodor., *Werdendes Quäkertum*, Stuttgart, 1937. Also Fogelklou, *James Nayler, The Rebel Saint*, pp. 21–23.

in the region about Preston Patrick in the Westmorland dales and the adjacent parts of northern Lancashire from Ulverston to Sedbergh that the Seeker movement crystallized into Quakerism most rapidly. A great enthusiasm for the new religious life seized upon the young farmers and villagers, both men and women. Some men of influence joined them—chiefly justices of the peace and Independents who had been in Cromwell's armies.

In the spring of 1652 Fox came to Ulverston in Furness. He engaged in controversy with the local priest and won the adherence of Margaret Fell which was a momentous event in the history of the movement. She was the wife of Thomas Fell, of Swarthmore Hall, who was a member of Parliament and a justice of the peace. A woman of unusual culture and spiritual insight, she was wealthy in her own right and had been a Seeker for twenty years.[9] Fox and his companions visited Swarthmore Hall where the whole household was won over. Judge Fell was away from home in London at the time, but on his return became favorable to Friends, although he never actually joined the Society. He allowed them to meet in the Hall and used his influence to protect them from hostility.[10] Swarthmore Hall became the unofficial center of the movement. Margaret Fell and her daughters kept in touch with the leaders by means of the travelling ministers and by correspondence. They wrote her of their needs, persecutions, imprisonments, successes and prospects; suggested fields to be occupied or opened up and places where the work should be strengthened. Funds were raised at Swarthmore and at Kendal to pay the expenses of travelling ministers and care for their families.[11] In these earliest years the easiest way to find or communicate with these Quaker aspostles often was to

---

[9] BBQ, 100.

[10] *Margaret Fell: Life and Work,* p. 8. She says "he became a kind of friend to Friends."

[11] BBQ, 135.

communicate with Swarthmore Hall.[12] In this way Margaret Fell became the "mother of Quakerism."

Within these first years the movement gained a solid hold in the north and gained its first group of active leaders; and the outlines of its organization, practices and concerns were sketched out. A vigorous itinerant ministry was carried on in the six northern counties during the next two years. According to Margaret Fell, some twenty-four preachers came out of Westmorland, Furness and north Lancashire before the middle of 1653. By the end of the year about thirty laborers had come out of the Westmorland meetings. Fox claims that by the spring of 1654 sixty or seventy ministers had been raised up and sent abroad out of the north.[13] In this work Fox, Farnsworth, Nayler and Dewsbury exercised a real but unofficial leadership.[14]

Among the converts in the north in the first two years of nascent energy (1652–1654) were many men of ability and influence who were to be leaders in wider fields. An increasing number of justices in the northern and Welsh circuits joined the movement or were openly sympathetic.[15] Other recruits had had experience under Cromwell, whose army was a school of religious agitation and discussion.[16] Among these were James Nayler, Edward Burrough and William Dewsbury. Others were men of culture and education and some had been clergymen: Thomas Taylor, Thomas Lawson, Samuel Fisher,[17] John Stubbs and Richard Farnsworth. In this work of "publishing Truth," there were many women who had an important place both in the

---

12 Harvey, *The Rise of the Quakers,* p. 50.

13 "The new Publishers of Truth were in most cases men of competent Bible knowledge and religious training according to the standards of the time. . . . They were men, moreover of a singularly advanced religious experience." BBQ, 94.

14 BBQ, 134.

15 For a list see FPT, 370.

16 See Fogelklou, *op. cit.,* pp. 16–40. Trevelyan, *op. cit.,* pp. 280–284.

17 BBQ, 59.

ministry of the word and the ministry of suffering.[18] Besides these should be mentioned many of less experience, the intensity of whose religious experience made them powerful exponents of the Quaker faith such as Mary Fisher, John Camm, John Audland and his wife Ann, Francis Howgill, Richard Hubberthorn, Dorothy and Jane Waugh.

In the year 1654 there was a second great expansion of the Quaker movement. To quote Harvey: "From the dales and fells and from the countrysides of the North went out a band of preachers whose names are hardly known to the historian, but whose lives and teaching had the deepest influence on seventeenth century England."[19] Of special importance was the campaign in the south of England. Francis Howgill and Edward Burrough went to London, John Camm and John Audland to Bristol, Richard Hubberthorn and George Whitehead toward Norwich and Thomas Holme into Wales. Friends had little success and met with much persecution in the Anglican and Puritan strongholds of Oxford, Cambridge and Norwich. In Bristol they fared better, preaching to great crowds.

In London, Burrough and Howgill did a notable work. The word spread through the city "that there was a sort of people come there that went by the name of plain North Country plowmen, who did differ in judgment to all other people in that city."[20] Camm and Audland had been in London in the spring of 1654 to see the Protector, and they reported the city to lie in spiritual darkness. Later two women from the north distributed one of Fox's tracts and found two meetings already in existence. Burrough and Howgill visited churches and conventicles of sectaries and held disputations wherever they could get a hearing. Finally (1655) a large room was secured at the old Bull and

[18] BBQ, 93.

[19] Harvey, *op. cit.*, p. 71.

[20] FPT, 163.

Mouth Tavern in Aldersgate where they held large meetings, "threshing among the multitudes" of sectaries, apprentices and curiosity seekers. As fast as they made converts they settled them in small quiet groups scattered about the city.[21] Later two such places for large meetings were secured. During the next two years workers came and went, aiding in the London campaign and spreading out at intervals for work in Bristol, Wiltshire, Dover, Norwich, Colchester, Suffolk, Plymouth, Sussex, Surrey and Bedfordshire.

In 1655 work was renewed in the Midland counties and London became the center of the widening movement. Meanwhile Fox visited, strengthened and extended the meetings in the south.[22] As a result of this work there were notable recruits: Amor Stoddart of London, an old Cromwellian soldier, Samuel Fisher, a former priest, now a Baptist, Luke Howard, and John Lilburne the Leveller. At Colchester James Parnell died in prison in 1656 at the age of twenty as a result of harsh treatment, the first martyr among the Publishers of Truth.

The work began in Ireland with William Edmondson who was among the Cromwellian "settlers" in Ireland. He had been converted by James Nayler in 1653 while on a visit to the north of England. Through his influence and that of his brother, the first Quaker meetings were settled about Lurgan in 1654. Pioneers in other parts of Ireland were James Lancaster, Miles Halhead and Miles Bateman. Richard Clayton from Swarthmore started one or two meetings in Ulster. In 1655–1656 many Quaker visitors arrived from England. Burrough and Howgill came from London, leaving the work in the English metropolis in the hands of Fox and Nayler. Howgill went into the southern provinces of Ireland and had some success among the English Protestant soldiers and officers there, while Bur-

21 BBQ, 184.
22 BBQ, 185.

rough continued to work in Dublin. William Ames was one of their prominent converts who was later a pioneer missionary in Holland. In Catholic Ireland Friends got no foothold, but at this time Ireland was under Cromwell's harsh government so that the army and "planters"[23] afforded better fields although the government was afraid of the political aims of the Baptists and Quakers.[24] Quakers made poor soldiers and were generally "cashiered" from the army. Quakerism nevertheless grew slowly, under the lead of William Edmondson and frequent English visitors. Before 1660 came Barbara Blaugdone, Richard Waller, Thomas Loe, John Burnyeat and Robert Masham of Yorkshire. During this period Quakerism also got a foothold in the Isle of Man.

There were Friends in Scotland as early as 1653 but Scotland proved almost as unreceptive as Catholic Ireland. The Presbyterian Church of Scotland had a strong hold on the people: it exercised vigorous discipline and discouraged sectaries. "A dominant type of religion was thus in possession of the country . . . which with all its sternness stood for morality and individual responsibility, and there was none of that confusion of opinions and little of that unsatisfied craving for a more vital experience which prevailed in England."[25] After 1651 Cromwell's army ruled a conquered Scotland, and as in Ireland, Quakerism found a limited hearing among the sectaries of the army; but the military authorities feared the effect of their teachings on discipline and in 1655 at General Monk's orders all Quakers were discharged from the army. Between 1653 and 1657 Scotland was visited by Caton, Stubbs, Howgill and Thomas Robertson. Small meetings were established at Heads, Badcow, Gartshore, Douglas in Dumbartonshire and at Edinburgh, Leith and Clydesdale. In 1657 Fox spent about five months in Scotland with Parker, James Lan-

23 JFHS, III, 961.
24 BBQ, 218.
25 BBQ, 226.

caster and Robert Widders. During this visit notable converts were Lady Margaret Hamilton and Edward Byllinge, afterward one of the proprietors of New Jersey.

Friends' work began in Wales as early as 1655. John ap John was the leader of the work and one of the ablest Quaker preachers. He was ably assisted later by Thomas Holme. The Puritan influence was never strong in Wales, but many of the justices appointed for the principality under the parliamentary government were liberal Puritans and a surprising number of them joined with Friends. Reports indicate that preaching in the Welsh churches was poor and the morals of the people low. During June and July, 1657, Fox visited every county of Wales, holding some large meetings and building up the Quaker groups which existed chiefly in south Wales in Tenby, Haverfordwest and Pontymoile.

Beginning about 1655, there was a most remarkable extension of Quakerism beyond the seas. The most productive work was that done in America. Mary Fisher and Mary Dyer came to Massachusetts in 1656. Rhode Island was an asylum for people of all beliefs and they got a strong hold there. They also got a foothold in New Amsterdam. The struggle with the Massachusetts leaders will be recounted elsewhere. As early as 1655 Quakerism went to Holland. Caton, Ames and Stubbs were the pioneers in Holland, where they came in contact with the Collegiants and the Mennonites. In 1654 and again in 1657, Friends went to France. Nearly all the Catholic countries of the Continent were visited by Quaker missionaries but to little effect. Mary Fisher went to the Sultan of Turkey, had an audience with him and got away safely. Between 1657 and 1660 several groups of Friends went to Palestine; prominent among them was George Robinson. John Perrot was a member of a party that set out for Turkey, but afterwards came back to Rome where he was imprisoned in the madhouse by the Inquisition.

The Quaker outlook at this time was world-wide and

their missionary zeal knew no limits beyond their leadings and power of accomplishment. "Fox would have sent Caton and Ames on still wider errands. At the end of 1660, when he was issuing epistles to Turk and Pope and even to the Emperor of China, he wrote of a seed of God to be gathered in Russia, Muscovy, Poland, Hungary, and Sweden, but Caton freely told him that he felt no call to go, still having much on him for Holland and the neighboring lands."[26]

In the spring of the year 1661, a second mission to the East was despatched by English Friends, consisting of John Stubbs, Henry Fell, Richard Scosthrop from the Craven district of Yorkshire, and Daniel Baker of London who had been a captain in a man-of-war. Fox tells us that the first three Friends were moved to go towards China and Prester John's country, and no masters of ships would carry them, so at last a warrant was got from the King, but the East India Company refused to obey it. Accordingly they crossed over to Holland, but found the same difficulty there, and had to content themselves with embarking for Alexandria, intending to complete the journey by caravan. They carried with them epistles from Fox, mostly in Latin and English, to the King of Spain, the Pope, the King of France, the magistrates of Malta, the Turk, the Emperor of China, Prester John, and, as a last epistle, one addressed "To all the nations under the whole heavens." There was also a letter from Stubbs and Fell in Latin and English to Prester John, who, it should be explained, was at this time identified with the Christian king of Ethiopa. They write as two apostles sent to all nations to visit God's vineyard, and they are satisfied that the Kingdom of Heaven must be known in all nations, though it be only as a grain of mustard seed.[27]

The first Quakers who came to America were almost wholly missionaries, impelled by the nascent enthusiasm of the Commonwealth period. The same zeal which sent them on a spiritual adventure to the countries of northern

---

26 BBQ, 415.

27 BBQ, 415, 429. For the range of missionary interest see the recommendation of the Skipton General Meeting in 1660, BBQ, 337.

and southern Europe, to Africa and to the "Great Turk," sent them also to the West Indian islands and the American colonies.[28] Later came colonists seeking to better their outward condition and also to have part in the experiment in free government and a Quaker social order in the Quaker colonies. Some came also to escape persecution in Great Britain, but the number of Quaker colonists, fleeing from persecution, was never proportionately so great as in the case of the Puritans who settled New England the preceding two decades. Emigration to escape persecution was on the whole discouraged.[29]

Barbados Island was the distributing point for most Friends coming to America.[30] A considerable Quaker community grew up there soon after 1656. In 1661 George Rofe calls it "the nursery of Truth." Besse gives the names of 260 Barbados Friends who suffered persecution.[31] As early as 1657 George Fox wrote a letter to them in which he expressed the first Quaker concern about Negro slaves.[32] By 1660 converts were made also in Bermuda, Jamaica, Nevis and Surinam (Dutch Guiana).[33]

The first Quakers to visit continental America were mostly women. Mary Fisher and Anne Austin began "the Quaker invasion of Massachusetts" in 1656. In 1657 Robert Hodgson, with four other Friends of whom three were women, crossed from Long Island to New Amsterdam. Persecution began when two of the women began preaching in the streets. Elizabeth Harris visited Maryland and Virginia in 1656 or possibly as early as 1655. During the next four or five years the stream of Quaker missionaries steadily increased in numbers, attracted by the possibilities

---

28 *Bicent. Jour.*, II, 251. JQAC, 91, 92.
29 JQAC, 357. BSPQ, 402, 411.
30 JQAC, 41.
31 *Sufferings*, II, 278, 371.
32 JQAC, 43, 44.
33 Fox, *Epistles*, no. 153.

of the new world and challenged by the hostility which they encountered in all the colonies except Rhode Island.

By 1660 Friends had visited all the existing colonies and had left converts in all of them except possibly Connecticut, most of whom were grouped in meetings for worship. The earliest monthly meeting in America appears to be that at Sandwich, Massachusetts. Scituate meeting was established before 1660.[34] In 1661 a yearly meeting was established on Rhode Island, which under the name of New England Yearly Meeting has been regularly held ever since. It is thus the oldest yearly meeting in the world.[35] Friends' meetings were early established on Long Island.

In Massachusetts the way had been prepared for the Quaker missionaries by the controversies with Roger Williams and Anne Hutchinson. Williams clashed with the Puritan authorities, denying that the civil government had any valid authority over the consciences of men; insisting that the colonists should pay the Indians for their land; and claiming that an oath, being a form of worship should not be tendered to an unregenerate person. He was banished by the authorities of Massachusetts Bay Colony and settled at Providence, Rhode Island, for which colony he secured a charter in 1644 and again in 1651. This colony, founded on the principle of religious toleration became an asylum for refugees from persecution in the Puritan colonies and in England.[36] Anne Hutchinson was the leader of a controversy with the Massachusetts authorities over the "covenant of grace" as against a "covenant of works." By the "covenant of grace" she meant the antithesis of a religion of external rules and commandments given long

---

[34] Thomas, *Hist.*, 6th Ed., p. 69.

[35] General Meetings were held in England as early as 1656 (Skipton) but the regular sessions of London Yearly Meeting did not begin until 1671. Thomas, *op. cit.*, 6th Ed., p. 52n.

[36] Two hostile ministers in New Amsterdam called it "the sewer of New England." JQAC, 225.

ago by an absentee God. She meant, to quote Rufus Jones,

> a religion grounded in a direct experience of God's grace and redeeming love, a religion not of pious performances, of solemn fasts and sombre faces, of painful search after the exact requirements of the law, but a religion which began and ended in triumphant certainty of Divine forgiveness, Divine fellowship, and present Divine illumination.[37]

She and her sympathizers were expelled from Massachusetts and a group of them founded a colony at Portsmouth on Rhode Island with the coöperation of Williams, to which came many other sympathetic exiles. These were prepared ground for the Quaker missionaries, and a large number of them became Friends. It was these controversies in part which made the New England Puritans so bitterly determined to keep the Quakers out of their colonies. The fear of witchcraft also influenced their attitude.[38] The coming of Mary Fisher and Ann Austin to Boston in 1656 caused great consternation. They were put in prison and their books burned. They were stripped and subjected to an outrageous examination for marks of witches.[39] They were closely confined in prison *incommunicado,* without light or writing materials for five weeks and then the authorities compelled the shipmaster which brought them to transport them to Barbados Island although at that time there was no law against Quakers either in the colony or in England. The Boston authorities proceeded to remedy this defect by a series of laws against Quakers and their sympathizers, characterized by an ever-increasing severity. They prohibited under heavy penalties any shipmaster from knowingly bringing Quakers into the colony. Quaker arrivals were to be whipped, imprisoned at hard labor, forbidden communication with outsiders and finally banished

---

[37] JQAC, 10.
[38] Bishop, *New England Judged,* p. 431.
[39] Bowden, *History,* I, 35.

from the colony. Fines were imposed for possessing Quaker writings, for attending Quaker meetings or for harboring Quakers. For returning after banishment Quakers were to be whipped, to have the right ear cut off, and to be deported again. Finally a law was passed (1658) making it a capital offense to return after banishment.[40]

These laws were a challenge to the faithfulness of the Quaker missionaries to their convictions. They were as deeply conscious of the sovereignty of God as the Puritans and felt sent by Him to bear testimony against their bloody laws with their lives, if need be. When no shipmaster could be found to bring them, they shipped to Rhode Island or provided their own ships. The voyage of the little *Woodhouse* from England with eleven Quakers, six of whom had been banished from Boston, is one of the romances of Quaker adventure. The master, Robert Fowler, sailed without astronomical observation or reckoning but, as the company were guided by the Spirit, they came safe to Long Island. After five passengers had been landed at New Amsterdam the others were carried on to Rhode Island,[41] from which place some of them went to Massachusetts Bay overland.

The authorities finally carried out their threat of death. In 1659 William Robinson and Marmaduke Stephenson were hanged on Boston Common. Mary Dyer was reprieved on the gallows but returned in 1660 and was executed. In the following year William Leddra suffered the same fate.

These executions and persecutions were called to the attention of King Charles II by Edward Burrough who told him that "there was a vein of innocent blood opened in his dominions, which, if it were not stopped would overrun all." The King replied, "But I will stop that vein." He sent the New England authorities an order that any Quakers

---

40 *Ibid.*, I, 160.

41 *Ibid.*, I, 60–67. A manuscript of the ship's log is in Friends Library, London.

liable to death or other corporal punishment should be sent to England for trial.[42] With fine irony, he sent the order by a banished Quaker, Samuel Shattuck. He arrived in time to save the life of Wenlock Christison, who was under sentence of death. The King's order put an end to the execution of Friends and brought relief from persecution for a time.[43]

Plymouth Colony, which is usually regarded as more tolerant than Massachusetts Bay, nevertheless fined, imprisoned and banished the Friends. The first Friends to visit Martha's Vineyard were expelled.[44] The Connecticut colonies also passed laws against the Quakers. Humphrey Norton, who visited New Haven in 1658 was imprisoned, whipped, branded in the hand, fined and banished. Other Quakers visited the Connecticut colonies, but were resolutely expelled and made but few converts.

Robert Hodgson and four others of the *Woodhouse* passengers reached New Amsterdam in 1657. In violation of the instructions of the Dutch proprietaries that all forms of religion should be tolerated in the colony, Governor Stuyvesant, probably under pressure from New England,[45] engaged in a determined struggle to keep the colony free from the Quakers. He proclaimed a law imposing a fine for entertaining Quakers, ordering the confiscation of ships bringing in Quakers, and revived a law against conventicles. Robert Hodgson was imprisoned, beaten, and starved until he almost died. The northern shores of Long Island had been settled by refugees from New England and from Europe. Among these groups persecuted Quakers from Massachusetts found refuge. Shelter Island at the east end of Long Island was purchased by Friends. The Quaker missionaries made numerous converts among these pre-

---

42 *Ibid.*, I, 237–240.

43 *Loc. cit.*

44 *Ibid.*, I, 69, 70. They were John Copeland and Christopher Holder.

45 JQAC, p. 223.

pared people. Prominent among these was Lady Moody, who had come from Lynn, Massachusetts, with a group of her neighbors.[46] Another influential adherent was John Bowne of Flushing. After being fined and imprisoned for keeping a conventicle in his house he was finally deported to Holland. There he appealed to the directors of the West India Company. Their letter to Governor Stuyvesant was as effective in stopping persecution as King Charles' missive to Governor Endicott.[47] They wrote:

> It is our opinion that some connivance is useful, and that the consciences of men ought to remain free and unshackled. Let every one remain free as long as he is modest, moderate, and his political conduct irreproachable.[48]

The first Friend to visit Maryland was Elizabeth Harris who made a number of converts there about Severn and Kent in 1656. Two years later Josiah Coale and Thomas Thurston came into the colony from Virginia on their way to New England and found a considerable response. In 1659 Thurston returned to Maryland. William Robinson, Christopher Holder and Robert Hodgson had large "convincements" as a result of their labors the same year. Coale came again in 1660. In the northern colonies most of the Quaker converts were people who had grown dissatisfied with the rigidity and externalism of the Puritan and continental Protestantism. In the southern colonies the converts were chiefly drawn from settlers on whom the churches had no hold. In Maryland there were many refugees from Virginia and a few from other places, who were neither Catholics nor Episcopalians. It was chiefly

---

[46] There were Quaker meetings established at Flushing, Gravesend, Hempstead, Jamaica and Oyster Bay.

[47] Bowden, *op. cit.*, I, 324–325. When in 1664 New Amsterdam passed into the hands of the English it became part of the treaty confirmed by the Duke of York that no one should be molested, fined or imprisoned for differing in judgment in matters of religion, JQAC, 228.

[48] *Ecclesiastical Records of New York,* I, 530. Cited in JQAC, 228. Bowden, *op. cit.*, I, 324–325.

from among these unchurched colonists that the Quaker converts came. In spite of the religious toleration guaranteed by Lord Baltimore's Charter, many Friends and their followers were imprisoned, fined, whipped or banished for refusal of oaths or military service, for keeping on hats in court and for entertaining Quakers. The persecutions were thus largely political rather than religious.

Most of the Quaker "public Friends" who visited Maryland had come from Virginia or passed on into the latter colony. Chesapeake Bay was a common way of entry for both colonies. Josiah Coale and Thomas Thurston were the Quaker pioneers in Virginia (1657) where they spent about six months and made converts. In the effort to maintain the Church of England as the sole religious organization in the colony, the authorities almost equalled the harshness of the New England Puritans. Laws had been enacted in 1642 against Catholics and for the banishment of Non-conformists in 1643. Coale and Thurston were imprisoned under these laws. In 1660 and 1662 laws were made especially against the Quakers, the latter modeled on the English Conventicle Act.[49] These testify to the growth of the Quaker movement. Thurston return in 1658. William Robinson, Christopher Holder and Robert Hodgson labored here the same year and probably Humphrey Norton the next year. As a result of these efforts Robinson wrote, "There are many people convinced." [50]

There was one martyr to the intolerance of the Virginia authorities. George Wilson and William Coale were put into "a nasty stinking, dirty" dungeon in Jamestown. Wilson was scourged and heavily ironed, so that "his flesh rotted from his bones and he died." [51] It was not until long after the Restoration in England that religious toleration was established in Virginia.

---

49 JQAC, 271.

50 Bowden, *op. cit.*, I, 346. See also Neill's *Virginia Carolorum*, p. 296. Cited in JQAC, 273.

51 Bishop, *op. cit.*, p. 351.

CHAPTER 4

THE PRINCIPLES OF FRIENDS

THE message which George Fox and his co-religionists brought to their contemporaries was not a system of doctrine. They had tapped afresh the sources of spiritual power in Christianity; they had found a new way of life, and they set out to live it uncompromisingly and to invite all men to share it.[1] For them Christianity ceased to be a set of forms and "notions" that left the moral life practically untouched. It became the basis of a new type of first-hand experience. There is an intense feel of reality in their messages. George Fox asserted that he knew his religion "experimentally." Nayler describes thus his experience: "This is not a notion of what was done in another generation, past or to come, hundreds or thousands of years distant, but that which leads to . . . a new birth to light, without which none can see the Kingdom of God, nor enter therein."[2] There must have been many in the churches of that generation, especially among the Puritans, to whom religion brought a vital experience. With most of them, however, the new energy was expended in personal piety expressed in the sanctioned religious forms; but with the Quakers the new experiences and devotion were channeled into new patterns of life.

The Quaker "publishers of Truth," as they styled them-

1 See *Bicent. Jour.*, I, 316.

2 *Works*, pp. 429, 430.

selves later, brought no system of theology. They used the language of the Scriptures, of the Puritans and of the mystical sects in trying to convey the nature and possibilities of their religious discoveries. They were like a robust man trying to explain the secret of his health and vigor with no scientific vocabulary or theories: who enjoys life but knows little of biology. It was left for Penn, Barclay and other learned men of the next generation to give theological expression to Quakerism.

Certain principles were nevertheless basic in their religion, and it is important to understand them before proceeding with the history. The theological background of their thinking was in general that of Calvinism. The points emphasized in their preaching were naturally those in which they differed from the Calvinistic system. When they did attempt to give a theological statement, as when they sought to disprove charges that they were atheists or heretics or "no Christians," [3] it was usually quite orthodox, except for the Quaker aberrations.

The Quakers were optimistic rather than pessimistic as to the purposes of God and the possibilities and destiny of men. They knew by sad personal and social experience the terrible nature, power and extent of evil in the world; [4] but they could not share the pessimism of Calvinism as to the power of the devil or the hopelessness of man. They believed in the sovereignty of God even as the Puritans, but to them he was a God of redeeming love. They knew the universality of sin but did not believe that God held men guilty because of an ancestor's sin. They believed that salvation was open to all men and that in spite of the evil in them, men were capable of apprehending and answering to the invitations of divine love. Fox saw an "ocean of darkness and death but also an infinite ocean of light and

---

[3] See Burrough, *Works,* pp. 439–443; Fox's letter to the Governor of the Barbados, *Camb. Jour.,* pp. 197–200; Nayler, *Works,* pp. 255–360.

[4] *Bicent. Jour.,* I, 14–22; 31–32.

love which flowed over the ocean of darkness." [5] They knew that where sin abounded, grace did abound much more. Their faith in divine power was a faith in the efficacy of the spiritual forces of truth, righteousness, justice, good will and love, so that Friends would not resort to physical force even to try to promote good causes. They did not believe that evil can be overcome except by good. As George Fox put it, they lived "in the virtue of that life and power that took away the occasion" of all outward evil.[6]

Friends were in the succession of a great mystical tradition.[7] They found the ultimate and final religious authority, both for belief and conduct, within the individual instead of in something outside the believer, whether an institution, person or book. George Fox had this among his early revelations: "Now the Lord God opened to me by his invisible power, that every man was enlightened by the divine light of Christ and I saw it shine through all; and they that believed in it came out of condemnation to the light of life, and became children of it; but they that hated it, and did not believe in it, were condemned by it, though they made a profession of Christ. . . . I was sent to turn people from darkness to the light, that they might receive Jesus Christ." [8]

Early Friends used many names for the inward source of their religious life and faith: the Light, the Light of Christ, the Light Within, the Spirit of Christ, the Spirit, the Seed, the Root,[9] "that of God within you," the Truth. In later times the expressions the Inner Light and "the universal and saving Light" came into use.

Early Friends never gave exact theological definition to the Inner Light. It represented an experience rather than a theological "notion." It is fairly clear from their writ-

[5] *Ibid.*, I, 12, 14, 17, 19, 20.

[6] *Ibid.*, I, 68, 69.

[7] Mysticism as used in this book means a religion of first-hand experience, of personal relations with God, known within the soul.

[8] *Bicent. Jour.*, I, 34, 35.

[9] Nayler, *Works*, p. xiv.

ings, however, that this phrase and its synonyms included at least three related ideas.[10]

(1) It stood for God as knowable to and within men. It meant that he is not a localized or absentee God but a God at hand and not afar off, that in him we live and move and have our being; that, to use a modern phrase, he is immanent in the world and in man, and so may be inwardly known to every man; that every soul opens inwardly onto God and is conjunct with him. Such an idea runs easily into a pantheistic confusion between Creator and creature, obscuring the difference between good and evil,[11] but the strong sense of God inherited by the early Friends from the Calvinists prevented that danger. Even Nayler, when his mind was most clouded, never quite lost the sense of the distinction between himself as a man and the Christ within him.[12] The immanence of God did not mean a confusion of personalities; and it implied no necessary goodness.

This truth involved important consequences in regard to worship. Communion with God cannot be restricted to times or places, nor limited to the mediation of a priestly class nor to a particular ritual nor to sacramental objects. It allows no inherent difference between sacred and profane. God is spirit and the only essential condition for communion with him is a true or right spirit. In the seventeenth century, this attitude was regarded as radical and heretical. The church buildings were considered holy ground where alone public worship could be performed; Sundays and other days were holy days; the church, through its priests and sacraments, provided necessary mediation between men and God.[13] The Friends did not deny that men might worship God by such aids,[14] but the

---

10 Cf. *World Conference of Friends,* 1937. Report of Com. I, pp. 23–26.

11 As it did among the Ranters.

12 Nayler, *Works,* pp. 27, 28.

13 *Bicent. Jour.,* I, 11, 90–91, 93. Cf. Bunyan, *Works,* I, 7, 8.

14 Barclay, *Apology,* Prop. XIII, § XI.

only way by which they could prove that religious life was possible without them was to discontinue using them.[15] The theoretic conclusion that such aids and mediators were not necessary was strengthened by the experiences of Fox and his followers who found truth, light and deliverance, quite apart from the ecclesiastical means of grace.[16] Social or public worship requires set times and places for assembling, but they are required by the limitations of men not by the character or requirements of God.

(2) It meant also the capacity in all men to perceive, recognize and respond to God—to his truth, his love and his will. This was emphatically a denial of Calvin's doctrine of human inability as a result of the Fall, according to which this ability was limited to the elect, to whom alone God gave the enabling "prevenient grace." The Quaker belief became the basis of a complete democracy as well as of universal philanthropy. According to it, all men and women have access to God; all are potentially children of God and of equal value in his sight. The universal consciousness of sin comes only from the felt presence of the Light.[17]

In neither of these senses did the Inner Light imply any inevitable salvation.[18] There are evil as well as good potentialities in human nature. Man's capacities for knowing God vary with individuals as do the keenness of their senses and each person knows him according to his capacity. This capacity can be cultivated and quickened moreover just as can the outward senses, by study, attention and exercise —by meditation, public worship, Bible study, by Christian counsel and by the practice of truth as far as known.[19]

---

15 Burrough, *Works,* p. 6, the Epistle to the Reader.

16 *Bicent. Jour.,* I, 35–38. GTD, 216, 217, 794.

17 Brayshaw, *Personality,* p. 157.

18 So Whittier later: "He giveth day, Thou hast thy choice to walk in darkness still."

19 See Howgill, *Works,* pp. 68–71. "Return home to within; sweep your houses all, the groat is there."

Friends appealed to "that of God" in all sorts and conditions of men—American Indians, criminals and oppressors, Negroes and Turks, regardless of sex, race or nationality—with faith that the divine potentiality for truth, righteousness, brotherhood and the knowledge of God is in all. Women were given an equal place with men as members and ministers in the Society.

It was on this ground fundamentally that Friends refused to conform to those social customs such as the use of the plural pronoun, doffing the hat and similar "courtesies" to social superiors, which implied or perpetuated social, political or religious differences or helped one class to exploit others for its own benefit.

(3) The Inner Light was also a designation for God as inwardly known; for a man's whole experience of God. It included a body of convictions as to God's nature, requirements and dealings with men, which grew up out of the pooled experience of Friends and gradually crystallized into their mode of worship, conduct of life and relations to the world, and which came to be called "the Truth" or simply "Truth." This was theoretically not a fixed datum; but one that would grow with enlarging experience and vary with changing conditions. In practice, however, the natural conservatism of religion has made it hard to change anything which has been sanctified by religious emotion.

Friends' attitude to the Bible and to the whole historic Christian revelation is important for, while Quakerism is a fundamentally mystical religion and broke away from much of historic Christianity, it is still a Christian mysticism. Early Friends never attempted to define this relationship with theological exactness.[20] It was enough to believe that the Spirit of God whom they knew personally through the Inner Light was the same Spirit who inspired the Scripture writers and who was supremely manifest in the his-

---

20 BBQ, 277. Cf. Grubb, *The Historic and the Inward Christ*, pp. 30, 31.

toric Christ.[21] In Fox's great experience, it was the Spirit of Christ who "spoke to his condition." In 1648 he described his mission as follows:

> I was sent to turn people from darkness to the light, that they might receive Jesus Christ: for, to as many as should receive him in his light, I saw that he would give power to become sons of God; which I had obtained by receiving Christ. I was to direct people to the spirit, that gave forth the Scriptures, by which they might be led into all truth, and so up to Christ and God, as they had been who gave them forth. I was to turn them to the grace of God, and to the truth in the heart, which came by Jesus; that by this grace they might be taught, which would bring them salvation, that their hearts might be established by it. . . . I saw that Christ died for all men, and was a propitiation for all; and enlightened all men and women with his divine and saving light; and that none could be a true believer, but who believed in it. . . . These things I did not see by the help of man nor by the letter, though they are written in the letter, but I saw them in the Lord Jesus Christ, and by his immediate spirit and power, as did the holy men of God, by whom the Holy Scriptures were written. Yet I had no slight esteem of the holy Scriptures, but they were very precious to me, for I was in that spirit by which they were given forth: and what the Lord opened in me, I afterward found was agreeable to them.[22]

Edward Burrough gives his testimony to the same effect: "And we believe that this God hath given his son Christ Jesus into the world, a free gift to the whole world, and that every man that cometh into the world is lighted by him that every one may believe and be saved." [23] A modern statement phrases it, "The central Quaker faith in the seventeenth century was a testimony that man may live in

---

[21] See Fox, *Epistles,* "An Epistle by Way of Preface by George Whitehead": "In many of the ensuing epistles he often mentions the seed, the life, the power of God, and the like; whereby he intends no other than what the Holy Scriptures testify of Christ."

[22] *Bicent. Jour.,* I, 34, 35.

[23] Burrough, *Works,* p. 439. (Also p. 6 of the "Epistle to the Reader.")

vital contact with the divine Life-stream and that that divine stream of Life can flow into expression through men."[24]

Thus Friends regarded God's manifestation in human life as a continuous stream of influence, inspiring the prophets and apostles, the writers of the Bible and becoming manifest supremely and without measure in Jesus Christ; and present with all men in all ages as the guide, teacher and redeemer of men, if and as they receive him.

The Calvinists conceived Christ's work of redemption as primarily historic and theological. It was a "transaction," performed to remove obstacles, which had been created by human sin, to God's forgiveness of men. Its primary efficacy was at the future judgment in determining men's eternal salvation. Salvation was primarily a judicial act rather than a moral one. It aimed at getting men accounted righteous by God. The emphasis of Friends, on the other hand, was upon the work of the inward Spirit of Christ in making men righteous by a moral transformation. They had no patience with a salvation that left men in sin and moral imperfection "for term of life," and which so emphasized faith as the condition of salvation that it left the impression that moral conduct was relatively unimportant. Fox himself had come up into the "Paradise of God," and he believed it possible for others to share the state of innocency that Adam was in before the Fall.[25] Salvation was thus a state of continuous living by the Spirit, rather than an isolated experience of "conversion" or a future judicial "justification."

The early Friends regarded the Bible as the record of men inspired by the Spirit of Christ; but they did not regard revelation as either ended with the Bible or confined to it. Nor did they believe men should be content with a

---

24 *Friends' World Conference, 1937*. Report of Com. I, p. 11.

25 *Bicent. Jour.*, I, 281.

second-hand knowledge of the gospel of Christ, even though acquired through the Bible. The Bible should be used as men use a guide book[26]—to help them find and experience for themselves the truths recorded in it. The Bible was not a substitute for the personal knowledge of God, nor a new law. Men understood the Bible and used it rightly as they were in the Spirit by which it was given forth originally and knew by experience the things it recorded. At Ulverston George Fox had challenged the reality of a religion taken only from a book, even from so valuable a book as the Bible. "You will say, Christ saith this, and the apostles say this; but what canst thou say? Art thou a child of the Light, and hast thou walked in the Light, and what thou speakest, is it inwardly from God?"[27]

Friends valued the Bible also as a means of testing religious beliefs and experience. Since the Spirit must be consistent with himself, a supposed revelation which did not agree with the teaching of the Bible was to be suspected of error. In early Friends' writings the language of the Bible is everywhere employed and they sought everywhere to convince their adversaries by quoting Scripture; not because it was a final authority to themselves but because their Protestant opponents did so regard it. It is noteworthy that all sects appealed to the Scriptures to support their peculiar views, so that in practice its use to validate any particular belief was hardly convincing. Friends could always fall back on the Inner Light as the ultimate authority as to the teaching of the Bible and were thus never in bondage to an interpretation that violated their sense of God and duty, for spiritual things are to be spiritually discerned.

The mysticism of Friends was a social mysticism. This is

---

[26] *Ibid.*, II, 512. Cf. also Fox to Cromwell: "I told him, 'that all Christendom (so-called) possessed the Scriptures, but wanted the power and Spirit that they had, who gave forth the Scriptures.' "

[27] *Ibid.*, I, 210.

true both in its worship and its work. They recognized that in all departments of human nature, knowing is a social process. This is particularly true of spiritual knowledge. While Quakerism often sounds like pure individualism, the existence of the Society of Friends indicates their faith that the highest knowledge of divine things is a social product. In corporate experience the will of God is known most fully and in social worship the Inner Light is apprehended most clearly. The pooling of experience in teaching and testimony and the quickening of the spiritual powers through common seeking of the Light enhance the accuracy of spiritual discernment and the richness of spiritual experience in all. The Friends' meeting for worship is therefore based on an informal seeking together, usually called a "silent meeting;" [28] until any member has a truth, experience or exhortation to be shared vocally. The business of the Society is also conducted in the spirit of worship, seeking a corporate judgment as to the will of God. The individual judgment as to truth, right and duty is thus checked against the common judgment.[29]

Quaker mysticism is also social in the sense that it is not wholly subjective nor chiefly concerned with the individual's own spiritual state or salvation. It was equally concerned with the welfare of others. God as revealed in Christ is a God of love, the universal Father. All anti-social impulses are therefore not of God. The cross of Christ is the supreme manifestation of God's sacrificial love for men. His Spirit sheds abroad in men's hearts the altruistic impulses to share with their fellow men and help them according to their needs. From this has sprung the Quaker sensitiveness to human need, and its reforming zeal, and

28 Not because they are wholly or even usually held in silence, but because the meeting is held "on the basis of silence," as other public worship is usually held on the basis of a continuously vocal order of service.

29 Friends under an "exercise" to do some unconventional thing, such as the "signs," usually asked counsel of other Friends.

it is the root of Quaker pioneering in philanthropy and reform.[30]

Mysticism is the greatest adventure of the human spirit. The inner life is a strange complex of the impulses of the beast and the aspirations of the sons of God. It is difficult at times to distinguish "that of God," amid the inner confusion, from impulses of the flesh and prejudices created and sanctified by pagan society. Most mystic sects have sooner or later, "run out" (as Fox said of the Ranters) into absurdities, puerilities, fanaticism or immorality.[31] Friends have been preserved in large measure from such a fate by the double safeguard of their attention to the historic Christian revelation and the social check upon possible individual vagaries.[32]

These principles have an important bearing on worship and the ministry. Worship is, as has been noted, not essentially a matter of time or place or form, but of a worshipping spirit. Because of the social nature of man it reaches its highest possibilities in social worship. Its forms and manner are always subject to spiritual guidance both in the individual and in the group. The ministry is not a matter of orders or official functions but of the divine gift or call. The Quaker ministry is essentially a lay ministry open to all and exercised as the Spirit may lead.

Early Friends were so occupied with attempts to order their lives according to their principles of spiritual autonomy and brotherhood that they did not attempt a thorough criticism of the political and economic order. They struggled against the abuses near at hand within these systems but rarely questioned the inherent nature of them as social systems. In their attitude toward the economic life Nayler was more nearly an ascetic; Fox, a capitalist, and Bellers,

---

30 See Whittier, *Proem.*

31 See *Bicent. Jour., Penn's Preface,* p. xxv. Jones, *Autobiography,* p. 22.

32 For a modern statement of these principles, see *Friends World Conference,* 1937, Report of Commission, I, pp. 17–22.

a philanthropist. Winstanley's "Digger" land communism did not appeal to Friends. Byllynge was a republican in politics,[33] and Lilburne, a Leveller. It remained for Penn to attempt in the second period to build a state on Quaker principles.

Persecution by the state in defense of a state church and religious requirements for public office which Friends could not meet gave Friends from the start a rather negative attitude toward government of resistance and aloofness, which colored their political attitude for two centuries.[34] However, they believed in the rightful authority and functions of government. Edward Burrough affirms:

> Concerning government and magistracy this I have to say: It is an ordinance of God, ordained of him for the preserving of peace among men; for the punishing and suppressing of evil-doers, and for the praise of them that do well; that men's persons and estates may be preserved from violence and wrong-dealing of evil men. . . . We know, whatsoever men profess to do yet they cannot perform any good thing nor rule for God in our nation till that themselves be reformed and ruled by Him, and have the spirit of God poured upon them for such a work. . . . If any one man or a number of men whatsoever shall have the spirit of the Lord poured on him or them and shall be anointed of the Lord for such an end and use, to govern this nation, under such a government shall the righteous rejoice and the whole land sing for joy of heart, when tyranny and oppression shall be clean removed, strife and contention and self-seeking utterly abandoned, and when peace and truth flows forth as a stream, and the Lord alone rules in thy rulers, and he the Principal amongst them; and under such men and such a government only and not under any other shalt thou, O nation, be happy, and thy people, a free people.[35]

Burrough does not raise the question of the use of force in dealing with anti-social men or aggressive nations. Both

33 See Brinton, *Children of Light,* pp. 109–131.
34 Burrough, *Works,* pp. 247, 248.
35 *Ibid.,* pp. 343, 604, 605.

he and Nayler seek the solution of the problems of government in the Inward Light as the guide of both rulers and subjects, but they seem to believe in the use of force against evil doers:

And so his government being according to that in every conscience, everyone that minds that in the conscience shall witness him and his government to be of God, and so he that resists, shall receive to himself condemnation, witnessed by that in the conscience. And all who own not that in the conscience which is pure, to obey the Lord therein, the sword of the Lord in the hand of his minister shall be upon such, and that of God to which he is subject, even the anointing he hath received, shall instruct him in the spirit of meekness, wisdom, and judgment, to find out the transgressor, and lay the sword upon him; and such shall not bear the sword in vain, but a terror to the Evil-doer shall be, without respect to the persons of men or any other thing, but only to the law of God, which is one with that in the conscience.[36]

All Friends were agreed, however, that the Christian is bound to refuse obedience to government when its requirements are contrary to those of God, while at the same time submitting peaceably to the penalties of disobedience. They did, however, use all peaceable means to convert their oppressors, to redress wrongs, prevent injustice and bring the political order into conformity with the principles of the Kingdom of Christ. Fox strongly admonished Oliver Cromwell to "lay down his crown at the feet of Jesus." [37]

---

36 Nayler, *Works,* p. 304.

37 *Camb. Jour.,* I, 260.

Chapter 5

THE PERSECUTION OF FRIENDS UNDER THE COMMONWEALTH

The Quaker "Publishers of Truth" were subject to persecution almost from the beginning. George Fox was imprisoned in Nottingham for some time in 1649 and put in the stocks at Mansfield Woodhouse shortly after his release for speaking in church. He spent a year in Derby jail for blasphemy and for refusing to serve in the parliamentary army. Cromwell sincerely tried to secure toleration for all sects except the Catholics, and the army on the whole supported him in this, for the core of the "New Model" consisted of Independents and other sects who believed that the war against the king was waged for religious as well as political liberty. This was the fundamental reason of their opposition to royalist Anglicans as well as to covenanting Presbyterians; for the Anglican prelates and nobles as well as the Presbyterian ministers were against religious tolerance of any but the established religion. A great deal of the persecution of Friends was instigated by the justices belonging to the country nobility and by priests of the Established Church, who sensed in the Quakers a threat to their privileges, honors and power. The Quakers, moreover, represented such a radical modification of the social order that the people were instinctively hostile. It was easy to incite a mob against them. In spite of Cromwell's best efforts,[1] they usually fared ill in the courts, and the later parliaments under the Protectorate were intolerant.

---

[1] Trevelyan, *op. cit.*, pp. 310, 311. FPT, 350–352.

The charges on which Friends were arrested, imprisoned and otherwise persecuted under the Commonwealth covered a wide range.[2] Disturbing public worship was one of the most common of them. Although the law allowed others to speak after the regular preacher had had his hour, the visiting "Publisher of Truth" was frequently so scandalized at the preacher's teaching that he interrupted the sermon. In either case the Quaker was usually mobbed, arrested and sentenced; for it was what he said which was objectionable rather than the occasion of it.[3] Women preachers were particularly insufferable in the churches.[4]

Non-payment of tithes. Friends stood out for a free ministry and refused to contribute to or recognize a "hireling ministry" in any way. They insisted at least that maintenance of a gospel ministry should be free and not forced.[5] The prosecutions instigated by priests whose tithes Friends refused to pay were one ground of the frequent charge that the ministers were mercenary.[6] For non-payment of tithes Friends' goods were often distrained in greatly excessive amounts.[7]

Refusal to honor magistrates. This charge was chiefly occasioned by Friends using "thou" instead of "you" in addressing them and by refusing to take off their hats in court. Because the English churches were not heated, men usually kept their hats on during the services, removing them only during prayer as a sign of reverence in the presence of God. Therefore Friends regarded removing the hat in the presence of civil and church officials as equiva-

---

2 See the partial list in FPT, 345–352. Cf. also Besse, *Sufferings,* I, 564, 565.

3 *Shorter Jour.,* pp. 9–14. *Camb. Jour.,* I, 108. BBQ, 194. FPT, 35, 36, 43–45. Bowden, *Hist.,* I, 77–81, 107.

4 Whitehead, *Christian Progress,* pp. 22, 23, 35, 68, 70.

5 *Bicent. Jour.* Penn's Preface, p. xxxi.

6 Burrough, *Works,* "Epistle to the Reader." *Camb. Jour.,* I, 178–180. Trevelyan, *op. cit.,* pp. 280, 311, 315.

7 *Camb. Jour.,* I, 178–180.

lent to paying them a reverence which belongs only to God. At heart the discontinuance of the customary "reverences" toward dignitaries was an expression of the democracy of Friends who would not show respect of persons by gesture, hat or language. These matters may seem trivial to us but the vigor with which magistrates and others insisted on such honors shows that they were not regarded as trivial on either side.[8]

The refusal to take oaths brought Friends much suffering. They usually quoted Christ's command "Swear not at all" as a justification; but the real reason for the refusal was the double standard of truthfulness which taking an oath implies.[9] During the Civil War and the Commonwealth the government was in continual fear of plots and insurrections and Friends' refusal to swear allegiance to the government created a suspicion of disloyalty. An old statute of Elizabeth, designed originally against the Catholics, was made more stringent in 1655 when Cromwell's oath of adjuration was imposed.[10] It provided an easy way to persecute the Quakers. When other charges were wanting or could not be substantiated against them, the justice could always tender the oath and impose penalties for its refusal, although Quakers were always willing to affirm their loyalty and disown plots and insurrections.

The charge of *vagrancy* gave hostile justices an equally good excuse to get rid of Friends. The Vagrancy Act was originally designed to correct abuses that grew out of the closing of the monasteries under Henry VIII and the turning of farm land into pastures under Elizabeth, both of which threw armies of beggars and unemployed onto the highways.[11] The law provided that "rogues, vagabonds and sturdy beggars" should be apprehended and whipped and

---

8 *Camb. Jour.*, I, 211–217, 267, 308, 341. Ellwood, *Life*, p. 55.
9 *Camb. Jour.*, I, 141; II, 483.
10 *Ibid.*, I, 191, 192, BBQ, 195.
11 Trevelyan, *op. cit.*, p. 23.

given a pass requiring the civil officers to pass them from parish to parish back to the place of their birth. In 1657 the Act was extended to include all persons wandering about or travelling without sufficient cause. The Quaker preachers were easily sentenced under the Act by justices seeking an excuse; for although they were not beggars or paupers, they were not legally preachers, neither had they lawful excuse to travel as journeymen, merchants, officials, or gentlemen.[12]

Sabbath-breaking was defined by three statutes as travel on the Lord's Day without reasonable cause or on days of public humiliation or Thanksgiving—except to or from a place of public worship or upon some other extraordinary occasion allowed by a justice—or vainly and profanely walking on the Lord's Day. Going to a Quaker meeting was thus technically Sabbath breaking.[13] For this Friends were frequently fined and on their refusal to pay, their horses or other property were distrained.[13a]

The refusal to conform to court procedure often brought upon Friends fines or imprisonment or abuse. They kept on their hats in courts (as mentioned above) and refused to plead in the regular forms. They would neither give security to keep the peace nor for good behavior, since this was construed to include abstaining from speaking in the churches and from holding Friends' meetings. They would not pay court fees when they regarded the proceedings as unjust. They were often abused in jail, placed in the foulest quarters, denied bedding, pen and paper, or the right to see their friends; they were often kept for days at a time without food, and detained in prison despite orders for their release because they would not pay the jailer's fees. According to law the jailer had to furnish prisoners bread, water and lodging. He expected to compensate himself by

---

12 Whitehead, *Christian Progress,* p. 104 and FPT, 348.

13 Ellwood, *Life,* pp. 66–70.

13a Besse, *Sufferings,* I, 565.

selling food, drink and other supplies to the prisoners or by fees from relatives for the privilege of supplying beds and food. The Quakers refused conscientiously to pay any fees to the officials of a government that denied them justice.[14]

Blasphemy was frequently alleged as the ground of persecution. The central Quaker doctrine of the indwelling Christ was easily misunderstood as a claim to divinity. Fox was imprisoned at Derby and Jane Waugh at Banbury on this charge.[15] The charge of heresy was closely related.[16] Friends were often suspected of being Jesuits in disguise.

The refusal to perform military service or to furnish a substitute brought imprisonment to many, especially in the American colonies. Under Cromwell, the Quakers were discharged from the army especially in Ireland and Scotland, often with penalties, for their pacifist attitude.[17]

The Quakers were often charged with *riot* (usually where the Quakers themselves were mobbed), *unlawful assemblies* and *plotting* against the government. George Fox was carried up to London in 1654 on a charge of plotting.[18]

Public indecency. A number of men and women were arrested and punished for public indecency because they appeared in public naked "as a sign." George Fox and other leaders defended the practice, when the doer felt it a religious duty to do so.[19] Usually the counsel of other Friends was asked beforehand and some Friend or Friends walked with the person thus exercised, carrying his or her clothes. The Quakers, like the Puritans, were much under

---

14 *Bicent. Jour.,* I, 62. BBQ, 200. Edmundson, *Jour.,* p. 46 (2d Ed.). Burrough, *Works,* p. 498. Whitehead, *Christian Progress,* p. 35. Bowden, *Hist.,* I, 106.

15 BBQ, 199. *Camb. Jour.,* I, 2. *Bicent. Jour.,* I, 169.

16 Bowden, *Hist.,* I., 102.

17 BBQ, 215, 216, 219, 228, 229. *Camb. Jour.,* I, 425n.

18 FPT, 345. *Shorter Jour.,* 38.

19 The suggestion of such a sign came apparently from Isaiah's walking "naked and barefoot three years" (Isa. 20:2, 3).

the influence of Old Testament prophecy and occasionally imitated their "acted prophecies." An age that whipped men and women or exposed them in the pillory stripped to the waist could hardly have been shocked by these occasional "signs" as much as people would be in later ages.[20]

The charge of witchcraft was sometimes made and in a period when thousands of women were put to death as witches in England and New England the charge could easily end seriously. In Massachusetts the first Quaker women, Mary Fisher and Ann Austin were stripped and searched for marks of witchcraft, but apparently no Quakers were ever convicted as witches.[21]

In Massachusetts and Connecticut Colonies a series of laws, growing always more stringent, were made expressly against "the cursed sect" of Quakers; so that the very severe persecution of Friends there was simply for being Quakers. In England under the Commonwealth there was no law against Quakers as such.

The penalties [22] suffered by Friends, legally and illegally, under form of law or without it, include mob attacks with stones, staves, Bibles or fists; personal attacks by rowdies, fellow prisoners or jailers; imprisonment, often in insanitary and unspeakably vile prisons; in many of them without protection from weather and without sanitary conveniences.[23] Under the Commonwealth, 3,173 Friends suffered imprisonment, of whom 32 died in jails, according to a paper sent Charles II in 1662 by Fox and Hubberthorne.[24] Friends suffered greatly from public whippings—chiefly as vagabonds. Many Friends, both men and women, were stripped and publicly whipped with knotted cords —ranging from ten to two hundred lashes. In Massachu-

---

20 *Bicent. Jour.*, I, 49. BBQ, 89, 126, 148–149.

21 BBQ, 67, 181.

22 GTD, 795–796.

23 FPT, 48.

24 BBQ, 464. Cf. *Camb. Jour.*, I, 192, 389, 390. *Bicent. Jour.*, I, 522.

setts and in Connecticut, women and even an eleven-year-old girl, were so treated. Two Friends were beaten in America until death seemed inevitable, but they recovered. Cassandra Southwick and other New England women, were beaten at the cart's tail from place to place.[25] The Massachusetts and Virginia laws provided heavy fines, for non-attendance at church, for entertaining Quakers or for attending their meetings. Friends were subjected to excessive distraints of goods for fines, fees and tithes.[26] Friends were often exposed in the pillory or stocks, even in inclement weather, for long hours or even overnight.[27]

Friends were often deported from a parish or city, usually as vagrants; a few were transported beyond seas. In Boston, the first Quakers were banished under penalty of being whipped and imprisoned if they returned and having an ear cut off. The imposition of a heavy fine on any shipmaster, who should bring Quakers, resulted in Friends coming by way of Rhode Island for the most part. The Boston authorities attempted to sell the two children of Lawrence and Cassandra Southwick and a few other Quakers into slavery in Virginia or Barbados but no shipmaster could be found to take them. Later some Quakers were banished from Massachusetts under penalty of death if they should return. Quite a number returned and lost their ears and four were hanged on Boston Common. These sufferings were on the whole light, compared with what the Society was to suffer in the Restoration period. They served to prevent weakness or compromise in the infancy of the movement; they attracted general attention to the Quaker character and message and generally won the sympathy of the masses, especially of their neighbors and friends who knew their personal character, by their patience and steadfast faith; and yet their sufferings were

---

25 Whitehead, *Christian Progress,* p. 68.

26 *Ibid.,* p. 69, 70.

27 BBQ, 197. Whitehead, *op. cit.,* pp. 69, 70.

not so severe as to exterminate the movement at the start nor drive all the Quakers to emigrate to America. This relatively mild character, it owes largely to the religious ferment of the early Commonwealth days and to Cromwell's later efforts for religious toleration. Many times he interfered to save or protect imprisoned Friends; there were many friendly justices, and about half the later major-generals were tolerant.[28]

---

[28] See Trevelyan, *op. cit.,* pp. 311–315.

CHAPTER 6

NAYLER'S DEFECTION

AFTER the departure of Burrough and Howgill from London at the mid-year 1655, the burden of the work in the metropolis was taken up by James Nayler, an able preacher and public disputant, who combined the appearance of a rustic with charm of manner, and intellectual power with a tender and sympathetic spirit and an almost excessive conscientiousness. He carried the burden of the work in London until the spring of 1656 when Edward Burrough returned.

Meanwhile some women Friends, of whom Martha Simmonds was the leader, had become disturbing elements in the meetings in London and elsewhere. They had refused to heed the counsels of Friends and had been reproved for their conduct by Burrough and Howgill. They appealed to Nayler for "justice." He took a very individualistic view of spiritual leading; this, with his natural sympathy, made him hesitate to condemn them. He came more and more under the influence of Martha and her companions, who flattered him and tried to set him against Fox and the other leaders who had condemned them, and they appealed to a latent jealousy of Fox's spiritual authority in Nayler who was overwrought with his London tasks.

These women and a few men Friends perverted the idea of the Christ within the believer, and persuaded Nayler that he was such an outstanding example of Christ manifest in the soul that worship could properly be paid to him. At the end of July he went to Bristol where his companions compromised him by bowing, kneeling and singing before him. Soon afterward he was arrested and thrown into Exeter jail, where his condition became pathological; he was much depressed and often fasted. Martha Simmonds persuaded him that Fox was trying to bury his name in order to exalt his own.[1] Some of his women followers wrote extravagant letters to him and some of them visited him in jail and knelt before him singing "Holy, holy, holy."

When Fox was released from Launceston jail in September he came to Exeter, but the breach between him and Nayler was widened. Both showed the physical and mental strain of their terrible imprisonments. Nayler's friends had consciously or unconsciously set one against the other. Fox had chafed helplessly in Launceston prison while Nayler's party, apparently with his approval, were bringing the Quaker movement into disrepute and anarchy. Fox later wrote a stern letter to Nayler; but Hannah Stranger and her husband sent him letters just before his release in which they called him "the only begotten Son of God" and asserted, "Thy name shall no more be called James Nayler but Jesus."

On October 24th Nayler and his party entered Bristol imitating the triumphal entry of Jesus into Jerusalem.[2] They were arrested, and arraigned before the scandalized authorities. The letters from his partisans and Fox's condemning letter were used against him. One of his companions had a copy of the apocryphal description of Jesus by Publius Lentulus, seeming to show that Nayler had deliberately copied the personal appearance of Jesus. In it all Nayler seems to have been an apathetic victim of his admirers' enthusiasm.[3] The Bristol authorities referred Nayler to Parliament. This Parliament was the second of

---

[1] See letter to him from M. Fell in BBQ, 249, 250.

[2] Fogelklou, *op. cit.*, pp. 175–178.

[3] "His chief fault appears to have been in allowing his followers to push him into a demonstration that seemed so logical an outcome of the doctrine of the Inward Christ that his enfeebled body and will could not

the parliaments set up by the Protector. It was filled with Presbyterians and the less tolerant Independents who were opposed alike to Cromwell's major-generals and his policy of religious toleration. The Nayler case gave them an opportunity to oppose the Protector's policies, especially as Nayler was regarded as the foremost of the Quakers. After long and heated debates and hearings in committee and in the House, Nayler barely escaped a death sentence. The sentence finally passed was savage enough:

> Resolved that James Nayler be set on a pillory, with his head in the pillory, in the New Palace, Westminster, during the space of two hours, on Thursday next, and be whipped by the hangman through the streets of Westminster to the Old Exchange, London, and there likewise, to be set upon the pillory, with his head in the pillory, for the space of two hours, between the hours of eleven and one, on Saturday next; in each of said places, wearing a paper containing an inscription of his crimes; and that at the Old Exchange, his tongue shall be bored through with a hot iron, and that he be there also stigmatized in the forehead with the letter B; and that he be, afterwards, sent to Bristol and be conveyed into and through the said city, on a horse bare ridged, with his face back, and there also publicly whipped the next market day after he comes thither; and that from thence he be committed to prison in Bridewell, London, and there restrained from the society of all people, and kept to hard labour till he be released by the Parliament; and, during that time, be debarred of the use of pen, ink and paper, and have no relief but what he earns by his daily labour.[4]

On hearing the sentence, Nayler said, "God has given me a body; God will, I hope, give me a spirit to endure it. The Lord lay not these things to your charge."

---

resist it. He never actually identified himself with Christ. Before the Parliament and at Bristol he testified after claiming (as Fox and others did) the title Son of God, 'I do abhor that any of that honor which is due to God should be given to me, as I am a creature.' " Fogelklou, *op. cit.*, p. 183.

[4] Cited in Fogelklou, *op. cit.*, p. 203.

During his imprisonment Nayler's mind cleared and his spirit finally triumphed over the misunderstanding, harshness, and estrangements of his experience. After nearly three years he was released by Parliament in 1659. In the meantime he had made a full acknowledgement of his fault. In a letter to Dewsbury in 1657 he expressed his regret at the divisions and disorders that had resulted and in 1658 he made an acknowledgement of his error in a letter to Parliament.[5] He had become reconciled to nearly all of the Quaker leaders before his release; but it was not until January, 1660, that Fox and he were reconciled through the active efforts of Dewsbury. Nayler preached again in London for a while but died on his way to his home in Yorkshire in October, 1660.[6]

The whole episode had far-reaching implications. It publicized Friends afresh in an unfavorable light and gave new impetus to persecution. The action of Parliament without his consent led to Cromwell's modification of the Instrument of Government, reinstating the House of Lords as a check on the powers assumed by Parliament.[7] During Nayler's imprisonment there were disturbances of meet-

---

[5] *Works,* Intro., pp. xxxv–xlvi.

[6] Toward the end of his life he said: "There is a spirit which I feel, that delights to do no evil, nor to revenge any wrong, but delights to endure all things, in hope to enjoy all things in the end; its hope is to outlive all wrath and contention, and to weary out all exaltation and cruelty, or whatever is of a nature contrary to itself. It sees to the end of all temptations; as it bears no evil in itself, so it conceives none in thoughts to any other; if it be betrayed it bears it; for its ground and spring is the mercies and forgiveness of God. Its crown is meekness, its life is everlasting love unfeigned, and it takes its kingdom with entreaty, and not with contention, and keeps it by lowliness of mind. In God alone it can rejoice, though none else regard it, nor can own its life. It's conceived in sorrow, and brought forth without any to pity it; nor doth it murmur at grief and oppression. It never rejoiceth but through sufferings; for with the world's joy it is murdered. I found it alone, being forsaken; I have fellowship therein, with them who lived in dens, and desolate places in the earth, who through death obtained this resurrection and eternal holy life." *Works,* p. 696.

[7] BBQ, 265.

ings in London and other places by Nayler's friends of Ranter tendencies, who denounced Fox and the more sober leaders. Nayler, however, seems to have had no responsibility for them and publicly disowned their proceedings.

The episode seems relatively trivial beside the attention which it received; but as such things often do, it crystallized problems that must sooner or later come to open issue. One was the danger of the doctrine of the Indwelling Christ, which without certain rational and social safeguards easily leads from a belief in the immanence of God to a kind of pantheism which implies personal infallibility. Fox had been preserved from that by his clear sanity[8] although he and some of his enthusiastic followers had used language very near to it and many early Friends had acted out "signs" and imitated Biblical events.[9] Nayler's lapse in allowing the extravagant demonstrations of his friends and his parody of the triumphal entry publicized the danger in a dramatic way. The cleavage between Fox and Nayler also raised the very difficult problem in Quakerism of the relation between individual and social guidance, between individual liberty and corporate authority.

Fox's personal authority had become almost unquestioned in the movement, although it had no official sanction. It is a question how far he had grown to assume as a right an obedience which had grown up because the leaders almost always saw eye to eye with him, and which actually rested on identity of guidance. He assumed to "judge" Nayler, while the latter, naturally enough, believed his light was fully as competent as that of Fox. When the "Inward Lights" of two saints disagree, how shall the matter be decided? Fox was inclined to believe that his judgment must be final. He was so nearly always right and continued so to win the approval of the Society, that it was

---

[8] Fogelklou, *op. cit.*, p. 109. During Nayler's trial Fox had sent a statement defending the doctrine of the divine immanence in men.

[9] BBQ, 254.

natural to feel that Nayler ought to have given in. Possibly it was this challenge of his primacy that Fox found so hard to forgive. We must remember also that Nayler gave (unintentionally) encouragement to anarchistic and destructive elements in the movement at a time when Fox was in prison, watching helplessly the apparent disintegration of a work which he could but identify with the cause of Christ. Nayler's defection thus raised issues beyond its intrinsic significance.

The episode was not wholly without compensations. Braithwaite remarks: "But while Nayler's fall prejudiced the work of Friends in many ways, which I have indicated, its most lasting effect was good, for it effectually warned the Quaker leaders of the perils attending the overemphasis which they had laid on the infallibility of the life possessed by the Spirit of Christ. Henceforth they walked more carefully, heedful of the special temptations which beset the path of spiritual enthusiasm." [10]

---

[10] BBQ, 271.

Chapter 7

BEGINNINGS OF ORGANIZATION

George Fox and his co-workers did not set out to organize a sect, any more than did Martin Luther or John Wesley; there was a world-wide scope in the thoughts and purposes of all three. The first Quaker converts, however, were drawn into close fellowship with each other by their common faith, experience and leadership. Their work, needs and the pressure of a hostile world required organized efforts.[1] The earliest groups of Friends were formed largely from Baptist, Seeker and other brotherhood groups, who already enjoyed a measure of group life and organization; they existed apart from the Established Church, disclaimed any relation with the state, and had some form of "business meetings"; [2] and they were accustomed to meetings for worship which were non-liturgical and often silent. These elements of religious group life were taken over by the Quaker movement, somewhat as the early Christian church inherited forms of organization from the Jewish synagogue.

The early organization of the Quakers was powerfully influenced by George Fox and other dynamic leaders, especially Farnsworth, Dewsbury and Nayler.[3] This leadership was not official but personal. William Penn says of Fox, "Though God had visibly clothed him with a divine preference and authority . . . yet he never abused it; but

---

1 *Bicent. Jour.*, I, 28.

2 Barclay, *Inner Life,* pp. 352, 353.

3 BBQ, 134. Fogelklou, *op. cit.*, p. 109.

held his place in the church of God with great meekness, and a most engaging humility and moderation. For upon all occasions, like his blessed Master, he was servant to all; holding and exercising his eldership in the invisible power that had gathered them; . . . because his authority was inward and not outward, and he got it and kept it by the love of God."[4]

Under the Commonwealth, Fox's influence was predominant in the Quaker movement. Because of his thorough acquaintance with all phases of it, especially the needs and abilities of the travelling ministers and the opportunities of various fields, his judgments were rarely questioned. They were so clearly right that his suggestions and requests were usually complied with without question; but Robert Barclay (the younger) has greatly exaggerated the degree and character of his direction and organization of the movement.[5] He also exercised a great unifying and stabilizing influence by his letters and writings.

Mention has already been made of the influence of Margaret Fell who made Swarthmore Hall a coördinating center of the work of the growing Society. Through her, the ministers kept in touch with the leaders, information and suggestions were distributed and the needy were helped spiritually, physically and financially. The "Kendal Fund" was raised and maintained by Westmorland and Lancashire Friends to help the work, and it was disbursed through Swarthmore. The expenses of the "Publishers of Truth" were paid where necessary: they were furnished with clothes and Bibles; and food and bedding were supplied to those in prison. Quaker books were bought and distributed. The campaigns in London and the south of England in 1654–1657 were largely financed by this fund. Gradually this kind of support was derived in larger part

---

[4] *Bicent. Jour.*, pp. xlix, l.

[5] Barclay, *Inner Life*, pp. 339–359.

from other parts of the nation, but Swarthmore Hall continued throughout this period as the great unofficial center.

Without the authority of official decrees or pronouncements the infant Society of Friends attained in a short time a remarkable unanimity as to its message, practices and organization. This was due in part to common ideas and practices in the sects from which most of the early converts were drawn. But finally, it was due to the Inward Light as a principle of personal and social guidance that this unanimity was arrived at. When thoroughly trusted, it proved able to bring the Friends into contact with spiritual reality with sufficient accuracy to form the ground of a common view of life, common ideals of conduct and programs of corporate conduct. It did not work equally well in different individuals or groups; there was no infallibility attained; and experience showed that it worked better when checked by the group judgment. The Quaker organization arose partly to secure such corporate aid in "sharpening the image" of the religious ideal and clarifying the spiritual leadings. In each group or congregation a few of the more able members, called elders, served as leaders. They were chosen by common consent, usually in consultation with Fox or other leaders.

The organized activities of the Society were of two kinds, centering in the meetings for worship and in the meetings for business, respectively. These were not distinct in the sense that one was sacred and the other secular. Worship and church business were both determined by the divine leading, individual and corporate. The meetings for worship were usually held on Sunday by small groups living in the same neighborhood. They met without any ritual or prearranged service to "wait upon the Lord in silence." These were called "silent meetings," because they convened "on the basis of silence." Any vocal exercises were expected to arise from the leading of the Spirit in individuals as conditioned by the group life and spirit.

The business meetings were usually held at rarer intervals and gradually came to be settled as monthly meetings, which normally included a number of local groups or meetings, situated in contiguous territory.[6] The monthly meeting became the local administrative or executive unit.[7] It arose out of the needs of and the demands on the first Friends communities. It provided for the necessities of the travelling ministers and their families, when necessary, and for expenditures for clothes, travel, Bibles and other books.[8] It looked after persecuted Friends, providing necessities for those in prison and making efforts for their release. As the Society grew the care of the poor among the members, and even of their poor neighbors, devolved upon it.[9]

Marriages came early under the care of the monthly meetings. Friends could not conscientiously be married by a priest, since this would seem to sanction a "hireling ministry." In 1650 Parliament had made a civil marriage valid,[10] but Friends believed that the only sanctions needed were the free consent of the parties and the sense of the divine presence and approval. So they simply took each other as husband and wife in the presence of the Lord and his people. The monthly meeting took care that in the case of each couple there were no legal impediments to marriage, that they were morally free from obligations to any others, and had the consent of their parents. A certificate was signed by a large number of witnesses of the marriage and the monthly meeting records were carefully kept to protect the legal and property rights of widows and children. The Quaker practice was really a common law marriage and was so declared by a decision in 1661.[11] The

6 BBQ, 141. FPT, 21.

7 BBQ, 330.

8 Barclay, *op. cit.*, 347. BBQ, 143, 186, 321.

9 *Ibid.*, 352.

10 BBQ, 145, 146.

11 *Bicent. Jour.*, I, 520.

monthly meetings also kept records of births and deaths among their numbers in lieu of parish records.

In this period there were no formal lists of members. Those who attended Friends meetings and conformed to Friends ways were generally regarded as Friends. If any such behaved in un-Quakerly ways, especially so as to bring moral or spiritual reproach to the Society, the meeting made every effort to restore the person to conformity, and if the efforts finally failed, they "disowned" him by publishing to the world the fact that although this person had associated with them, they no longer owned him as a Friend.

In addition to monthly meetings there were held "general meetings," made up at first chiefly of "public Friends," *i.e.*, elders and travelling ministers from wider areas. These took care of larger questions of concern to the movement, such as collections for the work overseas and on the continent of Europe, and the character of the ministry, to prevent abuses. The movement attracted some people of little judgment or ability, especially from the Ranters, who needed caution, advice and help. The aberration of Nayler and the extreme individualism of John Perrot later made such problems acute.[12] Fox issued a paper of advice to Friends about the end of 1656. A meeting of "elders" was convened at Balby in Yorkshire in November, 1656, which issued a careful circular letter of advice.[13] In it is the germ of the official "advices" on matters of conduct which became a feature of the later disciplines. Another general meeting was held at Scalehouse in 1657, to deal mainly with the collections for the work of Friends; and another similar one at Skipton in 1658.[14] Out of these, gradually developed both the later quarterly and yearly meetings.

Many of the elements of the Quaker organization came

---

12 BBQ, 319. Fox, *Epistles,* No. 131.

13 BBQ, 312, 313.

14 *Ibid.*, 322, 323, 325.

to their full fruition and many of its most significant features developed only after the end of the Commonwealth in 1660.

Reviewing the situation at the close of the Commonwealth period, the movement had spread all over the British Isles but had made its greatest headway in England. Braithwaite, basing his estimate largely on the statistics of imprisonments, estimates the number of Friends in the Restoration year "at from 30,000 to 40,000, out of a population of about five millions." A contemporary estimate is upward of 60,000.[15] They were "drawn principally from the trading and yeoman classes, though there were also some artisans and laborers, a fair number of merchants, and a few gentry." [16]

The movement was characterized by an apostolic fervor and by spiritual power and exaltation. Its springs were fed by a wonderfully vital sense of the presence of God. Its adherents were characterized by their mystic worship, their keen sensitiveness to human need and their conscientiousness in their dealings with one another. The movement had not yet crystallized into a formal organization, when it was suddenly plunged into a struggle for existence against both church and state, in which it could only rely on the power of an unformulated faith and an unorganized fellowship.

---

15 *Ibid.*, p. 512 and note.
16 *Loc. cit.*

CHAPTER 8

EARLY LITERATURE

THE "Publishers of Truth" used the press for spreading their message as well as the spoken word. They contributed their full share to the vast output of apologetic and controversial writings, in which the religious, intellectual and political ferment of the Commonwealth period found literary expression.[1] This activity was favored by Cromwell's efforts for religious toleration and by the lack of a vigorous and effective censorship of the press.[2] In spite of some arrests for owning, circulating or selling Quaker publications, and in a few cases the seizure or destruction of offending presses, there was a large output of printed matter. In the seven decades after 1653 there were 440 Quaker writers, who published 2,678 separate publications, varying from a single page tract to folios of nearly a thousand pages.[3] Fox exercised an unofficial censorship over Friends' publications which purported to represent the Society, because the custom grew up of submitting all such compositions to him in advance of printing.[4]

The Quaker leaders were naturally their first writers.[5] Through the press they reached wider audiences both at home and beyond the seas. They stated their principles in brief proclamations, epistles and addresses. They replied

---

1 Above chap. 2, "The England of George Fox," p. 12.

2 For the laws against unlicensed printing see BBQ, 303, 304.

3 Wright, *Lit. Life,* p. 8.

4 BBQ, 134.

5 Wright, *op. cit.,* p. 41.

(too often in kind) to the attacks of their adversaries upon them. They made use of the frequent periods of imprisonment to carry on their work by letters and pamphlets—at times so effectively that the prisoners were expressly forbidden to have pen and ink.[6] They spread their message by religious exposition, theological argument and by accounts of personal experiences and reports of controversies. Their writings also helped create a unity of thought and practice in the Society. They expounded their mystical concepts of Christianity and their practical ideals of Christian conduct. They attacked the mercenary and persecuting spirit of the clergy, their unspiritual preaching and soulless forms of worship. They exposed and denounced the officers of the courts for their unjust and cruel persecutions. They took exception to features of the prevalent Calvinistic theology.

In the three years, 1653 to 1655, Friends published one hundred and thirty-six tracts and broadsheets.[7] In general they adopted the sharp controversial tone and denunciatory style common to churchmen, Puritans and many of the sects. They showed the same or even greater vigor, assurance and missionary zeal. The style was often prolix, involved and repetitious. They used mainly the theological and religious vocabulary of the Puritans and mystics, although the Friends often used it in a peculiar sense. This style had a greater appeal in that day than it does today. It was also in part redeemed by the vital experience and glowing earnestness behind the verbiage. It was an age given to long caustic and satirical titles, even for short broadsheets. In these and the ensuing controversies a favorite device was for each side to call the other antichrist. The following representative titles are given by Braithwaite:

---

[6] Bowden, *Hist.*, I, 34, 45.
[7] Wright, *op. cit.*, p. 8.

For example, Fox, in 1653, had issued his "Unmasking and Discovering of Antichrist," and in 1654 "The Vials of The Wrath of God Poured forth Upon the Seat of the Man of Sin": Farnsworth in 1653 sent out "A Voice of the first Trumpet sounding an Alarme to call to Judgement," also "A Call out of False Worships," and "A Brief Discovery of the Kingdome of Antichrist, and the downfall of it hasteth greatly," whilst Margaret Fell in 1655 wrote "False Prophets, Antichrists, Deceivers . . . which hath been long hid and covered, but now is Unmasked, in these last dayes, with the Eternal Light which is risen." [8]

Nayler's defection in 1656 was the signal for a widespread and vigorous counter-attack on Friends. Priests, smarting under the interruptions and denunciations of the Quaker evangelists and embittered by the loss of tithes and members, rushed into print. Churchmen and others in high position, such as Richard Baxter, John Owen, William Prynne and Samuel Clarke, found the Quakers dangerous to the church and society. Leaders of the Baptists and other sects joined in the literary onset. John Bunyan's first work was an attack on Friends' doctrine of individual spiritual guidance.[9]

Although sometimes unequally matched in point of learning, Friends pitted themselves against any antagonist, armed against all comers by their living teaching respecting the Inner Light. Smith, the Quaker bibliographer, in his *Bibliotheca Anti-Quakeriana,* includes about ninety-eight adverse authors during the Commonwealth period, and the names of thirty-seven of these occur in the *Dictionary of National Biography,* clear proof of the importance in their own day of these obscure controversies. The zest with which Friends threw themselves into public disputing and polemics is, in fact, only another evidence of the large claims and wide ambitions of early Quakerism.[10]

---

[8] BBQ, 279, 280.
[9] *Ibid.,* 286, 287.
[10] *Ibid.,* 305.

The points of attack upon Friends were largely the eccentricities of some Friends and garbled reports as to their tenets and customs. At times these opponents resorted to personal slander. Some of these brochures were replies to Quaker attacks on the church and priests. There was little effort apparently on the part of most of them at understanding the real character of Quakerism. On the other hand, most people are prejudiced against new ideas and customs, and rarely take the pains to understand them. This is especially true where the old order is consecrated by religion. On the whole, the Quakers understood their opponents better; which is natural. They had grown up in the same theological and ecclesiastical circles as their opponents. There were sincere and vital differences between the Quaker writers and their opponents in regard to the authority of Scripture, the nature and function of the church, its ministry and sacraments, the nature of man, and spiritual guidance; but these questions were rarely discussed on their merits.

The hostile writings against Friends were not allowed to go unanswered; and frequently these attacks and counter-attacks stretched out through several literary generations.

For instance, Hubberthorne published the report of a public dispute with Thomas Danson, a well-known divine of the day: he replied with "The Quakers' Folly Made manifest to all men." George Whitehead, one of the disputants, retorted with "The Voice of Wisdom uttered forth against Antichrist's Folly and Deceit"; Danson took up the cudgels a second time with "The Quaker's Wisdom descendeth not from Above," and was answered by Luke Howard in "The Devil's Bow Unstringed," as well as by Samuel Fisher, the third of the disputants. One debate thus gave rise to six pamphlets, surely overmuch shedding of printers' ink. Or, again, John Stalham, an Essex minister, begins with "Contradictions of the Quakers"; Farnsworth replies with "The Scriptures' Vindication"; and is answered in "The Reviler Rebuked." Hubberthorne continues with "The Rebukes of a Reviler fallen upon his own head," to which Stalham rejoins in "Marginall Antidotes"; and Fox has the last word in a reply to "Marginall Antidotes," to be found in *The Great Mistery*.[11]

Edward Burrough carried on a controversy with John Bunyan regarding the Inward Light which extended through two pamphlets on each side.

On the Quaker side, the earliest controversialists were, like most of the "First Publishers," men and women of little education, but the movement soon enlisted a goodly number of educated and experienced men. The chief Quaker writers under the Commonwealth were George Fox, Edward Burrough, James Nayler, Samuel Fisher, Richard Farnsworth, Francis Howgill, Richard Hubberthorne, and George Whitehead.

Though many authors had received little formal education and were devoid of skill in writing, a fairly large number of the leaders had been trained at Oxford and Cambridge; a few like Giles Barnardiston and William Penn had been sent abroad to complete their education with foreign travel. Some like Samuel Fisher and Francis Howgill had studied divinity for the purpose of taking orders in the Church of England, and after becoming dissatisfied with Anglican doctrines, had preached for Independent congregations before joining the Friends. To their support of Quakerism such men brought the zeal that fresh inspiration and novel intellectual views can furnish as well as minds that had already been trained to organize and express thought.[12]

George Fox was naturally one of the earliest and most vigorous of the Quaker writers. His style was vigorous, simple and direct, in contrast with the involved sentences of Burrough and Fisher. Many of his early epistles and tracts are embodied in his *Journal*. He also gave close attention to the printed attacks on Friends. In 1659, in

11 BBQ, 283.
12 Wright, *op. cit.*, pp. 8, 9.

collaboration with Edward Burrough, he published a reply to one hundred of the most noteworthy of the anti-Quaker publications. Its long apocalyptic title begins: *The Great Mistery of the Great Whore Unfolded,* etc. The book follows the plan of citing a statement from the work to be answered or asking a question raised by a passage in it, and then proceeding to show its falsity. In addition to his own writing and his unofficial censorship upon the writings of other Friends, he watched over the progress and needs of the Society, often suggesting to his co-workers subjects to be treated, attacks to be met and incidents to be recorded.

Edward Burrough was probably the most prolific of the early Quaker apologists. From 1652, when as a young man of twenty he joined Fox, until his death in 1662, he found time for copious writings along with his vigorous ministry and hard travels. His collected writings under the long title beginning *The Memorable Works of a Son of Thunder and Consolation* contain about nine hundred small folio pages. He had no great learning, but understood how to reach the understanding and consciences of his contemporaries. He had great courage and was gifted with a natural eloquence.[13] His style is often prolix, but it is in part redeemed by his great sincerity, earnestness and prophetic fervor.

> Burrough's style varies from the plainest of unvarnished prose to vigorous invective, and to an occasional passage of highly emotional power, especially when he was "moved" to write of his mystical experiences with the Inner Light.[14]

James Nayler was, in many respects, superior to Burrough as a Quaker controversialist. He was more courteous, more sensitive to spiritual realities and had a better disciplined mind. On account of his later defection his writ-

---

[13] BBQ, 47.
[14] Wright, *op. cit.*, 47.

ings were not published until long after his death and then his controversial works proper were omitted.[15]

The most scholarly of the Commonwealth Quaker controversialists was Samuel Fisher. He had a university education, and had been an Anglican rector, a Puritan lecturer and then a Baptist preacher. His collected works fill a folio volume of about a thousand pages, three-fourths of which are taken up by his *Rusticus ad Academicos*. The work is devoted to a defense of the Quaker view of the Scriptures and was a caustic and defiant reply to the writings of John Owen, Thomas Danson, John Tombes and Richard Baxter, which expounded and defended the doctrine of the verbal inspiration and sole authority of the Scriptures. Fisher follows the method of question and answer, and writes in an involved style, with much citation of authorities and copious marginal notes. He anticipates many of the problems and methods of nineteenth-century Biblical criticism. He asks awkward questions about translations, the original manuscripts, the text and manuscripts, the canon and the apocryphal books. No reply to the book was ever written. The extent of its influence outside the Society is unknown. Among Friends it was never very popular. After all, the attitude of Friends toward the Bible rested on their experience of the Inward Light rather than on logic and learning.

Other able writers can only be mentioned. Howgill, Hubberthorne and Whitehead were not particularly distinguished. Howgill was tender and mystical; most of Whitehead's writings belong to a later period. Although Farnsworth was an effective writer, his works were never collected and reprinted.

Arrangements were early made for the wide circulation of Friends' writings. The travelling preachers carried literature to distribute. Friends in the North at first bore the

---

15 BBQ, 288.

cost of printing, taking six hundred copies of each book for use in their counties.[16] The Skipton General Meeting in 1659 directed that each monthly meeting pay for its own books except those sent to other nations.[17]

---

16 *Camb. Jour.*, I, 266.
17 BBQ, 316, 328.

Period II

Quakerism after the Restoration 1660-1691

CHAPTER 9

THE STRUGGLE FOR EXISTENCE

THE second period of Quaker history extended from the restoration of Charles II to the death of George Fox and was as truly conditioned by the Restoration Settlement as was the first period by the Commonwealth. The Restoration marked a great change in the spirit and history of the nation and affected profoundly the fortunes of the Society of Friends.

The primary cause of the Restoration was the dislike of the English people for the severity, strictness and cost of Puritan military rule, to which Cromwell had been driven by inability to secure a satisfactory parliament. The Puritans had failed in their effort to establish the kingdom of the saints. The sectaries had been disappointed by their failure to secure religious and civil liberty. After Cromwell's death his son Richard lacked the strength to hold the Commonwealth together. The army became divided and General Monk occupied London and declared for a free parliament as a first step toward the restoration of "a government of king, lords and parliament," which seemed the only kind of government upon which, in the emergency, the people could unite. From his exile in Holland

Charles II issued the Declaration of Breda, which reconciled the Nonconformists to his restoration by the promise of "a liberty to tender consciences, and that no man shall be disquieted, or called in question for differences of opinion in the matter of religion, which do not disturb the peace of the kingdom." The Convention Parliament called by General Monk, vented its spite on Cromwell's bones, executed the regicide judges, and recalled the Stuarts to the throne.

The position of Friends during the period was primarily determined by the efforts of parliament to secure the spiritual unity of the nation through uniformity of worship under the Established Church and the efforts of the Stuarts to restore the Catholic Church. The first parliament under King Charles II (commonly called the Restoration or the Cavalier Parliament) was actuated principally by three motives: (1) revenge for the loss of estates and livings and the persecutions which the Cavaliers and Episcopalians, who composed it chiefly, had suffered under the Commonwealth; (2) fear that the hated Puritans might regain control, and (3) dread of Catholic supremacy toward which the Stuart policy was directed.

The Cavalier Parliament proved to be the master of the nation. Charles was able in the interest of peace to curb its desire for vengeance, but he was too easy-going to risk his crown and the pleasures of his dissolute court to keep his word to the Nonconformists. The attitude of Parliament in regard to religion was primarily political; it was determined to secure the unity and peace of the nation, if possible. This was the purpose of its efforts to establish uniformity in religion. It feared with a certain historical justification that conventicles of religious sects would become nests of sedition.[1] The Thirty Years War on the Continent, which had only ended in 1648, and the English

---

1 BSPQ, 7.

Civil Wars showed what terribly destructive consequences religious differences could produce; and the later Revocation of the Edict of Nantes (1685) by Louis XIV of France and the expulsion of the Huguenots brought home to Englishmen the terrors of Catholic political power. The Northern Uprising in 1663 showed that Puritanism was still a potential menace, especially among the old Cromwellian soldiers scattered through the country.

The history of Friends in this period is primarily the story of their resistance to the efforts of the government to enforce uniformity in religion. They bore the brunt of the struggle for the toleration of Nonconformity, because they would neither abandon their meetings, nor meet in secret; because they would not take oaths of any kind, not even oaths of allegiance to the government, and would not conform in many other ways to the laws and usages of the land. The persecutions were not continuous throughout the period or the Society could hardly have survived them.

For several months after the accession of Charles, Friends enjoyed a relative liberty. This halcyon period came to a sudden end because of the uprising of the Fifth Monarchy Men.[2] They were a radical millenarian sect, who believed that the four monarchies of Daniel's visions, the Babylonian, Persian, Greek and Roman, having already come to pass, the fifth or Messianic monarchy was ready to be revealed, whenever the followers of Christ should begin the struggle to establish it. They stored arms in London and on the night of January 6, 1661, thirty-five of them, under the leadership of Venner, a cooper, issued from their hall and attempted to seize the city, crying, "King Jesus and their heads upon the gates!" They were put down by the city militia after having terrorized the city for four days. No one knew who or how many were involved in the attempted coup and persecution broke out

---

2 Trevelyan, *op. cit.*, 336.

against all sects suspected of sedition, especially the Baptists and Quakers. A proclamation was issued on January 10th "prohibiting meetings of Anabaptists and Quakers and Fifth Monarchy Men, and commanding justices to tender the oath of allegiance to persons brought before them for assembling at such meetings."[3] The following Sunday the London jails were crowded with Friends, arrested at their meetings, which they held as usual. In all parts of the country arrests were made, chiefly in the cities, until about 4,230 Friends were in prison.

Fox and Hubberthorne drew up a "declaration against plots and fightings" which was presented to the king and published in London January 21st, part of which reads as follows:

> Our principle is and our practices have always been to seek peace and ensue it; to follow after righteousness and the knowledge of God, seeking the good and welfare and doing that which tends to the peace of all. . . . All bloody principles and practices we as to our own particular do utterly deny, with all outward wars and strife and fightings with outward weapons for any end or under any pretense whatsoever; and this is our testimony to the whole world. . . . The Spirit of Christ by which we are guided, is not changeable, so as once to command us from a thing as evil and again to move unto it; and we do certainly know and so testify to the world that the Spirit of Christ, which leads us unto all truth, will never move us to fight and war against any man with outward weapons, neither for the kingdom of Christ nor for the kingdoms of this world. . . .
>
> For this we can say to all the world; we have wronged no man's persons or possessions; we have used no force nor violence against any man; we have been found in no plots nor guilty of sedition. When we have been wronged, we have not sought to revenge ourselves; we have not made resistance to authority; but wherein we could not obey for conscience'

---

[3] BSPQ, 9. See the vivid account of conditions in Newgate prison in Ellwood, *Life*, pp. 137–200 (1714 Ed.).

sake we have suffered the most of any people in the nation.[4]

The leaders of the insurrection exonerated Friends of any part in it and on January 25th by proclamation of the Lord Mayor, many of the London Friends were set free. By the middle of May all Friends who were "in prison for refusing oaths or for meeting contrary to the proclamation or for not giving sureties" were released by the king. Nevertheless the country justices, often incited by the priests, found means to persecute Friends.

Without special legislation, the magistrates had at hand a ready weapon against them in the Elizabethan writ of *praemunire,* which was originally aimed at "popish recusants" who refused to swear allegiance to the monarch as head of the church.[5] A person convicted under it was put out of the king's protection; his lands and goods were forfeited to the crown, and he remained a prisoner at the king's pleasure. This law was frequently invoked against Friends, when other charges could not be proved. The court could always tender the oath of allegiance, knowing that Friends would not take it.[6]

Special laws against Nonconformists were soon enacted by the Cavalier parliament. Within five years it enacted the so-called Clarendon Code which contained the following provisions:

By the Corporation Act (1661) the membership of the municipal bodies who ruled the towns and usually controlled the elections of their parliamentary representatives, was confined to those who would receive Communion by the rites of the Church of England.

By the Act of Uniformity (1662) 2,000 Puritan clergy were expelled from livings in the Established Church, for refusing to assert their "unfeigned consent and assent" to everything in the Prayer-book.

---

4 *Camb. Jour.,* I, 494–500, gives the 1684 text of the Declaration.

5 The name was taken from the Latin wording of the writ.

6 BSPQ, 112.

By the Conventicle Act (1664) attendance at meetings for religious rites, other than those of the Established Church, were punished by imprisonment for the first and second offense, and transportation for the third, on pain of death if the criminal returned.

By the Five Mile Act (1665) no clergyman or schoolmaster was to come within five miles of a city or corporate town, unless he declared that he would not "at any time endeavour any alteration of Government either in Church or State." As the Puritan congregations were principally seated in the towns, the great body of dissenters were hereby cut off from even private education or domestic encouragement in their faith.[7]

In addition to this code the Quaker Act of 1662 imposed heavy penalties on persons maintaining on religious grounds the unlawfulness of all oaths and on Quakers if they left their homes and assembled to the number of five or more for worship not authorized by law.[8]

With the passage of the Act of Uniformity and the Quaker Act, persecution broke out afresh, of which London was the storm center. Friends continued to meet as before and under the direction of Major-General Browne the meetings were raided and Newgate and other prisons crowded with Friends. At the ensuing trials in mid-summer the Quaker Act was put aside and the *praemunire* used against them. On the occasion of the new queen's arrival in London, the king ordered the release of all but ringleaders and preachers.

In September and again in October and November the jails were filled on the strength of rumors of plots. During this year twenty died in Newgate or shortly after their release from the effects of their confinement.[9] At one time thirty London Friends made an offer to lie in prison in place of the sick and poorest of their brethren, but the

---

[7] Trevelyan, *op. cit.*, 341.
[8] BSPQ, 22, 23.
[9] Besse, *Sufferings*, I, 388, 389.

authorities would not allow it.[10] Persecution was revived under the first Conventicle Act by the abortive Puritan Northern Plot in 1663. George Fox was *praemunired* at Lancaster early in 1663 and after fourteen months of exposure to cold and rain in Lancaster jail he was transferred to Scarborough, where he was confined in an exposed cell until 1666. Francis Howgill and Margaret Fell were *praemunired* at the same time as Geoge Fox but by special favor of the king Margaret's estates were not forfeited. Fox was released in 1668. Howgill lay in Appleby jail till he died in 1669. Others of the Quaker leaders were imprisoned as a consequence of the Northern Uprising and the passing of the Conventicle Act. The Society suffered from the cessation of the refreshing visits of the travelling ministers. Both the Quaker Act and the Conventicle Acts provided for transportation for a third offense. In all, some 109 men Friends and 44 women were sentenced to banishment under them, but from various causes the sentence was actually carried out in only a very few cases.

Persecution was relaxed, however, when public attention was distracted by the Great Plague in London (1665), the Great Fire (1666) and the Dutch War (1665–1667). Then the fall of Clarendon (1668) gave the Friends a breathing space of a few years. It was during this period that some of its ablest members joined the Society. Isaac Penington and his wife, Mary Springett Penington, had come to the end of their long search for religious satisfaction in 1658, and were largely responsible for the later adherence to the Society of Thomas Ellwood (1659). William Penn became "convinced" near the end of 1667 and shortly afterward Robert Barclay joined the Society. George Keith had joined in 1663. In 1668 William Penn wrote a book, *Sandy Foundation Shaken,* attacking the logical inconsistencies of the popular teaching on the Trin-

---

10 *Ibid.*, I, 381.

ity. At the instigation of the Bishop of London, he was imprisoned in the Tower for blasphemy, where he improved his time writing *No Cross No Crown*. It was evident that Penn's religious position was misunderstood by his persecutors. He was willing to suffer for his faith but could hardly afford to remain in jail on account of a misunderstanding. His next work *Innocency With Her Open Face* vindicated his essentially Christian faith and secured his release. Penn, Barclay, Keith, Ellwood and Penington brought the Society a combination of fresh enthusiasm, learning and social position—elements which were of inestimable value in the supreme struggles of the next decade.

The first Conventicle Act expired in 1669, but the English people sensed the growing Catholic influence at court, and their fear of it led Parliament to pass the second Conventicle Act the next year. The king was more and more indulging the Nonconformists as a pretext for suspending the penal laws against the Catholics. He had long been negotiating with the Catholic ecclesiastical powers and the King of France, and in 1670 he signed the secret Treaty of Dover, agreeing to help Louis XIV destroy the Protestant Dutch State in return for a large subsidy from the French, which would free him from the control which Parliament exercised over him through its power of the purse.

The Second Conventicle Act provided that a single justice could convict without the safeguard of a jury. The penalty of transportation was dropped. Under it justices could break into suspected houses and could use the militia to break up unlawful assemblies. Prosecution was limited to three months after an offense and a conviction barred prosecution for the same offense under other acts. Fines were imposed for attending or preaching at or harboring a conventicle. The most odious feature of it was the encouragement of informers, who were to receive a third of the fines, which were recoverable by distraint of goods. The purpose of the law was to ruin Nonconformists financially rather than to punish them.[11]

Friends continued to meet according to their custom in spite of the new Act. In London their meeting-houses were occupied by guards or were padlocked or dismantled. Friends continued to meet amid the wreckage of the furniture of their meeting-houses or in the streets in front of them until they were taken off to prison by the troops or constables. The attempt to pull down meeting-houses was quickly thwarted, however, by the wit of Gilbert Latey who installed a family in one.[12] Since the days of Magna Carta an Englishman's dwelling has been inviolate. From that time this clever arrangement was commonly adopted in meeting-houses.[13]

In August, 1670, William Penn and William Mead were arrested at the Grace Church Street meeting in London and soon after brought to trial in the Old Bailey Court under the new Act. The recorder, Richard Brown, together with the other justices was determined to punish the ringleaders of the Quakers. First of all the accused were fined for contempt of court for refusal to take off their hats. The prisoners pleaded not guilty to the form of the indictment, especially to the charge that they had assembled by force and arms and caused a riot; and demanded under what law they were charged. Instead of the Conventicle Act they were indicted under the common law. William Penn made a plea for the fundamental rights of Englishmen and when the recorder charged the jury in the absence of the accused, who had been sequestered in the bail dock, to bring in a verdict of guilty, Penn exhorted them to stand for their legal rights and to bring in a verdict according to their consciences. They brought in the

---

11 BSPQ, 66, 67.

12 BSPQ, 77.

13 To this day the older meeting premises in England have a residence for the caretaker in them.

verdict: "Guilty of speaking in Gracious Street," and refused to add the words "in an unlawful assembly" at the recorder's demand. In a rage Recorder Brown ordered them to bring in a positive verdict, and on their second refusal ordered them shut up without fire, food, drink, tobacco or other accommodation, until they brought in a verdict of guilty. On being called the next day and the next, they persisted in the verdict, "not guilty." The recorder finally fined them forty marks each and imprisoned them until the fine should be paid, and sent Penn and Mead to Newgate until they paid the fine for contempt of court. In November the jurymen were admitted to bail and after a year had passed, the case was reviewed by the Court of Common Pleas which unanimously decided that a jury could not be fined for its verdict. The decision became one of the bulwarks of English liberty.[14]

The persecutions from 1662 to 1672 put the Society of Friends to its severest test. They were felt in three ways with special severity: (1) in the financial ruin of its membership through fines and distraint of goods, the forfeiture of estates under the *praemunire* and the loss of wages and business during imprisonment; (2) in the breaking up of its meetings for worship through the imprisonment of their members and (3) in the lack of guidance and inspiration through the imprisonment and death of the leaders.

The work of the informers was particularly vicious under the Second Conventicle Act.[15] Braithwaite thus characterized their work:

> The informer had been encouraged under the Penal Statutes, because the ordinary Englishman, even when "dressed in a little brief authority," was averse to harrying his honest neighbors. But now the Bench, the magistracy, and the corporations were packed with the creatures of tyranny; and he

14 See Penn's account of the trial in *Works,* I, 7–14. Cf. Traill, *Social England,* IV, 363, 364.

15 BSPQ, 113, 114.

became the master of men's liberties and estates. He could invoke the Penal Laws against the Justice who had the temerity of independence to disregard his trumped-up charges: he throve on perjury and excessive distraints: if he pressed for fines rather than imprisonments, it was not from mercy but from greed: a bribe was the only passport to his indulgence; and he feared nothing but the raking up of his own past. He preyed upon the industry of the country; though with small profit to the King's Exchequer: his only talent was the art by which he exploited the tyranny of the times.[16]

The provision that the informer should receive one third of the fines and fees, appealed to men of vicious and unscrupulous character. They were often in league with officials of similar character and there was little restraint on their rapacity. They were often guilty of perjury against wealthy Friends.[17] The fines, which Friends refused to pay voluntarily, were secured by levying on their goods, often in excessive amounts, and in many cases the informers retained the shares that belonged to the government and the poor fund.[18] These professional informers became very unpopular. The Quakers' fellow-townsmen did not like to see their honest neighbors robbed for the benefit of rascals, and the tradesmen disliked to see their good customers ruined by rogues from outside.[19]

The financial losses of Friends were very great. The amounts of these fines and distraints are given by Besse by counties. Braithwaite summarizes a few of them:

In Somerset, distraints to the value of about a thousand pounds were made on Friends in 1670, often on false information. Suffolk escaped with half this amount. At Guildford 180 pounds in distresses were taken for meetings held in the street, when Friends were kept out of the meeting-house. In the North

16 BSPQ, 113, 114.

17 Ellwood, *Life,* 276–291; Besse, *op. cit., passim.*

18 For other cases see BSPQ, 113 note.

19 *Ibid.,* 80, 81.

Riding a Richmond innkeeper named William Thornaby kept a minute record, unique among rogues' diaries, of the service done by him and his agents during fourteen months. The booty in fines from seventy-nine meetings was two thousand pounds, often excessively levied.[20]

Friends in London enjoyed a relative immunity from persecution at this time and raised a fund of about a thousand pounds, which was increased by contributions from other quarters, to aid distressed Friends, but it fell short of the actual needs even when supplemented by local gifts.[21] The monthly meetings looked after their own members to the best of their ability, cared for the wives and children while the men were in prison, and in many cases maintained a "stock" or fund to provide materials for the prisoners to work at their trades, as they were usually allowed to do, and assisted them where necessary to market their products. In 1672 there were 125 *praemunired* Friends in prison and 60 under sentence of banishment.

It is less easy to estimate the spiritual losses from the imprisonments, which often included the majority of the adult members of meetings. The Society has always found its chief strength in the meetings for worship. Friends continued to hold these, often outside their closed meeting-houses, and sometimes in the jail where the majority of the membership were confined; but many of the members were separated by prison walls from their brethren. At Reading there were times when most of the men were in prison. In 1664, 1666 and again in 1670 the meetings were carried on mostly by women and children in spite of threats of arrest and abuse.[22] At Colchester also the meeting-house was wrecked and for weeks in succession during the winter of 1663–1664 the meetings were held in the

---

20 BSPQ, 79.
21 *Ibid.*, 79, 80.
22 *Ibid.*, 228, 229.

street, continually harassed by troopers.[23] The sufferings and ill usage put a great moral strain upon the judgment and faith of the Quakers. The monthly meeting records show that nearly every meeting had a few members not equal to the strain, who had to be "dealt with" and cared for. The unity of Friends in the early days was largely the work of the travelling ministers, who visited even the remote meetings and gave them the benefit of their counsel and faith, but during this period this uniting influence was largely lacking because so many of the ministers were in prison and their ranks were depleted by death.

The Camp of the Lord, which in the first years of Quakerism had issued forth two and two from the North, was by this time sadly reduced. John Camm had passed away after less than three years of lavish labour at Bristol. His yokefellow, John Audland, died in March 1664, worn out with service at thirty-four. Burrough and Hubberthorne had been persecuted to death; Caton and Ames were gone, and Howgill was ending his days in Appleby. The gloom and glory of James Nayler's life were over, and leaders from the South of England had been taken, like Humphrey Smith, George Fox the Younger, and the learned Samuel Fisher. . . .

Mystical movements, with their emphasis on inward experience, have seldom had much institutional stability. It would not have been surprising if Quakerism, with leadership and organization weakened by persecution, had languished and declined. But the quiet meetings, resolutely maintained up and down the land, remained centers of power, and offered an almost invincible resistance to the persecutors.[24]

The imprisoned leaders kept in touch with one another by correspondence and tried in some measure to encourage meetings and individuals by personal and circular letters.[25] The bulk of their epistles in the ponderous folios

---

23 Besse, *op. cit.*, I, 199–201.

24 BSPQ, 219, 225.

25 *Ibid.*, 223, for Dewsbury's correspondence.

of their collected works bears testimony to the diligence and extent of their correspondence. As the authorities got knowledge of this communication it became an additional ground of suspicion that Friends were secretly plotting sedition against the government.[26]

Friends obtained a sorely needed respite from persecution when, in 1672, Charles II claimed the power to dispense with the execution of the laws in matters ecclesiastical and issued a proclamation suspending the penal laws against Nonconformists and Popish recusants. It authorized meetings of Nonconformists in places and under teachers licensed by the government, and allowed Catholics to worship only in private houses. The proclamation alarmed the country, because of the fear that it was an excuse to tolerate Catholicism. Nevertheless the Nonconformists generally availed themselves of it. Many Friends were released under it, but those *praemunired* and under sentence of banishment could only be released by a royal pardon. The Great Pardon, which was accordingly secured from the king, contained 491 names, mostly of Friends. A few non-Friends were included, however, among them John Bunyan, who was lying in Bedford jail. A copy of it had to be presented to most of the jailers where Friends were confined to secure their release. In 1673 Charles was compelled by Parliament to cancel the Declaration, but the officials waited for a positive order before enforcing the laws again and it was not until 1675 that an Order in Council directed the more diligent execution of the laws against Noncomformists. Meanwhile Friends enjoyed a sorely needed respite for nearly three years.

During the latter part of the reign of Charles II, the king yielded to Parliament and Church regarding toleration, but a severe struggle followed between king and Parliament over the succession to the throne, which was inspired by

---

26 BSPQ, 218.

fear of the Catholics and which brought the country at times close to civil war. The attempt to bar the king's brother, the Duke of York, who was heir apparent and an acknowledged Catholic, from the throne finally failed. Charles got a subsidy from Louis XIV on his promise to turn Catholic and help destroy the power of Protestant Holland. This enabled him to carry on the government without summoning Parliament, and after the destruction of the Whig opposition, he ruled as absolute monarch until his death.

Religious toleration made progress, however, despite the successive repressive measures; and, following the Proclamation of Indulgence in 1672, Nonconformity got such a hold in English life that it could not again be suppressed. In 1673 a bill passed the Commons legalizing Nonconformist worship in some measure; but it was rejected by the House of Lords. In 1681 Parliament resolved, just before its dissolution, "That the prosecution of Protestant Dissenters upon the Penal Laws is at this time grievous to the subject, a weakening of the Protestant interest, an encouragement to Popery, and dangerous to the peace of the kingdom." [27] The decision of the Lord Chief Justice which released George Fox from Worcester Jail in 1675 practically stopped the use of the writ of *praemunire* against Friends.[28] Arbitrary judges and officials and perjured informers received a check by the Habeas Corpus Act of 1679.

Friends were to undergo yet one more severe trial. After the Whig influence had been destroyed by the perjuries of Titus Oates and by the Rye House Plot, the king secured the support of the church by enforcing the laws against the Nonconformists. The old law against Catholics provided that any person over sixteen years of age could be mulcted

---

[27] *Ibid.*, 97.

[28] *Camb. Jour.*, II, 285. Richard Davies, *Life*, 156–161.

of twenty pounds for each month of non-attendance at church or the king could take two-thirds of the offender's lands until he came to church. When the Tories turned on the Nonconformists in 1681, this law was used along with the newer acts against Friends.

Some Friends, led by William Penn, had taken an active part in trying to elect Whigs to the so-called Whig Parliaments because of Whig support of toleration. This was held against Friends by the Tories, some of whom frankly confessed that if the Quakers would not vote for parliament men against the king's interest, they might be freed from further persecution.[29]

The persecutions at this time were particularly violent in the cities. In Bristol two-thirds of the inhabitants were said to be Nonconformists. The Baptists in particular suffered from the efforts of the sheriff, but as the other Dissenters met in secret, the Quakers bore the brunt of the persecution. The prisons were crowded with them and continued so until 1685. So many Friends were in jail that it was customary to give the notices of intending marriages there. By mid-summer, 1682, about 150 were in jail and the meetings were held by the children and a few women. The children were abused, threatened, put in stocks and imprisoned contrary to law, but they carried on undeterred through the summer heat.[30] By the autumn of 1682 some 1200 Bristol Dissenters had been indicted, including 500 Friends. Warrants for distresses on 191 of them amounted to over 16,000 pounds, although not all the warrants were actually executed.

An old act of Elizabeth's reign, designed to drive the Separatists out of England was now revived and used to imprison Dissenters.[31] It provided that any person guilty

---

29 BSPQ, 112.

30 Whiting, *Persecution Exposed,* 76, 77.

31 It was declared still in force by the First Conventicle Act. See FPT, 359–361.

of attending an unlawful meeting should be imprisoned until he conformed. In default of his conforming within three months of conviction, he should forfeit his goods and lands to the king and abjure and leave the realm. The penalty for refusal was death. No Dissenters were actually put to death, thanks to the intervention of the king after a few were sentenced; but the Act was invoked to imprison Friends and other Dissenters. Under this Act also an unlawful conventicle became technically a riot, the penalty for which was imprisonment.

In London Friends continued to meet in the streets near their closed meeting-houses in spite of the extreme cold of the winters of 1683 and 1684, and the interference of the militia who continually broke up their meetings and arrested the speakers. At Norwich George Whitehead and Thomas Burr suffered a sixteen-weeks imprisonment for refusing the oath of allegiance.[32] In 1682 about 60 Friends were imprisoned in the Norwich Guildhall, chiefly in the underground dungeon. For nine months in 1682–1683 the monthly meeting there was held in the jail; the minutes showing that the chief business was the care of the poor. Ilchester jail had had a large number of Friends prisoners since 1661. In 1679 Friends meetings were held in the Friary, an annex to the Ilchester jail, even the quarterly meetings occasionally convening there.

There were many cases of great brutality on the part of jailers toward their Quaker prisoners, but the story would be incomplete without mention of the many instances where the jailers treated them with kindness and even permitted them great liberties. Some were allowed to be at large on their own cognizance or to live in hired houses in the county town. George Fox was permitted to attend yearly meeting in London during his imprisonment in Worcester.[33] Margaret Fox was allowed liberty from Lan-

32 Whitehead, *Christian Progress,* 524–536.

33 BSPQ, 428.

caster jail at times to look after her property and even to go to London.[34] Thomas Taylor, of Westmorland, during his ten years and a half in prison spent part of his time teaching school.[35] Richard Davies was allowed by a friendly jailer to go on an extended visit to Bristol and South Wales.[36]

The death of Charles II in 1685 brought a respite for Friends. When Admiral Penn was near death in 1670, he had asked the Duke of York, then High Admiral of the Fleet, to look after his son William. In consequence a friendship grew up between the duke and the younger Penn which continued when the former succeeded to the throne as James II. Together with Robert Barclay, who also had access to the court, William Penn was able to render suffering Friends a great service. George Whitehead, Gilbert Latey and Alexander Parker presented a petition to King James within a month of his accession, showing that 1,460 Quakers were in prison. He promised to release Friends and to stop the ravages of the informers.[37] The writs for seizing Friends' estates under the acts against recusants had been suspended already.

In 1686 the king's general pardon was proclaimed and the same month a royal warrant was secured directing the release of a list of Friends and the remission of fines for non-attendance at church; and the suppression of informers in the London area was undertaken. In 1687 James issued a declaration of indulgence suspending the penal laws against Nonconformists and removing religious tests for public office. This was an alarming and probably unconstitutional assumption of power. The churchmen regarded it as a part of the king's plan to make England

---

34 BSPQ, 262.
35 *Ibid.*, 223, 224.
36 *Ibid.*, 224, 225.
37 Whitehead, *op. cit.*, 570, 571.

Catholic and it contributed materially to the revolution which a few years later drove him from the throne. However, it brought welcome relief to Friends who had suffered for a quarter of a century from the perversions of law by government officers and from the injustices of parliament.

In explanation, if not in extenuation of their attitude, Braithwaite says:

> But to many of the Dissenters, and especially to the Quakers, harried by persecution for twenty-five years, the Declaration necessarily bore a benign complexion. They had suffered long and cruelly at the hands of an intolerant Parliament, acting in the interests of a narrow-minded Church ascendancy. The Commons of England, who should have been the custodians of liberty, had added weapon after weapon to the arsenal of tyranny; till the persons and estates of Friends lay at the mercy of a horde of Informers. Any lenitives had been due to the Lords or to the uncertain indulgence of the Crown. Their conventicles had been treated as seditions, when there was no sedition; they had been fined and imprisoned as Popish recusants, when they were no Papists; their peaceable meetings had been indicted as riots; they had rotted in prison with no legal charge against them; and been acquitted in Court, only to find themselves trapped with the tender of an oath on pain of a *praemunire*. No legal chicanery, no arbitrary proceeding had been too gross, if it had served the turn of their oppressors. In a word, they had been treated for a generation as outlaws, living and worshipping on sufferance, and only living and worshipping at all because cruelty is capricious and their honest neighbors refused to aid in their destruction. The law denied the Quaker the common rights of an Englishman. If strictly administered, his marriage was no marriage; he was disabled from giving legal evidence or taking up his freedom in the town where he traded; and in common with other Nonconformists, public offices were closed to him. It had even been held that Quaker burying-grounds seized by the King should have the bodies taken out and buried at the cross-ways. While preserving the shadow of freedom, a persecuting Parliament

had been incessantly destroying its substance. Can we wonder that Quakers feared the despotism of the majority in the Commons, more than the prerogative of the King?[38]

William Penn was now at the height of his influence with the king and used it to promote tolerance, to restrain the despotic policy of the king and the Catholic party and to prepare the way for a parliamentary act to grant legal tolerance. Penn may have been overcredulous as to the king's good intentions but there is no ground to charge him with insincerity or duplicity, much less with being a Catholic.

King James persisted in his plans to legalize the Catholic religion, in defiance of laws and Parliament. The result was that in 1688 William of Orange—who had married James' daughter, Mary—on invitation of seven of the English leaders of all parties, who were alarmed by the attacks on the universities, the trial of the bishops and the birth of an heir to James, landed in England, and James fled to France. William had already made a tardy pledge of toleration and a guarantee of a Protestant supremacy. In 1689 parliament passed the Toleration Act which gave Nonconformists a legal place in English life, and a limited tolerance to Friends.

It is difficult to estimate the number of Friends who suffered imprisonment or other legal penalties before 1689, in spite of the fact that from an early period Friends kept accounts of those who "suffered in the cause of Truth." Jeremy White estimated that during the reigns of the last two Stuarts the number of persecuted Dissenters was about 60,000, of whom 5,000 died as a result of their hardships.[39] Penn's estimate for all Dissenters after the Restoration was 15,000 families ruined and 5,000 who died as a result of imprisonment. These figures are probably too high. For

---

[38] BSPQ, 131, 132.

[39] Oldmixon, *History of England under the Royal House of Stuart,* 715.

Friends alone the indexes of Besse's *Sufferings* contain 12,-406 names for England and Wales, including sufferers under the Commonwealth as well as the Restoration. His indexes are imperfect in places and his lists incomplete. Braithwaite concurs in the estimate of Joseph J. Green, the Quaker genealogist, of about 15,000 sufferers under the later Stuarts, and about 450 who died as a result of imprisonment.[40]

---

40 For a complete count of the Friends who suffered imprisonment there should be added perhaps 5,000 under the Commonwealth. BSPQ, 114, 115.

CHAPTER 10

THE ESTABLISHMENT OF QUAKERISM IN AMERICA

AFTER the Restoration, Friends continued to be persecuted in New England, Maryland and Virginia in spite of colonial charters and the king's commands. There were no more executions in Massachusetts Bay Colony, but in 1662 the barbarous "Cart and Whip Act" was reënacted. Under it, many Friends, including women and children, were stripped to the waist, tied to the tail of carts and whipped through the towns, ten lashes in each, until they were out of the province. Besides, many were imprisoned and fined for attending Friends meetings, furnishing them meeting places or entertaining them. In 1664, Charles II addressed an injunction to the colonial magistrates,

> To permit such as desire it to use the Book of Common Prayer, without incurring any penalty, reproach, or disadvantage; it being very scandalous, [continues the admonition] that any person should be debarred the exercise of their religion, according to the laws and customs of England, by those who were indulged with the liberty of being of what profession or religion they pleased.[1]

About a year later the king sent a similar charge to the Connecticut authorities. While these orders did not include Quakers, they did make impossible the ideal of uniformity which supplied one motive for persecuting

---

[1] Bowden, *Hist.*, I, 278.

them. In 1665, the royal commissioners commanded the Massachusetts authorities that Quakers be allowed to go about their secular affairs unmolested. The last Quaker was whipped in 1677. In 1681 the laws against Quakers were repealed or suspended.[2] In the meantime the growing sympathy for Friends on the part of the colonists had relaxed the severity of the Massachusetts Bay magistrates, especially after the death of Governor Endicott in 1665. It was not until 1724 and 1728, however, that the New England Quakers were relieved from penalties for non-payment of tithes.

In Maryland, Friends were subjected to heavy fines, in 1677 and 1678, for refusing to take oaths. William Penn had a conference with Lord Baltimore about the grievances of Friends but the latter's promise to grant them relief was not fulfilled for ten years. An act passed by both houses of the Assembly in 1681 for their relief was not sanctioned by the Proprietor "for reasons of state." In 1688 they were relieved from penalties for refusing to swear.[3] In Virginia there was a relaxation, after 1672, of persecution for neglect or refusal to pay tithes, attend church or have children baptized, but there was a revival of severity against them between 1675 and 1680. "Distraints for priests' wages" were continued until the adoption of the Bill of Rights at the beginning of the Revolutionary War; fines and distraints for refusal of military service continued until 1766 and were revived during the Revolution.[4]

Quaker missionaries from England continued to visit all the existing colonies from 1660 to 1700 in spite of hostile authorities and the hardships of travel. Under their influence the existing meetings were augmented and strengthened and the Society extended into new territory. Friends visited Maine as early as 1662 and Quakerism grew in the

[2] Thomas, *Hist.*, 65; JQAC, 109, 110.
[3] Bowden, *op. cit.*, I, 382–384.
[4] JQAC, 412, 568.

colony for the next ninety years. In New Amsterdam a line of meetings extended through Westchester County northward between the Dutch "patroon estates" on the Hudson and the boundary line of Puritan Connecticut. On the "Eastern Shore" of the Chesapeake and in southeastern Virginia Friends meetings continued to grow in numbers and size into the eighteenth century.

William Edmundson worked in this latter area, where he found a few scattered Friends. Henry Phillips was the first Quaker colonist in North Carolina. He had not seen a Friend for seven years when Edmundson came into the northeastern counties in 1671 and established some meetings about Hertford, mostly among people who "had little or no religion" previously.[5] John Perrot had visited Virginia and Maryland about 1662 and his influence had a detrimental effect on the growth of Friends, since he discouraged regular meetings for worship and introduced a contentious spirit.[6]

The next important stage in the development of American Quakerism, after the coming of the first Quaker missionaries and their struggles for toleration, was the visit of George Fox to America. He had followed the struggles of the pioneers with great interest.[7] In company with twelve other Quaker leaders he sailed from England in 1671 for Barbados. He spent three months in this island, strengthening and extending the Society, during which time he wrote his well-known letter to the governor to refute "scandalous lies and slanders" and to show that Friends shared the fundamental doctrines of Christianity in regard to God, Christ and the Bible.[8] After a visit to Jamaica the party sailed to Maryland.

---

[5] Edmundson, *Jour.*, 59, 60.

[6] JQAC, 276, 302n. Burnyeat, *Jour.*, 188.

[7] His first epistle to Friends beyond the sea in 1657 concerned the treatment of slaves. Out of four hundred and twenty published epistles thirty-two were to Friends in America.

[8] *Camb. Jour.*, I, 155–158. The letter is printed in the Discipline of the Five Years Meeting of Friends in America.

John Burnyeat had been working in Maryland and had called a meeting for Friends in the province at West River in April, 1672. George Fox arrived in time for this meeting, which became the first "business meeting" for Maryland, the beginning of Baltimore Yearly Meeting.[9] Friends in America, both as individuals and as groups, had kept up a sporadic correspondence among themselves; but Fox seems to have initiated correspondence between English and American Friends.[10] He had an eager interest in the aborigines of America. While in Maryland he had his first meeting with a group of Indian chiefs. On his later travels to Rhode Island and return, he lost no opportunity to get acquainted with the natives and to preach to them.

From the Chesapeake country, Fox and Robert Widders made the trip overland chiefly on horseback across Delaware and New Jersey. His own account of the journey gives a vivid impression of its hardships.

> Wee passed by the head of Miles River and soe stered through the woods and then wee passed by the head of Wyes River and then wee passed through the head of Chester River and then wee made a fire and took up our lodgeing in the woods about the head of Chester River and then wee passed all a long through the woods [to a plantation called the worlds end] being very much tyred and one swimmed over our horses over Sasafras River and went over our selves in Canooes and from thence wee came to Bohemia River and swimmed over our horses and went over our selves in Canooes soe wee had 30 miles to goe in the afternoon to any Towne and they whose horses were week stayed in the woods and made themselves a fire but I and some others whose horses were stronger got to the Towne that night being a Dutch Towne [being the 9th of ye 3^{d} m^{o}] the Towne is called Newcastle being wet to the skin and from thence wee passed over a great water and boated our horses and were some of us in great danger of our lives and were very much troubled to get new guides which were

[9] See Thomas, Anna B., *The Story of Baltimore Yearly Meeting,* 14, 15.
[10] Bowden, *op. cit.,* I, 355, 377; JQAC, 271.

very chargeable and soe passed through the woods sometimes wee lay in the woods by a fire and sometimes in the Indian Cabbins through the bogs River & Creeks [and wilde woods we passed where it was said it was never knowne before for any man to ride] I came at last & lay at one Indian Kings house.[11]

He spent some weeks in Long Island, traversing it from Flushing to Shelter Island, organizing Friends, making converts, and dealing tactfully, and to a large extent successfully, with Ranter elements which were disturbing the western parts of the island. He passed over to Rhode Island where he found a series of strong Quaker centers and held very large meetings. The yearly meeting of that year was a memorable occasion in the history of New England Quakerism. Besides Fox there were in attendance six other eminent public Friends. They enjoyed such a precious religious fellowship and the attenders were "so knit and united," as Fox described it, that they took two days for leave-taking after the sessions closed.[12] He spent about two months in the colony, holding large and influential meetings. Here as well as on Long Island he had to deal with troublesome Ranters and was largely successful in winning them to the good order of the Society.[13]

The veteran Roger Williams challenged the Quaker leader to a public debate on fourteen propositions. Fox had left for Long Island before the challenge came, but Burnyeat, Edmundson and Stubbs took it up. Seven of the propositions were to be discussed at Newport and the others at Providence. The propositions were in fact accusations, as Burnyeat alleges. Among them were such as "that the Christ which the Quakers profess is not the true Lord Jesus Christ; that they do not own the holy Scriptures, and that their principles are full of contradictions

---

11 *Camb. Jour.*, II, 210–211.
12 *Bicent. Jour.*, II, 169.
13 *Camb. Jour.*, II, 222.

and hypocrisies."[14] Three days were consumed at Newport and one at Providence. As usual in religious controversies both sides claimed the victory.[15] Williams wrote an account of the debate, entitled *George Fox Digged out of his Burrows*. Fox and Burrough answered it in *A New England Fire-Brand Quenched*. Williams was evidently quite ignorant of the Quaker principles.[16] In violence of language and spirit the books are examples of the controversies of the time. Roger Williams calls Edmundson "rude" and Edmundson calls Williams a "bitter old man."[17]

On the return trip from New England, Fox visited Maryland Friends again on both shores of the Chesapeake where large numbers of the colonists flocked to the meetings.[18] He also held meetings again with the Indians. Leaving Maryland, Fox crossed Virginia in company with Robert Widders, James Lancaster and George Pattison. He held many meetings with the planters; made many converts, and strengthened the few Friends whom they found in those parts. It is estimated that the number of Friends in the colony was doubled by his labors.[19]

The company crossed into the north-east corner of North Carolina, enduring great hardships, travelling through the swamps and unbroken forests. They found some of Edmundson's converts and held many meetings, among the colonists, including public officials who were friendly. Here Fox followed his usual custom of holding meetings with the Indians. From Carolina he returned to Maryland, whence he embarked for England.

In the course of his American journey, he had visited the most important Quaker centers in the colonies; given the organization of the Society a powerful stimulus; quickened

14 Burnyeat, *Jour.*, p. 53.
15 Thomas, *Hist.*, p. 70.
16 *Loc. cit.*
17 Dexter, *As to Roger Williams;* cited by Thomas, *op. cit.*, p. 70.
18 Thomas, *op. cit.*, p. 81. Bowden, *op. cit.*, I, 374–377.
19 Bowden, *op. cit.*, I, 355.

interest in the Indians, added many members to the Society and given Friends a fresh impulse toward missionary expansion in America. He attended New England Yearly Meeting and aided in the organization of Baltimore Yearly Meeting, the establishment of a half-year's meeting on Long Island, the yearly meeting in Virginia and a quarterly meeting in North Carolina. The Virginia records state that they were begun in 1673 "by the motion and order of George Fox, that servant of God." At the beginning of these records is a copy of Fox's "Canons and Institutions." [20] On his return to Bristol he induced the monthly meeting there to correspond with Friends in Maryland and Virginia.[21]

The Society continued to grow in numbers in the colonies until the end of the century. In 1695, New York Yearly Meeting was organized by the authorization of New England Yearly Meeting.[22] George Fox wrote to North Carolina Friends in 1681 advising the establishment of a yearly meeting, but this was not done until 1698.[23] The next great phase in the development of American Quakerism was the establishment of the Quaker colonies, New Jersey and Pennsylvania, and the Quaker control in Rhode Island, Delaware and North Carolina. George Fox had followed the struggles of the Quaker pioneers in America with great interest; and beginning in 1659 he wrote epistles to Friends in Barbados Island, Virginia and New England, Jamaica, Maryland and Carolina.[24] As early as 1660 he had in mind the possibility of a Quaker refuge in America when he wrote to Josiah Coale to inquire about available lands near the Susquehanna River.[25] The idea

---

20 See Thomas, *op. cit.*, pp. 52, 53.

21 Bowden, *op. cit.*, I, 355, 377–379.

22 Thomas, *op. cit.*, p. 76. *American Friend,* II, 551, ff.

23 *Epistles,* no. 371, p. 462.

24 *Epistles,* nos. 178, 189, 196, 216, 244, 288.

25 A. R. Barclay, *Col. of MSS* in Friends Library, London, no. 53; cited in Bowden, *op. cit.*, I, 389, 390.

did not prove practicable at the time. When Fox returned from America in 1673 his interest in American Quakerism was greatly increased. It is not without significance that he went directly from Bristol, where he landed, to visit William Penn. It is not improbable that he quickened the idea of a Quaker colony in America in Penn's mind.

The opportunity for such a colony, however, came first in New Jersey. In 1664 the Duke of York granted the country between the Delaware and Hudson rivers to Lord Berkeley and Sir George Carteret. In 1674, not long after Fox's return to England, Berkeley's share, known as West Jersey, was acquired by two Friends, John Fenwick and Edward Byllynge. A disagreement between the partners led to William Penn being called in as arbitrator. Byllynge became financially embarrassed and conveyed his nine-tenths of the colony to three Friends: William Penn, Gawen Laurie and Nicholas Lucas.

Fenwick brought over a colony of Friends which settled at Salem in 1675. Meanwhile Penn and the other proprietors settled the boundary between East Jersey (still held by Carteret) and West Jersey[26] and drew up a plan of government called "Concessions and Agreements of the Proprietors, Freeholders and inhabitants of the province of West Jersey, in America." This "plan" anticipates the liberal principles which were afterward embodied more completely in the Pennsylvania charters. It is probable that Byllynge also influenced the type of government adopted.[27] The proprietors wrote to the colonists:

> There we lay a foundation for after ages to understand their liberty as men and Christians, that they may not be brought in bondage, but by their own consent; for we put the power in the people, that is to say, they to meet and choose one

---

[26] It ran from Little Egg Harbor to latitude 41° on the Delaware (opposite Stroudsburg, Pa.).

[27] See Brinton, *Children of Light,* chap. V.

honest man for each proprietary, who hath subscribed to the concessions; all these men to meet as an assembly there, to make and repeal laws, to choose a governor, or a commissioner, and twelve assistants to execute the laws during their pleasure; so every man is capable to choose or be chosen. No man to be arrested, condemned, imprisoned, or molested in his estate or liberty, but by twelve men of the neighbourhood. No man to lie in prison for debt, but that his estate satisfy as far as it will go, and be set at liberty to work. No person to be called in question or molested for his conscience, or for worshipping according to his conscience. . . .

"No men, or number of men upon earth, hath power or authority to rule over men's consciences in religious matters," says chapter xvi; "therefore it is consented, agreed, and ordained, that no person or persons whatsoever, within the said province, at any time or times, hereafter, shall be any ways, upon any pretence whatsoever, called in question, or in the least punished or hurt, either in person, estate, or privilege, for the sake of his opinion, judgment, faith or worship towards God, in matters of religion; but that all and every such person and persons, may from time to time, and at all times, freely and fully have and enjoy his and their judgments, and the exercise of their consciences, in matters of religious worship throughout all the said province." [28]

In 1677 a colony of Friends settled at Burlington and another shipload came in 1678. By 1681 at least 1400 colonists, mostly Friends, had come into the colony. They were careful to buy the land of the Indians, to prevent the sale of liquor to them, to organize meetings for worship and business, and to build meeting houses.

In 1679 Carteret's widow offered East Jersey for sale and it was acquired by twelve English Friends, to whom were soon added a number from Scotland. Robert Barclay, the Quaker apologist, was elected governor, but he never visited the colony, being represented by a deputy.[29] A

[28] Bowden, *op. cit.*, I, 395, 396.
[29] Bowden, *op. cit.*, I, 407.

yearly meeting was established at Burlington in 1681 which ultimately became Philadelphia Yearly Meeting. In 1702 the proprietors of the two Jerseys, now united under one Council of Proprietors, surrendered their political rights to Queen Anne.

It was in 1681 that William Penn received from Charles II the grant of Pennsylvania colony in settlement of a debt which the king owed his father, Admiral Penn, for whom the colony was named by the king. The Duke of York showed his friendship for Penn by adding the "three lower counties," which later constituted the state of Delaware. Penn's ideals of government were remarkably progressive. How far he was influenced by John Locke and Algernon Sydney, is an unsolved problem. His Quaker principles were in any case his chief guide. He wished not only to establish a refuge for his persecuted co-religionists, but to make a "holy experiment" in applied Quakerism. He was consciously trying to give the nations an example of a free democracy. His definition of a free government was: "Any government is free to the people under it, whatever be the frame, where the laws rule and the people are a party to those laws; and more than this is tyranny, oligarchy or confusion."[30] Penn was not quite free to do as he pleased with the colony, however, since his arrangements were subject to the royal veto. He was not allowed to do away entirely with the death penalty, nor a militia, nor to abolish the slave trade. The colony was called upon from time to time to make grants to aid the British government in its frequent wars.

The first colonists under the Quaker regime arrived in 1681. Penn himself came the next year. He secured the friendship of the Indians by fair treatment; he purchased their lands,[31] protected their interests in trade, and made

---

30 Janney, *Life of Penn,* p. 187.

31 The Dutch had already established the practice of buying land of the Indians and the Quakers had done the same in New Jersey. JQAC, 367.

the famous treaty at Shackamaxon—in Voltaire's happy phrase, "the only treaty never sworn to and never broken." When he landed from the *Welcome* at Upland (now Chester), he called together an assembly of the settlers to whom he submitted the proposed plan of government and code of laws, which were speedily adopted. They guaranteed freedom of conscience and worship for all; but the right to hold office was restricted to Protestant Christians. They allowed the substitution of an affirmation for the legal oath; and abolished the death penalty except for treason and murder, at a time when there were over two hundred capital offenses in England. All freeholders were allowed to vote for officers and for members of the legislative assembly. By August, 1683, two general assemblies had been held and at least seventy laws passed.[32] These constituted a strikingly liberal penal code; but they were Puritan in their attitude toward personal vices and public amusements. They forbade swearing, duelling, drunkenness, cock-fighting, lotteries and stage plays.[33]

Philadelphia was laid out by the proprietor on generous lines as the capital and metropolis of the province. When he left the colony for England in 1684, the city had three hundred and fifty-seven houses. Meeting-houses were established from the very beginning not only in the city but in the settled townships; schools were opened in 1683, and in 1684 the city had a printing press. A monthly and quarterly meeting were set up in 1682. In the next year a yearly meeting for ministers was established. At first the Pennsylvania settlers attended the yearly meeting at Burlington, N. J. From 1683 to 1685 yearly meetings were held at Philadelphia as well as at Burlington. The two were united in 1686 and held alternately at Burlington and Philadel-

---

Penn followed the Indians' ideas by paying them again and again for their lands. Kelsey, *Friends and the Indians,* pp. 4, 39.

[32] JQAC, 476.

[33] *Loc: cit.*

phia for the next seventy-five years. In 1684 epistles were sent to London Yearly Meeting and to Friends in other parts of America. The Women's Yearly Meeting also addressed an epistle to women Friends in England.[34]

Shortly after Penn's arrival in the colony, he visited New York, New Jersey and attended the yearly meeting in Maryland. He also visited Lord Baltimore and made an unsuccessful attempt to settle the boundary between their two colonies. The difficulty was that, owing to the royal ignorance of American geography, the grants to the two proprietors overlapped.[35] The matter was not finally settled until 1762 when the surveyors, Mason and Dixon, ran the famous boundary line.

In 1683 the yearly meeting approved a plan, which doubtless originated with Penn, to hold a general meeting of American Friends "from New England to Carolina."

> Epistles were sent to London and to Carolina, Virginia, Maryland and New England: "That it may be presented to them if possible from these remote provinces they may send two or three for each province to our Yearly Meeting here being as a center or middle part that so communion and blessed union may be preserved among all." [36]

Two years later representatives attended from Rhode Island and Maryland. In 1686 and 1687 Friends from Long Island, New York and Maryland were in attendance. The invitation for a general American yearly meeting was revived in 1686, but the time was not ripe for such a union of Friends in one organization. The chief obstacles were probably the difficulties and expense of travelling.

The proprietors issued a prospectus setting forth the attractions of the new colony, which received wide attention in Great Britain and on the Continent. Penn also

---

34 Bowden, *op. cit.*, II, 25.
35 JQAC, 419.
36 *Ibid.*, 437.

made visits to Holland and the Rhineland partly in order to interest prospective colonists. The first emigrants were chiefly from England and Wales. Numbers came also from certain persecuted German sects, Mennonites, Schwenkfelder and German Baptists. A colony of former Dutch Mennonites from Krefeld and Krisheim, whose conversion to Quakerism was begun by William Ames in 1659, emigrated in a body and settled Germantown, now a suburb of Philadelphia. Their leader was Francis Daniel Pastorius,[37] a German scholar, who became a Friend under Penn's influence. This Germantown meeting issued in 1688 the first official protest of a religious body against slavery.[38] The Welsh immigrants settled in a "barony" of 40,000 acres to the west of Philadelphia along what is now the "Main Line" of the Pennsylvania Railroad. Later came the Scotch-Irish immigrants who settled further to the west and north. Most of the earlier settlers were Quakers or (in the case of the continental sects) members of religious sects who were sympathetic with many Quaker principles and practices. The Scotch-Irish settlers, on the other hand, constituted a vigorous population generally opposed to the Quaker pacifism, tolerance, and friendship with the Indians.

In the last decade of the seventeenth century the Society in Pennsylvania and New Jersey was disturbed by a schism led by George Keith. He was a Scotch Quaker, one of the ablest scholars among the early Friends, and a friend and co-worker of Robert Barclay. In 1689 he came to New Jersey as surveyor of the colony and established the boundary line between East and West Jersey. When the Friends' Public School was established in Philadelphia in 1689 he

[37] The "Pennsylvania Pilgrim" of Whittier's poem. On the history of these colonists see Hull, *William Penn and the Dutch Quaker Migration to Pennsylvania,* chap. IV.

[38] Thomas, *op. cit.,* 113.

was made headmaster, a position in which he was not very successful and which he gave up after a year.

He began to advocate unusual doctrines[39] and became critical of his co-religionists. He charged them with laxity in discipline and with denying the divinity and offices of the historic Christ. Friends generally, both in England and America, protested against his innovations and criticisms; but there were many of the second generation, to whom Quakerism was an inheritance more than a vital experience, who were attracted by Keith. Keith's spirit was more objectionable to Friends than his doctrines; he was "brittle" in temper, disputatious and belligerent. Efforts on the part of a group of ministers to conciliate him failed. He organized a separate society which he called "The Christian Quakers." Their discipline was stricter than contemporary Quaker practice and contained some provisions which have since become part of Quaker policy. His "Society" soon disintegrated.

Keith was fined for sedition in consequence of publishing some violent criticisms of the colonial magistrates who were also Friends. William Bradford was also indicted for printing his pamphlets; but he was not convicted, and the trial is notable as the first case where it was ruled by the court that the jury should be judge of the seditious character of a publication as well as of the fact of publication—a rule which is now the basis of the freedom of our press.[40] In 1692 Philadelphia Yearly Meeting "testified against" Keith; and his followers were disowned. In 1693 his case was carried to London Yearly Meeting which decided against him chiefly on account of his violent temper and divisive spirit. Finally he joined the Church of England and in 1702 was sent to America as a missionary to Friends.

39 He was influenced by van Helmont's doctrine of the transmigration of souls. JQAC, 446.

40 JQAC, 451.

The Keith controversy led to a greater emphasis among Friends on the historic Christ. In 1695 a statement of Friends' beliefs on the points involved in the controversy was issued by Philadelphia Yearly Meeting.[41]

The Quakers exercised a strong influence in certain other colonies besides those which they actually controlled. They made Rhode Island their asylum in the early days, where their influence became sufficient to exempt them from oaths and military service. Many men of influence in the colony joined the Society. Three of its great colonial governors were Quakers—Nicholas Easton, William Coddington and Henry Bull—as well as several deputy governors. King Philip's War occurred during the governorship of William Coddington. It put him in an awkward position, but he refused to join in the war against the Indians. This displeased Roger Williams' Providence Plantation which had the least Quaker population and was most exposed to the hostile Indians. While it did not entirely escape damage from the Indians, Rhode Island suffered less severely in this war than any other New England colony. The Quaker officials in Rhode Island were also embarrassed by their obligations to the English government and its demands upon them for help in its wars.

The Quaker officials in the Rhode Island Colony were in every instance devoted to the maintenance of peace. They exerted themselves to the utmost to keep the Colony out of actual war; but they seem to have settled it as their policy to stay in office, when they were put there by the people, even though they found themselves compelled, by unavoidable conditions and circumstances, to perform public acts of a warlike nature. When they found that the great current of events could not be forced to take the course which in their vision seemed the ideal one, they faced the stubborn conditions that existed and did the best they could with them. They discovered, what all practical workers discover, that the achievement

[41] Cf. Bowden, *op. cit.*, II, 28–33, where the document is given.

of great ends and high ideals can be won only by slow stages and by graceful bends around obstacles which are for the moment immovable. There has always been in the Society of Friends a group of persons pledged unswervingly to the ideal. To those who form this inner group compromise is under no circumstance allowable. If there comes a collision between allegiance to the ideal and the holding of public office, then the office must be deserted. If obedience to the soul's vision involved eye or hand, houses or lands or life, they must be immediately surrendered. But there has always been as well another group who have held it to be equally imperative to work out their principles of life in the complex affairs of the community and the State, where to gain an end one must yield something; where to get on one must submit to existing conditions; and where to achieve ultimate triumph one must risk his ideals to the tender mercies of a world not yet ripe for them. John Woolman, the consummate flower of American Quakerism in the eighteenth century, is the shining type of the former principle, and the Rhode Island governors are good types of the other course.[42]

Next after Rhode Island, Friends were influential in the Carolinas. There the Friends were the first organized religious body and in many places the only organized body. The North Carolina Friends were mostly recruited from people who had lost touch with organized Christianity. John Archdale, one of the proprietors, was Carolina's great colonial governor. Under him Friends' scruples were respected and a number of Friends were elected to the assembly, so that they virtually controlled the Carolinas during the last decade of the seventeenth century. Even after Archdale resigned they continued to be an influential part of the population.

In Maryland Friends exercised considerable influence, though they were greatly in the minority. It was founded as a Catholic colony, but Lord Baltimore's charter guaran-

---

[42] JQAC, 175, 176.

teed religious freedom. In the course of time the Episcopalians became strong enough to try to establish the Church of England as the only lawful religion; but the Quakers held the balance of power between the Catholics and the Episcopalians and prevented this threat to the religious freedom of the colony. By this means also they finally secured exemption from the requirements of oaths and military service.

By the year 1700 Friends meetings had been established in all the English colonies. Friends owned or had recently owned the Jerseys, Pennsylvania and Delaware; they had a controlling influence in Rhode Island and the Carolinas; they had considerable influence in New York, especially on Long Island, and in Maryland; and they had won the struggle for toleration in New England and Virginia. At that time Friends were the greatest single religious organization in the English colonies as a whole, both in their influence and in their promise. It is an important question why they failed to hold their place or fulfill this promise. One reason may be the increase through immigration, even in the Quaker colonies, of the non-Quaker population.

A second reason is that Friends lacked trained leaders to cope with new situations. Other religious bodies established colleges and trained their ministers, while Friends had no one who could compete with them in presenting their truths in a striking and effective way, because they neglected higher education. There was a lack of well educated men and women especially among Friends who could look at problems from other than the traditional points of view. This was especially vital in Pennsylvania where Friends had no leaders who were highly educated in religious matters after the first generation died. In England the children of the wealthy Friends were tutored at home but in America anything above common school education was rare. Another reason for the decline of the influence of Friends was the growth of Quietism which made them reluctant to assume the responsibilities incident to government and which also led them to desist from vigorous efforts to convert their non-Quaker fellow colonists to their own faith and principles.

As to the number of Friends in the colonies in 1700, estimates vary. Some give the number of Friends in Pennsylvania colony at fifteen thousand. Possibly there were twice that number in America as a whole. Friends continued to grow in numbers for the next fifty years and it is estimated that about 1750 there were fifty thousand in the colonies.[43]

---

[43] JQAC, 524.

Chapter 11

ORGANIZATION

The persecutions which the Quakers suffered under the later Stuarts led to the organization of the Quaker movement into the Society of Friends. Under the Commonwealth a loose organization had developed for the promotion of evangelization and worship, the care of the poor and imprisoned and the oversight of the moral and spiritual welfare of the Children of the Light.

The general persecutions and illegal status of Friends after the Restoration increased the need that they should be able to bear a common witness and give one another mutual support. The imprisonment of the leaders interfered with the travelling ministry which had been the chief source of unity and power. The strain of persecution developed weaknesses in the membership and exaggerated tendencies to eccentricity in some members. Out of these needs grew the fuller organization of the movement, in order to provide a structure strong enough to withstand the external pressure and internal weaknesses and at the same time to resist the tendencies toward unrestrained individualism which were inherent in Quaker mysticism. The development of the Quaker organization during the Restoration period was conditioned chiefly by the struggle between these centrifugal and centripetal forces in the movement.[1]

During the Commonwealth period the Nayler episode

1 BSPQ, 228.

had raised the question of the proper balance between individual liberty and social control in the Quaker group. The problem was underscored just after the Restoration by a movement fostered by John Perrot. He was a former Baptist of Waterford, Ireland, who had been convinced by Edward Burrough in 1656. He was a man of fine spirit, idealistic and emotional—the stuff of which martyrs are made. He was a member of the apostolic band which set out for the East in 1657. In the following year he was imprisoned by the Inquisition in the madhouse in Rome, where he barely escaped death as a heretic.[2] From his prison he wrote letters to Friends in England in an affected style, signing himself "I, John" after the fashion of the author of the book of Revelation. He was released in 1661. He carried the Quaker revolt against religious customs and traditions to an extreme. He wrote a letter protesting especially against the custom of men Friends removing their hats during public prayer.[3] After his return to England he pressed his opposition to this custom by voice and pen.

In the unheated English churches the custom prevailed of keeping on the hat during public worship, removing it only during prayer as a sign of reverence. This custom Friends continued and it was the basis of the refusal of "hat honor" to men however exalted their social, political or ecclesiastical station. Perrot claimed a higher revelation than any yet granted Fox and the other Quaker leaders. He carried the idea of individual guidance to a narrowly logical conclusion, ignoring the social element in it. He

---

[2] Ellwood's statement regarding him represents the disillusionment of a former sympathizer: "This man came pretty early amongst Friends, and too early took upon him the ministerial office, and being though little in person yet great in opinion of himself, nothing less would serve him than to go and convert the Pope." Ellwood, *Life* (1714 ed.), p. 241.

[3] The original is in the *Swarthmore Collection,* Friends Library, London. It is undated but was probably written prior to November 8, 1661. See BSPQ, 232, 233.

objected to all set customs, or prearrangements in religious life, especially in worship. Only when the individual felt immediately moved to any religious exercise did he think it allowable. He would have no fixed times or places for public worship, no "judging" of the conduct of fellow members of the Society. His fine spirit and helpful ministry gave him at first considerable influence. Thomas Ellwood, Isaac Penington, John Crook and even George Whitehead were for a time among the "hat men." They were attracted by the idea of possible new revelations beyond those of Fox, as well as by Perrot's logic and spirit.

In strict logic Perrot's position was unassailable. If the Inward Light in the individual is an ultimate and adequate guide in things religious, must it not be trusted hour by hour for all requirements? The immediate "moving" ought to be sufficient. If it is right for Friends to meet for worship at a given time and place, would they all not be moved to go there at the time? But the chief leaders of the Society rejected these conclusions. Early Friends claimed "immediate" guidance as against the "mediated" knowledge of God's will and grace which sacerdotal and sacramental religion offers; but Perrot took the word "immediate" to mean guidance "on the spur of the moment." Early Friends believed too largely in the immanence and unchangeable purposes of God to limit his revelation of his will for human conduct to the moment beforehand! Fox and the other "founders" knew from experience that there is a revelation of God's will regarding customary action and regular church order as well as regarding particular duties and they were deeply conscious of the social element in individual guidance as well as the experience of corporate spiritual guidance. Farnsworth gave the clearest exposition of the errors of Perrot's position.[4]

In England after many conferences, practically all the

---

[4] *Works,* 219.

"hat men" acknowledged their error. Perrot went afterward to Barbados and to America where he exercised a rather wide and disintegrating influence, which was only overcome by the visit of Fox and his companions in 1671–1672. In 1665–1666 John Burnyeat found some disciples of Perrot in Virginia who had "become loose and careless" and who did not attend meeting once a year.[5]

George Fox spent nearly three years in Lancaster and Scarboro jails in 1664–1666. During that time the need of a more thorough organization to safeguard and promote the life of the Society was apparently borne in upon him and its outlines took shape in his mind.[6] He tells us in his *Journal* how the Lord moved him to these measures:

> Then I was moved of the Lord to recommend the setting up of five monthly meetings of men and women in the city of London (besides the women's meetings and the quarterly meetings) to take care of God's glory, and to admonish and exhort such as walked disorderly or carelessly, and not according to truth. For whereas Friends had had only quarterly meetings, now truth was spread, and Friends were grown more numerous, I was moved to recommend the setting up of monthly meetings throughout the nation, and the Lord opened to me what I must do, and how the men's and women's monthly and quarterly meetings should be ordered and established in this and in other nations; and that I should write to those where I did not come, to do the same.[7]

The need of a more thorough organization which Fox felt was anticipated by an epistle drafted by Farnsworth and issued in 1666 by a special meeting of leading ministers in London. Braithwaite claims that this document marks the point where Quakerism narrowed itself into a religious Society.[8] The most important paragraph of it is as follows:

---

5 Burnyeat, *Jour.*, pp. 34, 35.

6 See Hodgkin, *George Fox,* p. 205 for this suggestion.

7 Ellwood, *Life,* p. 245. *Camb. Jour.*, II, iii.

8 BSPQ, 247, 248.

So dear Friends and brethren, believing that your souls will be refreshed in the sense of our spirits and integrity toward God, at the reading of these things, as we were, whilst we sat together at the opening of them; and that ye will be one with us in your testimony, on behalf of the Lord and his precious Truth, against those who would limit the Lord to speak without instruments, or by what instruments they list,—and who reject the counsel of the wise men, and the testimony of the prophets, whom God sanctified and sent among you in the day of his love, when ye were gathered,—and would not allow Him liberty in and by his servants, to appoint a place wherein to meet together, to wait upon and worship Him (according as He requires) in spirit, but call this formal, and the meetings of man;—we say, believing that ye will have fellowship with us herein, as we have with you in the Truth, we commit you unto God, and to the word of life, that hath been preached unto you from the beginning; which is neither limited to time, nor place, nor persons, but hath power to limit us to each, as pleaseth Him:—that ye with us, and we with you, may be built up in the most holy faith, and be preserved to partake of the inheritance, which is heavenly, amongst all those that are sanctified.[9]

The organization which took shape under Fox's guidance was largely a systematizing of various meetings already in existence; and its complete working out was a labor of years. He began by setting up five monthly meetings in London in addition to the Two Weeks Meeting already in existence.[10] In other places there were monthly meetings, as mentioned above, although some of them were held every six weeks, or only quarterly. In addition, there had been regional gatherings of travelling ministers or elders at various times.[11] These regional meetings seem sometimes to have been called quarterly meetings. General meetings

---

9 *Letters of Early Friends,* pp. 323, 324.

10 This latter meeting grew into Gracechurch Street monthly meeting which came to have special charge of marriages in the London Meetings.

11 BBQ, 309–322, 338; *Camb. Jour.,* I, 355–356 seems to refer to these meetings.

for the whole nation were held also.[12] These appear to have been of two kinds; those attended by ministers which were chiefly religious, and those for business attended by elders only. There are records of general meetings of the latter type for the northern counties at Skipton in 1657, 1659 and 1660; at Scalehouse in 1658 and at Kendal in 1661. These are often referred to as yearly meetings, but were only regional in scope. In connection with these there were held meetings of "ministering Friends" at John Crook's near Balby in Yorkshire in 1658, in London in 1659 and at Warmsworth near Balby in 1660, and again in London in 1661.

The Two Weeks Meeting in London was a gathering of elders rather than ministers, established about 1656. Its functions were practically those of a monthly meeting:—to provide meeting places, to care for the poor, the sick and the unemployed; to settle differences between Friends or between a Friend and a non-Friend; to keep records of births, marriages and burials; to see that marriages were properly performed; to keep a record of Friends' sufferings; and to advise with the women's meetings.[13] In London there were also two women's meetings.[14] The Women's Two Weeks Meeting for the care of the poor, sick, disorderly, prisoners, etc., which finally became the women's counterpart of the men's Two Weeks Meeting; and the Box Meeting, which collected funds in a money box for such charitable purposes.

Women took a prominent part in the establishment of the Quaker Society. Elizabeth Hooten was one of the first preachers and Margaret Fell furnished the movement an invaluable home and organizing center at Swarthmore. Her material and spiritual contributions to the movement were as important as that of the travelling "Publishers of

12 *Letters of Early Friends,* pp. 310–317.
13 *Ibid.,* pp. 287–310.
14 Fox, *Epistles,* p. 6.

Truth." According to Quaker theory women were entitled to an equal place in all phases of the Society's life and work, but the status of women in English society in the seventeenth century made the realization of this a slow process. Fox's efforts in completing the organization of the Society were directed chiefly to the establishment of men's monthly meetings and of women's meetings coördinate with them. Before this, women had participated in the existing business meetings to some extent. Fox realized that lack of experience in public affairs and modesty alike would prevent the adequate participation of the women in the affairs of the Society; and so he violated logical consistency in deference to actualities. The matters that claimed the attention of the women's meetings are enumerated in "An Epistle from the Women Friends in London to the Women Friends in the Country, also Elsewhere, about the Service of a Woman's Meeting" (1674) as follows:

> These services have been and are;—to visit the sick and the prisoners that suffer for the testimony of Jesus; to see they are supplied with things needful;—and relieving the poor, making provision for the needy, aged, and weak, that are incapable of work;—a due consideration for the widows, and care taken of the fatherless children and poor orphans, (according to their capacities) for their education and bringing up in good nurture and in the fear of the Lord; and putting them out to trades in the wholesome order of the creation. Also, the elder women exhorting the younger, in all sobriety, modesty in apparel, and subjection to Truth; and if any should be led aside by the temptations of Satan any way, endeavoring to reclaim such;—and to stop tatlers and false reports, and all such things as tend to division amongst us; following those things that make for peace, reconciliation and union. Also admonishing such maids and widows as may be in danger through the snare of the enemy, either to marry with unbelievers, or to go to the priest to be married or otherwise, and so, to bring a reproach or scandal upon Truth or Friends. And that maid servants that profess Truth and want places, be

orderly disposed of and settled in their services; and likewise, that the savoury life and good order of Truth, be minded between mistresses and their maids.[15]

It was more than two centuries before the long apprenticeship of women Friends in their own meetings and the improved intellectual and social status of women in the Anglo-Saxon world led to the discontinuance of separate women's meetings and their equal participation in the Society's affairs. At the beginning even among Friends there was objection to the innovation of women's meetings.[16]

At first there seems to have been little distinction in function between monthly and quarterly meetings.[17] Gradually the latter term was applied to the less frequent meetings of Friends from a larger territory. There was a tendency to make the county the unit for the quarterly gatherings[18] and for them to be more concerned with the spread of the Quaker message, its social and religious applications, and the oversight of the ministry.[19]

The first meeting of national scope appears to have been one held at Skipton in 1660, which was composed of representatives from the principal Quaker sections of England and Wales.[20] Fox calls this a yearly meeting. After this the yearly meeting was moved to London, where a meeting chiefly for the ministry was held in 1661. After this there was an interval during which such general gatherings were

---

15 *Letters of Early Friends,* pp. 344, 345.

16 BSPQ, 274.

17 *Ibid.,* 291.

18 *Ibid.,* 358.

19 The Six Weeks Meeting in London is in many respects unique. It was instituted in 1671 to consider matters not deemed suitable for the Two Weeks Meeting. It was composed of a select group of men and women, sixty-eight in all, and served as a court of appeal for the London monthly meetings. Later it was composed of representatives appointed by the men's and women's monthly meetings.

20 *Camb. Jour.,* I, 353–355.

impracticable on account of persecution. In 1666 and again in 1668 special meetings were summoned. There was no regular annual meeting of ministers like the 1661 Skipton meeting till 1668. An epistle issued at the close of the latter states the intention to set up an annual meeting:

> We did conclude among ourselves to settle a meeting, to see one another's faces, and open our hearts one to another in the Truth of God, once a year, as formerly it used to be; and once in two years for Friends in the ministry, that go in all parts beyond the seas, to come up and meet with us in London. The next meeting will be about the time called Easter, in the year 1670, in London.[20a]

Out of these meetings grew the annual gatherings called London Yearly Meeting. In 1671 it was decided to establish a central body of representatives from the counties to meet annually "to advise about the managing of the public affairs of Friends throughout the nation," which ministers were to be allowed to attend. After 1673, however, for four years only ministers attended; but after that the meeting of representatives from the quarterly meetings and the minister's meeting met separately each year.

The settlement of the yearly meeting thus occupied nearly ten years. Such a central body was a novelty in that age and roused much adverse criticism. It was not established swiftly and surely, under strong religious concern, as had been the case with the setting up of the monthly meetings; it was superadded to an existing system, and was due, at first, to the practical convenience of calling in representatives to bring in reports of sufferings, control collections, and to settle the proportions in which the counties should receive Quaker books. Its higher value lay in training and consolidating the membership. To bring together from all parts of the country the men of most weight in the movement, for conference and fellowship and the rekindling of vision, was a true way of developing

---

20a *Letters of Early Friends,* 325.

a corporate life which should carry the Society forward in one common service.[21]

There was no women's yearly meeting in England until nearly a century later (1784).

In 1668 George Fox prepared the first draft of the plans for the Quaker organization, which was afterward called by some who opposed it, the "Canons and Institutions." It served for a very long time as the discipline of the Society. It was arranged under nineteen different heads, and summed up the practices, advices, and organization, which had grown up or which the leaders had instituted up to that time.[22]

The organization of this hierarchy of meetings was not consciously suggested by the Presbyterian system nor in conscious imitation of it. Yet the gradation of monthly, quarterly and yearly meetings, each with special functions, higher authority and larger jurisdiction is curiously analogous to the Presbyterian system of presbytery, synod and general conference. The chief difference is that the Presbyterian bodies are wholly representative, whereas in theory the Quaker meeting is a gathering of the whole membership. Any Friend who is a member of a monthly, quarterly or yearly meeting may attend the official gatherings and take part in the deliberations. Representatives are appointed to the higher meeting by its subordinate constituent bodies, but only for the purpose of insuring attendance.[23]

Friends' business meetings were regularly preceded by a meeting for worship and when the business of the meeting was taken up, it was with no feeling of turning from the sacred to the secular. Christ was felt to be present as the directing Head of the church and the official action of the

---

21 BSPQ, 278.

22 The text is in Beck and Ball, *The London Friends' Meetings,* pp. 47 ff. For the substance see Fox, *Epistles,* pp. 276–293.

23 BSPQ, 279.

meeting was taken only as His will was sought and found. There was no president, but only a clerk, who introduced the business which claimed the attention of the meeting and recorded its conclusions, which were reached, not by voting, but by an agreement as to the "sense of the meeting." The spirit and method of procedure is stated by Burrough in his advice to London Friends (1662) as follows:

> Being orderly come together, not to spend time with needless, unnecessary and fruitless discourses; but to proceed in the wisdom of God, in such things as may upon occasion be moved amongst you, for the service of Truth and the good order of the body; to hear and consider, and if possible to determine the same in justice and truth,—not in the way of the world, as a worldly assembly of men, by hot contests, by seeking to outspeak and over-reach one another in discourse, as if it were a controversy between party and party of men, or two sides violently striving for dominion, in the way of carrying on some worldly interests for self-advantage; not deciding affairs by the greater vote, or the number of men, as the world, who have not the wisdom and power of God;—that none of this kind of order be permitted in your meeting. But in the wisdom, love and fellowship of God, in gravity, patience, meekness, in unity and concord, submitting one to another in lowliness of heart, and in the Holy Spirit of truth and righteousness, all things to be carried on . . . and to determine of things by a general mutual concord, in assenting together as one man in the spirit of truth and equity, and by the authority thereof. . . . And if at any time, any matter or occasion be presented to the meeting, which is doubtful or difficult, or not within the judgment of Friends there assembled, they not having full knowledge or experience of the matters depending,—that then on such occasions the judgment be suspended.[24]

---

[24] *Letters of Early Friends,* pp. 305, 306. The whole document extends from p. 294 to p. 310. It is possible that Friends' custom of estimating the "weight" of opinions in making up the sense of the meeting is an adaptation of the old custom in the English Parliament, where the rank of the members counted as well as numbers.

Two other central organizations were formed during this period. "The Morning Meeting" (shortened from "Second-Day's Morning Meeting") grew out of the custom of the Quaker ministers who were in London meeting on Monday mornings to consult about their "concerns" for the ministry in the London meetings so that they would "not go in heaps." [25] The earlier custom of consulting Fox or other leaders before publishing Quaker books or pamphlets had been interrupted by the Restoration persecutions. In 1672 the yearly meeting appointed a committee of ten to supervise Quaker publications. A year later Fox set up a weekly "Second-day Morning Meeting," chiefly for the purpose of combining these two functions: distributing the ministry in London and vicinity and supervising publications. This meeting came to have many functions both because of the "weight" of its membership and because of the frequency of its meetings.[26] It collected a library of two copies of all books written by Friends, as far as possible, and a copy of all books "written against the Truth from the beginning." The meeting was consulted as to setting up new meetings in the London area, dealt with ministers charged with moral lapses and in emergencies acted for the whole Society.

It is evident that with respect to the message of Friends, whether spoken or written, the Morning Meeting was a body of the first importance. It fostered controversial polemic overmuch, according to our ways of thinking. Its criticism, on the other hand, seems usually to have been moderate and sensible. But, in any case, controversy and criticism alike were an intellectual education to those who attended, and did much to keep the flame of learning alive. Ministers from all parts had

---

[25] This began as early as 1670; the travelling ministers when in London were accustomed to make Gerrard Roberts' house their headquarters and keep in touch with one another. BSPQ, 279, 280 and note.

[26] See Fox's letter to London Women Friends 1676. *Swarthmore Collection,* V, p. 9.

the right of entry, and, when in London, took a large share in the business. This kept them in touch with the thought of Quakerism; and it also helped to vary and freshen the thought of the Morning Meeting.[27]

Its prestige was strengthened by a letter left by Fox at his death requesting Friends who had been accustomed to write him about sufferings or asking advice to write to the Morning Meeting.[28] Ellis Hookes, the clerk of the yearly meeting became clerk of the Morning Meeting, which soon made his "chamber" or office its meeting-place. Until 1681 he labored with great industry and patience as librarian, critic, censor, editor, proof-reader and author at the task of providing the Society with an adequate literature. He also served as clerk of a half-dozen other committees and meetings.

The Meeting for Sufferings originated in the need of a representative body capable of acting for the Society when the yearly meeting was not in session. In 1660 Ellis Hookes undertook to digest the accounts of Friends' sufferings which were sent up from the counties, but was hampered by the difficulty of getting exact and business-like reports. To assist him the yearly meeting of 1675 arranged for a representative conference on the subject. One outcome of this conference after considerable discussion was an arrangement for a "meeting for sufferings" consisting of London Friends appointed to correspond with the counties, the Morning Meeting and at least one Friend from each county, who would be ready to attend when required. This body was to meet in London before each of the quarterly law terms in order to bring to the attention of the authorities the sufferings of Friends and to make efforts for their relief. In the intervals there was to be a weekly meeting attended by one fourth of the London members, the

---

[27] BSPQ, 281.
[28] *Letters of Early Friends*, pp. 353, 354.

attendance changing each quarter so as not to be unduly burdensome. The meeting gradually assumed wider functions, largely because of its representative character and frequent sessions and came to be the legal representative of the yearly meeting *ad interim*. The London representatives had the right to summon the whole body at need.

As Quakerism spread, especially in America, the essential features of the organization in England except the Morning Meeting were transferred to other countries.[29]

---

[29] In America the name, Meeting for Sufferings, has been discontinued generally. It is called the representative meeting, or, in the Five Years' Meeting, the permanent board.

CHAPTER 12

INTERNAL TROUBLES

THE organization of the Quaker movement described in the last chapter was not accomplished without protest. The strain of persecution created tensions between leaders and revealed flaws in judgment and temper. Many converts brought with them from the Ranter movement an impatience of social control. The travelling ministers whose force of conviction and personal winsomeness had moulded and unified the ideals and practices of Friends were prevented by imprisonment, illness and death from circulating freely between 1662 and 1672, and the local congregations or county groups became more or less isolated from the larger activities and tendencies in the Society. Their attitudes tended to become congregational rather than national.[1] Their expenses were chiefly for their own poor and persecuted members.

The effort to organize the Society more thoroughly and on a national scale was accompanied by a gradual revival of the travelling ministry, at first to revive and sustain the existing membership and then to extend the borders and increase the membership. The scheme of organization was primarily intended by Fox, not as a means of restraint but to give spiritual support in the absence of the leaders to isolated meetings under persecution, and to enlarge their opportunity to have an active part in the responsibilities and activities of the Society as a whole. It was at heart an

---

1 BSPQ, 217.

attempt toward a more democratic society. Fox's draft of the so-called "Canons and Institutions" began with the words, "Your fellowship is in the spirit." He believed that the new organizations would be instruments of service rather than fetters upon the soul.

There were elements in the Society, however, who took the other view and set themselves to oppose Fox's plans. Back of particular issues there was the fundamental problem of adjusting individual liberty to the authority and discipline of the organized church. Sippel finds the particular genius of the Quaker movement in its combination of prophetism with mysticism.[2] The prophetic spirit has a consciousness of a call and commission to witness to God's will; an assurance of direct divine authority to say "Thus saith the Lord." The prophet's ministry is a life-work. He is a minister to God's people, an organizer and director. Only the message and form of service vary. On the other hand, the mystic waits on the movings of God's spirit as an individual. If he has a message for neighbor or meeting, it comes, when and where God wills, and when the message is given or the service rendered, he resumes the common tenor of life and waits on God's moving for other service. In Quakerism there has always been a tension between the leaders with their consciousness of being commissioned as prophets to the people; and the mystically minded members feeling themselves taught of God and needing not to be taught of men; jealous of any authority but that of the Spirit in their own souls; and more conscious of the liberty of the children of God and the priesthood of believers than of the fellowship of believers and their organized coördination in the body of Christ. Between the two tendencies within the Society there was not a sharply drawn division; they were all Friends; all believed in the Inward Light as the authority in belief and conduct; all shared the fellow-

---

[2] *Werdendes Quäkertum,* pp. 103, 104.

ship of the Children of Light. The difference was a difference of polarity; between those to whom the individual spiritual judgment was primary and ultimate and those to whom the group judgment was to be regarded as superior. Such differences usually find overt expression in concrete matters of conduct which derive their importance from the principles they involve.

The resistance to the new organization broke out in Westmorland in the Preston Patrick region where the Society got its first great accessions. The leaders were John Story and John Wilkinson, two able preachers among the first Publishers of Truth. Story was the stronger character and real leader. The Conventicle Act of 1670 imposed heavy fines on preachers at conventicles and on the owners of houses where conventicles were allowed. Contrary to Friends' general practice some of the Westmorland Friends met secretly in the hills or woods. Human motives are hardly ever unmixed; possibly they did this partly to protect the owners of the houses where they were accustomed to meet from the heavy fines; possibly in order to escape the informers and officers. Fox and other leaders of the Society at large realized the danger of such a course. In a moral struggle nothing jeopardizes a cause like the suspicion of deceit, insincerity or self-interest. Many of the leaders felt called to testify by letters or personal visits against the secret meetings; and when the new organizations added their censure, the Wilkinson-Story faction came out in opposition to the new system of meetings and separated from them. By 1675 the situation had become acute. Separations have a way of spreading; especially if they involve ideas or issues that are widely diffused; and all those who chafed under the old leadership or the new order were encouraged to join the Westmorland faction. Sympathizers with Story and Wilkinson were especially numerous in the West, where Bristol became their stronghold and William Rogers, a Bristol merchant of some learning and ability, became their champion.

The chief matters to which this faction objected, in addition to the condemnation of secret meetings, were: (1) the exercise of authority of one meeting over another or the right of a meeting to "judge" the acts of members publicly. They wished to allow this only when the member consented. They wanted all meetings to be composed of appointed representatives only. (2) Separate women's meetings except in large cities for the care of the poor. (3) The requirement that engaged couples should lay their intentions of marriage before the women's meeting. There were some who wished to marry before priests so as to protect the legitimacy of their heirs. (4) The raising of funds to pay the expenses of travelling ministers. (5) The authority of the Morning Meeting in London to supervise Quaker publications and the expenses of Friends travelling abroad in the ministry. (6) Fox's leadership and acknowledged authority. (7) The practice in some meetings of "groaning, singing or sounding" while a Friend was praying or speaking in meetings for worship. (8) The prohibition of the payment of tithes by members to avoid fines or imprisonment, when the individual felt free to do so.

After various efforts of Fox and other Friends to compose these differences by private correspondence and conferences, they came before the Yearly Meeting of Ministers in London in 1675, which issued a letter which dealt largely with the issues raised by Story and Wilkinson and on most points condemned their positions. Leading Friends continued efforts for reconciliation, and in 1676 got leaders of both sides together at Draw-well near Sedbergh, where an understanding seemed to be arrived at. Story and Wilkinson afterward paid a satisfactory visit to Fox at Swarthmore. William Rogers of Bristol was at the

Draw-well meeting, but was not satisfied with a published report of it, and the controversy broke out afresh. Rogers charged Fox with desiring to play the part of Moses to the Quakers and become their lawgiver, and charged that Story and Wilkinson were being persecuted because they would not submit to his orders.

At the Yearly Meeting of Ministers in June, 1677, a strong condemnation of the attitude of Story and Wilkinson was issued, signed by sixty-six leading Friends,[3] reproving their "jealous, rending and separating spirit," and denying any intention of all or any to set up "a worldly or arbitrary power over God's heritage." The controversy spread through other sections of England during the next five years, with Bristol as the chief center. There were sympathizers with the Wilkinson-Story faction in Wiltshire, Hertford and Reading. The monthly meeting records of Upperside Monthly Meeting near Old Jordans and of Norwich showed adherents there also.

In 1678 on his return from a visit to the Continent Fox went to Bristol, where prolonged discussions took place between Rogers, William Ford, Arthur Ismeade and John Maltravers, on one side, and Penn, George Whitehead and William Gibson, on the other. Fox and Story were present. Afterward Rogers circulated a biased account of the meeting, which indulged in petty personalities and attacks on Fox's character. In 1680 Rogers published an elaborate summary of the whole case, its history, causes, arguments, documents, etc., called *The Christian Quaker Distinguished from the Apostate and Innovator.* It is often pettifogging in argument, more anxious to make a partisan case than to find the truth, and full of invective and personalities. Fox is charged with having hidden to avoid imprisonment, with securing his property from informers,

[3] Whitehead did not sign it, because it might hurt his service; nor George Fox who purposely kept in the background. BSPQ, 309.

with living on the fat of the land while his poorer brethren suffered and, along with other leaders, with being domineering and intolerant, misusing Scripture in his defense of separate women's meetings[4] and violating his own rules of procedure at his own marriage.[5]

The great majority of Friends sided with Fox in support of his plans for organization. Practically all the great founders of the Society stood by him; not that they regarded him as infallible; but that his character and judgments were preferable to those of his opponents, in whom they sensed something of worldliness, self-interest and jealousy. Three of the finest spirits among the Quaker leaders were Isaac Penington, William Dewsbury and William Penn. All of them had suffered much for the cause. Penington was the sensitive mystic; Dewsbury, the great reconciler and apostle of unity; and Penn the statesman among them. They all believed in Fox's sincerity, integrity, and constructive ability and their judgment is trustworthy as to the merits of the personal attacks on Fox. Aside from this both Penn and Barclay believed that the fundamental issue was that of church authority against anarchy.

Roger's *Christian Quaker* was not allowed to go unchallenged. Ellis Hookes published a reply on behalf of the Morning Meeting. Penn and George Whitehead also published replies which called forth three more sections of *The Christian Quaker* in addition to the original five. Rogers resorted finally to doggerel verse in replying to Whitehead, in the course of which he made an attack on the Morning Meeting, especially its demands for funds for the travelling ministry and its alleged control over their movements. General collections for books and service beyond the seas were set on foot by the ministers' meetings in 1668, 1672 and 1676 and by the yearly meeting in 1679,

---

4 *Christian Quaker,* Part V, pp. 33, 39.

5 Barclay, *Inner Life,* p. 443.

when Rogers began the publication of his *Christian Quaker*. To quote him:

> Then the Gospel loud did cry; our Law's the Light,
> Liberty of Conscience is Men's Right;
> But when that Fox, about Church Government,
> More than the Gospel, Time and Labour spent,
> I' th' stead of Liberty of Conscience, He,
> Said Liberty of th' Gospel, it must be.
>
> ** ** ** ** ** **
>
> When He had framed i' the Church a Government,
> Preachers, approved by Man, beyond Seas went,
> Who when they wanted Moneys to proceed,
> The Church her Cash then did supply their Need,
> If they their Motion freely did Submit,
> To the London Church, and do as She thought fit.
>
> ** ** ** ** ** **
>
> The Spirit's motion in a home-bread Swain,
> Without a city stamp, seem'd but in Vain;
> And yet sometimes, 'gainst such as Fox had sent;
> The Church Dar'd not to shew Her discontent.
>
> ** ** ** ** ** **
>
> At length, Her Papers, like to Briefs did cry
> For Money, Money for the Ministry.[6]

To which Ellwood replied in kind in his half-humorous *Rogero-Mastix:*[7]

> May none beyond Seas go, but who can spare
> Sufficient of their own, the charge to bear?
> Must Christ be so confined, he may not send
> Any, but such as have Estates to spend?
> God bless us from such Doctrine, and such Teachers,
> As will admit of none but wealthy Preachers.

---

6 *A Second Scourge for George Whitehead.*

7 *Rogero-Mastix: A Rod for William Rogers, in Return for his Riming Scourge*, etc. (1685), p. 19.

Friends' contention against the priests of their day was not that they lived by the gospel; but that, as they believed, they were not a truly called and spiritual ministry and therefore not worthy of support; and they objected also to the compulsory payment of tithes and other fees.[8]

The controversy had run out into absurdities, quite alien to the spirit of men engaged in unselfish service and suffering for great truths, concerned not with petty personal rights and liberties but with the Kingdom of peace and love. It practically disappeared with the death of its leaders (Story in 1681 and Wilkinson a few years later), the renewal of persecution at the end of Charles II's reign and especially with the revival of the travelling ministry which followed the Declaration of Indulgence of 1672 and the Great Pardon in 1786. Most of the Separatists finally returned to the fold or were lost to Friends altogether, although a few of the separated meetings continued until the next century.

A revival of religion in Cumberland and along the Scottish border began in 1672 and continued through the remainder of the century. In this Christopher Story and John Wilkinson of Cumberland were prominent. Ministers visited Scotland and Ireland at the exhortation of Fox.[9] Charles Marshall spent the two years 1670–1672, "running through the nation," during which he attended about four hundred meetings. Itinerancy revived and the Quaker movement felt again the inspiration of the travelling apostles in all sections of England and Ireland. John Burnyeat visited America and Ireland and travelled constantly in England 1673–1682. John Banks did a great serv-

---

[8] See Penn's Preface to *Bicent. Jour.*, p. xxix, V. "They believe all compelled maintenance, even to gospel ministers, to be unlawful, because expressly contrary to Christ's command, who said 'Freely ye have received, freely give'; at least that the maintenance of gospel ministers should be free, and not forced. The other reason of their refusal is, because those ministers are not gospel ones, in that the Holy Ghost is not their foundation, but human arts and parts."

[9] See *Epistles*, #283, directed to Bristol Friends.

ice in Ireland and the North of England. Leonard Fell was often Fox's travelling companion. John Gratton was a Baptist convert who preached with power through the Midlands and Peak District. In company with Barclay, Penn and Keith Fox visited the Continent in 1677 and he made another visit there in 1684.

The controversies were not so much settled as forgotten in the absorption of the new work and renewed growth of the movement. Nevertheless they were not wholly in vain. The nature of church organization and of church government were involved in them and the leaders were compelled to think out more thoroughly the basis of church authority and its relation to the Inward Light; to try to adjust individual autonomy to the group judgment and corporate activity.

During the controversies two works had appeared which were only indirectly connected with the Story-Wilkinson-Rogers contentions, but which involved the fundamental problems precipitated by Fox's organization of the Society. In 1673 the issue raised by John Perrot was revived by a pamphlet published anonymously called, *The Spirit of the Hat.*[10] Aside from much personal bitterness against Fox and his co-laborers[11] (such as Rogers displayed), it puts the case for religious individualism forcefully and subjects the position of Fox to a keen criticism. A rigorous application of its principles would prevent all collective action, in so far as that requires common agreement as to rules of procedure or prearrangement as to time or place, unless the Inward Light is of such nature that its movings and revelations in the individual can be relied on as a basis

---

[10] Its chief author was William Mucklow. See Barclay, *Inner Life*, p. 436. Also Smith's *Catalogue.*

[11] He charges Fox and some fellow-ministers with extravagance in their mode of living and insinuates immoral relations with women on the part of many eminent ones in the ministry, if not on the part of Fox himself, pp. 29, 34, 43.

of common action. In strict and narrow logic, the Inner Light as the ultimate guide in the individual might be a basis of social action also, but common sense and experience do not find it so. The Light in its working is not divorced from the senses, the constructive imagination, logical reason and social judgment. *The Spirit of the Hat* generated a fresh controversial literature. It was answered by Penn in *The Spirit of Alexander the Coppersmith;* which brought a reply in *Tyranny and Hypocrisy Detected;* to which Penn rejoined in *Judas and the Jews.* In the same year also Mucklow wrote a pamphlet on *Liberty of Conscience* to which George Whitehead replied in *The Apostate Incendiary Rebuked.* It can only be said in extenuation of the acrimonious language of these brochures, of which the titles are a fair indication, that it was rather milder than that of other controversial religious literature of the age.

In 1674 Robert Barclay wrote an exposition and defense of the Quaker system, which became, with slight modifications, the classical statement. It appeared just after *The Spirit of the Hat* and preceded the general interest in the Story-Wilkinson controversy, of which Barclay was ignorant when he wrote. Its doctrinal background was the extreme individualism of the Ranter spirit, which suggested the title *The Anarchy of the Ranters.*

Robert Barclay belonged to a strong Quaker group at Aberdeen in Scotland. It included his father, David Barclay the laird of Ury,[12] Alexander Jaffray, Patrick Livingstone, a convert of the earlier Quaker visitors to Scotland; and George Keith, who was a graduate of Aberdeen University and one of the most learned and able thinkers of early Friends. He contributed much to the intellectual formulation of Quakerism and was especially helpful to Robert Barclay. All members of the group were convinced

---

[12] See Whittier's poem, *Barclay of Ury.*

in mature life, had thought deeply upon religion, and brought to the Society a background of the theological emphasis and tenets of Calvinism.

Robert Barclay belonged to the second generation of Quakerism. He experienced, however, a vital religious experience when he was "convinced" in 1666 at the age of eighteen. He described his convincement in the *Apology:*

> Of which I myself, in a part, am a true witness; who not by strength of arguments or by a particular disquisition of each doctrine, and convincement of my understanding thereby, came to receive and bear witness of the Truth, but by being secretly reached by this life. For, when I came into the silent assemblies of God's people, I felt a secret power among them, which touched my heart; and as I gave way unto it, I found the evil weakening in me and the good raised up; and so I became thus knit and united unto them, hungering more and more after the increase of this power and life whereby I might feel myself perfectly redeemed. And, indeed this is the surest way to become a Christian.[13]

He had been brought up under a strict Calvinistic discipline; and was sent to Paris to study under his uncle who was a Catholic and a Professor in the Scots Theological College. Here he got a thorough training in scholastic logic and philosophy, in Catholic theology, in the Church Fathers, the Bible and the Latin and French languages. His mother was afraid he would become a Catholic and in accordance with her dying request, his father brought him home in 1663. He did not return to the Presbyterian fold, however; but sampled various religious groups, associated with men of liberal views, and finally joined Friends.[14] This preparation fitted him preëminently to become the theologian of Quakerism.

In his *Anarchy of the Ranters* Barclay attempts to find

---

13 *Apology*, Prop. XI, § VII.

14 *Works*, "Universal Love," Sect. I.

a *via media* between the unrestrained individualism of the Ranters and the absolute authoritarianism of the Roman church. He finds the basis of church authority in the manifest presence, leading and authority of the Holy Spirit, which was common ground for all Friends.

Barclay distinguishes between the authority of the church in "temporals" and in "spirituals." In regard to outward things he finds the warrant of the church in Christian love. "Love and compassion," he says, "are the great, yea, and the chiefest marks of Christianity." [15] Since the Spirit is the spirit of love, he leads Friends, as they are led of the Spirit, to meet together about the care of the poor and other outward needs of members.

Who will be so unchristian, as to reprove this good order and government, and to say it is needless? But if any will thus object: "May not the Spirit lead every one of you to give to them that need? What needs meeting about it and such formalities?" I answer, the Spirit of God leads us so to do; what can they say to the contrary? Nor is this a practice any ways inconsistent with being inwardly and immediately led by the Spirit; for the Spirit of God doth now, as well as in the days of old, lead his people into those things which are orderly, and of good report; for he is the God of order, and not of confusion.[16]

In regard to spirituals, he finds the authority to consist in the Spirit of Christ manifest in and through the church. In this he seems to hold a high view of the authority of the church.

I affirm, and that according to Truth, That as the Church and Assembly of God's People may and hath Power to Decide by the Spirit of God in matters fundamental and weighty (without which no Decision nor Decree in whatever matters is available), so the same Church and Assembly also in other

---

[15] *Anarchy of the Ranters,* Sect. V.

[16] *Loc. cit.*

matters of less moment, as to themselves (yet being needful and expedient with Respect to the Circumstances of Time, Place and things that may fall in) may and hath Power of the same Spirit, and not otherways, being acted, moved, and assisted, and led by it thereto, to pronounce a positive Judgment: Which, no Doubt, will be found obligatory upon all such, who have a Sense and Feeling of the Mind of the Spirit; though rejected by such as are not watchful, and so are out of the Feeling and Unity of the Life. And this is that, which none that own Immediate Revelation, or a being inwardly led by the Spirit to be now a thing to expected or dispensed to the Saints, can without contradicting their own Principle deny.[17]

Barclay acknowledges, however, that such a church can exist and the members can recognize its authority, only when both church and individual members are really led by the Spirit.

The only proper Judge of Controversies in the Church, is the Spirit of God, and the Power of deciding solely lies in it; as having the only Unerring, Infallible and certain Judgment belonging to it; which Infallibility is not necessarily annexed to any Persons, Person or Places Whatsoever, by Virtue of any Office, Place or Station anyone may have, or have had in the Body of Christ.[18]

The power of decision, he affirms, will ordinarily rest with those whose religious interest, activity in religious work, and approved judgment in religious matters give them a position of leadership; shown, however, in their ability to gain the assent of the body.

This may seem to beg the question; but it is only stating the perennial problem of democracy. Political democracy will only work where the citizens are both public-spirited and politically intelligent, and where the political author-

---

[17] *Works* (Ed. 1718), vol. I, pp. 381–382. (*Anarchy of the Ranters,* Sect. VI, Question II).

[18] *Works,* p. 225.

ity is evidently wise and just. In actual practice Friends' polity has usually worked well on the assumption that the Light in the individual and church are from the same Spirit and can be perceived by both with sufficient clearness; as long as the members are spiritually alive and active, and more concerned to maintain Christian brotherhood than to carry through a particular policy or achieve some outward end. Barclay explains the nature and value of group leading by a famous figure.

> And as many Candles lighted, and put in one place, do greatly augment the Light, and make it more to shine forth; so when many are gathered together into the same Life, there is more of the Glory of God, and his Power appears, to the refreshment of the Individual; for that he partakes not only of the Light and Life raised in himself, but in all the rest.[19]

In our time we turn most naturally to the analogy of the scientific method by which scientists pool their knowledge, verify one another's experiments and observations and correct one another's mistakes; so that each is wiser for the contribution of others and the whole group speak with the authority of the common knowledge and experience.[20]

In situations where the individual judgment differs radically from the decision of the church, Friends have never reached a clear judgment as to the principles which should obtain. Barclay and the leaders of his day were inclined to believe that in such a case the member was in error and should submit to the judgment of the "weight of the meeting." This problem was involved in the Perrot and Story-Wilkinson controversies, but complicated there by the manifest bad spirit of the champions of the right of the individual. Such cases have been relatively rare in Quaker history. Fundamentally the individual Light is both primary and ultimate. However much one's spiritual appre-

---

[19] *Apology,* Prop. XI, § XVII.

[20] *Ibid.,* Prop. II, Statement of Thesis.

hension is quickened and clarified by group consideration, in the end the group judgment as to the mind of the Spirit must be composed of the assent of the individual members. The individual member who cannot share the conviction of the group may in humility acquiesce in their decision out of deference to their greater experience, or he may allow the group to proceed as they are led without protest, or he may do his utmost to bring them to his view; but, in the end, his own action as an individual must be according to his own conviction of God's will; and the church has no right to expect him to do otherwise nor to try to compel him to do so. On the other hand, the group acting in a corporate capacity as a church must act according to its corporate judgment. It should always have a tender respect for the individual leading or the individual "concern"; it may decide to postpone action out of deference to dissenting individuals in the hope of reaching a united judgment in future on receipt of further light; but when it feels that it must act, it must act on its best light, and the individual has no right to demand that it violate its own convictions and follow his.

In later writings Barclay modified his position somewhat, reflecting in them the clearer understanding of these problems which came to Friends generally and to the leaders of the Society in particular out of the prolonged discussions and painful experiences of these controversies.[21]

---

[21] BSPQ, 345.

Chapter 13

QUAKER EDUCATION

The educational ideals of the leaders of the first generation of Friends were lofty and original, fostered by their enthusiasm for humanity and their faith in the possibilities of human nature. They did not have to struggle against the conviction of human depravity, nor overleap a barrier between sacred and secular, nor overcome a prejudice against the natural (as distinguished from the supernatural) as if it were inherently ungodly. Their break with the rites and dogmas of the historical churches as well as with many social customs and political ties, gave them original and fresh viewpoints and encouraged educational pioneering and adventure. In an age when education was almost exclusively classical and theological, Friends generally felt the claims of "useful" and "natural" learning and aimed at the development of personality.

Two noteworthy projects in the first period of the Society's history represented educational ideals which were only partially realized in later Quaker education. One was the development of nature study and practical subjects in the curriculum. George Fox proposed that "William Tomlinson should set up a school to teach languages, together with the nature of herbs, roots, plants and trees." This idea was apparently much on Fox's mind. His initial experience brought him a sense of a new world. It baptized him into a fresh sympathy with all life and gave him a conviction of intuitive insight into the meaning of the material world. "Now I was come up in spirit through the flaming sword, into the paradise of God," he said of his great experience.

All things were new; and all the creation gave unto me another smell than before, beyond what words can utter. I knew nothing but pureness, and innocency, and righteousness; being renewed into the image of God by Christ Jesus, to the state of Adam, which he was in before he fell. The creation was opened to me; and it was showed me how all things had their names given them according to their nature and virtue. I was at a stand in my mind whether I should practice physic for the good of mankind, seeing the nature and virtues of things were so opened to me by the Lord.[1]

His interest in education was doubtless later increased by a sense of his own lack of schooling. Many of the early leaders, who had received their education before becoming Friends, did not fully realize the value of it to them, simply because they had never attempted to do their work without it. There was even a tendency to depreciate it, because their school learning had not brought them to the great central experience of Quakerism nor helped them consciously on the way to it. George Fox, however, realized his own lack and knew how much better he could have pleaded the cause of Quakerism if he had had more schooling.

The following passages show the character and scope of Fox's educational ideals.

Then, returning towards London by Waltham, I advised the setting up a school there for teaching boys; and also a women's school to be opened at Shacklewell, for instructing girls and young maidens in whatsoever things were civil and useful in the creation.[2]

I would not have any to think that I deny or am against schools for the teaching of children the natural tongues and arts whereby they may do natural things; but all natural tongues and languages upon the earth make no more than

1 *Bicent. Jour.*, I, 28.
2 *Camb. Jour.*, II, 119.

natural men; and the natural man knows not the things of God.[3]

"At his death Fox desired that a part of the Philadelphia property given to him by Penn should be enclosed 'for a garden, and to be planted with all sorts of physical plants, for lads and lasses to learn simples there, and the uses to convert them to distilled waters, oils, ointments, etc.' "[4]

Penn's educational ideals were broad and enlightened, with an emphasis upon the development of personality that was in advance of his times. He wrote to his wife in 1682, concerning their children:

> For their learning be liberal . . . but let it be useful knowledge, such as is consistent with Truth and godliness, not cherishing a vain conversation or idle mind, but ingenuity mixed with industry is good for the body and mind, too. I recommend the useful parts of mathematics, as building houses or ships, measuring, surveying, dialling, navigation; but agriculture is especially in my eye; let my children be husbandmen and housewives; it is industrious, healthy, honest and of good example, like Abraham and the holy ancients, who pleased God and obtained a good report. This leads to consider the works of God and nature, of things that are good, and diverts the mind from being taken up with the vain arts and inventions of a luxurious world. It is commendable in the princes of Germany and the nobles of that empire that they have all their children instructed in some useful occupation. Be sure to observe their genius and do not cross it as to learning; let them not dwell too long on one thing, but let their change be agreeable, and all their diversions have some little bodily labour in them.[5]

In *Some Fruits of Solitude* the individualism of Quakerism is still more emphasized: "the genius of the child is

[3] GTD, 653.
[4] BFHS, III (1909), pp. 100–101.
[5] Janney, *Life*, p. 199.

not to be crossed in its education," he wrote again. He also appreciated the importance of activity in education and of the experimental and ethical in true learning:

We are in Pain to make them Scholars, but not Men! To talk, rather than to know, which is true Canting.

The first thing obvious to children is what is sensible; and that we make no part of their rudiments.

We press their memory too soon, and puzzle, strain and load them with words and rules; to know Grammar and Rhetorick, and a strange Tongue or two, that it is ten to one may never be useful to them: Leaving their natural Genius to Mechanical and Physical, or natural Knowledge uncultivated and neglected; which would be of exceeding Use and Pleasure to them through the whole Course of their Life.

To be sure, Languages are not to be despised or neglected. But Things are still to be preferred.

Children had rather be making of Tools and Instruments of Play; Shaping, Drawing, Framing and Building, etc., than getting some Rules of Propriety of Speech by Heart: And those also would follow with more Judgment, and less Trouble and Time.

It were Happy if we studied Nature more in natural Things; and acted according to Nature; those Rules are few, plain and most reasonable.

Let us begin where she begins, go her pace, and close always where she ends, and we cannot miss of being good Naturalists.

It is pity therefore that Books have not been composed for Youth, by some curious and careful Naturalists, and also Mechanics, in the Latin Tongue, to be used in Schools, that they might learn Things with words: Things obvious and familiar to them, and which would make the Tongue easier to be obtained by them.

Finally, if Man be the Index or Epitomy of the World, as Philosophers tell us, we have only to read ourselves well to be learned in it. But because there is nothing we less regard than the Characters of the Power that made us, which are so clearly written upon us and the World he has given us, and can best tell us what we are and should be, we are even Strangers to our own Genius: The Glass in which we should see that true instructing and agreeable Variety, which is to be observed in Nature, to the Admiration of that Wisdom and Adoration of that Power which made us all.[6]

Penn's provisions for education in Pennsylvania are mentioned elsewhere.[7]

A statement issued by Ellis Hookes, for many years clerk of the Morning Meeting in London and Christopher Taylor, the schoolmaster, is characteristic: "We deny nothing for children's learning that may be honest and useful for them to know, whether relating to divine principles or that may be outwardly serviceable for them to learn in regard to the outward creation." Thomas Lawson refers to an original educational project:

> Some years ago, George Fox, William Penn and others, were concerned to purchase a piece of land near London for the use of a garden school-house and a dwelling-house for the master, in which garden one or two or more of each sort of our English plants were to be planted, as also many outlandish plants. My purpose was to write a book on these in Latin, so, as a boy had the description of these in book-lessons and their virtues, he might see these growing in the garden or plantation, to gain the knowledge of them; but persecutions and troubles obstructed the prosecution hereof, which the Master of Christ's College in Cambridge (Ralph Cudworth, who was keenly alive to the advantages of a study of nature) hearing of, told me was a noble and honorable undertaking and would fill the nation with philosophers. Adam and his posterity, if the primitive original station had been kept, had had no book to mind, but God himself, the book of life and the book of the creation; and they that grow up in the knowledge of the Lord and of His creation, they are the true philosophers . . . His work within and His works without, even the least of plants, preaches forth the power and the wisdom of the Creator; and, eyed in the spark of eternity, humbles man.[8]

---

[6] *Some Fruits of Solitude.*

[7] Above chap. 10, pp. 118, 120.

[8] Letter to Sir John Rodes, *A Quaker Post-bag.* pp. 20–23.

This idea of nature study was much in advance of the times. The modern study of natural phenomena was then just in its beginning and even among Friends it had to wait for a more scientific age for its realization.

The second noteworthy educational project was proposed by John Bellers, who has been called the "father of Socialism." His idea was the forerunner of the many modern attempts to combine theoretic instruction with practical activities. In 1697 the London Meeting for Sufferings took up his "Proposals for Raising a College of Industry, with Profit for the Rich, a Plentiful Living for the Poor, and a Good Education for Youth," which he had prepared in 1695. The scheme provided for a regulated work-colony in which there should be a mixture of book-learning with industries and agriculture. All the workers should help in agriculture with the "peak-load" at harvest time; and during the slack-season, use their labor in the industries.

The children would have an English education, with manual training from four or five years old, and careful moral supervision throughout. Those of pregnant understanding it may be worth encouraging to the furthest degree, but for most "it's labour sustains, maintains, and upholds, though learning gives a useful varnish." "There may be a library of books, a physic-garden for understanding of herbs, and a laboratory for preparing of medicines." "The hand employed brings profit, the reason used in it makes wise, and the will subdued makes them good." "Young men should be apprenticed in the institution till 24, and young women till 21 or marriage. The older people must keep the rules, the restraints of which will not be more, or so much, as the best-governed 'prentices' are under in London. The elder men are to do less work, and, if suitable, to be made overseers."

By a curious lapse from wisdom, Bellers proposes to allow the Founders to keep a nominee at the College, either without working, or only doing partial work, though he may be expelled "in case of exorbitancy." [9]

[9] BSPQ,. 579. Quotations are from Bellers' *Proposals &c.*, pp. 15–20.

The institution established by London Friends at Clerkenwell in the suburbs of the capital in the effort to carry out Bellers' plan proved only partly successful. Its management was not efficient, the pensioners of the managers proved a disturbing factor, and the manual labor was overemphasized to such an extent that the educational features were neglected. In 1811, it was transformed into a *bona fide* school, which was transferred first to Croydon, and finally to Saffron Walden.[10]

Early Friends made great efforts to educate their children. The yearly meeting epistle of 1695 advised "that Schools and Schoolmasters who are faithful Friends and well-qualified, be placed and encouraged in all Counties, Cities, Great Towns or places where there may be need." [11] Their elementary schools were frequently held in empty rooms of meeting houses. English Friends established at least a score of higher grade schools, many of them Latin schools. In Ireland during this period there were a number of excellent Friends' schools. The character of the curriculum in such schools is shown in the following summary by a pupil of his five years' schooling at Sidcot School: "I have learned in grammar, Latin Testament, Corderius, Castalion, Textor and Tully, and am got through Arithmetic, except one rule, and also have learned merchants' accounts." [12]

Friends labored under many handicaps in the effort to carry out their educational ideals. Nonconformists were excluded from the universities. They would not have attended the theological schools, even if they had been open to them. Education was still considered a function of the Established Church, and the laws often put obstacles in the way of Quaker teachers and schools. Available textbooks

---

[10] Bellers also made very advanced proposals looking toward public health and socialized medicine in *An Essay Towards the Improvement of Physick* &c. (1714).

[11] *London Epistles*. Cited in Graham, *The Faith of a Quaker,* p. 173.

[12] Knight, *Sidcot School,* pp. 9–17. Cited in BSPQ, 531.

were mostly written by non-Friends. This mattered most when they dealt with Biblical and other religious subjects. Friends made some efforts to provide textbooks of their own, more in consonance with their ideals, but their efforts apparently did not meet with great success. Braithwaite records one of these attempts:

> Taylor obtained the assistance of a learned and devoted German Friend, John Matern; and, at the instance of the Six Weeks' Meeting, who desired "a book for teaching children at the schools Court hands, Lawyer's Latin, etc., the better to enable them to read a writ and other Law process," published in 1676 *Institutiones Pietatis,* to which the chief principles of Latin were added. With Matern's help he also produced a *Compendium Trium Linguarum,* an abridgment of Latin, Greek and Hebrew, "in a short and easy method for the use of the studious and Christian youth." The book lays aside "all the old, corrupt, heathenish books and grammars thence educed," and illustrates the languages from scripture.[13]

A number of the Quaker scholars of the first generation became schoolmasters. There were Christopher and Thomas Taylor of Skipton, men of great abilities and learning, who were pioneers in Quaker education. Alexander Arscott had a university education, which he put to similar use. Other able schoolmasters were "the learned Richard Richardson," who was the first master of the Devonshire House school for the children of poor Friends; and Edward Plumstead, Ambrose Rigge, and John Field, Latin teachers in or near London. Richard Scoryer had a normal school in Southwark and afterwards at Wandsworth (1681) where he offered to train Friends *gratis* who wished to become teachers.

These scholars brought to the Society trained minds, better able because of their education to grapple with the very complex problems of the Quaker polity and policies.

---

[13] BSPQ, 526.

They had in some measure an understanding of religious history so that they could see contemporary problems in perspective and in the light of the religious experience of the past. This was a safeguard against the narrowness and fanaticism that are an ever present danger to mysticism. Their learning gave them an understanding of the religious temper and thought of their own times; and their ability to speak to their contemporaries in a religious vocabulary which they understood made them all the more effective Publishers of Truth.

After all allowance has been made for the difficulties under which early Friends worked, there remain two serious defects in their educational ideals and efforts. First, they did not attempt to provide for higher education of collegiate grade. Shut out from the universities, they provided no institution to take their place. When the university-trained men of the first generation died, there were none to take up their mantles. Friends did not have means to found a great university, to be sure; and it would have seemed a daring thing to start even a small one. But in other lines, Friends were not afraid to attempt daringly original things.

The second defect lay in the absence of provision for religious education beyond the very rudiments. The members of a religious democracy, such as the Society of Friends, needed more religious training, not less, than those of other bodies having a professional ministry or specialized leadership. With every member a priest and preacher, all needed to be informed as to the history of Christian ideas and institutions, the range of Christian experience, and the all-too-common dangers that beset religious people—the danger that love be lost in theological contention, that rites and ceremonies become merely camouflage for spiritual bankruptcy, that emotionalism be induced to compensate the lack of morality, and that subjective religion lose touch with practical life when it loses touch with the historic Christian revelation in the Bible. "To be bred at Oxford or Cambridge was not enough to qualify one to be a minister," as George Fox discerned; [14] but the Society did not see soon enough that ignorance of religious things is equally inadequate for an effective ministry; that at times in history "zeal not according to knowledge" has proved quite as dangerous to the Christian cause as learning without spiritual experience. Friends had to learn by sad experience that the "Inner Light" is not an easy substitute for the encyclopedia; that God does not give by inward illumination the truths that He has given men intelligence to learn; that even the Children of Light must "dig for wisdom as for silver" and get mental as well as bodily food by the sweat of the face.

---

[14] *Bicent. Jour.*, I, 11.

Chapter 14

LITERATURE AND DOCTRINE

THE writings of Friends during the post-restoration period were marked by greater intellectual ability and wider outlook, but the intense struggle for existence made practically all Quaker writing during the final Stuart period primarily controversial and apologetic. Attacks on current abuses, accounts of Friends' sufferings, replies to literary attacks, and doctrinal writings alike were intended to justify Friends' customs, commend their beliefs and defend them from misrepresentation, no less than the formal apologies, which were explicitly addressed to king or Parliament. Toward the end of this period (and in the early part of the next) there grew up a copious literature of biographies (with their accounts of conversions and religious experiences) and histories, which were also part of the Quaker propaganda.

The apologists were in the main men and women of education and culture, belonging themselves to the ruling class, who had the ability as well as the necessity to expound Friends' principles to the rulers of church and state, who were their principal antagonists. Penington, Penn and Barclay were able and prolific exponents and defenders of Quakerism in terms that appealed to the theologian and statesman. As the leaders began to succumb to the hardships of their imprisonments and itinerant ministry (as most of them did rather than to old age, for the majority of them died before middle life) their writings were collected, edited and published under the care of the

Morning Meeting. Howgill, Nayler, Burrough, Penington and others had their testimony thus preserved and their work continued.

Much of this writing was done in prison and published and circulated amid difficulties and dangers. By the Licensing Act of 1662, unlicensed printing was punishable by severe penalties. The public licenser of printing rarely authorized the printing of Nonconformist works. Often the Quaker printers were arrested and their stocks and presses confiscated.[1] To reduce the risk of total loss in this way a book was sometimes printed in sections by different printers. Usually the printer's name was omitted, although it is boldly given in a surprising number of cases.[2] The Quakers made a notable contribution to the struggle for freedom of the press as well as for freedom of speech. The total number of Quaker tracts circulated before 1725 has been estimated at from two and a half to four million.[3]

In the early days, as has been noted, Friends' compositions were submitted in advance to George Fox. After 1672 the Morning Meeting took over the function of Quaker censorship. Ellis Hookes was for a long time secretary of this meeting and to him fell the arduous duties of reader, censor and editor of Friends' publications under the direction of the Morning Meeting. This meeting had a standing order to procure and keep copies of all books against Friends and to provide answers to them "with all convenient speed." [4]

During this period certain types of Quaker writing began to be settled and the general ideals of style, subject matter and treatment which were to characterize Quaker literature for nearly two centuries were established, and

---

1 BSPQ, 418, 419.

2 Wright, *Lit. Life*, pp. 95, 96.

3 *Ibid.*, p. 8. Cf. *Camb. Jour.*, I, 447n.

4 Wright, *Lit. Life*, p. 99. Cf. *A Quaker Post-bag*, pp. 118, 126, 135-138 &c.

gave it a remarkable homogeneity.[5] They are pretty well described by William Penn in his *Preface to the Reader,* prefixed to the collection of the works of John Whitehead.[6] Penn cautions the reader (1) not to expect "the learning of the schools," (2) nor a "nice polished stile" "to give lustre" or "varnish" to the subject matter, but (3) to try to realize in himself the truths which the Quaker author expresses out of his own experience. Friends thus eschewed efforts at a display of learning and at fine writing. They had the practical purpose of bringing spiritual knowledge and personal convincement. Their literature in all its forms remained by and large a part of their missionary effort, a part of their "witness" and proclamation of religious truth.

The anti-Quaker literature[7] amounted to a considerable body of writing. Smith catalogues about 1200 titles before 1725. Among the most noteworthy of the later literary opponents was Francis Bugg (who apostasized from Friends in 1684), who wrote a score of books against Quakerism. The most important were his autobiography, *The Pilgrim's Progress from Quakerism to Christianity* (1693) and *The Quakers' Yearly Meeting.* Charles Leslie, an Irish priest of the Established Church, wrote an even more important book *The Snake in the Grass* (1696), to which George Whitehead replied in *An Antidote against the Snake in the Grass* and Joseph Wyeth in *Anguis Flagellatus* or *A Switch for the Snake.* Leslie kept up the controversy through a dozen other works. Wright notes that, "Whereas the earliest criticisms against the Friends had been launched largely by the Presbyterians, Baptists and other sects, those at the close of the century were for the most part produced by Anglican churchmen."[8] Some of the severest critics, however,

---

5 *Ibid.,* chap. V.

6 *The Written Gospel Labours of John Whitehead,* 1704.

7 See Joseph Smith's *Bibliotheca Anti-Quakeriana.*

8 *Op. cit.,* p. 55.

were Quaker apostates, notably Bugg and George Keith. The latter, in the estimation of Braithwaite

> was the most formidable of all the antagonists of Quakerism, alike from his knowledge of the Society, his learning, his sincerity, and the general moderation of his writings. He no doubt lost his temper under provocation, and probably never understood sympathetically the spiritual side of Quakerism; but in confronting the Society of Friends with the claims of historic Christianity much of his criticism was salutary medicine, which did not altogether fail of effect.[9]

The works of Bugg and Leslie after those of Keith were the most effective of the host of attacks on Quakerism, but they presented no new points of valid criticism after Keith. They were mostly a rehash of stories of Quaker fanaticism, perversions of Quaker practices, charges of heresy, popery and of tyranny on the part of the leaders, and personal slanders. They seem to have made little or no effort to get at the truth or falsity of the scandalous stories or to understand the real character and beliefs of their opponents. The Quaker leaders were called Jesuits in disguise, plotters against the government and even atheists. One writer interprets the custom of monthly meetings appointing a committee to see to the proper accomplishment of intentions of marriage to mean that they were to be witnesses of the consummation itself! The purpose of these attacks was in the main simply "to render Truth and Friends odious."[10]

These attacks had the general effect of making Friends more careful to restrain manifestations of fanaticism and led them to emphasize their orthodoxy. They worked along with other tendencies toward bringing Quaker doctrinal expressions into harmony with conventional Protestant theology; and made for the suppression of individualism as well as eccentricity. The literature of the controversies

---

[9] BSPQ, 493.
[10] *Ibid.*, 488.

within the Society, especially that of the Wilkinson-Story controversy and its aftermath has been treated in connection with the account of these controversies.[11]

Two phases of Quaker literary activity, biography and history, belong chiefly to the latter part of this period and the first part of the next. They come naturally after the period which they record.

In the early Quaker literature full biographies were comparatively rare. Noteworthy among them are those of Gilbert Latey, Thomas Aldam, and John Roberts.[12] Closely allied with them, perhaps the germ from which they grew, were the "testimonies" to the character and service of deceased Friends by their meetings or friends. These were usually entered on the records of the monthly meeting and prefaced to their published works. Another source of the biographical type is the record of "sufferings" "in the service of Truth," which were carefully kept from early days.[13]

Since deprivation and imprisonment bulked very large in the lives of practically all of the "ministering" Friends as well as of others in their constituency, the subject of suffering found expression first in tracts, then in letters of protest, and a generation later in memoirs. The constant and methodical recording of sufferings was based on the clearly defined objective of acquainting the public first with the sufferings of the group, and secondly with the body of beliefs that made the Friends willing for the sake of conscience to endure religious persecution. Added to these was an additional wish to assure whatever government was in power that the Friends held no ill will against it, but were only seeking freedom of speech and of the press that they might worship and preach as their consciences dictated.[14]

In 1656 Thomas Salthouse and Miles Halhead issued an eighty-page tract: *The Wounds of An Enemy in the House*

[11] See chap. 12. Also BBPQ, 488.
[12] *Ibid.*, pp. 117, 118.
[13] Fox, *Epistles* no. 141.
[14] Wright, *op. cit.*, pp. 88, 89.

of a Friend. The title of a contemporary Irish tract begins *A Brief Relation of some Part of the Sufferings &c.* In 1682 a record of the sufferings of a thousand Quaker prisoners was presented to the king. Later the records of Friends' sufferings preserved in local meetings were collected and preserved in Devonshire House in London which had become the Quaker headquarters. Although the worst of the sufferings ceased after the Toleration Act, it was not until 1753 that Joseph Besse produced from these records of persecutions his painstaking and monumental record of the *Sufferings of the Quakers* which are such a fruitful source for Quaker historians.

The earliest Quaker histories belong naturally to the second stage of the movement; but they may be treated here since they are part of the literary process we are recording. The first of them was by a Dutchman Gerard Croese; it was published in Latin (1695) and translations into Dutch and English appeared in 1696 and into German in 1697.[15] It was on the whole an inaccurate and unsympathetic book and at the request of leading Friends, the English publisher allowed them to add a forty-page reply to certain points as an appendix.

The most important of the early histories was *The History of the Rise, Increase and Progress of the Christian People Called Quakers* by Willem Sewel, a Dutch Quaker, published in both Dutch (1717) and English (1722). It was a painstaking compilation of extracts from journals, official documents and Quaker records. It has gone through many reprints and editions and is one of the best known Quaker books. In 1694 William Penn wrote his brief history of *The Rise and Progress of the People Called Quakers,* which appeared first as the preface to Fox's *Journal.* It has been frequently reprinted as a separate work and widely circulated. During the seventeenth century Quaker historians

15 Hull, *Willem Sewel of Amsterdam,* pp. 115, 136, 137.

confined themselves chiefly to Quaker history but a few ventured into other fields. Thomas Ellwood wrote a condensed account of Biblical history under the title *Sacred History;* William Caton abridged Eusebius Pamphilus' *Ecclesiastical History;* and Ellis Hookes composed *The Spirit of the Martyrs Revised* which is a short Christian martyrology, modeled after Fox's *Book of Martyrs.*

The practice of gathering up and publishing Friends' writings began in 1662 with the issue of the writings of George Fox the Younger who died only the year before. The unknown editor who signs himself simply J. P. adopts an apologetic tone for the novelty of such a publication: "Surely I need not study a motto," he pleaded, "nor dive into invention to fetch up an inscription to be engraven on the tomb, since the names of the faithful are in the book of God, and the glory is in Him forever." [16]

This literary example was followed in the collected works of Hubberthorne (1663), Burrough (1672), Howgill (1676), Fisher (1679) and Penington (1681). These earlier collections usually have fancy titles, such as *Balm from Gilead* (William Smith), *The Dawnings of the Gospel Day* (Howgill), *A Handful After the Harvest Man* (Richard Samble), and *The Memorable Works of a Son of Thunder and Consolation* (Burrough). The later collections bore on the whole more prosaic titles, such as *Truth Vindicated* (Elizabeth Bathhurst, 1691); *The Works of the Long-Mournful and Sorely-Distressed Isaac Penington; The Christian Progress of George Whitehead* (1725); and *Truth Triumphant through the Spiritual Warfare, Christian Labours and Writings of the Able and Faithful Servant of Jesus Christ, Robert Barclay* (1692). Practically all the collected works have long titles (of which those quoted are but the beginning) and which constitute a sort of summary of the contents.

---

16 BSPQ, 418.

After his return from America George Fox found time during nearly two years' rest at Swarthmore to arrange his papers and dictate his *Journal.* His other writings were later collected and published in two volumes: his *Epistles* and *Gospel Truth Vindicated* usually called his *Doctrinals.* These were not published, however, until after his death.

The Quaker "journals," as their autobiographies are usually called, are the distinctive Quaker literary form. They almost created a new and distinct type of literature. This is natural since the essence of Quakerism is the individual religious experience of God and spiritual truth. It finds its highest expression in the personal life rather than in theologies or institutions. The "lives" or "journals" were written and published, therefore, as Wright notes, as examples of a group experience. The motive of the writer of the autobiographies is usually evangelistic—to commend the Quaker faith by the story of the author's "convincement," experience, sufferings, providential deliverances, labors in the ministry, and attainment of inward power and peace. They constitute, along with official records, the main source material of Quaker history. Many of the earliest histories were little more than extracts from them.

Before 1725 Friends had "published over eighty religious confessions and journals, a number probably greater than all the non-Quaker autobiographies printed in England during the preceding seventy-five years."[17]

> The autobiographies and the religious confessions of the early Friends contain the most complete revelation to be found in their writings of the Quaker attempt to make religion both practical and spiritual. In addition to out-numbering the journals of "the world's people" which found their way into print, the Friends injected into their autobiographies a marked degree of introspection, and so composed their life histories

[17] Wright, *op. cit.,* p. 110.

that they served the double purpose of unfolding the experiences of the writers and of the group they represented.[18]

The journals were frequently expansions of autobiographical accounts of early religious struggles, convincements, imprisonments, travels, etc. Usually they were compiled by the aid of "confessions," diaries and letters which the early Publishers of Truth carefully kept.[19] The publication of Friends' journals began later than that of the collected writings, the first being that of William Caton (1689). In his preface to Burnyeat's journal (1691), William Penn justifies the practice as follows:

"The account of his own convincement," says Penn, "is sweet, lively, instructive and persuasive to others to try, as he did, and to embrace the holy Truth. Then follows a relation of his travels and ministry in these nations and beyond the seas, as Luke presented the Churches with the Acts or travels of the apostles in their infancy—a pleasant and seasoning lecture both for the young who love to hear of voyages, to excite them . . . to journey towards . . . Jerusalem; and to quicken those more aged to shake off their dust, the earth . . . and to lift up their eyes and see the fields, how white they are to harvest, and how few labourers there are to take it in.[20]

By 1725 twenty-six Quaker journals had been published. These established a literary type which was to prevail until modern times.[21]

The printing of Fox's *Journal,* in 1694, edited by Thomas Ellwood, was, beyond question, the most important literary event in the history of Friends. Others of that age could have written, with somewhat less learning, Barclay's *Apology,* or compiled, with somewhat less industry and fairness, Sewel's *History;* but the vital inward experience and the vitalizing service of the Founder of Quakerism were the central spirit

18 *Ibid.,* p. 155.
19 *Ibid.,* 193–197.
20 Cited in BSPQ, 421.
21 Wright, *op. cit.,* p. 160.

and expression of the movement, a treasure much of which would have been lost beyond recall, unless preserved in the artless and sincere record of the Journal.[22]

The Quaker apologists grew out of the necessity of meeting the charges of heresy on the part of their opponents and of giving theological expositions of the doctrinal implications of the Quaker faith. In contrast to the overemphasis on doctrine by the Puritans, Friends never regarded any creed or theological formulation to be an essential part of the Quaker religion, as William Penn carefully noted:

> It is not opinion, or speculation, or notions of what is true, or assent to, or the subscription of articles or propositions, though never so soundly worded, that . . . makes a man a true believer or a true Christian; but it is a conformity of mind and practice to the will of God, in all holiness of conversation, according to the dictates of this Divine principle of light and life in the soul, which denotes a person truly a child of God.[23]

When the Friends attempted to express their convictions in theological terms they naturally used the vocabulary of contemporary Puritan and mystic sects.[24] The first apologetic writings were short statements put out to meet specific situations. The earliest of these is believed to be the one issued by Christopher Holder and John Copeland from the prison in which they were confined in Boston (1657).[25] This was to meet the charge of the New England Puritans that the Quakers were atheists and infidels. A similar docu-

---

22 BSPQ, 427.

23 *A Key &c.* Sec. 2. Cited in BSPQ, 379. Cf. Mekeel, *Quakerism and a Creed,* p. 7.

24 See Smith, *A Preservative from Quakerism.* Preface pp. x, xi. "And they having so many new-coined words and strange notions and phrases and figurative mysterious ways of speaking, peculiar to themselves or which they have taken from the Ranters and Familists and other former enthusiasts."

25 Bowden, *Hist.,* I, 90, 93. But see Mekeel, *op. cit.,* p. 10.

ment was the letter of George Fox to the governor of Barbados (1671). A fuller and much more adequate statement of Friends' beliefs was composed by George Whitehead, and published by the authority of the Morning Meeting at the time of the Keith controversy (1693) to satisfy outsiders of the orthodoxy of Friends' beliefs about Christ's person and work.[26] Most of the Quaker apologies, however, attempted to state and defend the moot points merely between the Friends and their critics. None of them is a complete statement of Quaker doctrinal beliefs. All of them agree in insisting that theological belief is not the essence of religious faith, which is a matter of a spiritual experience and a working faith.

Penn and Barclay proved the ablest and most prolific of the Quaker apologists of this period, with Penington, Keith and Whitehead close behind them. Penn, Barclay and Keith were all theologically trained. Penington stresses the mystical side of Quakerism and has relatively less of Calvinism in the background of his religious thinking, although he did not wholly escape it when he tried to formulate a doctrine of the Light Within. His writings are not theologically systematic; they spring from his own inward experiences and are the fruit of devout meditations. He has had a great influence in presenting the mystical side of Quakerism to sympathetic souls. He was greatly helped by his wife, Mary Springett Penington, whose long experience as a Seeker brought her a similar understanding of the mystic way.

William Penn's earlier writings were theological. He had studied theology at Oxford and in Paris and had studied law in the Temple in London. His radical and somewhat crude criticism of the doctrine of the Trinity in *The Sandy Foundation Shaken* led to his imprisonment in the Tower. He modified his attitude later, making a more

---

26 Sewel, *Hist.*, II, 497–508.

positive and constructive statement in *Innocency With Her Open Face* which led to his release. His *No Cross No Crown* is a scholarly and vigorous presentation of the democracy of Quaker customs and the underlying Christian ideals. Penn's later writings dealt more with ethics and with social and political problems than with theology. His *Frame of Government* for Pennsylvania and his *Essay Towards the Present and Future Peace of Europe* have had great influence upon political thinking and especially on the constitutional development of England and America.

One of the keenest minds among the scholars attracted to the Society of Friends was George Keith, a Scotch theologian and schoolmaster and a friend of Robert Barclay, whose thinking he undoubtedly influenced to a great degree. His later abandonment of Friends made him a very keen critic of the Quaker position and also destroyed almost wholly the influence among Friends of his earlier doctrinal writings.

It is to Robert Barclay that the Society owes its most thorough and influential doctrinal defense of Quakerism. His education in Scotland and in the Jesuit Scots College in Paris had given him a full understanding of both the Calvinistic and Catholic positions. After he joined Friends (1666) he became the foremost theologian of the Society. We have already noticed his *Anarchy of the Ranters* in which he expounded the Quaker ideal of church government. His chief work was the *Apology for the True Christian Divinity* which grew out of a public disputation between Barclay and Keith on one side and a group of students of the University of Aberdeen. In medieval fashion he formulated his contentions in sixteen theses or propositions, which were later expanded into the *Apology,* which was first published in Latin on the continent in 1676.[27] It is natural that in this book he should show the influence of medieval scholasticism and of the doctrines

---

[27] BSPQ, 386. Wright says the *Apology* was published in Amsterdam in 1678 and "Englished" in 1680. *Lit. Life,* p. 56.

of Scotch Presbyterianism as well as the onesidedness of theological statements born of controversy. The style is not attractive to modern readers, because of a tedious use of formal syllogisms, and his scholastic vocabulary.

After stating the fundamental propositions at the beginning of each section Barclay proceeds to prove them, first by Scripture, and then by reason and lastly by citing authorities from the Church Fathers or other accepted religious writers. By this method Barclay makes an appeal to the three great divisions of Christendom. The appeal to Scripture is for the benefit of the Protestants to whom the Bible is the ultimate authority. The appeal to reason is for the benefit of Socinians and other rationalists. The appeal to the Church Fathers is for the benefit of the Roman Catholics to whom tradition embodied chiefly in their writings is the final authority.

It is interesting to compare the propositions of the *Apology* with the chapters of the Westminster *Confession of Faith* which was adopted by the Westminster Assembly in 1647. The *Apology* has fifteen Propositions against thirty-three chapters in the *Confession*. Many of the latter deal with subjects omitted by Barclay, the reason being that there was no serious controversy between the Quakers and the Calvinists on these subjects, or that the subject is completely alien to the Quaker system, such as "Church Censures" and "Synods and Councils." For example, Barclay has no propositions dealing with "God and the Holy Trinity," "God's Eternal Decrees," "Creation," and "Providence"; nor with "Christ the Mediator," "Free Will," "Effectual Calling," "Assurance of Grace and Salvation" and "The Law of God." Likewise he does not treat of "The State of Men after Death and the Resurrection of the Dead" nor of "The Last Judgment." It is evident, therefore, that Barclay is dealing principally with the points which were radically at issue between himself and the Calvinists.[28]

---

[28] Cf. *Prop.* III, § 1, where he refers to the Westminster *Confession.*

The fundamental difference comes out in the opening sections of the *Apology* and the Westminster *Confession.* The latter begins logically with a long section on the Holy Scriptures, since the Scriptures were for the Presbyterians the ultimate source of religious knowledge. Barclay's first Proposition, on the other hand, deals with "The True Foundation of Knowledge"; the second is on "Immediate Revelation," and it is only in the third section that he comes to deal with Friends' doctrine of the Scriptures. This order of Barclay's reveals the beginnings of modern religious thought which seeks the primary source of knowledge within the individual as the Quakers made the Inner Light the primary religious authority.[29] He gives a high position to the Scriptures which he calls a secondary rule of faith, as a source of instruction and comfort and as the only outward judge of theological controversy between Christians, and he admits them as a test of pretended religious guidance; but he insists that they cannot be the ultimate religious authority since they are only the product of the inspiration of the Spirit of God, so that the Spirit who is the source must be the ultimate authority rather than the product.

All the early Friends' writings were to some extent under the influence of the Calvinistic conception of the sinfulness of human nature although they did not accept the idea of inherited guilt. Instead of abandoning this conception, as did some of the mystical sects and the Cambridge Platonists, they tried to combine the dogma of human depravity with the belief in the Inner Light. By this means they escaped the Calvinistic dogma of the universal doom of mankind except for a few elect, since the Inner Light provided for the possibility of universal salvation. However, Barclay in his attempt to combine the doctrine of

---

[29] Barclay was undoubtedly influenced by the philosophy of Descartes, whose epistemology abandoned the Scholastic reliance on external authorities and sought the ultimate basis of truth in the mind itself. BSPQ, 392.

human depravity with that of the universal and saving Light resorted to an artificial means. He makes the Inner Light a part of human nature, but only as a special spiritual organ of divine revelation and salvation, which he called a *vehiculum Dei,*[30] a term which he seems to have got from Keith. In one respect this spectacular explanation is immaterial because if the Inner Light is in all men, it does provide for knowledge of God in all and the possibility of universal salvation. However, Barclay's explanation seemed to make the Inner Light, as the organ of God's work in the soul, something thrust into human nature by a special grace rather than an original and integral part of it. It seems to leave human nature, as such, outside the scope of the Divine in man, and especially to lead to the depreciation of the human reason and the body and its appetites as something essentially depraved and sinful. This made it difficult for Barclay and his successors to do full justice to the incarnation of Christ and cast suspicion upon the processes and products of human reason. His theology, which in the next period of Quaker history became the accepted theological standard, provided for the development of Quietism; and later it furnished the theological basis for the Evangelical movement of the early nineteenth century.[31] Barclay's theology was also defective in that he found no satisfactory way to combine the belief in the atonement with the doctrine of the Inner Light. He regards justification as signifying the process or act of making man righteous, rather than the treatment of the believer as though he were righteous, which is the usage of Paul and Luther. However, Barclay's interpretation of salvation as necessarily involving righteous character was fundamentally involved in the Quaker religion, which could never be content with anything short of deliverance from the power and dominion of sinfulness.

---

30 *Ibid.,* Prop. VI, § XIII. The expression *vehiculum Dei* is omitted in all the American editions, as far as I have examined them.

31 BSPQ, xxxiii–xliii.

II

The Age of Quietism
1691-1827

Period 1

The Aftermath of Toleration 1691-1737

CHAPTER 15

THE REACTION

THE Revolution of 1688 marks a turning point in the history of English Quakerism. The frank attempt of James II to bring about a Catholic reaction and the tyrannical measures used to accomplish it finally alienated practically all classes of the nation so that leaders of all parties invited William of Orange and Mary his wife, daughter of James, to become joint sovereigns.

William's experience as a Dutch ruler and his anxiety to unify his new kingdom led him to favor toleration, the comprehension of all Protestants in the national church and the revision of the Test Acts. He failed to accomplish the latter, but in 1689 the Toleration Act was passed, which changed the legal status of all the Nonconformist bodies. At the beginning the king was hostile to Penn and suspicious of the Quakers because of the friendship which James II had for them, but he was gradually convinced of their loyalty.

The Toleration Act merely suspended the penal laws against the Nonconformists, provided their meeting places were registered and they worshiped with unlocked doors. It did not include Popish recusants, nor persons denying the Trinity. Tithes were still required and the oaths of supremacy and allegiance and the declaration against Transubstantiation were still obligatory.

A special act met Friends' scruples against oaths by providing the following affirmations in addition to the declaration against Transubstantiation.

> I, A.B., do sincerely promise and solemnly declare before God and the world that I will be true and faithful to King William and Queen Mary. And I do solemnly profess and declare that I do from my heart abhor . . . that damnable doctrine and position, that Princes excommunicated or deprived by the Pope . . . may be deposed or murdered by their subjects or any other whatsoever. And I do declare that no Foreign Prince, Person, Prelate, State, or Potentate, hath or ought to have any Power . . . ecclesiastical or spiritual, within this realm.
>
> I, A.B., profess faith in God the Father, and in Jesus Christ, His eternal Son, the true God, and in the Holy Spirit, one God blessed for evermore; and do acknowledge the Holy Scriptures of the Old and New Testament to be given by Divine Inspiration.[1]

These acts relieved Friends from persecution as Dissenters and legalized their worship. They were no longer subject to punishment for refusing oaths. They were, however, still under great disabilities. They were still required to pay tithes and their goods were subject to distraint in order to collect them; informers were outlawed, however, and new laws protected Friends to some extent against arbitrary and excessive seizures. They could not hold public office and were excluded from the universities.[2]

---

[1] BSPQ, 155.

[2] It is at this date that Besse concludes his record of Quaker "Sufferings." The yearly meeting of 1689 issued the following advice which proved to be the keynote of the Society's policy for more than a century:

"Walk wisely and circumspectly towards all men, in the peaceable spirit of Christ Jesus; giving no offense nor occasions to those in outward government, nor way to any controversies, heats, or distractions of this

To the end of Queen Anne's reign (1713) English internal history is the record chiefly of the completion of the Revolution of 1688 and the working out of the forces and principles involved in it;[3]—the end of the royal claim of Divine Right, the Bill of Rights, parliamentary government, the Protestant succession, the superior powers of the Commons over the Lords, party cabinet government, religious toleration, freedom of the press and the union of Scotland and England. A high church and Tory reaction in 1713 threatened to give the Church a monopoly of education, but the death of Queen Anne nullified the Schism Act which had just been enacted; and with the accession of the Whigs to power under George I the danger passed and the Act was repealed.

The new era in Quaker history which began with the Revolution was fraught with peculiar dangers. Most of the founders had passed on. Fox died the next year. Margaret Fell Fox lived on a few years to regret changes which she regarded as unwholesome. William Penn was for a while under suspicion, then imprisoned for debt and at last his mind gave way six years before his death in 1718. These calamities much diminished his active influence among Friends. Among the leaders who survived, George Whitehead had perhaps the greatest influence on the fortunes of the Society for the next quarter of a century. He gave himself chiefly to the task of adjusting the Society to the new order. Rufus Jones characterizes his influence as

---

world, about the kingdoms thereof. But pray for the good of all, and submit all to that Divine Power and Wisdom which rules over the kingdoms of men. That, as the Lord's hidden ones, that are always quiet in the land, and as those prudent ones and wise in heart, who know when and where to keep silent, you may all approve your hearts to God; keeping out of all airy discourses and words, that may anyways become snares, or hurtful to Truth or Friends, as being sensible that any personal occasion of reproach causes a reflection upon the body." *London Epistles*, p. 35. Cited in BSPQ, 160.

3 See Hulme, *A History of the British People*, chap. XVIII.

follows: "George Whitehead and those who joined with him in the patient work of securing 'tolerations' and 'privileges' for Friends were, without knowing it, preparing for a different type of person and were passing over from a movement charged with potential energy to a stage of arrested development and cooling enthusiasm. George Whitehead was a good man, and he was a real success in securing happy adjustments, but he marks, nevertheless, the end of an era, and is in his own person the exhibition of a changed ideal." [4] In the two decades after Toleration the great work of recording the history and publishing the lives and writings of the Quaker worthies of the earlier period was mostly completed. A second generation of Friends came on the scene, more uniform in their ways of life and thought, and very devoted to their Quaker inheritance; but it had cost them less than the earlier generation had paid to acquire it, and their Quakerism had not been so fashioned and tested in the fire. They settled down to a tolerated and quiet place in English society. The Quaker, to quote Braithwaite, "had passed from persecution into peace. His weatherbeaten Ark which had stoutly ridden out the storm found itself by a miracle in calm waters. It seemed a time for refitting the ship not for the fresh heroic adventure of launching forth into the deep." [5]

The relief granted Friends by the Toleration Act was sorely needed. The Society was like an army after a great battle, which needs time to bury the dead, care for the wounded, bring up reserves and replenish its supplies. Since 1661 Friends had been in a continuous and exhausting struggle. The widows and orphans of those who had died in jail or as a result of imprisonment were to be cared for as well as the aged and infirm. Many had lost their estates, shops, trades and patronage. Even after Toleration

---

[4] BSPQ, xlvi, xlvii.
[5] BSPQ, 160, 161.

came it took tedious legal processes and exhausting travels to get imprisoned Friends set free. Those who had been *praemunired* could only be released and their estates restored by a royal pardon.[6]

The aggressive evangelization and missionary work that characterized the first decade of the Society's history had been slowed down to a considerable extent by the necessities of the struggle for existence after the Restoration. There was naturally an even greater pause for recuperation after 1689. The vigor of their attacks on current evils and their proselytizing zeal abated. They became more concerned to preserve the "testimonies" which they had inherited.[7]

This relaxation of Friends was a part of the general reaction of English society from the Puritan struggles and the persecutions of Dissenters. King William promoted Latitudinarianism and worked for the comprehension of all Protestants within the National Church. He did not succeed in the latter, but his efforts were indicative of the temper of the times. There was a tacit agreement among Englishmen not to bother one another much about religion. It became bad taste to discuss personal religion or to try to make converts. "Fanaticks" were in disrepute, the butt of witticisms in the coffee houses and the theaters. Walker describes the general situation as follows:

> The end of the struggles of the seventeenth century had been marked by a general spiritual lethargy in the Establishment and among Dissenters alike. Relationalism had penetrated all classes of religious thinkers, so that even among the orthodox, Christianity seemed little more than a system of morality supported by divine sanctions. Butler may stand as typical. His frigid probabilities may have convinced some intellects, but they can have led few men to action. There were able preachers, but the characteristic sermon was the colorless essay on

[6] BSPQ, 114, 115.
[7] See JLPQ, 1–6.

moral virtues. Outreaching work for the unchurched was but scanty. The condition of the lower classes was one of spiritual destitution. Popular amusements were coarse, illiteracy widespread, law savage in its enforcement, jails sinks of disease and iniquity. Drunkenness was more wide-spread than at any other period in English history.[8]

This tendency away from religious earnestness was furthered by the rise and spread of Deism. Locke's *Essay on the Human Understanding* laid the foundation for the age of rationalism. A generation of poets and essayists were critical and formal rather than creative. Reason was made the ultimate test of religious beliefs. "Natural" religion was preferred to "revealed" religion. The credible beliefs were chiefly belief in God, in immortality and in the moral law. Nature was the norm of what was credible. Miracles and supernatural revelation were ruled out. Naturally such an attitude was not conducive to religious activity beyond mild theological controversy. With this exception sermons dealt with moral and political subjects.

The Deists were not a particularly gifted group but they applied the fundamental Protestant principle of private judgment relentlessly. Their chief weakness lay in their limited knowledge of nature and history. Their world was still a small world. Little was known of Asia, Africa and America. Their ideas of "natural" religion and the "natural" man were largely idealizations of American savages, undisturbed by facts. The natural sciences were still in their infancy. Men's ideas of what is reasonable depend on the assumptions contained in their premises; and there was much in heaven and earth not dreamed of in the assumptions of Deism. However, for the moment, Deism was a plausible theology, especially in the absence of great upheavals of religious faith and experience. It created an attitude and atmosphere suited to the wearied state of the

---

[8] Walker, W., *A History of the Christian Church,* p. 507.

Friends although deistical doctrines did not receive serious attention among Friends until near the end of the eighteenth century.

Friends engaged in a most vigorous controversy over the Affirmation Act. By the Act of 1689 Friends were allowed an affirmation in place of the oath of allegiance, but they still suffered disabilities because of their unwillingness to take oaths. "Without these, they could not sue for their debts, nor carry through their transactions with the customs and the excise, nor defend titles to property, nor give evidence in court: they were, in strict law, unable to prove wills or be admitted to copyholds, or take up their freedom in corporations, and in some places they were kept from voting at elections. Nor could they answer prosecutions in ecclesiastical courts for tithes and church-rates."[9] It was difficult to frame a bill which would satisfy both Friends and the government. The matter was frequently discussed in yearly meeting and finally as a result of the efforts of the Meeting for Sufferings and the personal influence of George Whitehead an Affirmation Act was passed by Parliament in 1695.[10] The law was for seven years. It legalized the following form of affirmation: "I, A.B., do declare in the presence of Almighty God, the Witness of the truth of what I say, etc." The affirmation was not to be accepted, however, in criminal cases nor from jurors nor in lieu of an oath of office.

The form of this affirmation was not satisfactory to many Friends. They regarded any phraseology calling God to witness as in effect an oath and the form adopted was accepted reluctantly. The Society was divided into two parties over the issue, the "Satisfied" and the "Dissatisfied." The latter consisted largely of the more conscientious, active and spiritual sections of the Society.

---

9 BSPQ, 181.
10 *Christian Progress*, pp. 646–655.

In 1702 the Act was renewed until 1715 over the protests of the "Dissatisfied." The question now became involved with other controversies in the Society. The "Dissatisfied" corresponded largely with those who were opposing the growing worldliness in the Society and who pressed for the more rigorous exercise of discipline. The "Satisfied" Friends were largely those who wanted to get along with the government, both because they were prosperous in trade and were Whig in their sympathies. Penn was the leading "Jacobite," as the "Dissatisfied" leaders came to be called. He had allowed in Pennsylvania a simple affirmation and was dissatisfied with the English Act.

Reconciliation between these parties became increasingly difficult. Champions of both sides took to print.[11] The yearly meetings of 1712, 1713 and 1714 were long drawn out owing to the difficulty of agreement. In the first year of George I the old act was repassed without a time limit and extended to Scotland and to the colonies.

The subject was kept alive during the following years, but the heat of controversy abated with a growing disposition toward patience on the part of the "Dissatisfied" and a willingness on the part of the "Satisfied" to continue efforts toward securing an affirmation which would ease the consciences of their fellows. The sufferings of the "Dissatisfied" had been considerable because of their refusal to use the legal affirmation. Many had lost property and a few had been imprisoned. The Whig government was more favorable to Dissenters. In 1718 the Schism and Occasional Conformity Acts were repealed. In 1719 a Toleration Act for Ireland was passed. Finally in 1722, with the united support

---

11 As early as 1692 Fisher's *A Position and Testimony Against All Swearing,* against the Declaration of Fidelity was published. In 1713 appeared the anonymous, *A Letter from a Satisfied to a Dissatisfied Friend;* and Skidmore's *Essay Upon the Vth of Matthew, From Verse 33d to 37th.* This was answered by Claridge's *Novelty and Nullity of Dissatisfaction* in 1714. Skidmore replied the same year with *Primitive Simplicity Demonstrated.* The controversy was kept up in letters both circular and private.

of all parties in the yearly meeting, Parliament passed an act which prescribed an affirmation acceptable to all Friends. It omitted all reference to God and read simply: "I, A.B., do solemnly, sincerely, and truly affirm, etc." [12]

Even before the Revolution many Friends had been growing in wealth in spite of persecution. After the Toleration Act their industry in agriculture and business, their honesty in trade and the simplicity of their mode of living brought a rapid gain in wealth. With wealth came worldliness and departures from the primitive plainness. Toleration removed the winnowing effect of persecution and made it easy for less devoted members and leaders to join the Society or to remain in membership. The advices of the monthly meetings, the writings of non-Friends and the journals of travelling Friends all give evidence of this change. It occurred not only in London but in the northern counties and in Ireland as well.[13] The spiritually-minded leaders all regarded this prosperity as a menace to the Society.

Attempts were made to deal with this situation by corporate discipline and by definite rules. One of the earliest of these attempts was made in Ireland. In 1698 at a special sitting of the Leinster Provincial Meeting it was agreed:

> That a competency of the lawful things of this world is sufficient for every one, and is the right bounds, with a due consideration of every one's charge, station, place and service; and that mind which will not be content with this bears the character of covetousness, and renders such unfit to rule in the Church of Christ; and there was an unanimous consent, one by one, to offer up ourselves to the judgment of the Province Meeting, or other approved elders, as the Province Meeting shall think fit, if in anything we do exceed those bounds. . . . Not that we intend to deprive any of the moderate and lawful

---

12 BSPQ, 203.

13 *Ibid.*, 499–502.

use of the things of this world, or to take from any man his possessions or to invade and take away property; but to bring all things into right bounds and set them in their right places.[14]

In Ireland it was already the custom to appoint "faithful Friends" in each meeting to make inquiry as to members' manner of life and report to the Province meeting.[15] The meetings thus assumed supervision over the outward life of the members. This led gradually to the conversion of the peculiar testimonies of earlier days into essentials of the Quaker life and to the establishment of regulations regarding property, business, furniture and dress. Plainness was defined by rules and enforced by the discipline. In Ireland this was gladly accepted for the most part in the glow of religious brotherhood. Very few were disowned and disownment was the only penalty for refusal to conform.

There were no formal lists of membership as yet. Persons who associated with Friends and conformed to their religious customs were regarded as members unless the meeting disowned them. This only meant that they would be excluded from attending the business meetings. The Irish disciplinary ideals and methods were soon carried to England by travelling ministers who found much to admire in this zeal and strictness.[16]

The meetings in the north of England took up the matter of dress with great care. A protest was made against extravagant feasting, gifts of food and other superfluous expenditures at births, marriages and funerals. Gradually restrictions were placed on making and dealing in superfluities and luxuries.

---

14 Cited in BSPQ, 504.

15 These were the forerunners of the overseers ultimately provided for in the Quaker discipline everywhere.

16 See Gratton's *Journal* for 1696. Rutty's *History*, pp. 166–168. Chalkley's *Journal* for 1707.

The new instrument of Church government was a ready means for retrenching extravagances which gave insidious entrance to the spirit of the world; and zealous Friends did not see that they were substituting legalism for liberty, the control of the form for the control of the Spirit. Nor did they perceive that every legalism that fenced in the Jew would bar out the proselyte, till Quakerism would become a self-contained, introspective sect, out of touch with the world that it should be conquering for the Kingdom of God. But, however radically imperfect was the method adopted, they were right in seeking to preserve a vital Church by waging a crusade against the worldly spirit that threatened to overwhelm it; and it is significant that Ireland and the Quarterly Meetings in the North of England and Scotland which followed the Irish lead were the districts which refused the compromise of the Affirmation of 1696 and possessed at the time the greatest spiritual life.[17]

This tendency to legalism did not go without protest. Margaret Fell Fox voiced a vigorous reminder of the essential Quaker principles.

> But Christ Jesus saith, That we must take no thought what we shall eat or what we shall drink or what we shall put on; but bids us consider the lilies, how they grow in more royalty than Solomon. But, contrary to this, we must not look at no colours, nor make anything that is changeable colours, as the hills are, nor sell them, nor wear them. But we must be all in one dress and one colour.
>
> This is a silly, poor gospel. It is more fit for us to be covered with God's eternal Spirit and clothed with His eternal Light, which leads us and guides us into righteousness; and to live righteously and justly and holily in this present evil world. This is the clothing that God puts on us, and likes, and will bless. This will make our light to shine forth before men . . . for we have God for our Teacher; and we have His promise and His doctrine; and we have the apostles' practice in their day and generation; and we have God's Holy Spirit to lead us

[17] BSPQ, 516–517.

and guide us; and we have the blessed Truth that we are made partakers of to be our practice. . . .

This is not delightful to me, that I have this occasion to write to you; for wheresoever I saw it appear I have stood against it for several years; and now I dare neglect it no longer. For I see that our blessed, precious, holy Truth that has visited [us] from the beginning, is kept under; and these silly, outside, imaginary practices is coming up, and practiced with great zeal, which hath often grieved my heart.[18]

There were ministers belonging to this period who likewise raised their voices against the growing legalism, but their protest was too largely a voice out of the past and went for the most part unheeded. The growth in luxury and the decline both in spiritual life and in Quaker strictness are well attested by the journals of most of the travelling ministers and by the monthly meeting records of the period. Samuel Bownas gives the following account of the state of Friends in Ireland (1740) which seems fairly characteristic of Friends in England and America as well:

I found in that nation a brave, zealous and living people in the root of true religion and discipline, or church government, well qualified with experience in divine wisdom; but there were also some who seemed very perfect in the form, and appeared to the outward very exact and zealous against pride and worldly customs, but for all that, the inside was not right, so that I found often very close exercise among them in warning them against the leaven of the Pharisees, which was equally, if not more hurtful to religion than that of the Publicans; and in some places, shewing that it was needful to be good examples in plainness of speech, as well as apparel, which many had deviated from; but nevertheless such there were, who though plain, and otherwise strict, were too much taken up with the world, and the riches of it, making haste to increase their substance, which was a very great hindrance to their growth in the life of religion, and made them dwarfish therein; setting

[18] Paper dated 1700, Friends Library, Portf. 25, no. 66. Cited in Crosfield, *Margaret Fox of Swarthmoor Hall*, pp. 198, 199.

forth that a form, without life, whether by education or otherwise, would not avail.[19]

The unity among Friends, which had been created by the personal influence of George Fox and the other founders of the Society, was maintained during the ensuing period mainly through the discipline of the monthly meetings and the influence of the travelling ministers. The great distance between the American colonies and the mother country together with the freedom of pioneer life in America would have made it easy for the two main branches of the Society to grow apart. During this period there was no printed discipline and the Society was largely governed by custom and tradition. The writings of the founders were widely circulated, but it would be easy for divergent interpretations of them to spring up, as did happen in the nineteenth century.

Within the first half-century after Toleration, there was raised up a succession of able men and women, who travelled widely in the Society and thus brought all sections of it under their unifying influence. Practically all had been born well back in the creative period of the Society's history between 1675 and 1700; they had known some of the Founders, and their ideals had been shaped within the creative period. They carried over to the next generation the memories, personal impressions of the Founders, the passions and convictions of the period of the Society's rise and so bridged the gap between the first and second divisions of Quakerism. All of them visited Friends on both sides of the Atlantic. After George Keith had been disowned by Friends, he joined the Church of England and was sent back to America as a missionary to "gather the Quakers from Quakerism to the Mother Church, the good old Church of England."[20] He recognized so fully

---

19 *Life,* pp. 274–275 (1805 Ed.).

20 Richardson, *Life,* p. 87.

the important part which the itinerant ministry played in the development of the Quaker movement that he proposed "as a means to prevent the growth of Quakerism, as he called it, the making of a law to restrain Friends from travelling, save to their own meetings; for he said it was travelling preachers that kept the Quakers up so strong in countenance." [21] The most important of these travelling ministers for the life of the Society as a whole in this period were: Thomas Wilson (1653–1725), James Dickenson (1658–1741), Thomas Story (1663–1742), John Richardson (1666–1755), Thomas Chalkley (1675–1741), John Fothergill (1676–1744), and Samuel Bownas (1676–1753). These men were essentially conservative; their purpose was to preserve and extend the principles and organization which had been created for them by the founders of the Society. Rufus Jones says of them:

> There was, I am inclined to think, no striking decrease of zeal. There was rather a change of aim and purpose towards which the zeal was directed. We shall see in the succeeding chapters that men and women still existed in large numbers who devoted life and all they had to the cause of Quakerism with no limit to the degree of their sacrifice. Their fundamental conception of the Quaker mission had altered. Their outlook was a different one, but they were still ready to die daily for their faith.[22]

All of these leaders had had a vital personal experience of God which made them into new men. This did not so much involve new views as it did for the first generation. It meant the personal acceptance of the religious ideals in which they had been brought up, but to which they had been heretofore indifferent or hostile. The transforming experience usually came after a struggle. They had no intellectual doubts to wrestle with; their primary concern

---

21 Bownas, *op. cit.*, p. 170.
22 JLPQ I, 3.

was as to their relation to God; how to learn his will and do it. They all had a definite and decisive call to the ministry, against which they often struggled, fearful of themselves or lest they should be presumptuous in undertaking so august a mission without warrant. They struggled to keep their ministry fresh and genuine; they were fearful of "running ahead of their Guide"; of speaking "in the will of the creature"; of expressing more than was given. They were often "shut up" or "dry" in meetings without a clear sense of why no message was given. They were careful students of their own messages, trying to learn from their expriences how to make their ministry more effective, not by homiletic or literary art, but by the demonstration of the Spirit and power. They were all well versed in the Scriptures and used Biblical language and illustrations constantly in their preaching. One could almost gather from the journal of Samuel Bownas a manual of mystical method for a Friends minister. He had a special concern for the ministers, and usually attended their meetings at yearly meeting time, although he often discussed the ministry in the yearly meeting proper because he felt that the ministry should be a concern of the whole church.

In repeated journeys these men visited most of the Quaker centers in England, Scotland, Wales, Ireland and America. They show us that during this period Quakerism was still growing, especially in the north of England, Ireland and the American colonies. They had disputes with priests and Dissenters, chiefly Presbyterians and Baptists. They suffered persecution in petty ways still, because they would not pay tithes or because other denominations feared their inroads upon them.[23] Convincements still con-

[23] Samuel Bownas was kept in prison on Long Island nearly a year in 1702–1703 at the instigation of George Keith on a charge of "speaking scandalous lies of, and reflections against, the Church of England, as by law established." The grand jury refused to indict him in spite of the threats of the justices. After nearly a year, during which two other juries refused an indictment, he was set at liberty. *Life,* pp. 100–150.

tinued and the Society grew throughout their generation, especially in America. There large numbers of outsiders or the world's people flocked to hear the visiting preachers. Very generally Friends were able to hold their young people, and to this cause Bownas attributes principally the great increase in the size of meetings in America between 1706 and 1726.[24]

[24] *Ibid.*, pp. 269–270.

Chapter 16

THE SECOND PERIOD OF AMERICAN QUAKERISM

THE Second Division of Quaker history in America began about 1700 and lasted until 1756.[1] Among the causes that prolonged this period in America were the work of pioneering which absorbed a large part of Friends' energies in constructive work; the steady increases in membership through convincements and immigration; the problems created by growth and expansion such as the building of new meeting-houses and the organization of new meetings; the care of the Indians; the treatment of Negro slaves; and the application of Quaker principles to the conduct of government in those provinces where Friends participated to a greater or lesser degree in political affairs.

The frequent visits and letters of travelling ministers constituted the chief unifying influence, supplemented and confirmed by epistolary correspondence between yearly meetings. These official letters usually dealt with common religious problems, for the most part in general and formal language, or were devoted to exhortations to faithfulness to Quaker principles. They served as symbols of the inward unity of the loosely organized Society and promoted its community feeling. Bownas at the beginning and Samuel Fothergill at the end of this half-century visited practically all Quaker communities in America. Their visits and epistles were the more important because there

1 See *Introduction*, pp. xxii, xxiii.

was as yet no Quaker periodical literature to disseminate and inculcate Quaker views. The writings of the founders of the Society had become Quaker classics and were very widely circulated and read. The leaders at least were very thoroughly versed in the Bible, which was in more general use than in the next three-quarters of a century.

Between 1700 and 1756 the records show that seventy ministers from abroad visited within the limits of Philadelphia Yearly Meeting. Besides these there were nearly always one or more American ministers on religious visits in their own or other yearly meetings.[2] James Dickenson visited America in 1691, 1696 and 1714. Thomas Wilson visited America twice (1691–1693 and 1713–1714). John Fothergill made three visits to America (1706, 1721 and 1722–1724). Thomas Story visited all the settlements in the American colonies in 1698 and Thomas Chalkley first visited the country the same year. He moved to Philadelphia in 1701, but his business as a shipmaster made him a Quaker missionary in many parts of the world. Of these men, four were chiefly instrumental in the great expansion of Quakerism in New England: Chalkley, Richardson, John Fothergill and Thomas Story; the first three being the founders of the Quaker community on Nantucket Island, which afterward had a great influence on Quakerism in North Carolina and the West through the migration of its members. On his second visit Bownas visited all Friends meetings in America except seven.[3] Whatever beneficial changes or new developments occurred in one section of the Society were by these means brought to the attention of the other sections by which they were usually adopted.

The Great Awakening in New England under the influence of Jonathan Edwards and Whitefield seems not to

---

[2] See JQAC, 540–543, for a list.

[3] *Life*, p. 259.

have influenced the Friends consciously.[4] But the revival of interest in spiritual religion which it aroused must have been partly responsible for the increased attendance at Quaker meetings in New England and New Jersey in particular in the decade following Whitefield's southern journey (1739). This influence coinciding with the outbreak of the Spanish War, which was critical in the attitude of Philadelphia Yearly Meeting of Friends toward war and of the Pennsylvania Friends toward the colonial government, did not mark any new era in the history of the Society. Samuel Fothergill's ministry in America, especially in New England, when the influence of the Great Awakening began to subside, apparently met the needs of groups of people still hungering for a vital religious experience.

The Society continued to spread into new territory and to grow in membership throughout this period. Noteworthy expansions occurred in New England, especially in Maine and on Nantucket Island; in New York northward along the Hudson river; and in Virginia and North Carolina. About 1725 there began a migration of Friends from Pennsylvania and New Jersey which led to the establishment of a chain of meetings in western Maryland, the Valley of Virginia and in the Piedmont of North Carolina especially in Guilford and Randolph counties. This movement was begun probably from economic motives.[5] About 1730, groups of Friends from Salem, New Jersey, and Nottingham, Pennsylvania, established Monoquesy Meeting in western Maryland. In 1732 Alexander Ross led a company of Pennsylvania and Maryland Friends into

[4] See Whittier's "The Preacher." Whittier asserts that the Quakers remained "asbestos amid the fires" of the Whitefield revival in New England. Contemporary Quaker writers hardly mention him. Samuel Fothergill says Whitefield hurried ahead of him into Georgia to protect his flock. *Memoirs*, p. 173. See JQAC, 128–130.

[5] The descendants of these settlers who remained in these and neighboring counties were of substantial Quaker stock and constituted the main strength of North Carolina Yearly Meeting. John Griffith, *Jour.*, p. 375.

northern Virginia forming Hopewell Monthly Meeting (1735). The immigration into this region grew until there were five monthly meetings which were united in Fairfax Quarterly Meeting.

About the same time there began a movement of eastern Friends into central sections of Pennsylvania and New York. The Pennsylvania movements were westward from near Reading and from Caln Quarterly Meeting toward Lancaster. The later migrations in New York followed the Mohawk valley toward the Great Lakes. These blazed the way in the next period for a later migration from New England.

It is difficult to estimate accurately the number of Friends in America during the first half of the eighteenth century, since the meetings had no formal membership and reported no statistics. Visiting English Friends mention the increase in the size of meetings and the building of new meeting-houses in the large Quaker centers. There were numerous convincements, but meetings were still held in private houses where the Quaker population was small. Thomas estimates the number of American Friends about 1760 at about 50,000.[6] Estimates for the year 1700 indicate a Quaker population of 20,000 in Pennsylvania.[7] This is probably too large. Sharpless estimates the membership of Philadelphia Yearly Meeting, including as it did Friends in the neighboring colonies of New Jersey, Delaware and Maryland, at about 30,000 at the outbreak of the Revolution.[8] An estimate of 50,000 in 1700 for the six yearly meetings—New England, New York, Philadelphia, Maryland, Virginia and North Carolina—is probably too liberal rather than too conservative.

During this period Friends constituted the largest religious body in Rhode Island; in 1700 they formed about

---

6 Thomas, *Hist.*, pp. 102, 103.

7 JQAC, 522.

8 *Ibid.*, 524.

half the white population of the colony and they continued to take an active interest in the government. In 1714 Walter Clarke died, after having served twenty-three terms as deputy governor and four terms as governor. William Wanton "was almost continuously in some public office between 1704 and his death in the governorship in 1733, to which he was twice elected, having previously been Speaker of the Assembly for seven years."[9] John Wanton, his brother, was an official of the colony from 1712 till his death, serving as governor seven times. Other prominent Friends in Rhode Island politics during this period were Gideon Partridge, long the foreign agent of the colony in England (1715–1759); and Stephen Hopkins, whose services were of exceptional influence on the fortunes of the colony and the American nation. He served the colony in many capacities in the Assembly and on the Supreme Bench and was elected governor in 1755.

Friends lost control of New Jersey with the accession of Queen Anne in 1702 when the proprietors surrendered the charter, but they remained an influential element in the population and powerfully influenced the policies of the government.

Friends kept control of the Pennsylvania Assembly until 1756 in spite of the rapid growth of the non-Quaker population, largely through the steadfast support of the German element, who liked the Quaker tolerance and pacifism. During most of this period the colony was governed by deputies sent out by the proprietors. Many of these were not happy choices. James Logan was the most influential person in the colony during the first half of the eighteenth century as the agent of the proprietors. David Lloyd represented the distinctly Quaker and democratic tendencies, usually in opposition to Logan. There was a good deal of

[9] JQAC, 202. The Wanton brothers were not members of the Society during part of their public careers, although they were born in a Quaker home and died in the faith. *Ibid.*, pp. 201–203.

stickling for petty rights among the settlers and bickering with the proprietors over liberties and authority. It is difficult for people who have been oppressed to learn quickly the limitations and obligations of liberty.

On the whole, however, the colony prospered. Sharpless describes the three decades after Penn's incapacity as follows:

> For thirty years following 1710 we have a state, satisfied, at peace, enjoying popular liberty and security for its continuance. It was prosperous, too, beyond precedent. The ravaged and outraged dwellers in the Rhine Valley, the battle ground of Europe, the vigorous Presbyterians of Ulster who were threatened with the invasions of Episcopacy, heard of a land where wars were unknown, where taxes were light, where land was plentiful and cheap, and where every man worshipped as he pleased. The streams from both lands, little rivulets at first, but strengthening with each decade, settled the province at an unprecedentedly rapid rate. The government was simple and inexpensive, making very little demand on the people. Fortunately England made no calls on her colonies for warlike aid. Oaths were settled so that the question made no trouble. The wise arrangements of Logan kept peace and amity with the Indians. A scheme of paper money supplied the medium of pay for the importations of a growing colony, yet was so cautiously issued, that Pennsylvania probably alone among the provinces always maintained it at par. The parties of the early days were forgotten. Lloyd and Logan preserved, if not friendship, at least decorous intercourse. The Friends carried everything their own way in the state, the governors selected by Hannah Penn being widely responsive to prevailing desires and their councils made up of judicious and clear-headed men.[10]

Friends came into increasing difficulties with the Crown over the demands of the latter for grants of men and money for military purposes. The Quaker Assembly was

---

[10] JQAC, 485–486.

willing in 1701 to make grants of money so far as their religious convictions permitted. In 1711 the Assembly voted £2000 for the Queen's use, leaving to her the responsibility for the manner of its use. This seems to have been the settled attitude of the Quaker majority in a difficult situation. From 1739 until 1763 England was almost continuously at war with Spain or France. As the French strengthened their hold in Canada and gained the support of the embittered Indians, the problem of war and peace became more and more a question of colonial defense rather than merely one of theology. At the outbreak of the war with Spain in 1739, John Kinsey, as spokesman for the Quaker Assembly, carried on a long debate with Governor Thomas. In the end the Governor charged that the Quaker principles were inconsistent with government and recommended that the Crown disqualify Friends from holding office in the colony. James Logan advised that all Friends holding scruples against voting aid to the government for warlike purposes should voluntarily resign from the Assembly. The yearly meeting refused to consider the proposition, and in the election of 1742 the Quaker party triumphed. In 1745 the Assembly reaffirmed its peace attitude, but voted the king £4000 for "bread, beef, pork, flour, wheat, and other grains," instead of military supplies. In succeeding years money was voted "for the King's use," usually exacting in return some enlargement of the liberties and powers of the colonial government. Quaker officials in Rhode Island had similar difficulties with royal demands for military grants and preparations.

The mere record of members, organizations, travelling ministers, meetings, and political activities does not give the full history of the Quakerism of the period. It involved not merely doctrinal and ecclesiastical changes but a transformation of ethical and social relations amounting to the development of a new social order. The meeting for worship was the vital and creative unit of this new order.

The augmented forces of faith and worship worked out from it to all the relations of life, creating and sustaining a *Society of Friends,* a brotherhood of the spirit, having its basis in neither external compulsion nor institutional authority, but in the inner spiritual forces of faith, love, justice and good will. Its peculiar customs were "testimonies" to great truths of the Christian Gospel—universal divine love, the divine potentialities in all mankind, and human brotherhood regardless of race, class, nationality, or sex. Friends abjured and opposed whatever they realized to be injurious to human beings whether in personal conduct, social custom, or institutional order.

Friends urged tavern keepers against allowing too much liberty for excessive drinking; tried to prevent the sale of liquor to the Indians, and drunkenness among the colonists, as well as the carousing and fighting that usually went with drinking bouts; they opposed gambling and lotteries because of their "hurtful consequences" to the participants; they insisted that taxes (except for military purposes) be scrupulously paid and that the king's revenue be not defrauded; that Friends keep their promises, pay their debts, and be honest in trade. The sale of "unmerchantable beef" was looked into; care was taken that parties to a marriage were clear of other engagements and that quarrels be composed and slanders avoided. Persons guilty of sexual irregularities were rigidly "dealt with," and those who took part in war or warlike exercises were disowned.

In keeping with Puritan ideals, "worldly amusements" were regarded as hurtful to the higher life and consequently were discouraged or proscribed. Friends were warned against dancing, horse racing, attendance at fairs, shooting matches, wrestling and other such hurtful diversions; and were admonished to avoid profanity, gossip and indecent conversation.[11]

---

11 Chalkley, *Jour.,* p. 177.

The efforts of Friends for a better social order were not merely negative. They worked for positive results. They were concerned for religious training of the children in the home and in meeting; to teach them by example as well as precept to observe Friends' customs, to attend carefully to the "Inward Monitor," and to read the Scriptures. Youths' meetings were frequently held, usually in connection with the quarterly or yearly meetings. Education was fundamentally religious. Children were taken to meeting by their parents as a matter of course.[12] The travelling ministers frequently visited the families of all members of particular meetings.[13] These unofficial pastoral visits not only helped to keep up the interest of the members but had often profound influence on the children. The Quaker classics and occasionally new books, as they appeared, were purchased by or supplied to the monthly meetings for the use of the members.

During this period there was a decline in educated leadership as compared with the formative period of the Society. Frontier life was inevitably unfavorable to education, but Friends gave earnest attention to establishing elementary schools in practically all Quaker communities, so that their general literacy was above that of the colonists in general. Care was taken to secure Quaker schoolmasters and to have the children trained in the principles of Friends and in practice of their "testimonies." Often the school was held in the meeting-house. The William Penn Charter School in Philadelphia was kept up and strengthened under the care of Philadelphia Monthly Meeting. Small elementary schools were often started as private ventures of Quaker schoolmasters with the encouragement and help of the monthly meetings. In 1746 Philadelphia Yearly Meeting adopted the following minute in order to extend the movement for general literacy:

---

12 Cf. *The Gospel Labours of John Churchman*, p. 1.

13 *Ibid.*, pp. 24–31.

> We desire you, in your several Monthly Meetings, to encourage and assist each other in the settlement and support of schools for the instruction of your children, at least to read and write, and some further useful learning, to such whose circumstances will permit it. And that you observe, as much as possible, to employ such masters and mistresses as are concerned, not only to instruct your children in their learning, but are likewise careful in the wisdom of God and a spirit of meekness, gradually to bring them to a knowledge of their duty to God and one another; and we doubt not such endeavors will be blessed with success.[14]

The Friends in Pennsylvania and New Jersey, in following out the policy of Penn, devoted themselves especially to the protection and care of the Indians. Between 1733 and 1751 Friends are reported to have spent £8366 for the benefit of Pennsylvania tribes; and great efforts were made to prevent the sale of alcoholic liquors to them and to protect them from being cheated in trade.[15] Treaties with the Indians were often made in Friends meeting-houses[16] and many of the travelling ministers visited Indian settlements and held meetings with them. Among these missionaries were Thomas Turner, Thomas Story, John Richardson, Thomas Chalkley, and John Woolman. They were received hospitably and heard with respect; but in spite of a fancied likeness between the Indian belief in the Great Spirit and the Quaker doctrine of the Inner Light few Quaker converts were made among them.[17]

The Pennsylvania Indians and neighboring tribes remained faithful to Friends; but a series of acts of the proprietors gradually alienated them from the government of Pennsylvania. The most noteworthy of these was the Walking Purchase in 1737. The origin of the matter was as follows:

---

[14] JQAC, 528, 529.
[15] Thomas, *Hist.*, p. 111.
[16] JQAC, 502.
[17] *Ibid.*, 498, 499.

There was an old agreement, of doubtful authenticity, made in 1686, which conveyed to William Penn certain land in Bucks County and extending northwards as far as a man could walk in a day and a half. With the understanding of the time, this would mean abount thirty miles, and would carry the purchase to the junction of the Delaware and Lehigh rivers where Easton stands.[18]

Thomas Penn desired land north of the Lehigh River for sale to prospective settlers. Since the resident Indians refused to sell, the proprietor resorted to trickery. The prescribed walk was arranged to mark the extent of the purchase. Paths were cleared, boats provided to cross the streams and horses to carry equipment, so that two trained athletes covered sixty miles in the specified time. Then surveyors slanted the northern boundary line to the Delaware so as to include all the coveted territory. The Indians, conscious of the fraud, refused to leave the land until the proprietors finally got their Iroquois overlords to compel them to move. After this the process of encroachment on Indian rights was continued. Chiefs were plied with liquor and made to sign away lands. Settlers crowded in on lands not yet purchased. In 1754 the proprietors purchased nearly the whole of western Pennsylvania from the Iroquois, without consent of the Delaware tribes. Meanwhile the colony was filling up with Scotch-Irish Presbyterians who had no patience with the Quaker attitude to the Indians; and the French took advantage of the Indians' resentment at their mistreatment to fan their hostility. The outbreak of the French and Indian War in 1755 marked the end of the long peace between the colony and the Indians.

After the initial protest of the Germantown Friends against slavery in 1688 and that of the Keithians in 1693, the opposition of the Friends to slavery developed very

---

[18] JQAC, 501.

slowly. Some Friends owned slaves and even engaged in the slave trade. In 1696 Philadelphia Yearly Meeting advised Friends "not to encourage the bringing in of any more negroes." Penn directed, in the will which he made on leaving Pennsylvania in 1701, that his slaves should be set free, but his instruction was not carried out.

Chester Meeting had a persistent concern against the slave trade and especially the encouragement to the trade given by the purchasing of slaves. Between 1711 and 1729 this meeting memorialized the yearly meeting at least five times. At last in 1730 the purchase of imported slaves was made a disownable offense. In 1711 the importation of Negroes into the province was prohibited, but the law was rejected by the Royal Council. Meantime, in 1712, William Southerby had petitioned the Assembly to abolish slavery in the province. Instead, it laid a duty of £20, intended to be prohibitive, on each slave imported. This bill was also vetoed by the Queen's Council. In 1729 Ralph Sandiford published a paper against slavery. The yearly meeting noted with satisfaction that the reports showed that Friends were fairly free from encouraging the importation of slaves, and exhorted the subordinate meetings to continue their care in the matter. Five years later a query on the subject was directed to be answered in the yearly reports as follows:

> Are Friends clear of importing or buying negroes; and do they use those well which they are possessed of by inheritance or otherwise; endeavoring to train them up in the principles of the Christian religion? [19]

In New England slavery was particularly common around Narragansett bay, and some Friends even owned or imported slaves. A few Friends grew uneasy about it early in the eighteenth century and, in 1717, New England Yearly Meeting at Newport advised merchants to "write

---

19 JQAC, 515.

their correspondents in the [West Indian] islands and elsewhere to discourage their sending any more [slaves] in order to be sold here."[20]

The anti-slavery movement received an impetus about 1742 from Thomas Hazard of Rhode Island who came to believe that slaveholding was wrong and quietly spread his views. In 1743 the New England Yearly Meeting took up the subject, and in 1744 advised the members to refrain from buying Negroes when imported, and directed the quarterly meetings to report how the advice was observed. In 1747 the movement against slaveholding received a great impetus from a visit by John Woolman. In other colonies the development of a conscience and testimony against slavery came chiefly in the next period.

Friends continued their struggle for relief from oaths, tithes and military service in those colonies where their refusal of these still entailed fines, imprisonment and political disabilities, especially in Massachusetts, Connecticut, New York, Maryland and Virginia. In 1724 three Quaker assessors of Dartmouth were imprisoned for refusing to assess taxes for the support of the ministry. They appealed to the king, and the Privy Council ordered their release and the remission of the taxes. After 1746 Friends were free from all charges for support of ministers in New England. Relief from distraints for non-payment of tithes did not come in Virginia until the Revolution in 1776. The right to substitute an affirmation for an oath in the court was granted slowly, following the Affirmation Act in England; but the gradual withdrawal of Friends from public life in Pennsylvania, New Jersey, Rhode Island and North Carolina during the first half of the eighteenth century made the problem of the oath of office of little practical importance.

---

[20] Cited in JQAC, 157.

Period II

The Peculiar People
1737-1784

Chapter 17

THE COMPLETION OF THE DISCIPLINE

There were many signs of change in English society toward the end of the first third of the eighteenth century. The reaction from the struggles of the Puritan period was coming to an end. The Stuart dynasty was definitely finished; the last serious attempt of the Jacobite Pretender to the throne had been decisively defeated. The second George of the Hanoverian line had succeeded peaceably to the throne. A new generation had arisen and new issues were demanding attention. Fresh areas of English society were ripe for a spiritual harvest, which was to be gathered, however, not by Friends but by the Methodist and Evangelical movements. Puritanism won its spiritual victory in the Wesleyan movement after the failure in the previous century of its military and political struggles.[1]

Other events, indicating a change in the religious climate, were the publication in 1727 and 1735 of translations of works of continental Quietists,[2] the early writings of William Law, and the visit of Count Zinzendorf, the

---

1 Green, *A Short History of the English People,* III, 307, 308.

2 Hobhouse, *William Law and 18th Century Quakerism,* p. 151.

founder of the Moravian Brethren, to England in 1750. In America we have already noted the religious stirrings of the awakening in New England and Whitefield's revival.

The two most definite beginnings of the revival of religious life and interest were the publication of Bishop Butler's *Analogy*[3] and John Wesley's decisive religious experience. Butler's work (1736) marked the turning point in the theological struggle between orthodoxy and Deism. Bishop Butler met the Deists on their own ground and attempted to show that orthodox Christianity was both rational and according to nature. Against his argument Deism, as a theological system, never successfully rallied;[4] but the victory was purchased at the cost of a surrender to the demand for a rational faith and the abandonment of church or Bible as the ultimate ground of religious doctrine. It marks the point, however, at which reviving religious interest made the church aggressive again instead of lying passive under the attacks of Deism.[5]

John Wesley's transforming experience came in 1738, when in the Moravian Chapel in Fetter Lane, London, his

---

[3] *Analogy of Religion to the Constitution and Course of Nature.* Butler had been preceded by William Law's *The Case of Reason or Natural Religion* (1731) and Bishop Berkeley's *Alciphron or the Minute-Philosopher* (1733).

[4] The rationalistic movement continued, however. It was inextricably involved with the philosophical school of Locke and Hume; and it acted as a corrosive in the fields of the natural sciences, history, archaeology and literary criticism. Its influence filtered down among the people in the latter half of the century as a rationalizing of doctrinal and moral nonconformity. The name came to be applied to all sorts of heresy, liberalism, and radicalism in religion, much as in the post-war period of the twentieth century Bolshevism covered and damned all deviation from "standpat" political and social ideals. Cf. Churchman, *Gospel Labours,* pp. 14, 15. Griffith, *Jour.,* p. 123. "In a sense, the 'deism' of William Savery's time was the forerunner of the later unrest, the vague stirrings of discontent at the antiquated forms, arid theology and grafting politics of a bishop-ridden church." Taylor, *op. cit.,* p. 317.

[5] Butler's *Analogy* had apparently no immediate effect on the thinking of Friends but in the next century it had considerable influence on Joseph John Gurney and through him on sections of the Society.

"heart was strangely warmed." This supplied to the Wesleyan group the religious fervor which the Holy Club at Oxford had lacked. Wesley had been powerfully influenced by the Pietism of the Moravians since his Georgia days (1735–37). He owed much to the fervent piety and mysticism of William Law, whose *Serious Call to a Devout and Holy Life* (1729) made him the John Baptist of the new era. He called the new generation to sincerity, conscientiousness, simplicity, and self-denial—to put off the old man and put on the new, and work in the way of the cross. After 1733 Jacob Boehme's works "opened his eyes," deepened his experiences of spiritual forces, and shifted his emphasis from doctrine to life. Law exercised a powerful influence on John Wesley for eight or nine years after they met in 1732, contributing much of the "inwardness" of Methodism.[6]

The Wesleyan movement spread with great rapidity in England and later in America. It had certain features closely akin to Quakerism, including its insistence on first-hand religion and on the inward witness as the basis of assurance, its proselytizing zeal, its joyousness, its non-ecclesiastical character and its practical program of human betterment. After Quietism became prevalent among Friends both assumed the depravity of human nature. Wesleyanism was destined to have a great influence on Quakerism in the next century through the Evangelical movement in England and the Great Revival in America; but, at the outset, the differences in customs, theological expression, and ecclesiastical development prevented any sympathetic coöperation between them.

Friends shared the general religious awakening in the second third of the eighteenth century but with them the new religious zeal took the direction of the completion and enforcement of the discipline. The laxity, of which the travelling ministers increasingly complained during the

---

[6] Hobhouse, *William Law and 18th Century Quakerism*, p. 308.

preceding decades, seemed to them to be due to departures from Friends' "testimonies" and to the failure of the leaders to enforce the discipline. The cure, therefore, was more and more sought in the strict observance of the disciplinary requirements and a succession of able ministers set themselves to the revival and enforcement of them. These new spiritual energies were particularly manifest in the younger generation and gradually led not only to the completion and dominance of the discipline, but to the spread of Quietism and to the fine flowering of Quaker philanthropy.

The beginning of the new era in Quaker history is marked by the establishment of birthright membership in 1737 and the first written book of discipline in England in 1738. The adoption of birthright membership was perhaps all the more significant in that it was unintentional. Heretofore the membership of a monthly meeting consisted loosely of those who associated with Friends, attended meetings for worship and conformed generally with their customs. From this loosely defined membership a selected number were invited to participate in the business meetings.

Friends were accustomed to care for their own poor, and the minute of London Yearly Meeting which established birthright membership was occasioned by the difficulty in some cases of determining which meeting was responsible for the care of particular widows, orphans and other needy Friends. The minute read:

> All Friends shall be deemed members of the Quarterly, Monthly and Two-Weeks meeting within the compass of which they inhabited or dwelt the first day of the Fourth Month, 1737 . . . and the wife and children to be deemed members of the Monthly Meeting of which the husband or father is a member, not only during his life but after his decease.[7]

---

[7] Cited in Barclay, *Inner Life*, p. 520; Thomas, *Hist.*, p. 109.

It had been the custom to regard the children of Friends as part of the Quaker community and as objects of their religious care; but this minute for the first time included them in the membership. Heretofore the Society had been regarded as a fellowship of the Children of the Light; of people set apart by personal religious experience and dedicated to the religion of the Spirit. While the minute only included the children of Friends as members to be cared for when needy, it suited the temper of the period to count them as members for all purposes. It was expected that Friendly nurture and the influence of the meeting would lead them to become Friends by conviction, but no distinction was made whether they did or not. Thus birthright membership was fastened upon the Society and gradually wrought a great change in its fundamental nature.

The vast importance of this step was not appreciated for some time. It changed the Society of Friends from a church of believers, at least in theory, to a corporation or association of persons some of whom always would be of those who were not spiritually minded. Youth had been no hindrance in the early days, provided the person was believed to be spiritually minded; after the adoption of this regulation membership for a large number had no connection with change of heart.[8]

It also marked a great change in the ideas and activities of Friends. They no longer looked to a resumption of the earlier evangelistic activities to build up the membership but depended more and more on the children of Friends to keep up the Society.

George Fox had instituted separate monthly meetings for women against much opposition; and the system was never completely carried out in England although it seems to have prevailed in America. In some places women Friends were invited to "sit with the men" in their monthly meeting. Toward the middle of the century an effort was

[8] Thomas, *Hist.*, p. 109.

made to establish women's monthly meetings throughout Great Britain.[9] In America there were separate quarterly and yearly meetings for women from the beginning.[10]

Since the business meetings were "select," it was the custom to hold a "general monthly meeting" every three months to which the whole membership was invited (including women and servants) for reading the advices and for exhortations. "Youth's meetings" were also held for the younger members in connection with the quarterly meetings and in many places both in England and in America one quarterly meeting in each year became a popular gathering where the local and visiting ministers had a special opportunity to preach to members and "the world's people." These were often called yearly meetings but must be carefully distinguished from the yearly meetings which were the highest legislative and judicial bodies in the Society. They correspond to the "circulating meetings" held at the different points in the quarterly meeting limits in the central counties in England.[11]

At the beginning of London Yearly Meeting it was composed chiefly of "public Friends." In America the regular yearly meetings for business were more democratic in character so that separate meetings for those especially concerned with the public ministry seemed more necessary. The custom of holding such meetings to consider the problems and character of the ministry and for mutual encouragement originated in Philadelphia Yearly Meeting in 1685.[12] In time the attendance was limited to ministers

---

9 JLPQ, I, 107.

10 *The Friend* (Phila.) xviii, 134. Cited in Thomas, *Hist.*, p. 95.

11 The most notable of these were in Cornwall, Devon, Somerset, Wilts, Dorset, Gloucester, Hereford, Worcester, and Warwick. Boisterous crowds of non-Friends often attended these and they were finally discontinued. Similar meetings at Jordans, Brigflatts and Armscot continued until recent times. The annual popular quarterly meeting still exists in places in America.

12 JQAC, 538.

certified as acceptable by their monthly meetings. In 1714 the monthly meetings were authorized to name a few "prudent solid Friends" to sit with the ministers in these meetings. Such "meetings of ministers and elders" became general in course of time on both sides of the Atlantic Ocean. They were naturally joint meetings of men and women, since ministers were of either sex.

In 1753 Samuel Fothergill, who had spent many years travelling in America proposed the establishment of a meeting of ministers and elders for London Yearly Meeting, which was done the following year. The new meeting was to "give account of the state of the ministry in their respective counties and of the unity subsisting one with another and with their meeting," but was not to interfere with any part of the exercise of the discipline of the church belonging to the yearly meeting of business held in London.[13] This meeting took over the function of giving certificates to ministers with concerns for service beyond the seas which had formerly been done by the Morning Meeting.

The system of meetings was completed in England by the establishment of the women's yearly meeting.[14] Large numbers of women Friends had been accustomed to go to London at the time of yearly meeting to attend the meetings for worship and to meet informally to consider matters of special concern to them, but their gatherings had no official standing and they could take no part in the yearly meeting proper. In 1753, under the influence of two American Friends who were then in England, William Brown and John Pemberton, the women petitioned for a yearly meeting. The request was not granted, either at this time or in 1766, when it was renewed. The concern of the women was kept alive, however, through three decades.

---

13 JLPQ, I, 112, 113.

14 The women's yearly meeting in Ireland was established in 1679. *Ibid.*, p. 113n.

It came up again in 1784 in connection with the proposal to rebuild the yearly meeting premises at Devonshire House. The women wanted a meeting room for their yearly meeting in the remodeled buildings. A number of American Friends were again present and pressed the subject. This time the petition of the women Friends was granted. The minute adopted by the yearly meeting was as follows:

> This Meeting, after a solid and deliberate consideration of the proposition brought in from the Women's Meeting, held annually in this city, agrees that the said Meeting be at liberty to correspond in writing with the Quarterly Meetings of Women Friends; to receive accounts from them, and issue such advice as, in the wisdom of Truth, from time to time may appear necessary and conducive to their mutual edification. For this purpose it will be expedient that the said meeting be a meeting of record, and be denominated the Yearly Meeting of Women Friends held in London; yet such meeting is not to be so far considered a meeting of Discipline, as to make rules nor yet alter the present queries, without the concurrence of this meeting.[15]

In 1756 at the outbreak of the French and Indian War, Philadelphia Yearly Meeting established a "Meeting for Sufferings" as an executive body to represent the yearly meeting when not in session. The other American yearly meetings followed Philadelphia's example in this regard within the next two decades. The system now completed, consisting of preparative, monthly, quarterly and yearly meetings for business, together with the corresponding women's meetings, meetings of ministers and elders, and meetings for sufferings remained practically unchanged for more than a century.[16]

The development of the official classes or "office-bearers" in the Society was a gradual process. They were merely

---

15 Cited in JLPQ, I, 117.

16 The London Morning Meeting stood outside the system.

functionaries but never "orders" within the church. Ministers were regarded as men and women definitely called of God to preach the gospel and equipped spiritually for the service. The Society only recognized the gift and recorded its recognition. When special meetings of ministers were established the question arose as to the scope of their membership. In England the Morning Meeting in London, which had oversight of Friends who desired to travel in foreign counties, kept a book in which ministers visiting London signed their names. If the name was not challenged, the minister became an accepted member of the proper meetings of ministers. In America ministers who had the approval of their monthly meetings or who had minutes from them to travel in the ministry were accepted members of the meetings of ministers. In 1722 William Gibson appealed from the decision of the London Morning Meeting that he was not entitled to membership in it to London Yearly Meeting, which decided that ministers must produce a certification from their own monthly or quarterly meeting before they could be enrolled as members of the Morning Meeting. The latter, therefore, requested the monthly meetings to furnish lists of recognized ministers. Thus the custom of "recording" ministers arose in London Yearly Meeting. The initiative in recording ministers was to be taken by the meeting of ministers and elders of the monthly or quarterly meeting according to a minute of London Yearly Meeting in 1773.

In the formative stage of the Society "public Friends" were called either ministers or elders. This use of the term "elder" fell into disuse when the first generation passed away. The elders of subsequent Quakerism were "solid, weighty and experienced" Friends appointed by the monthly meetings to sit with the ministers in the ministers meeting to consider the state of the ministry, to aid young ministers and finally to have oversight of spiritual conditions in the church. This custom began, as has been already mentioned,[17] in Philadelphia Yearly Meeting as early as 1685. Irish Friends provided for the appointment of Friends from each province to meet and consider the condition of the ministry and worship. Elders were appointed by some English quarterly meetings as early as 1700. The distinct class and function of the elders was defined by a minute of London Yearly Meeting in 1727 as follows:

> A Proposition from ye Friends of Wilts relating to ye Extending a Care of Friends to young Ministers, etc., being read, this Meeting desires all Monthly Meetings to appoint serious, discreet, and judicious Friends, who are not Ministers, tenderly to Encourage and help young ministers and advise others as they shall in ye wisdom of God see occasion: and yet where there are meetings of Ministering friends, such friends so chosen be admitted as members of such Meetings of Ministers, and Act therein for the Good purposes aforesaid.[18]

For some years the functions of the elders were not clearly differentiated from those of the overseers, who were later charged with the oversight of the moral conduct of the membership, including the observance of the "testimonies."[19] In an attempt to stem the tide of worldliness and laxity in discipline, Irish Friends had, as already noted, appointed committees to labor with negligent Friends.[20] This plan was adopted in parts of London Yearly Meeting, but later fell into disuse. Such functions were often exercised by the elders.[21] In 1751, however, the custom was revived and Friends were appointed to have general oversight of the membership. They were called overseers or

---

17 Above, p. 218.

18 Cited in JLPQ, I, 122–123.

19 Such as the plain dress and speech, marriage, refusal of tithes, oaths, military service, etc.

20 See above, chap. 15, p. 192.

21 See the Yearly Meeting Epistle of 1744 where the elders are exhorted to "advise and assist the weak and to use their Christian endeavors to restoring such as may have wandered and gone astray." *London Epistles,* p. 203.

sometimes "interval Friends" because they looked after the membership in the intervals between monthly meetings. In 1755 London Yearly Meeting adopted a query to be answered by the quarterly meetings: "Have you two or more faithful Friends deputed in each particular meeting to have the oversight thereof, and is care taken when anything appears amiss that the rules of our discipline are put in practice?" In 1789 the yearly meeting in response to a question from Warwickshire Quarterly Meeting, decided that the offices of elder and overseer are distinct and that overseers as such are not entitled to sit in the meeting of ministers and elders. By this slow process the threefold official system was completed.

It was the eldership, however, which became the dominant influence in the history of Quakerism for a century after 1750. The elders acquired the position of influence in the affairs of the Society which the ministry had previously occupied. By many Friends of later generations they have been held responsible for the decline of the Society in members and influence during this period. It is almost a law of Quaker history that the Society has been vigorous and growing when the ministry is dominant and has declined when the elders were in power.[22] This explanation of the fluctuations of Quaker history has a measure of truth in it but is too simple an explanation to be acceptable. On the whole the elders were the ablest men and women of the Society; they were spiritually minded and devoted to Quakerism, as they understood it, and possessed of shrewd corporate judgment. Their function of nourishing, advising, and safeguarding the ministry in the course of time took a secondary place. They became the guardians of tradition and as such were a conservative force. They became the repositories of sound doctrine, the interpreters of the Quaker literature and the ruling class in the Society.

---

22 Cf. Barclay, *Inner Life,* chap. XXII.

They were not, however, spiritual pioneers, prophets or apostles of progress.

These classes gradually developed unwritten and written principles and rules of procedure and judgment. The most used and most valuable of these were the advices and queries.[23] As these were regularly and solemnly read before the membership, they were a powerful influence in maintaining standards of conduct and character and in moulding the ideals of Quaker youth.

The discipline, the final stages of which we have traced, was gradually reduced to writing and finally printed. These books of discipline were largely based on the so-called "Canons and Institutions" of George Fox with the addition of yearly meeting decisions, extracts from epistles, rules, regulations, principles, queries, and advices. In 1738 on the request of the Yorkshire Quarterly Meeting, manuscript copies of the discipline were prepared and distributed to the quarterly meetings. Parts of the discipline were printed for circulation from time to time—regulations for removals from one meeting to another in 1729 and for procedure in marriage in 1754. In 1762 John Fry printed an unofficial edition of the whole discipline, but it was not until 1783 that the official *Extracts from the Minutes and Advices* was published and distributed to the monthly meetings.[24]

There was a revival of religious life and interest in American Quakerism in 1755, especially in New England, largely under the influence of Samuel Fothergill, which, as in Great Britain, took the form of stricter discipline. The English rule in regard to birthright membership was gen-

---

[23] These originated in the early days of the Society and have been added to from time to time. Largely through the influence of David Hall, who labored among Irish Friends in 1736–37, a revival of religious interest led to the revision in 1740 of the queries used there. In 1755 London Yearly Meeting revised the queries, providing separate sets for the quarterly and monthly meetings. In 1792 the two sets were combined.

[24] *Minutes,* XVIII, 133, 414. Cited in JLPQ, I, 143.

erally adopted, the membership was overhauled and all who could not prove their right of membership were required to apply for admission. Fothergill's suggestions to New England Friends seem to have been generally followed in all the colonial yearly meetings.

It appears to me the likeliest method to know who are of you, will be to consider that all such who have a birthright in the Society, or have been admitted upon request, or been employed in offices of the Church, must be deemed members, and under the care of Friends, and that a visit be payed to all such as frequent meetings, and have not a right to membership by the means aforesaid; the visitors taking the queries agreed to last Yearly Meeting, and solidly reading them to the parties, may acquaint them those queries, or the substance thereof, are universally agreed to amongst Friends everywhere, as the rule of their outward conduct; and if they desire to be accepted as members, it is expected they concur therewith, conduct, and be governed thereby; if such submit thereto, and testify their concurrence by a personal appearance at the Monthly Meeting, or to Friends' satisfaction, a minute may be made of their being deemed and accepted as members of the Church.[25]

Manuscript books of discipline were adopted by the American yearly meetings as follows: Philadelphia 1704, 1719 and 1762; Virginia 1758; Baltimore 1759; New England 1739 or 1740.[26] All of them issued printed editions shortly after New England led the way in 1785. Philadelphia's first printed book of discipline came in 1797. The American disciplines showed a greater tendency than that of London toward systematic logical arrangement. In America these manuscript disciplines were, in general, kept

---

25 Crosfield, G., *Memoirs of Samuel Fothergill*, p. 174.

26 Thomas, *Hist.*, p. 106. Philadelphia issued a printed *Paper of Discipline* in 1689. As early as 1704 the yearly meeting advices and instructions were partly arranged as a discipline. JQAC, 535. The queries were adopted in 1725; systematized in 1743 and in 1755 definite answers were requested. JQAC, 536–538. Cf. BFHS, XXIV, 12–23.

in official hands and private possession of them was discouraged.[27]

From this time onward the discipline was enforced very much as in Great Britain.

> Now began the general expulsion of members for marrying non-members, the severe rules in regard to dress and language, and many of those customs and outward practices which later generations have supposed were peculiar to Friends from their foundation.[28]
>
> The increased attention to the Discipline, valuable and important as it was, was too often associated with too rigid an adherence to forms, and a tendency to multiply rules, and to make the exact carrying of them out, in a degree at least, a substitute for that patient and discriminating wisdom tempered with love, which should ever characterize Christian discipline.[29]

From this period Friends regarded themselves as a people apart; their ideal was to be a "quiet" and "peculiar" people, set apart to bear a testimony for certain great principles by their message and mode of life; living in the world but not of the world. Their common designations for non-Friends were "the world's people" or "persons not in profession with us."

With the completion of the discipline and the definite establishment of the three classes of "office-bearers," the leaders of the revival of religious interest had at hand the instruments for the renovation and standardizing of the Society. This two-fold revival of interest in personal religion and in the discipline was chiefly the work of a group of ministers who travelled widely throughout the Quaker world in this period. The most influential of them were: John Churchman (1705–1775), William Reckitt (1706–1769), John Griffith (1713–1776), Samuel Fothergill (1715–1772), John Woolman (1720–1772), James Pemberton

---

27 Thomas, *op. cit.*, p. 132n.

28 *Ibid.*, p. 105.

29 Braithwaite, *Memoirs of J. J. Gurney*, II, 14.

(1723–1809), Catherine Payton Phillips (1726–1794), John Pemberton (1727–1795), and Samuel Neale (1729–1792).

Woman travelling ministers had nearly ceased since 1700, but after about 1750 there was a noteworthy succession of very able women engaged in this service. The journals of these men and women are full of stories of hardships of travelling; of hairbreadth escapes from privateers and from the dangers of starvation, foundering in storms or disease on the seas; of spiritual wrestling with religious indifference and opposition to reforms; of long absence from home and family in Truth's service; of financial loss and the death of absent loved ones. The mysticism, the ideals of character and service, and the discipline of the Society in the eighteenth century were chiefly their creation. In spite of the defects of both Quietism and discipline, their faithfulness, their sterling character and the fine fruits of their religious endeavors and philanthropic pioneering were noteworthy contributions to their world.

These Friends preached to many non-Friends, both to those who attended the regular meetings of Friends and those for whom special meetings were appointed in whatever meeting places were available, in courthouses, private houses, Baptist and Presbyterian churches and often in barns. There is evidence that their work resulted in many convincements; perhaps enough to replace the losses of disownment. Those attracted by Friends' mode of worship and ethical principles were largely deterred from joining the Society, however, by the "peculiarities" on which membership was conditioned and by the lack of organized effort to gather them into membership. Another obstacle to larger convincements by the ministry of these itinerants was the fact that their primary concern was to preserve a religious heritage and revive the zeal of a past generation. They had no living fresh message for the new age; they did not attempt to put the Quaker life and faith in new wine skins.

In 1755 London Yearly Meeting recommended that all the families within its membership be visited.[30] In 1760 a committee was appointed by the yearly meeting, largely through the efforts of Samuel Fothergill, to visit the subordinate meetings and try to improve the "discipline and good order of the Society." [31] The committee did its work in patient thorough-going fashion during the next three years. Fothergill himself spent three months with the section which visited Ireland.[32] The religious revival again put the spirit of personal piety and sacrificial devotion into the Quaker forms for a substantial section of the membership. The Quaker type of outward life and moral character was thus standardized as it was known and respected for a century, but at the expense of much of its original independence and its progressive elements.

The non-conforming remnant, after being "dealt with," were rigidly disowned. The grounds for disownment were a mixture of ethical and ecclesiastical transgressions. They ranged all the way from neglect of the plain dress and speech and "marrying out of the meeting" to drunkenness, sexual immorality and rendering military service. On the whole those who were disowned for nonconformity were members untouched by the religious revival, and their continued membership would have been of little value to the Society.

In some cases the disowned Friends were deeply attached to Friends' ideals of worship and continued to attend Friends meetings; and their character and ways of life exercised a profound influence on their descendants, often producing original tendencies or susceptibilities toward spirituality, social initiative, or philanthropic reform. The loss of many of these finer characters to the Society proved the riches of the world, for many of them made great contributions to human progress.

---

30 Cf. Catherine Phillip's *Memoirs,* p. 149.

31 *Minutes,* XII, pp. 92, 103. Cited in JLPQ, I, 137, 138.

32 Cf. Fothergill *Memoirs,* pp. 173–174, for his ideals.

A noteworthy example of this was Thomas Paine, the son of an English Quaker. He was never actively identified with Friends, but acknowledged his profound debt to his Quaker training. He revolted early against the Evangelical theology and, coming to America in 1774, threw himself into the movement for independence. His *Common Sense* and *The American Crisis* exercised a profound influence on the struggle. An ardent democrat, he went to France later and espoused the revolutionary movement.

He was not a profound thinker but had a bold trenchant style which popularized radical ideas. He differed from Friends chiefly on points of theology and on the War for Independence. Quaker influences are shown in his opposition to the slave trade, to oaths, duelling, warfare in general, and to privileged classes and titles of honor and distinction. He advocated entire freedom of religion and conscience and universal suffrage. "In Paine's pages are found early mention of graduated income taxes, school taxes for the education of the poor, old age pensions and maternity benefits." [33]

In 1794 he published *The Age of Reason*. It was a crude, cynical and popular expression of French Deism, which largely eclipsed his contributions to humanity and democracy.[34] He is an example both of the liberalizing influence of a Quaker inheritance and of the lengths to which the Quaker individualism and social non-conformity may go, if not combined with a vital experience of spiritual realities, such as was central in the Quaker view of life.

---

[33] Taylor, *Life of Wm. Savery*, p. 158.

[34] In 1797 William Savery and David Sands had an interview with Paine in Paris in the course of which Savery is reported by Sarah Rawes to have said "I knew thee, Thomas, when thee lived a few doors from my Father, when thee wrote the book, entitled *Common Sense,* and if thee had left off there, perhaps thee mightest have been set down as a man of understanding, but since,"—"Ah," said he, "I see you have been reading *that Book.*" Taylor, *op. cit.*, p. 247.

CHAPTER 18

QUAKER QUIETISM

MYSTICISM is the religion of direct personal relations between man and God inwardly revealed and known. In the history of Christianity there have been many types of mystical experience and worship, varying according to the ways in which the direct relationship with God was sought and in which its character and consequences were expressed. Quietism is a form of mysticism which starts with the assumption of the essential moral ruin and religious incapacity of human nature. This means more than the sinful disposition and impulses of human nature, which Paul calls "the flesh." It is something other than the selfishness and willfulness of personal human desires set over against the will of God. It implies that all of the "human creature," as distinct from the divine manifestations in the form of supernatural "motions," "breathings" or inspiration, is wholly and unworthily "other" than the divine. Quietism believes, therefore, that God can work within and through the human spirit only when the usual activities of the "creature" are "quiet"; that only in the "silence of all flesh" can God make himself heard; that only when all "creaturely activities" of reason, forethought, planning and organization are suspended can God work in and direct the soul through some invasion, a "breaking in" or "prevailing" of the Divine. To quote Rufus Jones:

It must be understood at the outset that Quietism does not spell lethargy and inaction; it does not mean folded hands and a little more sleep; it is not a religion for lotus-eaters. The Quietist may, and often did, swing out into a course of action that would make the rationally centred Christian quail with fear and slink to cover. It is not a question of action or of non-action; it is a question of *the right way to initiate action.*[1]

In practice, among Friends and other Quietists, the emphasis came to be laid on the negative aspect of Quietistic experience, for the fear of "creaturely activity" and the effort to attain the "quietness" requisite for worship, guidance or enabling, came in time to overshadow all else. This view of human nature and of the conditions of religious life was common to both Protestant and Counter-Reformation Catholic theology. Its influence was widespread in Europe in the latter half of the seventeenth and the first half of the eighteenth centuries; and this constituted part of the religious atmosphere of early eighteenth-century Quakerism, although, as usual, Friends were slow to respond to it. The writings of Molinos, Antoinette Bourignon, Thomas a Kempis and Madame Guyon were in general circulation in England; and their phrases and ideas were familiar to English readers throughout the century after 1688. It was only toward the end of the eighteenth century, however, that Catholic Quietism consciously influenced Friends. Quaker Quietism was a parallel growth in this eighteenth-century religious soil and was well developed before its kinship with the Catholic Quietism of Molinos, Fenelon and Madame Guyon consciously reinforced it.[2] It had four principal sources.

The first was in Barclay's doctrine of human nature,[3] which laid the doctrinal basis for the Quietist fear of the

---

1 JLPQ, I, 35.

2 Dr. John Rutty refers in his *Diary* to Law's *Serious Call to the Imitation of Christ,* to St. Theresa and the Port Royallers (probably Pascal). Under date of 12 mo. 23, 1761 he hails a new translation of *The Imitation.* Woolman writes with appreciation of *The Imitation of Christ* in his *Journal,* p. 132.

3 Above, chap. 14, pp. 179.

impulses of the natural man and of creaturely activity and for its working faith that only in the suspension of the normal impulses, reasonings, desires, and activities of human nature could the leading and power of God become effective. A second source, strangely enough, was the lingering influence of Ranterism in the Society.[4] On the surface, Ranterism and Quietism have nothing in common; but both sought divine leading in definite feeling; the one in strong unchecked impulses and the other in carefully tested "impressions" of duty and truth. The journals of the Quietist leaders are largely records of how they "felt" in meetings and on their journeys. Among those not "recorded" as ministers, who yet occasionally spoke in meeting, the frequent explanation of breaking the silence was that they had to do so "to relieve their minds." Both were also extremely individualistic in their theory of divine guidance.

The individualistic Ranterism of men like Perrot, Wilkinson, Story and Rogers of an earlier age had failed to prevent the growth and dominance of the corporate discipline of the Society; but their idea of personal guidance by "immediate" strong impressions of duty triumphed in Quietism. The shift in the meaning of "immediate" guidance from "unmediated" or direct guidance to guidance "at the moment," tended to eliminate preparation, plans, purposes and programs from the lives and service of Quietist Friends, since these could not be "immediate" in the new sense and therefore constituted activities "in the will of the creature."[5]

The third source was the mood of reaction already described, which followed the period of the rise of Quakerism.[6] The religious relaxation and the cessation of evan-

---

[4] Cf. Churchman, *Gospel Labours,* pp. 130, 159. Griffith, *Jour.,* pp. 31, 62, 133.

[5] Above chap. 12, pp. 148, 149. Cf. Brayshaw, *Quakers,* pp. 226, 240, 241.

[6] Above chap. 15, pp. 186, 187.

gelistic effort formed a favorable nursery for the Quietist attitude. A congenial institution or mode of life usually develops a philosophy to justify it. The principles of Quietism were too much in consonance with the passive temper of Friends to be critically examined "in the light of eternity." As early as 1702 Hugh Turford published a little book called *The Grounds of a Holy Life,* which powerfully stimulated the growth of Quaker Quietism. It ran through twenty-eight English editions besides others in America and in continental countries. In 1725 Benjamin Holme of York published a booklet, *A Serious Call,* which was a rather colorless combination of Quietist attitudes with the doctrine of the Inner Light and evangelical theology.

The writings of certain continental Catholic mystics constituted a fourth source of Quaker Quietism. Among these Molinos, Fénelon and Madame Guyon were the most influential; their writings were translated and printed for Friends from 1772 to 1813, most of them by James Gough, a noted Quaker schoolmaster of Bristol.[7] They interested Friends chiefly because of their kinship with views which they already held in some measure and which these works powerfully reinforced. In 1813 William Backhouse and James Janson compiled, chiefly from the writings of Molinos, Fénelon and Madame Guyon, a little manual of Quietist devotion with the title *A Guide to True Peace,* or a *Method of Attaining to Inward and Spiritual Prayer.* The compilers used no quotation marks and gave no indication of sources except the mention on the title page of the writings of the three named above. It exercised an

---

[7] "*The Life of Lady Guion,* written by herself in French, now abridged and translated into English, etc. (Bristol, 1772); *The Life of Armelle Nicholas* (translated by James Gough, Bristol, 1772); *Select Lives of Foreigners, Eminent in Piety* [Peter Poiret, Antoinette Bourignon and others] (Bristol, 1773); reprinted with the addition of *The Life of Francis de Sales, Discourses of Dr. Taulerus, Life of Fenelon, Michael de Molinos and Thomas à Kempis* (Bristol, 1796). These books were published anonymously, but they were all by James Gough." JLPQ, I, 57n.

influence toward the end of the period of Quietist development comparable to Turford's *Grounds of a Holy Life* at its beginning. The characteristic Quietist attitude is expressed in the following quotation from it:

> We must retire from all outward objects, and silence all the desires and wandering imaginations of the mind; that in this profound silence of the whole soul, we may hearken to the ineffable voice of the Divine Teacher. We must listen with an attentive ear; for it is a still small voice. . . . But how seldom it is that the soul keeps itself silent enough for God to speak.[8]

Rufus Jones has described the influence of these continental mystics as follows:

> The Quietism of these Quaker ideals is not an exact copy of the Quietism of the continental experts. It was never a conscious imitation or the following of external teachers. It was a normal maturing and unfolding of a central religious principle—common both to Quakers and to Quietists—with a later intensification of the Quietistic tendency under the influence of religious leaders who were deeply impressed by the discovery of the writings of men and women outside their Society.[9]

In the journals of the most prominent Friends from 1737 to 1827 one finds an inner record of the development and nature of Quaker Quietism in the period when it was the dominant type. The outstanding names with the dates of birth and death are given in the following list. The ministry of some of these ran over into the next period but it seems best to treat them as representatives of Quietism here. It is difficult to get exact statistics as to the number of Friends who travelled in the ministry. Rutty's list of "Friends in the ministry" who visited Ireland 1654–1751 contains 341 names of Friends from foreign parts for the half century 1700–1750.[10] Many of these made repeated

[8] First American Ed., p. 6.

[9] JLPQ, I, 103.

[10] Rutty, *Diary*, pp. 351–363.

visits, James Dickinson recording eleven visits in his *Journal*. Sharpless gives a list of Friends from abroad who were "engaged in religious visits" in Philadelphia Yearly Meeting 1684–1773, which contains thirty-one names for the half century 1700–1750.[11] Besides these there were numbers of travelling ministers from American yearly meetings.

Some of the most noted of these were: John Rutty (1698–1775), an Irish physician whose *Diary* is a unique revelation of a Quietist's inner life; John Churchman (1705–1772); James Gough (1712–1791), translator and publisher of the works of continental mystics; John Griffith (1713–1776), New England evangelist; Samuel Fothergill (1715–1772), member of a distinguished and influential family which included his father, John Fothergill; and his brother, Dr. John Fothergill, the chief founder of Ackworth School; John Woolman (1720–1772); Catherine (Payton) Phillips (1726–1794); Richard Shackleton (1726–1792); John Pemberton (1727–1794), who died in Germany after a long ministry in the British Isles and on the Continent; Samuel Neale (1729–1791); Samuel Emlen (1730–1799); George Dillwyn (1738–1830); Rebecca Jones (1739–1817); Martha Routh (1743–1817); David Sands (1745–1818) and Thomas Scattergood (1748–1814).

In contrast with the noted figures of the preceding period, these were all born after 1700 and represent a generation that did not know the Founders in the flesh. They were all Friends by convincement in the sense that after "youthful follies," they came into a vital Quaker faith and later into the ministry after severe spiritual struggles. It is chiefly due to these men and women that Quakerism was revived, preserved and disciplined in the latter half of the eighteenth century. All of them labored among Friends in both hemispheres. Many of them carried on their ardu-

---

[11] JQAC, 540–543.

ous travels in foreign parts, especially on the Continent of Europe and the American frontier, in spite of primitive means of travel and poor accommodations, in spite of the perils of the seas, and of chronic or recurring ill-health which afflicted some of them, notably Thomas Chalkley, John Griffith, Catherine Phillips, Martha Routh and Mary Dudley. They were often absent from their families for long periods. Many of them spent a great deal of time and labor "visiting families," especially among the membership of scattered meetings in America and isolated Friends of Europe. Most of them kept intimate journals or diaries of their religious experiences and their travels, and carried on an extensive correspondence.

A few of them were Friends by convincement, notably David Sands, Mary Dudley, Rebecca Jones, Job Scott and Stephen Grellet. Many of them had an extensive ministry to non-Friends, and were filled with a genuine missionary zeal. Especially active among these were Samuel Fothergill, William Savery, Martha Routh, David Sands, Mary Dudley, Catherine Phillips, Job Scott and Thomas Shillitoe. Mostly, however, their ministry was among Friends in the established meetings, and their chief efforts were to revive the spiritual life of Friends and secure conformity to the discipline. They agonized in spirit over the seeming indifference, spiritual deadness and falling away which they sensed in many places; they wrestled with the spirit of unbelief; they waded through deep waters on behalf of the Society, besides the inward struggles to keep their own wills "pure" against the "will of the creature."

There seems a tendency in the earlier part of the period to take the neglect of the discipline and "testimonies" as evidence of a decline in religious life and interest and, toward the latter part of it, to regard conformity to the discipline as an index of reviving life. Probably both assumptions were fairly correct. John Griffith voices the common conviction of these Quietist preachers:

An earthly lofty spirit had taken too much place in some of the professors; the tendency whereof is, by darkening the understanding, and blinding the judgment, to account various weighty branches of our Christian testimony small trifling things. Here the flesh, that warreth against the spirit, having the ascendency, its language is quite opposite thereunto. The flesh saith, there is little in dress; religion doth not consist in apparel; there is little in language; there is little in paying tythes &c. to the priests; there is little in carrying guns in our ships, to defend ourselves in case we are attacked by an enemy. To which, I think, it may be safely added, there is little or nothing in people, who plead as above hinted, pretending to be of our Society; for if they can easily let fall the beforementioned branches of our Christian testimony, I am fully persuaded, they will maintain the others no longer than they apprehend it will suit with their temporal interest. I have often wondered why such continue to profess with us at all. They are not really of us who are not concerned to maintain those principles and testimonies the Lord hath given us to bear.[12]

Quaker Quietism developed a technical language, which was derived partly from the Quaker vocabulary of the Founders, partly from the continental and English Quietists and partly from the Bible.[13] The latter element came chiefly from a common symbolic use of Biblical incidents and figurative language. Some Friends (Samuel Fothergill, for example) used such language almost exclusively not only in preaching but even in correspondence. Among such expressions are the cloud remaining on the tabernacle, to withhold more than is meet, to dig for the springs, to

---

12 *Jour.*, pp. 124, 125.

13 Many of their sermons were in large part *catenae* of scripture texts loosely strung together. "Gallery Scripture" was a popular term for misquotations or citations of non-scriptural phrases as Scripture. JFHS, XXVI, 78. Comstock, *Life,* pp. 12–18. The ministers usually used an unnatural sing-song "tone." This was regarded as the proper mode of speaking under guidance. The elders sometimes encouraged a novice to speak with "unction." Kersey, *Narrative,* &c., pp. 38, 39. JFHS, XXII, 92.

turn the fleece, to run before one is sent, to outrun the Guide. Others used the more general technical Quietist vocabulary, in which the following expressions were common: to center down, to dwell deep, to be low, deep wading, "pure" leading or prayer, to be shut up or to be dry or barren, to travail with the suffering seed, to be stripped, the turnings of God's hand. A striking characteristic also is the habit of using general designations, phrases and circumlocutions instead of the words God, Lord, Christ or even the devil. One finds continually such expressions as the Creator, the Author of our being, the Source of unerring wisdom, our blessed Savior, the author of all evil, the enemy of all righteousness. In reading some of their journals and epistles one almost needs a glossary!

There was a tendency in the Society in this period to magnify silence as a form of worship and almost as an end in itself. John Griffith and Job Scott travelled extensively in the ministry and often sat in silence through meeting after meeting, explaining their being "shut up" by the need of famishing congregations who had grown too fond of words. Griffith came to feel that his mission was twofold—to reform the Society along the lines of the discipline and to teach Friends the value of silence. The silent meeting in the literal sense became the norm of worship. To "appear in" vocal prayer or testimony frequently laid one open to the suspicion of acting "in the will of the creature." Only a powerful conviction of duty laid on one could justify vocal service; and it was customary to apologize for breaking the silence. Dr. Rutty records the fact that for twenty-two consecutive meetings in Dublin, Ireland (1770) the silence was broken but once.[14] Job Scott visiting meetings in New Jersey and Pennsylvania (1785) attended fifteen meetings in twenty days not daring "to open his mouth in one of them."[15] These cases were regarded as

[14] *Diary*, p. 390.
[15] *Jour.*, p. 174 (N. Y. 1797).

exceptional, however. John Griffith gives the following fine expression of his ideal of the attitude of the worshipper.

> I was, through unspeakable kindness, when I sat down in a meeting, mostly enabled to say, "Thy will be done, whether in making use of me as thy instrument to sound an alarm to the people, or to set them an example of silent waiting upon thee." What shall I say or return to the Lord of everlasting loving-kindness for preservation, by sea and by land, in many perils; I am at a loss for expressions to set forth his bountiful goodness, and the greatness of his love and mercy to those who trust in him. I therefore humbly desire with silent reverence, or otherwise as ability is afforded, to magnify, worship and adore him, who is glorious in holiness and fearful in praises, working wonders, who alone is worthy now and evermore! Amen.[16]

Among these travelling ministers there were varying degrees of Quietistic temper. Many of them had practical concerns to which they gave themselves so steadily that they precluded extremes of introspection and the paralyzing fear of "creaturely activity." Samuel Fothergill and John Griffith had rather steady interest in the work of disciplinary reformation; Woolman was largely absorbed in his anti-slavery work. Most nearly typical of Quietist Quakerism were John Churchman, Job Scott and Thomas Shillitoe. These men sought to know the "pure" mind of God not merely in religious service but in all circumstances of life; and were especially fearful that in their religious ministry they would either be false to duty or "run ahead of their Guide" and "act in the will of the creature." The call to the ministry, each separate concern to "travel in the service of Truth," and freedom to return home when the service was complete; the choice of a travelling companion, the appointment of each meeting or family visit, whether to speak or not, and the nature of the message—the Lord's

---

[16] *Op. cit.*, 423.

servant must be "clear" as to each of these, before he could "go forward"; and often the clear intimation of duty came only after long waiting, agonizing effort or painful uncertainty. Job Scott confesses that

> in that dependent state, I often felt as empty of anything divine, any sight, sense or knowledge of things, as if I had been totally blind and insensible—and indeed who is so blind as the Lord's servant, and so deaf as the messenger whom he sends? And it is necessary it should be so, in order that his message to the people through them may be wholly in the fresh openings of divine life, without any mixture of man's fallen wisdom. . . .
>
> We were helped through to profit and relief in them all; though mostly in a way much to the subjection of our own creaturely wills. Oh! what need there is to lie low, and rise only as the pure life arises, lest we be found offering strange fire, or lifting up a tool on the Lord's altar.—Contentment in a lowly state, and moving on gently in the real necessity, is highly acceptable to him, without whom we can do nothing. Here we acknowledge his might, his right to command even faithfulness in the little, which fails not, if we rightly obey, to make us, in his own time, rulers over much.[17]

The Quietist attitude was unsuited for great spiritual building, adventure or conquest.[18] Its distrust of human nature—not merely of human sinfulness but of its frailties, finiteness, and natural faculties—tended to produce religious hesitancy and paralysis and consequently hobbled the energies of the Society. It dared not trust God's Spirit to inspire long-term plans nor to organize for vigorous spiritual conquest nor make use of all the faculties of the human mind nor trust the fruits of study and education. Even in their early philanthropies, such as the educational and religious work for the Negroes and Indians and their

---

17 *Jour.*, pp. 240, 263.

18 Cf. Rutty, *Diary*, p. 221: "So here are the pruners; but where are the waterers, planters and builders?"

interest in a scattered remnant in Europe, there was no attempt to organize for the carrying out of the individual concerns.[19]

On the positive side, however, the Quietist travelling preachers did revive and preserve the Quaker testimony, its literature and ideals. As in a cocoon, the discipline enveloped successive generations, devoted to the will of God and earnestly waiting on Him and carried over the ideals and literature of Quakerism to a more aggressive age. It developed souls of fine spiritual discernment, brave unworldliness, human tenderness and rare beauty of character. It gave some of its devotees a singularly true and helpful discernment of individual religious "states" and rare skill in "speaking to their conditions." The system or ideal which flowered in the philanthropic zeal, moral pioneering and social daring of the next period had a worthy place amid the formalities, frivolities and immoralities of the middle eighteenth century.

---

[19] Cf. Taylor, *Life of William Savery,* p. 31: "There was no attempt to organize this movement or to make it more than the operation of an individual concern." It should be noted, however, that "The Friendly Association for gaining and preserving Peace with the Indians by pacific measures" and the Tunesassa Indian mission were exceptions to the general Quietist fear of organized efforts.

Chapter 19

THE QUAKERS AMID INDIAN TROUBLES, THE REVOLUTIONARY WAR AND SLAVERY

There remain to be considered the influence of the French and Indian and Revolutionary wars upon American Friends and the work of the Friends during this period for the Indians and slaves. The development of the discipline was hastened by these events and by pioneer conditions which had delayed its serious beginnings. On the other hand, certain distinctive phases of Quaker philanthropy were developed earlier than elsewhere by the peculiar relations of the colonies to the Indians and Negro slavery.

The outbreak of the French and Indian War brought about a sharp change in the position and character of Pennsylvania Quakerism. The Indians had been alienated, the colonists on the exposed front were out of sympathy with the Quaker pacifism and Indian policy, the British government was impatiently demanding military supplies and defense measures of the colonies, and the governor declared war on the Delaware Indians. These conditions, not of their own making, placed the Quaker minority in the Assembly in an impossible position. The yearly meeting and a delegation of English Friends advised the Quaker assemblymen to resign in order to prevent the English government from imposing an oath of office which would have excluded Friends from all offices in the colonies. Most of them resigned or refused reëlection, and thus the direct participation of Friends in the colonial government practically ceased.

The opposition of Friends to war was kept alive during the colonial period by struggles against serving in the militia and by their refusal to pay war taxes. Their property was often levied on and sold for taxes or to hire substitutes. Their peace principles were put to the test afresh during the French and Indian War, and they had to turn to non-political means of working out their ideals. They closed up their ranks, revised their membership and completed their discipline.

After Friends gave up control of the Pennsylvania Assembly in 1756, they formed "The Friendly Association for gaining and preserving Peace with the Indians by pacific measures." New Jersey Friends also organized in 1757 the "New Jersey Association for Helping the Indians," which rendered effective aid to the Indians on the reservation at Brotherton, on which they were placed by treaties. The Pennsylvania Friends agreed to expend more for pacific means than war taxes would amount to. By the time peace was finally arranged the Association had expended about £5000. Its greatest work, however, was in connection with the negotiations which ended the Indian wars.

They began with the Northern Delawares under the great chief Tedyuscung, a diplomatist of no mean order when sober, and a reliable friend to the Quakers. The first conference was at Easton in 1756. Israel Pemberton, the leader of the movement, and a large number of other Friends were present, though evidently not desired by the Governor. The Indian was very plain. "This very ground that is under me [striking it with his foot] was my land and inheritance and is taken from me by fraud." He could not forget the "Walking Purchase" and the enforced emigration. All sorts of compromising suggestions were thrown in his way, but with the aid of the Friends he kept a clear course. . . . He finally got some kind of a recognition that the "walk" was unfair, was given compensation for his stolen land, and a peace was declared, cemented by the Friendly presents.

The Western Indians were also brought into peaceful lines. The Assembly was short of money, and though now not made up of Friends was thoroughly sympathetic. When the Association offered to lend them money, the House accepted the loan with thanks "for the friendly and generous offer." They sent some £2000 of goods to Pittsburgh for the Indians, and acted as agents of the British government in forwarding another consignment for the same purpose. Peace for a little time through their efforts settled down over Pennsylvania. It was a great work well done.[1]

In 1763 John Woolman, with only one companion, made a visit to an Indian village on the upper Susquehanna on a mission of peace and Christian love.[2] Friends in other colonies were not disturbed by the Indians during this period; but in Virgina in 1757 some who had settled on land not purchased from the nation fled eastward across the mountains in fear.[3] In 1763 a mob of frontiersmen, mostly Scotch Irish, massacred a small peaceable group of Conestaga Indians living in Lancaster County, Pennsylvania. The "Paxton Boys," as the mob was called, accused these Indians of giving information to the hostile tribes to the west, but the real motive was hostility to the Quakers for befriending the Indians and opposing military expenditures. The "Boys" were not brought to justice, because of public sentiment on the frontier, and they next threatened to massacre a band of Moravian Indian converts who had been brought to Philadelphia for safety. They marched to Germantown and threatened the Quakers, and especially Israel Pemberton, if they interfered. The city rose to arms to protect the Indians and after a

---

1 JQAC, 503–504. The best account of these proceedings is Thomson, *The Alienation of the Delaware and Shawnese Indians.*

2 *Jour.*, chap. VIII, pp. 186–207.

3 Reckett, *Life,* 61.

delegation led by Benjamin Franklin had negotiated with them, the invaders withdrew. Many young Friends joined the bands who rushed to arms, "and it being a cold winter day the meeting-house served as barracks, and the guns were stacked in the gallery."[4]

The conduct of these young men disturbed the Society profoundly. Philadelphia Monthly Meeting carried on proceedings against them for several years and a few acknowledged that they were in the wrong. None were disowned and some of them later came to accept the Quaker pacifist position. Others were among the "Fighting Quakers" of the Revolutionary War. "The Paxton Invasions" also gave occasion to a long pamphlet controversy between "Presbyterian" and "Quaker" sympathizers, which had now become party names, over the Quaker non-military policy. The last service of the Friendly Association was in connection with the Pontiac Wars which came to an end in 1768.

Friends continued after the French and Indian War to have an active interest in the welfare of the Indians, not alone in Pennsylvania, but in Maryland, New York and New England. All the yearly meetings gave attention to protecting and helping them. They tried to prevent their being debauched, or cheated in the courts; and some care was taken to pacify them.

The Revolutionary War brought fresh testing to Friends, especially in Pennsylvania. After Friends retired from the Assembly in 1756, there was a "Quaker party" in the colony led by James Logan, Isaac Norris 2nd and Benjamin Franklin. The Quakers, who took part in it, believed in defensive warfare, if necessary. The Revolution found this group divided. Some drew back, partly from a real preference for remaining under the Crown; others because they could not participate in war even for the ends of liberty. The most noteworthy of these was John Dickinson, who

---

[4] JQAC, pp. 506–508.

was a leader in the American cause up to the Declaration of Independence.[5]

When the Revolution began the Society rigidly maintained its testimony against war and any preparation for it, and disowned promptly all who deviated from this position. Representatives from New England, Virginia and North Carolina came to Philadelphia to consult with the yearly meeting as to the course to be pursued.[6] Friends suffered from the suspicion and hostility which always fall upon neutrals in a conflict. Their property was seized to pay for substitutes in the army and for war taxes. The Continental government arrested a number of prominent citizens of Philadelphia on suspicion of disloyalty in the fall of 1777 and sent about twenty Friends[7] who were among them to Winchester, Virginia, where they were confined through the following winter. They were returned home then with an acknowledgement of their innocence.[8]

After the British occupation of Philadelphia was over, the radical revolutionists sought vengeance on all suspected Tories including some Quakers. Two Quakers were hanged on a slightly supported charge of treason; moderates like Robert Morris, James Wilson and Thomas Mifflin barely escaped with their lives, and a mob broke Quakers' windows and hooted them in the streets. Sharpless estimates the direct property loss to Friends because of distraints and levies during the Revolution at about £50,000.[9] About 1779 the Assembly enacted a law requir-

---

[5] JQAC, pp. 559, 560. He came of Quaker ancestry and Friends furnished his fundamental philosophy of life. During his public career he was not active in the Society, and was for a time a soldier in the Continental armies. He was never disowned and in his later years he took an active part in the meeting in Wilmington, Del. He was not married after the manner of Friends but by his own request he was buried in the Friends burying ground.

[6] Bowden, *op. cit.*, II, 298–307.

[7] JQAC says 20 (p. 567); Thomas, *Hist.*, 18; and Taylor, *op. cit.*, 21. Elizabeth Drinker lists 21 (*Jour.*, pp. 45, 46).

[8] Gilpin, *Exiles in Virginia.*

[9] JQAC, 568.

ing a test oath of school teachers, which virtually shut Friends out from educating their own children. Some closed their schools; others kept them open and suffered the penalties. In smaller measure Friends in other colonies had the same experiences as in Pennsylvania.

The Friends who were disowned for participation in the war for the most part accepted the action passively. In general they had little interest in the Society in any case. A few "condemned their action" and were reinstated in membership. In Philadelphia, however, a small group formed a separate meeting, calling themselves "Free Quakers." A meeting-house was erected by popular subscription for them at Fifth and Arch Streets, but their membership gradually dwindled until the meeting in the house ceased in 1836.[10]

Beginning in 1777 Philadelphia Yearly Meeting attempted a reformation of the morals and life of its members which was carried through during the remaining years of the war. Isaac Sharpless estimates that

> the Revolutionary War left Philadelphia Yearly Meeting more moral internally, more devoted to moral reforms, more conservative of ancient tradition, customs, and doctrine, more separate from the world, more introversive in spirit, than it found it.[11]

The efforts of American Friends to get rid of slavery were due chiefly to the influence of John Woolman and a small group of kindred spirits which included Anthony Benezet, Ralph Sandiford and Benjamin Lay. As early as 1729 Sandiford had published a treatise against slavery. Benjamin Lay, an eccentric dwarf, waylaid Friends going and coming from meetings and denounced them in dramatic fashion for tolerating slavery. Benezet's influence was

---

10 Betsy Ross was the last of the original members. Cf. Wetherill, *History of the Free Quakers* (1894).

11 JQAC, 579.

largely outside the Society of Friends.[12] Between 1762 and 1771 he published three influential books on the slave trade. Philadelphia Yearly Meeting transmitted his *Caution and Warning to Great Britain and Her Colonies* to London Yearly Meeting with a request that it be circulated. His account of Guinea had a great influence in interesting Thomas Clarkson in the anti-slavery cause. Benezet corresponded extensively with influential persons at home and abroad with a view to interesting them in the anti-slavery cause. He was one of the founders and supporters of "The Society for the Relief of Free Negroes Unlawfully Held in Bondage" (1775).[13]

Woolman gave a great impetus to the anti-slavery movement by his visits to New England (1747), New York (1760), Maryland and Virginia (1746) and again to the southern colonies in 1757. In 1754 he published a pamphlet on *Considerations on the Keeping of Negroes.* At Philadelphia Yearly Meeting in 1758 he brought the question to a decisive issue. To those who would temporize or avoid the issue he said:

> My mind is led to consider the purity of the Divine Being and the justice of His judgment, and herein my soul is covered with awfulness. I cannot forbear to hint of some cases where people have not been treated with the purity of justice and the event has been most lamentable. Many slaves on this continent are oppressed and their cries have entered into the ears of the Most High. Such are the purity and certainty of His judgments that He cannot be partial in our favor. In infinite love and goodness He hath opened our understandings from one time to another concerning our duty toward this people; and it is not a time for delay. Should we now be sensible of what He requires of us, and through a respect to the private interest of some persons, or through a regard to some

---

[12] Cf. Brookes, *Friend Anthony Benezet,* chap. VI.
[13] *Quaker Biographies,* III, 94.

friendships which do not stand upon an immutable foundation, neglect to do our duty in firmness and constancy, still waiting for some extraordinary means to bring about their deliverance, God may by terrible things in righteousness answer us in this matter.[14]

This appeal was followed by a lengthy minute which earnestly advised Friends individually who owned slaves to free them, "making a Christian provision" for them, appointed a committee of which John Woolman was named first, to visit and treat with slave-holding Friends; and advised the monthly meetings not to allow recalcitrant Friends to sit in business meetings or "to be employed in the affairs of Truth" or to receive from them any contributions for the relief of the poor or any other services of the meeting. The yearly meeting patiently renewed its pressure again and again until in 1776 it directed that those who persisted in holding slaves be disowned. By 1780 no slaves were held by members of the yearly meeting except in cases where legal difficulties prevented manumission.

Friends of other yearly meetings moved in a parallel way. In 1758 and again in 1769 New England Yearly Meeting adopted strong minutes against slave-holding. In 1772 it was directed that slave-holders be disowned, and by 1782 no slaves were held by New England Friends. In New York it became a disciplinary offense to buy, sell or hold slaves in 1776. North Carolina took similar action the same year; Baltimore followed the next year and Virginia in 1784.

By the close of the eighteenth century there was not a slave in the possession of a Friend in good standing except where slaves were held by trustees, and state laws did not allow them to be set free.[15]

---

14 JQAC, 517.
15 Thomas, *Hist.*, p. 115.

The emancipation of the slaves was always accompanied and followed by provision for their economic welfare and efforts to educate them.[16]

The liberation of the Society from the curse of human slavery was chiefly due to the devoted efforts of John Woolman. His faith in "that of God" in all men made the Negro slave seem worthy and capable of full human freedom and opportunity, and it also gave him a working confidence in the possibility of convincing the slave-holders of the wrong of slavery and leading them to free their slaves voluntarily. He commended and practiced a new method of moral and social progress—the voluntary abdication of privilege from Christian motives by the exploiting classes. Unlike the later Abolitionists he did not denounce the slave-holders as essentially brutal nor try to impose abolition on them against their will by political and military force; nor did he rely on the class struggle of the exploited to wrest their rights from their oppressors. He laid the question of the righteousness of slavery before "the Light of Christ" within them and left them to answer, not to John Woolman but to God. He bore his testimony to its unchristian character by sincere living as well as by tender words.

Woolman's philanthropy was broader than the anti-slavery movement. His love of men and faith in them operated in all the relations of life. He would not add to his own enjoyment by diminishing the sweetness of life of any of God's creatures. Ending his days in England (1772), he had a foreboding of the inhumanities of the impending industrial revolution and characteristically addressed a *Word of Caution and Admonition to the Rich* to use their wealth and social and political power in Christian and humane ways.[17]

---

16 In 1770 Philadelphia Monthly Meeting established a "School for Black People and their Descendants." *Quaker Biographies,* III, 96.

17 The original title was *A Plea for the Poor.* Cf. Gummere, *The Journal and Essays of John Woolman,* p. 402.

He was the "fine consummate flower" of Quaker Quietism. He felt a sympathy with the mystics of all ages and felt especially near Meister Eckhart and the author of *The Imitation of Christ*. He pursued his work from no social or political theory but from careful attention to the "Inward Guide." He limited a growing business in order to be free to travel in the service of Truth. He waited carefully for an inward call before any undertaking or any religious mission, and at each step waited for inward assurance before he spoke or acted. His simple and sincere *Journal* has extended his influence far beyond the Society of Friends.

Period III

Philanthropy and the Transition to Evangelicalism 1784-1827

Chapter 20

QUAKER PHILANTHROPY

The sub-division of the Age of Quietism, which was *par excellence* the period of philanthropy, extended from 1784 to 1828. The disciplinary period in America was shortened partly because the continued growth of the Society in the early eighteenth century did not allow its crystallization quite so early as in England; and partly because, when the disciplinary crystallization did start in America, it had the advantage of the example of some twenty years' development in England. In America the disciplinary and the philanthropic periods partly overlapped, due perhaps to the fact that the practice of Negro slavery and the problems of the Indians kept alive and stimulated the philanthropic spirit.

Though the interests and activities of Friends were pretty well limited by Quietism and its traditions, happily they had traditions which justified philanthropic labors without stirring up the bogey of "creaturely activity." The principles of Friends in the early days had always involved them in social interests and obligations. The doctrine of the potential divine sonship of all men provided for large social applications of Christianity. George Fox and his co-workers had early manifested interest in the disinherited, disabled and down-trodden people; they had an intimate knowledge of prisons and prisoners during the persecutions of the first period; from the first they were opposed to war, and suffered for their unwillingness to participate in warlike measures. This pacifist attitude was kept alive and Friends' sufferings were increased because both England and America were involved in wars almost continually from 1755 to 1815.

The rich flowering of humanitarian interests in this period was due fundamentally to the Quaker concepts of God's universal love and the supreme worth and potential divine sonship of all men. But these were held in earlier periods. The mystic worship of the Friends meeting even in its quietist forms seems to have been an important influence. Since the "silent meeting" and the passion for human welfare went hand in hand, it is natural to infer that there was a causal connection between them; that the exceptional way of worship was in large measure responsible for the exceptionally high average of Quaker pioneers in philanthropy and social reforms. The connection is too close for mere coincidence. The silent meeting constituted a favorable nursery for sensitive spirits who "felt their brother's pain and sorrow as their own." The attitude of waiting on God alone fostered personal responsibility and initiative; it did not blunt the growing points of the soul by regimentation nor drown the still small voice by outward voices nor distract attention from the motions of the Spirit by too constant outward exercises. It emancipated the will in unusual measure from the thralldom of custom and public opinion. In the group worship and business meetings the individual life was enriched by the pooling of experience and collective wisdom.

Quaker susceptibility to new social situations and new human needs was increased in this period by additions to its membership by convincement. These new members brought fresh points of view and ways of thought, coming as they did from different backgrounds. A number of these influences were of French origin. Anthony Benezet (1713–1784) was a native of France, born in a Huguenot family which escaped to Philadelphia in 1731 by way of Holland and England. He became a Friend by "convincement" when quite young but there is no record of the date when he joined the Society.[1] He was a valuable teacher in the William Penn Charter School (1742–1755) and afterward established a private girls' school. He reformed educational methods, wrote textbooks, and gave a new impetus to education among Friends. In his influence on the anti-slavery movement in the Society, he was second only to John Woolman. Another Huguenot influence came through the family of William Savery. Two generations after the revocation of the Edict of Nantes (1685) his father, already a Quaker, established himself as a cabinet maker in Philadelphia. More important was the influence of Stephen Grellet, a French nobleman and refugee from the Revolution. Concerning his attitude and influence Taylor remarks:

> These French immigrants carried with them a glamor and romance, born of suffering and exile, that caught the imagination of all classes. Especially was this the case with exiled nobility of whom Stephen Grellet was typical. With world problems pressing for solution on a mammoth scale and on every hand, it was only probable that the concerned members among Friends should first endeavor to make clear their own action and then carry to the world the Gospel message that appeared to them all sufficient, in itself, for the healing of the nations.[2]

A number of influential men and women were converts from other denominations in mature life. Although

---

[1] Brookes, *Friend Anthony Benezet,* p. 23.

[2] Taylor, *Life of William Savery,* p. 31.

these conformed with the zeal of proselytes to the outward ways and Quietist attitudes of Friends, they inevitably brought a knowledge of the outside political and religious world, usually denied to birthright Friends; and there persisted in them ways of religious thought and standards of value, interests and susceptibilities hardly to be found among the birthright members. They more or less unconsciously gave new meanings to the Quietist words and phrases. Among these who became ministers were, in addition to those already mentioned, David Sands, a former Presbyterian, Rebecca Jones from the Church of England, Mary Dudley who came from the Church of England by way of Methodism, Thomas Shillitoe whose family were Anglicans, Job Scott who, although a birthright Friend, had been under the influence of the Baptists, together with Joseph Lancaster the educator and Daniel Wheeler, both from the Church of England. Certain "gay" Friends who became "plain" Friends by conviction, had been subjected to broadening influences by educational and social contacts, such as Elizabeth Fry, and her brother, Joseph John Gurney.

Association with non-Friends in the promotion of educational and philanthropic causes, brought a number of leading Friends in England into close contact with Evangelicals of the Church of England. Such were Clarkson, Wilberforce and Buxton in the Anti-slavery cause; Bishop Bathhurst, Henry Venn, Charles Simeon and others in the British and Foreign Bible Society; and others of less influence in education and prison reform. The effects of this Evangelical influence will be treated in the next chapter. A liberalizing influence came also through a group of Quaker scientists, such as Dr. Rutty of Ireland, Dr. John Fothergill, William Allen, and John Dalton.

In England Anti-slavery sentiment was slow in developing since slavery was not a pressing domestic problem. The

Anti-slavery movement which developed during this period was not initiated by Friends. None of the great leaders, Clarkson, Wilberforce and Buxton was a member of the Society, although T. Fowell Buxton's mother was a Friend and he married Hannah Gurney, sister of J. J. Gurney and Elizabeth Fry. His sister married William Forster, who first interested Buxton in the Anti-slavery cause. Clarkson first became interested in the slave trade through Benezet's *An Historical Account of Guinea.* Wilberforce and Buxton used their influence as members of Parliament effectively on behalf of the abolition of slavery.

Individual Friends gave vigorous aid to these leaders and London Yearly Meeting threw the whole weight of its influence in favor of the movement after 1784. In 1727 it had censured the slave trade and in 1758 it warned its members against reaping profits from "the iniquitous practice." The influence of American Friends was an important factor in creating this interest. Woolman's influence is shown in the London epistles of 1772 and 1774; and in 1783 at the urgent request of Philadelphia Yearly Meeting, London petitioned Parliament to stop the exportation of Negro slaves from Africa; and by 1787 no slaves were owned by any British Friend in good standing.[3] In 1805 a bill for the abolition of the slave trade failed of passage in the House of Commons by only seven votes; but two years later Parliament prohibited the importation of slaves into the British colonies after March 1, 1808—the same year that the United States Congress abolished the slave trade.

Then began the more difficult task of abolishing slavery in the British dominions. William Forster called upon Buxton to become the advocate of the slave on his election to Parliament in 1818. Six years later the aging Wilberforce called upon Buxton to assume the leadership of the

[3] Clarkson, *History of the Abolition of the Slave Trade,* I, 146.

Anti-slavery movement. The year before London Yearly Meeting had opened the struggle for abolition by a petition to the House of Commons which was presented by Wilberforce. Joseph Sturge now took up the championship of the cause within the Society as well as through the Anti-slavery Society. He was for immediate and total abolition of slavery; for to him it was not fundamentally a question of political expediency but of moral principle. In 1830 the yearly meeting directed the Meeting for Sufferings to petition Parliament "for the immediate and total abolition of slavery in the British dominions." The matter was delayed by the great agitation over the Reform Bill; but the year after its passage (in 1832) the Abolition Bill was adopted. It freed between 700,000 and 800,000 slaves, but was marred by provision for a system of apprenticeship for seven years before abolition became complete. It was not until 1838 that, under the leadership of Joseph Sturge, the apprenticeship system was abolished.

During this period Indian troubles on the northwest frontier again called for the services of American Friends. The Treaty of Fort Stanwix in 1768 had fixed the boundary between the whites and Indians at the Ohio river. Settlers pressed beyond it, however, and located in western Pennsylvania and Ohio. The national government was unwilling or unable to prevent these encroachments and the Indians resorted to attacks on the border settlements. Two expeditions which were sent to punish the hostile tribes met defeat. In 1793 and 1794 efforts were made to negotiate peace with the northwestern tribes and the Iroquois. At the request of the Indians and the government, Philadelphia Yearly Meeting appointed five delegates, of whom William Savery is best known, to attend the conferences in the interest of fair play and conciliation.

The first conference, which was held at Sandusky proved fruitless. The situation had greatly changed since the days of Penn. The government was willing to buy the Indians' lands, but the latter were no longer willing to sell. Their hunting-grounds were already greatly reduced, they maintained, and there was no room for them westward. The Friends had no other basis for a treaty to offer. All parties were confronted with the irresistible land hunger of Europe. The second conference at Canandaigua ended in a compromise treaty, to which the Iroquois acceded only because news had come of General Wayne's victory over the northwestern Indian coalition.

Out of these Quaker embassies there arose in the minds of Friends the plan of educating, civilizing and Christianizing the Indians.[4] In 1795 a committee was appointed, which undertook a definite work of this character. After a preliminary experiment on the Oneida reservation in New York State, the work was transferred to the Senecas and finally the mission station was located at Tunesassa in 1804,[5] where a large farm was purchased and schools for boys and girls were established which are still maintained by Philadelphia Yearly Meeting (O). This undertaking stimulated efforts to aid the Indians by other yearly meetings. New England undertook work for the Indians in Maine; New York supported work for the Brotherton Indians in New Jersey and the Onondaga tribe in New York. Baltimore directed its efforts toward the restriction of the sale of alcoholic liquors to the Indians in northeastern Ohio, and finally undertook a mission for the Shawnees at Wapakoneta (near Lewistown, Ohio) similar to that at Tunesassa. Later when Ohio and Indiana yearly meetings were "set up," they joined in the support of this work, which was only discontinued in 1832 when the Shawnee Indians were removed to a new reservation in the state of Kansas.

This period witnessed some significant gains in Quaker

---

[4] Taylor, *op. cit.*, pp. 154, 155.

[5] Thomas gives the date as 1803. *Hist.*, p. 111. Cf. Kelsey, *Friends and the Indians*, pp. 97, 98.

education. In England Friends schools had come to be largely schools for the well-to-do. A great many families were wealthy enough to hire tutors for their children; but there was need for schools for the children of the less favored. The new philanthropic and educational interest in England led to the establishment of Ackworth School for them (1779). This was largely due to the interest and efforts of Dr. John Fothergill, brother of Samuel and a prominent member of a family which powerfully influenced the course of Quaker history in the eighteenth century. He was a member of a committee appointed by London Yearly Meeting in 1777 to take forward steps for the education of the children of Friends not in affluent circumstances.[6] Friends acquired a building originally constructed for another purpose which was large enough to house three hundred children, and the school was opened in 1779. The school fee was fixed at eight pounds a year including board and clothes. Pupils were received at seven years of age and returned home at thirteen. The curriculum consisted at first of "reading, writing and arithmetic for the boys and for the girls the addition of necessary female employments." It was not until after 1800 that geography and grammar were added. It was considered by many Friends a most revolutionary movement and was criticized sharply, but its success silenced its critics. The style of the building had a marked influence on the architecture of later buildings for Quaker boarding schools, notably Haverford College, New Garden (N. C.) Boarding School, and Friends Boarding School (Richmond, Ind.).

Friends made a significant contribution to popular education both in England and America through the work of Joseph Lancaster (1778–1838). Education in England was, until late in the nineteenth century, essentially aristocratic,

---

[6] See Fothergill's account in *A Letter to a Friend in the Country Relative to the Intended School at Ackworth,* London, 1778.

the perquisite of the privileged classes. Lancaster's work began at the neglected end of the social scale. He was born in London and was fond of reading the Bible from childhood. At fourteen years of age Clarkson's *Essay on Slavery* inspired him to go to Jamaica to teach the Bible to the Negroes, but he returned to London at his mother's urgent request. His parents were not Friends and he did not join the Society until after his educational work developed. At twenty he began a school for neighboring children in his parents' home. He fitted up a schoolroom with his own hands and soon had a hundred pupils. He received many children of poor parents without fees. He devised the monitorial system by which the older and more advanced pupils oversaw and taught the others because he was unable to hire assistants. His school grew so large that he had to build a building for it; then from 300 pupils it increased to 800 boys and 200 girls. In the period of depression during the Napoleonic wars he had to provide food for the children of suffering families which he was able to do by the aid of Peter Bedford and other Friends.

Lancaster proved to be an impractical enthusiast, however. He was vain and irresponsible; he quarreled with his friends and finally faced a debtor's prison. Joseph Fox, William Allen and other Friends then formed an organization to promote his work and paid his debts amounting to £5000.

The educational movement which he started grew rapidly, however, under the management of Friends and with royal patronage so that it attracted wide attention. His ideas and methods of cheap, popular education spread rapidly through England and extended to Ireland and even to America, to which Lancaster himself removed in 1818. His system was later opposed in England in the interest of sectarian education, chiefly by representatives of the National Church. His most valuable educational work was in popularizing the idea of educating the children of the poorer classes in England and other countries. The Royal Lancasterian Society was finally absorbed into the non-Anglican British and Foreign School Society which continued to promote popular education. The National Society did a similar work under Anglican auspices.

One of Lancaster's helpers, Dr. Thomas Pole of Bristol, began at the Friars Meeting House in Bristol a school for women, as part of a scheme of adult religious education. Within two years the Bristol schools had grown to 1500 men and women and the movement spread through the central and northern counties of England and into Ireland. The work was quite limited in character since pupils could remain in the schools only until they could read the Bible, but it was a precursor of the later Adult School Movement.[7]

The Friends of Philadelphia Yearly Meeting began to improve the education of their children about the close of the Revolutionary War. The city children were already fairly well provided for, but the children of the country Friends were neglected. A concern for them took hold of the yearly meeting in 1779, as a result of a passage in the London epistle, which led to the appointment of a committee on education. Owen Biddle, George Dillwyn who had recently visited Ackworth, and John Dickinson, who gave the first large contribution toward the project, were leaders in working out the plan for a boarding school for boys and girls which was finally opened at Westtown, Pa. in 1799. Moses Brown of Rhode Island was active in interesting Owen Biddle and other Philadelphia Friends in this plan. Meanwhile he pushed plans for a boarding school for New England Friends, which, after an abortive attempt at Portsmouth, R. I. in 1784–1788, led to the establishment of the New England Boarding School at Providence, R. I. in 1819, which now bears his name.

---

7 JLPQ, II, 678, 679.

In New York City a group of Quaker women formed an association for the relief of the poor, which opened a public school in 1801 for poor children of the unchurched who were not eligible for admission to any of the charity schools of the city. Later the city took over the management and support of these schools. The Public School Society, which became the parent of the New York City free public schools, owed its inception in 1805 to two Friends, Thomas Eddy and John Murray.[8] A school on the Lancasterian model was established in Philadelphia in 1809 on the initiative of Thomas Scattergood. After nine years it became a school for Negro children.[9]

About 1776 the Friends became interested in the condition of prisons and the welfare of the prisoners. The Philadelphia Society for Relieving Distressed Prisoners was organized in Philadelphia, but the Revolutionary War so overshadowed other interests that it did not bear important fruit at the time. However, in 1787 the Society was reorganized and undertook the administration of the Walnut Street Prison in Philadelphia in 1790. The revival of interest in the prisons was due to a general situation. When William Penn founded the colony, there were more than two hundred capital offenses under English law. In America and especially in Pennsylvania the number of capital crimes was enormously reduced. Under the old regime the jail was merely a place of detention, not of punishment. Punishments under the early English laws were largely what were called "bloody punishments." Criminals were flogged, mutilated, put in stocks, transported, branded, hung or even drawn and quartered. There was a strong movement in the latter half of the eighteenth century to abolish these tortures. The Constitution of the United States forbade "cruel and unusual punishments."

[8] Wood, W. H. S., *Friends in the City of New York*, pp. 29–31. Cf. JLPQ, II, 686.

[9] Scattergood, Thomas, *Jour.*, pp. 460, 461.

The abolition of the "bloody" punishments and the substitution of fines and prison sentences made the jail more and more a place of punishment and therefore a place of residence. This created a new interest in the prisons, which had never been designed for human habitation.[10] Sensitive souls realized the inhumanity of sentencing people to live for long periods in the existing horrible conditions.

John Howard's earlier work had marked an advance in prison reform in which he had the aid of Friends, especially of Dr. John Fothergill and a few travelling ministers such as Catherine Phillips who had visited prisons in America in 1754–1755.[11] The Walnut Street Prison was intended to be primarily a place of reformation and was called a "penitentiary." Each cell opened out into a little garden and on the inside into a central court where a guard could oversee the occupant. Each of the prisoners was given some useful occupation. The solitary confinement was in order to give them opportunity to meditate and so to lead to "penitence." These arrangements and ideals were far ahead of the ideals and practices of the time.

Stephen Grellet became interested in the Philadelphia ideas of prison reform and on his extensive travels in the ministry, he visited prisons both in America and in Europe. In 1813 he visited Newgate Prison in London in company with Peter Bedford and William Forster, who had already begun religious work for the prisoners. They were shocked by the horrible conditions prevalent. Grellet went to Elizabeth Fry to get help in providing clothes for destitute children whose mothers were imprisoned there.[12] She became interested in the inmates; she secured work for the prison-

---

10 Robinson, L. N., *Penology in the United States,* pp. 70, 71.

11 *Memoirs,* pp. 106, 131.

12 Authorities differ as to the primary responsibility for interesting Elizabeth Fry in the case. Grellet claims to have done so. *Mem.,* I, 224. Hare (*The Gurneys of Earlham*), p. 257 and JLPQ, I, 350 give William Forster the credit. The *Life of Elizabeth Fry,* edited by her daughters (p. 179) and Forster's *Memoirs,* edited by Seebohm (I, 142) are indecisive.

ers, organized them under monitors of their own choosing to keep order, arranged classes for instruction and came regularly to read the Bible to them herself. To her the prisoners were human beings worthy of Christian care. In 1817 she organized an association for the improvement of female prisoners in Newgate. Her account of the Newgate experiment and other writings gave great impetus to prison reform. After she had convinced the officials that this was practical, she made journeys about England and later on the Continent, advising the education and better treatment of prisoners, and suggesting means to accomplish it. Her work was ably supported by prominent Friends, especially by her brother, J. J. Gurney and by William and Anna Forster and T. Fowell Buxton. After Margaret Fell, Elizabeth Fry was probably the greatest woman the Quaker movement has produced.[13]

Friends pioneered also in the intelligent and humane care of the insane. One of the first efforts to treat the insane as sick people was in Philadelphia. In 1709 Philadelphia Monthly Meeting took steps toward the establishment of a hospital for the sick and insane, which finally bore fruit in the Pennsylvania Hospital in 1757. Benjamin Franklin and Dr. Benjamin Rush were largely influential in the final success of this effort, but they had the active support of Friends who were the largest contributors to the fund for building the Hospital and who have always constituted a majority of the Board of Managers.[14]

In 1796 the "Retreat" just outside the city of York was founded for the care of the insane. The occasion was the case of a woman Friend confined in an establishment for insane persons near York. Her relatives and friends were not allowed to visit her and she soon died. Dr. William Tuke was led by the incident to plan a place under the care of Friends where more humane and milder treatment

---

13 Cf. Whitney, *Elizabeth Fry: Quaker Heroine.*

14 JLPQ, I, 371 n.

could be used and attempts at cure practiced.[15] The results were so gratifying that the idea spread rapidly. Up to that time the insane had been feared and abused as demon-possessed people; they were often kept in prisons with criminals or chained in mad-houses. A similar institution was the Frankford Asylum which was opened near Philadelphia by Friends in 1813 in consequence of a proposal made to the yearly meeting in 1811 by Thomas Scattergood who had visited the Retreat in York.[16]

An account of the Quaker philanthropy of this period would be incomplete without some notice of a group of English and American men and women, who shared in practically all the great humanitarian movements of their time. The work of some of these Friends has already been mentioned—e.g., Elizabeth Fry, Thomas Scattergood, William Tuke and Joseph Lancaster—and a future chapter will deal with the work and influence of J. J. Gurney. The English Quaker philanthropists were closely associated with a group of American Friends of similar interests, which included George Dillwyn, Samuel Emlen, Stephen Grellet, Rebecca Jones, John Pemberton, William Savery, Samuel Smith, and Nicholas Waln. Rebecca Jones was in a sense the center of the Philadelphia group and she had wide contacts with English Friends. She began attending a Friends meeting in Philadelphia when but a child. She was powerfully influenced by Catherine Payton Phillips, whom she heard when in her 'teens. She later travelled in the ministry, spending over four years (1784–1788) in the British Isles, becoming especially attached to certain women ministers there, Mary Dudley, Sarah R. Grubb, Hannah Cathrall, Mary Peisley, Christiana Hustler, Margaret Routh and Esther Tuke. During her later life, she was a semi-invalid, but kept up an extensive correspond-

[15] Tuke, *Description of the Retreat, An Institution near York for Insane Persons of the Society of Friends* &c., Phila., 1813, pp. 18, 19.

[16] Cf. *Friends Asylum for the Insane*, Phila., 1913.

ence with the travelling Friends in England and America. Like a second Margaret Fell her home was a center of the activities and interests of the Society. She kept in touch with the leaders in their travels and at home and gave them advice and encouragement; she served as the distributor of charitable funds for many Friends in Philadelphia and interested herself in reviving Bible reading and providing Bibles for poor Friends.

These philanthropic Friends reached the stage of organized concerns and coöperation with non-Friends in humanitarian reforms. English Friends led the way in these methods, especially in the Anti-slavery cause.

Not only did London Yearly Meeting, through its committees, engage directly in anti-slavery work, but the individual Friends began to agitate outside of the Society and in company with people of other denominations. Wilberforce and Clarkson, though not Quakers, were so closely in accord with the Quaker position, that they almost seem to be so.

The incidental importance of this agitation was twofold. Within the Society were developed independent committees or associations that carried on reform work, whether or not the Yearly Meeting as a whole approved. By this means progress was possible, even though official Quakerdom (which in those days was much narrower in personnel) did not go along, and that, too, in the name of the Society. This method became very common in America where the splits, diversities and divisions were much more pronounced than in England. Only in our own day has the influence of these collateral organizations waned, as they tend, one after another, to merge their work with a willing official body that in less favored days spurned such unauthorized and creaturely activity.[17]

Perhaps the most versatile and widely influential of the English group was William Allen (1770–1844). After the usual spiritual struggles of adolescence, during which he was at one time greatly helped by the counsel of Rebecca

---

[17] Taylor, *op. cit.*, pp. 378, 379.

Jones of Philadelphia, he came into a dedicated life. His primary concern was always for his spiritual duties with which he allowed none of his other interests to interfere. Like John Woolman he renounced the hope of riches for the sake of his religious and humanitarian interests.[18] His passion for mankind grew out of his religion. At eighteen he became deeply interested in the Anti-slavery movement and became later a lifelong friend and co-worker with Clarkson and Wilberforce. For forty-three years he went without sugar, because it was a product of slave labor, and he only resumed its use when the Abolition Bill was passed in 1833. At twenty-two he entered thc Plow Court Chemical firm and undertook to become a scientist. He became a lecturer on chemistry at Guy's Hospital in 1802 and a Fellow of the Royal Society in 1807.

In 1812 when there was great distress among the unemployed silk weavers of Spitalfields, a London suburb, because the Napoleonic Wars cut off the silk supply from Italy and the East, he joined with Peter Bedford and others in organizing "soup kitchens" to aid the starving weavers. He gave a great deal of time to the Lancastrian Schools, in which he became associated with the Duke of Kent. The latter was so impressed with his financial ability that he asked him to undertake the management of his embarrassed finances. William Allen worked out a plan by which the duke was able to live within his income and pay off his debts. He was the founder of the distinguished quarterly journal *The Philanthropist* (1811), and in 1814 formed a partnership with Robert Owen and others to buy the New Lanark cotton mills to carry out on a larger scale an advanced scheme for the improvement of the condition of factory laborers.

---

18 He refused a contract to supply the Russian army with drugs. Cf. Robinson, *Friends of a Half-Century,* p. 23.

In 1818 he went with Stephen Grellet on a religious visit to various countries in Europe including Russia where they had a memorable interview with the Czar. William Allen had already become acquainted with the Czar Alexander in London in 1814 and had gone with him to a Friends meeting. They talked of spiritual religion; he asked their advice about prison reforms; and the interview ended with a silent meeting and prayer. They had opportunities to advise Russian officials about religious education and the use of the Bible. William Allen remained a lifelong friend of the Czar and made in all seven journeys to the Continent.

Among other causes to which he devoted time and thought were the abolition of capital punishment, civilizing the American Indians, Sunday schools, the British and Foreign Bible Society, peace, and the Religious Tract Society. In his later life he was much occupied with an agricultural colony in Sussex, with proper housing, gardens and industrial schools. In much of his philanthropic work, especially that growing out of conditions in Spitalfields, he was closely associated with Peter Bedford, and with William Forster, who devoted himself to helping the poor and improving the condition of prisoners, in whose religious needs he, like Stephen Grellet, was deeply interested.

Peter Bedford (1780–1864) was a neighbor and associate of William Allen in most of his undertakings and, like him, a devoted Christian. He was a silk manufacturer and devoted much time and money to alleviating the condition of the workers in Spitalfields which was a typical manufacturing slum. He turned his attention to the problem of juvenile delinquents, to the education and training of the children of the poor, and to the reform of the criminal code and especially to efforts to abolish capital punishment. Together with William Allen and others he organized the "Spitalfields Soup Association and the Association for the Relief of Distress among the Industrious Poor."[19]

---

[19] Cf. Tallack, *Peter Bedford the Spitalfields Philanthropist*. The Bedford Institutes, named for him, still carry on work in that area for the working class. JLPQ, I, 349n.

Chapter 21

THE GREAT WESTWARD MIGRATIONS

FRIENDS in America have been a migratory people. It is not merely that their excess population has followed the frontier and that in the newly settled regions Quaker ministers and missionaries have made converts and established new meetings as other denominations have done; large sections of the Society have migrated from one section of the country to another—sometimes almost in a body—resulting in a great loss of members, meetings and meeting-houses in the older regions, and putting a great strain upon the financial means of Friends to build new homes, meeting-houses and schools in the new communities. Many members have been lost to the Society in these migrations because they settled in neighborhoods where no other Friends came. The Society has suffered also from the loss of the settled traditions and local interest of the older meetings,[1] while gaining, on the other hand, freedom from the dead hand of the past.

Mention has been made already of certain migrations of Friends from New Jersey, Pennsylvania and New England, beginning about 1725.[2] An important section of these migrants came from New England communities which had been largely dependent on the whale fisheries, such as New Bedford and Nantucket Island. A large proportion of these Friends moved southward, settling in Virginia, North Carolina and South Carolina. Later in the century there

[1] Cf. Forster, *Mem.*, I, 333.

[2] Above chap. 16, pp. 201, 202.

was a great movement of population from New England, eastern New York and central Pennsylvania into the western part of the two last-named states, that carried many Friends with it. In New York these settlements of Friends followed the upper Hudson and the Mohawk valleys. The migrations into western New York and Canada began about 1790 when Abraham Lapham moved from East Hoosac Monthly Meeting (Adams, Mass.) to the Genesee Tract west of Seneca Lake, against the vigorous protest of his meeting. Others followed within the next two decades. Monthly meetings were established as follows: Farmington, 1803; Scipio, 1808; De Ruyter, 1809; Hamburg, 1814; Junius, 1815; Collins, 1820; Hector, 1821; Rochester, 1825, and Elba, 1837.

This Quaker migration crossed early into Canada. Adolphus Preparative Meeting was set up in Upper Canada in 1798 and other Quaker meetings appeared rapidly along the border.[3] The western movement continued on both sides of the border until it reached as far as Raisin Valley, Michigan. In 1827 the three western quarterly meetings in the United States and Canada—Farmington (1810), Scipio (1825) and Canada requested New York Yearly Meeting that they might form a new yearly meeting to be called "Ontario Yearly Meeting." There were at that time about 4300 Friends in Farmington and Scipio quarters alone.[4] The distractions and division of forces of the separation of 1828 put an end to this plan.

Many of the settlers in western New York had already been pioneer settlers or were children of pioneers in eastern New York or in New England, who felt the "curse of the wandering foot," which afflicted generations of Americans

---

[3] On account of the interruption of communications between Canadian and New York Friends during the War of 1812, Hamburg Monthly Meeting was established for New York Friends who had formerly belonged to Pelham Monthly Meeting in Canada.

[4] JLPQ, I, 433.

unable to resist the lure and promise of the unknown West. One result of the rapid growth of the Quaker population of western New York was the depletion or complete extinction of older meetings in western New England or eastern New York, such as Peach Pond (N. Y.) and North Adams (Mass.).

During the latter years of the eighteenth century the opening up of western Pennsylvania attracted great numbers of Quaker settlers, many of whom came from Maryland and northern Virginia. Redstone Quarterly Meeting (near Uniontown, Pa.), comprising meetings on both sides of the Monongahela River, was established in 1797 and became the distributing center for the subsequent westward migrations into the Ohio valley. Up to this time these movements had been largely motivated by the spirit of adventure and the desire for economic betterment. Joshua Evans, who visited the Monongahela settlers in 1797 wrote:

> It seems to me they have in too general a way come over the western mountains to settle, for the sake of this world's treasure. Many of them appear to have obtained this, and are eagerly pursuing after more. Their minds are so overcharged with cares of this kind, that the better part hath been wounded, both in parents and children. A great part of their conversation is about *more land, new countries, and the things of this world.* I laboured to turn their minds to a consideration of their latter end.[5]

Attempts were made by Friends both in New York and North Carolina to discourage these removals, but with no final success.[6] By an arrangement between Philadelphia and Baltimore yearly meetings, Friends west of the Susquehanna had been transferred to Baltimore in 1789. These migrations, as a whole, resulted in declining country meetings in the older Quaker centers, and in an almost contin-

---

[5] *Journal,* in *Friends Miscellany,* X, 183.

[6] JLPQ, I, 401, 404, 431.

ued loss of members in the eastern meetings throughout the nineteenth century.

The second great migration of Friends occurred chiefly in the early nineteenth century, when great numbers of Friends removed from Virginia and the Carolinas into the Northwest Territory in order to escape from the influence of slavery and to obtain better lands. The position of Friends in the slave-holding states was rendered more and more difficult after they ceased to hold slaves. As the importance of slavery increased in the economic and social life of the South after the invention of the cotton gin, legislation was enacted making it more difficult for Friends to free their slaves and for free Negroes to keep their freedom. Friends came to be looked upon by their slave-holding neighbors as an alien and hostile influence in their social system. It became more and more difficult for them to support themselves in a slave-holding society, which put a social stigma upon manual labor; and to bring up their children according to their principles in such an environment.

The establishment of the Northwest Territory in 1787 as free territory from which slavery was forever excluded, offered Friends an opportunity to escape from this situation without too great material sacrifices, for the losses involved in selling their farms and the cost and perils of the long journey to the new territory were compensated by the great natural resources and wonderful fertility of the soil in the Ohio valley.[7]

Before this movement got fully under way there was a small migration from North Carolina over the Appalachian mountains into the valley of east Tennessee. The Lost Creek settlement began in 1784. In spite of efforts of the home meetings to discourage the movement, Friends continued to move to the Tennessee valleys.[8] In 1805 William

[7] For a statement of motives, see the letter of Borden Stanton in *Friends Miscellany*, XII, 216–219. Cited in JLPQ, I, 406–408.

[8] See Weeks, *Southern Quakers and Slavery*, p. 252.

Williams visited upward of fifty families in Lost Creek Monthly Meeting. Lost Creek Quarter including ten local meetings had been set up by North Carolina Yearly Meeting in 1802.[9]

The first Friend to explore the region north of the Ohio River seems to have been Thomas Beals from Western Quarterly Meeting in North Carolina who became interested in the new country through a visit to the Indians of the Northwest in 1777[10] in company with William Robinson and two other Friends. He removed with his family to Ohio in 1779. In 1796 George Harlan moved to Ohio and in 1797 Jesse Baldwin and Phineas Hunt followed. Soon after this the trails northward were pretty well blazed and the trek of Friends to the northwest set in in full force. Sometimes it involved whole communities. In 1799 John Dew returned to his home meeting, Trent River Monthly Meeting in North Carolina, from exploring the Ohio region and prophesied to his neighbors: "I see the seed of God sown in abundance, extending far northwestward." The members decided it would be right for them to move to the free territory. After obtaining the consent of Contentnea Quarterly Meeting, they closed the records of their meeting and moved to Redstone, where they deposited their certificates of membership, before moving on into eastern Ohio and settling at Short Creek in 1800.[11] In less than a year two preparative meetings and Concord Monthly Meeting were established.

Similar movements spread through the slaveholding states. Zachariah Dix, a member of New Garden Monthly Meeting in North Carolina, in 1803 travelled extensively among Friends in South Carolina and Georgia. He had

---

9 Now Friendsville Quarterly Meeting. It was transferred to Wilmington Yearly Meeting in 1897. These remote settlements of Friends were visited by Joshua Evans in 1797 and Stephen Grellet in 1799.

10 Levi Coffin, *Rem.*, p. 10. Gilpin, *Exiles in Virginia,* p. 183. Dr. Harlow Lindley gives the date as 1775 in Brinton, *Children of Light,* p. 308.

11 *Friends Miscellany,* XII, 219, 222.

been profoundly stirred by news of the massacres in San Domingo and warned Friends to escape from slavery and its consequences. His influence on Bush River Meeting (S. C.) led to a practical duplication of the Trent river removal. The great majority of the Bush River Friends removed in a body to the Little Miami valley near Waynesville, Ohio, where they settled on a tract already purchased by two of their members, Abijah O'Neall and Samuel Kelly. In 1802 these Friends requested their certificates of membership sent to Westland Monthly Meeting, Redstone Quarter, although they apparently took the more direct route to the Ohio country by way of the Kanawha valley, West Virginia.[12] Within a year or two the Bush River meeting dwindled entirely away as its members moved to the Miami valley settlement.

These are extreme cases, but in smaller numbers the meetings in the slave states lost their membership and the Quaker population in western Pennsylvania, Ohio and Indiana grew. Within three decades Georgia and South Carolina were stripped of their Quaker population. Virginia Yearly Meeting was so weakened that it was laid down in 1845 and the meetings remaining (chiefly in and near Fairfax county in the northwest and Suffolk county in the southeast) were joined to Baltimore Yearly Meeting.[13] North Carolina Yearly Meeting lost a large part of its membership. It has been estimated that from 1800 to 1860 not less than 6000 Friends emigrated from the southern states.

Meantime the development of the Society in Ohio was phenomenal. Concord Monthly Meeting (1801) was divided in 1804, the new meeting being called Short Creek. To quote Rufus Jones' summary of the development of the Ohio settlements:

---

[12] See the story, *Bush River*, by Wilson S. Doan in *The Quaker*, vol. I (1920).

[13] Weeks, *op. cit.*, p. 271.

Meantime the stream had been going farther west and settlements of Friends were forming along the fertile banks of the Miami River—both Great and Little Miami. So rapidly did this drift toward western Ohio grow in volume that Miami Monthly Meeting was set off by Redstone Quarterly Meeting, 13th October 1803. Miami Monthly Meeting, with the central settlement at Waynesville, Ohio, became the great Mecca of Quaker migration between 1803 and 1807. No less than eighteen hundred and twenty-six removal certificates of Friends were received by that Monthly Meeting in that four year period. Eight hundred and ten of this number came from Bush River and Cane Creek Meetings in South Carolina and from Wrightsborough, Georgia. Forty-five came from six Monthly Meetings in Pennsylvania, and sixty-nine came from seven Monthly Meetings in New Jersey. Middletown Monthly Meeting was also set up in 1803 and Salem followed in 1805.

In 1805 Concord and Short Creek Monthly Meetings requested liberty of Redstone Quarterly Meeting to hold a Quarterly Meeting of their own. In 1806 this request was granted, the Quarterly Meeting being named Short Creek Quarterly Meeting and being subordinate to Baltimore Yearly Meeting. In 1807 Salem and Middletown Monthly Meeting were granted the privilege of holding a Quarterly meeting named Salem Quarterly Meeting, and the same year Miami and Centre Meetings were granted the privilege of holding a Quarterly Meeting, called Miami Quarterly Meeting. In 1810 a request was made by Friends on the west side of Great Miami River, composed of West Branch, White Water and Elk, to have the privilege granted them of holding a Quarterly Meeting. This was granted in 1812 and the meeting was called West Branch Quarterly Meeting. At a later date West Branch and White Water became separate Quarterly Meetings.[14]

In 1812 in response to a request of Ohio Friends Baltimore Yearly Meeting, having asked counsel of Friends from Philadelphia and Virginia yearly meetings, authorized the establishment of Ohio Yearly Meeting to meet at Short

---

14 JLPQ, I, 411–412. BFHS, XII, I, pp. 4, 5.

Creek and to include all the quarterly meetings west of the Alleghenies including meetings in Indiana Territory. The number of Friends in the new yearly meeting has been estimated at twenty thousand, of whom probably one fourth came from Philadelphia Yearly Meeting.[15]

The westward stream of Friends' settlements early crossed into Indiana Territory, which became a state in 1816. David Hoover from Randolph County, N. C., who had lived a few years in the Stillwater valley (near Dayton, O.),[16] was one of the first Quakers to explore the Indiana wilderness with a view to settlement (1806). The same year there was a small settlement of about twenty Friends at Whitewater near the present site of Richmond, of which city their leaders, Jeremiah Cox and John Smith, are the reputed founders. They came apparently by way of Miami Monthly Meeting which received their removal certificates in 1806 and 1804 respectively. This settlement was visited by John Simpson of Philadelphia Yearly Meeting in 1806 while on the way for a conference with the famous Indian chief Tecumseh. William Williams from Lost Creek, Tennessee, visited Whitewater in 1807; he returned in 1810, and finally moved to Elkhorn Creek near Richmond in 1814. In 1807 an "indulged meeting" was granted to the eighty-four Friends in that territory and the year following a log meeting-house was built. In 1809 Miami Quarterly Meeting established Whitewater Monthly Meeting with two hundred and sixty-five resident Friends,[17] which from this time took the place of Westland and Miami as the distributing point for Friends adventuring farther into the Indiana wilderness.

It has been estimated that twelve hundred Friends from the southern states principally from North and South Carolina, emigrated to the Whitewater region during the

---

15 JLPQ, I, 411–412.

16 David Hoover, *Memoirs; Friends Review*, XI, 506, 507.

17 *Centennial of Whitewater Meeting*, pp. 34–39.

decade from 1809 to 1819.[18] West Branch Quarterly Meeting, held alternately at Whitewater and West Branch, was established in 1812. Other important Quaker centers in Indiana were Lick Creek, Blue River (in southern Indiana), White Lick (near Mooresville), Middle Fork and West Grove. One line of settlements ran to the northwest from Whitewater as far as New London (near Kokomo). Another extended along the Wabash river into Parke, Vermilion and Montgomery counties and another extended northward from White Lick through Marion and Hamilton counties to New London.[19]

In 1821 Ohio Yearly Meeting set up Indiana Yearly Meeting, which met in the newly built meeting-house at Whitewater. The rapid growth of the Society in central Indiana continued, however, so that in 1858 Western Yearly Meeting was set up composed of the central quarterly meetings, to which were added Raisin Valley Quarter in southern Michigan, and Vermilion and Chicago quarterly meetings in Illinois.

These new meetings were composed of diverse elements, coming as they did from both eastern and southern meetings, and it took time for them to become fused together.[20] The conditions of life on the frontier were primitive and equipment was meager. Each household had to provide most of its own food, clothing and furniture out of forest and field by their own hands. Providing the sheer necessities of physical life occupied most of their energies. They had to fell the forests, build homes, get fields under cultivation and construct fences and roads. Yet Friends quickly built meeting-houses and provided for schools. Most of them walked or rode long distances to the meetings for worship twice a week.

West of the Allegheny mountains Friends meeting-

---

18 Weeks, *op. cit.*, p. 271.

19 Brinton, *op. cit.*, p. 313.

20 Grellet, *Memoirs,* II, 165, 166.

houses assumed a fairly uniform type of architecture. They were log or frame buildings, rectangular in shape, with partitions which contained movable "shutters" dividing the building into two equal rooms, one for the women and the other for the men. At meetings for worship these "shutters" were open, throwing the whole into one room; but for business meetings which were held separately they were closed. The benches or seats extended the whole length of the entire building. Usually three benches on one side, each raised a little higher than the one in front of it, constituted the "gallery" where the preachers and elders sat. The lowest of these seats was called "the facing bench," because it "faced" the congregation directly. The main body of the house was occupied by benches facing toward the gallery, and occupied by the "body of the meeting." Sometimes there was an upper or upstairs gallery along the back of the rooms or even running around three sides. The rooms were usually heated by iron stoves, although sometimes, especially in the warmer sections of the country, fireplaces served. The rooms lacked any attempt at decoration and the windows were of plain glass.

A number of ministers underwent the hardships of frontier travel to visit these Quaker outposts in Ohio and Indiana. William Williams and John Simpson visited these regions before finally settling there. William Forster visited Friends as far northwest as the Wabash river in 1821, although he arrived in Richmond from the east too late to attend the opening of Indiana Yearly Meeting. In 1824 came Stephen Grellet. These were the first of a long line of distinguished eastern and English Friends who braved the hardships of the western forests under a concern for the spiritual welfare of the Quaker pioneers. They supplied the comparative lack of a strong local ministry, kept Friends in touch with trends in the Society at large, visited and encouraged isolated families and sought to revive and reclaim the indifferent or irreligious. They found religious conditions far from ideal. In many places they reported the spiritual life "low" and the meetings for worship lifeless. Business meetings were irregularly carried on in places. Friends' minds were too much occupied with the struggle for material things. Many were negligent of the testimonies. Many were "under dealings" for laxity and immorality as well as for "marrying out of meeting." There was happily another side to the story.

It would be a serious historical mistake to point out the existing defects and derelictions, which probably prevailed at this period to about the same extent as in the other sections of the Society, without at the same time emphasizing the qualities of strength and beauty that were exhibited in the best Quaker lives in the settlements west of the Ohio River. Most of the Friends who left their old homes to create new ones in the free Northwest Territory had gone forth, in high faith and in obedience to what they believed was divine light, to escape the environment of slavery and to help make a great area for freedom in the uncontaminated West. They loved truth, they hated unrighteousness and they had a clear leading and a real vision of a better social order which could be constructed in a region where ancient habits and customs were lacking. Most of these Friends lived what they professed. Many were sensitive in their consciences and tender in their spirits. They aimed to follow their best light and to be true to the highest that they knew. They were good material for the formative soil of a new community, and they did their part to make that growing community a spiritual one. Their venture, as they rode out from their old homes in their wagons and ox-carts, was a brave one, and they did yeoman service in the early work of building the new civilization beyond the Alleghenies.[21]

---

[21] JLPQ, I, 430.

Chapter 22

CAUSES OF THE SEPARATION OF 1827-1828

The third period of "The Middle Ages of Quakerism," as the age of Quietism has been called,[1] marked not only the culmination of the ascendancy of Quietism and the discipline, but it forms the introduction to the third division of Quaker history. It was a transition period, within which the Evangelical movement developed along with other causes of the separation of 1827.

The religious life of Friends during this period was generally "low," according to the judgment of the travelling ministers. This is borne out not only by the records of disciplinary proceedings against members for nonconformity in "dress and address" and disownments for marrying out of meetings; but by the astonishing number of disownments for moral delinquencies, not only in the frontier settlements but in old established meetings.[2] The records disclose disownments for "corrupt language," "fighting their fellow creatures," violating the Quaker testimony against military training or paying war taxes, using "spirituous liquors to excess," and fornication.[3] The minutes of Miami Monthly Meeting add to this list using

---

1 Tanner, William, *Three Lectures on the Early History of the Society of Friends* &c. (1858), p. 264. Thistlewaite, William, *Lectures on the Rise and Progress of Friends* (1865), pp. 91–97. Rowntree, John Stephenson, *Quakerism Past and Present* (1859), p. 126.

2 JLPQ, I, 395, 396.

3 *Ibid.*, I, 395n.

profane language, bearing false witness, spreading slanderous reports, failing to settle contracts, threatening a man with a gun, dancing and subscribing to a singing school,[4] and violating the peace testimony by paying muster fines or furnishing a substitute for the militia.

Friends laid great stress on external conformity to the discipline in outward matters, and with less stress they were devoted to certain traditional philanthropies. The ministry had come to be largely hortatory. Members were exhorted to be faithful to the testimonies, to "mind the Light," to follow their leading, and to "dwell deep." Outward strictness was balanced by inner freedom to follow inward spiritual leading. There was almost no teaching ministry in the meetings and little doctrinal instruction elsewhere. The Bible was, of course, not read in meeting, for fear it would become a lifeless form, or that the regular reading of the Bible would interfere with the leading of the Holy Spirit. A similar fear of "creaturely activity" prevented *regular* family worship or any organized efforts to teach the Bible. There were some families in which the Bible was read frequently, but many did not even possess a copy of it. The younger generation was thus without Biblical knowledge or doctrinal guidance.[5]

At the time we are considering the exercise of the authority in the Society rested mainly with the elders. The Meeting for Sufferings, which was largely made up of elders, grew in power at the expense of other elements in the Society. It had the supervision of publications, which gave it a sort of doctrinal censorship. The Select Meeting, as the meeting of ministers and elders was called, had practically the control of the meetings in its hands. Its members had grown accustomed to identify their policies with Quakerism. They had come to believe that the

4 JLPQ, I, 414-415.

5 Cf. Forster, Wm., *Mem.* II, 43n. Thomas, *Hist.*, p. 121. Kersey, *A Treatise* &c., p. 112.

"weight" of the meeting lay with them. In the large cities where Friends were numerous, such as New York, Baltimore and Philadelphia, the city Friends dominated the Meeting for Sufferings, the Select Meetings and the yearly meeting because of their wealth, culture, education and their habit of managing men, and because it was easy for them to communicate with each other. This was especially true in Philadelphia Yearly Meeting, where the city elders were a strong, intelligent group with common ideals and purposes. It had become the custom for some of the country meetings, especially those in the state of Delaware and on the Eastern Shore of Maryland, to appoint Friends resident in Philadelphia to represent them in the Meeting for Sufferings, since travelling was difficult and it was important that they should always be represented at the meetings, which were held in the city.

The separation of 1827–1828 which ushered in the modern period was the result of the collision of historical forces working within the Society in the half century following the outbreak of the American Revolutionary War. Of these the four most important had their roots in important movements outside the Society, the influence of which on Friends' history was retarded by the general aloofness of Friends from contemporary life.

First among these in time and importance was a new spirit of democracy and of personal freedom. The social philosophy, which asserted the natural rights and the political equality of men, originating with John Locke, had become widespread in America before the Revolutionary War. Jefferson embodied it in the Declaration of Independence. The American and French Revolutions affected profoundly the thinking of all classes. Even a group as isolated as Friends came in contact with the new spirit directly or indirectly in many ways. Friends were not indifferent to the demands of the revolutionists in France for liberty, equality and fraternity, however much they repudiated the warfare and bloodshed by which it was sought to secure them; nor was the Society untouched by the struggle for freedom of speech and the press against the Alien and Sedition Acts under John Adams' presidency at the end of the eighteenth century. Gradually Quaker tongues grew accustomed to such phrases as "inalienable rights," "consent of the governed," "liberty and equality." The younger generation even in the country meetings grew to be, to the minds of the elders, "raw and undisciplined." [6]

After a half century these influences led to a revolt against the discipline and arbitrary authority of the elders.[7] From this point of view the separation was a belated Quaker "French Revolution." In the manifesto put forth by John Comly and his sympathizers in Philadelphia in 1827, it was declared that early Friends "were made powerful instruments in opening the door of gospel liberty, and removing many of the fetters that had been formed in the dark night of superstition and error that preceded them. Hence they were prepared to promulgate the glorious truth, that *God alone in sovereign Lord of conscience,* and with this inalienable right no power, civil or ecclesiastical should ever interfere." [8]

The elders felt these new tendencies but had no idea of their true nature nor of the powerful forces behind them. It was easy to confuse them with immorality or unbelief, which seemed all too prevalent in the world. They attempted to repress them by more rigid discipline; for the successful use of external discipline tends to beget blind faith in outward compulsion and skepticism as to the worth and power of spiritual forces. The result was a revolt in the name of freedom.[9]

This tendency was reinforced by a second movement,

---

6 Hicks, *Jour.*, pp. 64, 74, 78.
7 Grubb, *Separations*, p. 15.
8 Comly, *Jour.*, p. 628.
9 Cf. Backhouse, H. C., *Journal*, p. 92.

closely allied to it. The French Revolution was a revolt against arbitrary authority in the church as well as in the state. The Bourbon dynasty and the Catholic hierarchy in France hunted heretics and revolutionists together. Both were enemies of liberty. The struggle for freedom against both was carried on in the name of reason. Men demanded the right to believe and follow what was reasonable. This idea of religious freedom passed over from the English Deists to France where it became identified with the struggle for personal rights and liberties, led by Rousseau, Voltaire, and the Encyclopedists. Butler's *Analogy* had conceded that religious beliefs must be rational.[10] Paley's *Evidences,* published in 1805, which made the same concession, exercised considerable influence among Friends on both sides of the Atlantic.

These various rationalistic influences were strong in sections of America, where they touched Friends at many points. In 1795 when Timothy Dwight became president of Yale College, he could find only twenty students who would confess that they were Christians; it was the common assumption that a scholar could not consistently be a Christian. Since Yale drew the bulk of its students from the surrounding territory, this indicates a rationalistic tendency in the younger generation in Connecticut, southeastern New York and on Long Island. Unitarian influences were at work in the same region. The American Unitarian Association was organized in 1825. Paine's *Age of Reason,* a crude version of Voltaire, was widely read in America in the first quarter of the nineteenth century. Elias Hicks found a Quaker community in Virginia which was quite under its influence. Certain rationalistic tendencies early in the nineteenth century, such as the Irish Separation, the case of Hannah Barnard of New York and the "New Light" movement in New England, greatly

---

[10] Foster, *Report,* I, 22.

alarmed the orthodox element among Friends and created a new sensitiveness to theological doctrines and a new fear of "unsoundness."

The leaders of the revolt against arbitrary authority in the Society were neither Deists nor Freethinkers. They insisted merely that religious doctrines should be in accordance with reason and that men's minds should not be subjected to arbitrary dogma. Elias Hicks in his travels frequently came in contact with Deists and atheists and expressed his abhorrence of both.[11] He was positively and profoundly religious after the Quaker pattern of the eighteenth century. But the new tendencies did influence him.[12] He regarded any manifestation of religious intolerance with abhorrence, and, like a Quaker Butler, he attempted to rationalize the doctrine of the Inner Light. His theology was not important in itself, since it was never adopted even by the section of the Society which championed his right to think for himself and which has been sometimes called by his name. It was, especially in its negative aspects, merely the occasion of the conflict which led to the separation—a conflict which would probably have arisen over some other issue in any case.

A third cause of the separation, although of less importance than the others, is to be found in the growing differences between country and city Friends. In the half century following the Revolutionary War there was a great increase in wealth and culture among city Friends, especially in Philadelphia, Baltimore and New York. In consequence there were departures from pioneer simplicity, an increase in luxury and a growing spirit of worldliness which John Woolman and Job Scott both noted with misgivings. John Comly, a country Friend, complains of

---

11 *Jour.*, p. 70.

12 He was acquainted with Priestley's *History of the Corruptions of Christianity* (1782, Rutts Ed. 1818) and with *The Celestial Magnet*. Cf. Foster, *Report*, I, 112, 115, 116.

these changes especially in New York and New England.[13] To be sure, the city Friends still wore the "plain" clothes, but the materials were more expensive and their homes were more luxuriously furnished. They were, as a rule, better educated and were influenced by the newer literature and modes of thought.

On the other hand, life in the country remained more nearly stationary. Roads were poor and travel slow and difficult.[14] Country people produced nearly all they needed on the farm and in the home. They rarely visited the city and had few means of keeping in touch with the wider world. The monthly meeting schools were elementary and inadequate. Consequently country and city Friends drew apart. When the country Friends came to the city to attend quarterly or yearly meeting, they felt strange among their city brethren. In the luxurious homes where they were entertained, they were ill at ease and under restraint. In many topics discussed and opinions expressed at their hosts' tables they sensed worldliness and non-Friendly innovations. In the business meetings they found the minds of city Friends already made up on issues new to them. The clerks paid little attention to their views, but attached chief weight to the words of the city elders and recorded the sense of the meeting accordingly. Samuel Bettle, the clerk of Philadelphia Yearly Meeting, testified in court after the separation, that as clerk he was accustomed to give no weight whatever to the opinions of practically all who afterward became leaders of the separation, who were mostly country Friends.[15] When the country Friends returned to their homes, confused and baffled by their experiences, they felt that policies to which they were opposed had been adopted by sharp practice on the part of the autocratic city leaders.

---

13 *Jour.*, pp. 156, 163, 164, 282.

14 Cf. Dewees, *History of Westtown Boarding School,* pp. 39, 46.

15 Foster, *Report,* I, 82.

Elias Hicks was a Long Island farmer as well as a Friends minister. He travelled very extensively under a religious concern and made frequent circuits of the country meetings, especially in New York, Philadelphia and Baltimore yearly meetings. He sat at the farmers' tables as one of them; his simple logic appealed to the plain people; and he spoke the familiar language of eighteenth-century Quaker Quietism. When late in life he incurred the disapproval of the Philadelphia elders, some of them followed him on his country visits, trying to undo the harm they believed he was doing. But their broadcloth clothes and shiny hats "queered" them with the country Friends, who came to look on Elias as the champion of the common people against the usurpations of the city elders.[16]

The fourth of these tendencies, which culminated in the separation, is the "Evangelical" movement. This movement —which must be distinguished from the common Protestantism which is called evangelical Christianity in the wider sense—had a long history, running back to Wiclif in England and to the Pietists on the Continent. It became a powerful force in England with the Wesleyan movement about the middle of the eighteenth century, and later it produced the "Low Church" or "Evangelical" movement within the Church of England. It led to a great revival of religious life and activity both in England and America and carried with it new programs and methods of religious work. The Wesleyan movement included revival meetings, class meetings, Bible classes and temperance work. The later Evangelicalism included in its program foreign missions, poor relief, Sunday schools, savings associations and Bible societies. It produced a number of leaders of antislavery and prison reform movements. It has always been interested in popular religious education and eager to convert the world. It has been about equally insistent on the

[16] Grubb, *Separations*, p. 38.

necessity of personal religious experience and on doctrinal orthodoxy as the conditions of saving faith. It has promoted education of a circumscribed type while at the same time afraid of liberal learning and intolerant of free thought.

The Evangelical movement began the wider reconstruction of American religious life about the beginning of the nineteenth century. About this time Timothy Dwight, in a series of sermons, converted Yale College into an Evangelical stronghold. The great Kentucky revival broke out in 1801. The famous "Haystack prayer meeting" at Williams College (1803) marks the beginning of a new vital interest in foreign missions. The American Bible Society was organized in 1807.

The main points of the "Evangelical" creed in the narrower sense are (1) the plenary (or even verbal) inspiration and final outward authority of the Bible; (2) the total depravity of human nature as a consequence of the Fall; (3) the "deity" of Christ and (4) his "substitutionary" death on the cross; and (5) the necessity of a definite personal religious experience.

Evangelicalism had certain important points of contact with Quakerism: its insistence on religion as a vital personal experience; its gospel of salvation for all men, even of the neglected classes and the heathen nations; and its passion for morality and social reforms. But its doctrines of the final outward authority of the Scriptures and the total depravity of human nature were radically opposed to the early Quaker doctrine of the Inward Light, and its new vocabulary and program were alien to eighteenth-century Quaker Quietism both in methods and spirit.

The Evangelical movement influenced Friends in England in many ways. Mary Dudley, a friend of John Wesley in her youth, joined Friends and united the Evangelical passion and theology with the Quaker mystical worship and "prophetic" ministry. Even more influential in this direction was Thomas Shillitoe, who came into the Society from the Church of England. As noted above many English Friends were associated with Evangelicals of the Church of England in the Anti-slavery movement. Other Quaker leaders were similarly associated with Evangelicals in the Bible Society and in prison reform work. Charles Simeon, Henry Venn and Bishop Bathhurst of Norwich, leaders of the Evangelical wing of the Church of England, were close friends of Joseph John Gurney. Through such contacts English Friends gradually absorbed Evangelical views and ideals.

In America the Quaker leaders had no such vital contacts with outside religious workers. But there was a strong group of ministers who came into the Society from other denominations, bringing new susceptibilities, concepts and religious terms. They brought an increasing emphasis on the sinfulness of human nature, on future rewards and punishments as a motive of religious faith, on the use of Scripture and on the atoning work of Christ in salvation. Rebecca Jones of Philadelphia came from the Episcopal Church and parallelled in America the work and influence of Mary Dudley in England. She had a profound sense of sin as a child and a deep evangelical experience of conversion. The following passage from her *Memoirs* is characteristic:

> Acknowledging with gratitude and in humility of soul the tender and infinite mercy of the Lord Almighty, which has in numberless instances been signally vouchsafed and displayed for my redemption from sin and the wages due thereto, and his preservations and deliverances by sea and by land; hoping, through the merits of my blessed Saviour and Redeemer Jesus Christ, to be admitted into his holy kingdom when I shall put off this earthly tabernacle; and in peace and unity with his Church under every name.[17]

---

[17] *Mem.*, p. 358.

David Sands had been a Presbyterian and Stephen Grellet, the son of an exiled French nobleman, had been a disciple of Voltaire. When these two became Friends, they brought a doctrinal consciousness new in Quaker experience. The former felt a special mission to cry out against Deism, and the latter almost leaned backward in his reaction against his former infidelity. These ministers were closely associated with the leading Friends, especially in Philadelphia and New York, and kept in touch with leading English ministers by travel and correspondence. Most of them combined an evangelical fervor with a deep philanthropic interest. There was a close exchange of ideas and interests among them both in England and America. Stephen Grellet was first interested in Quakerism by Deborah Darby and Rebecca Young, two Friends ministers from England. William Savery was instrumental in Elizabeth (Gurney) Fry's "conversion." Stephen Grellet (with William Forster) first got her interested in Newgate prison. Rebecca Jones helped William Allen at a critical stage in his religious experience, as she herself had been powerfully influenced by Catherine Phillips in her youth.

On becoming Friends these converts reacted in different ways. Some added an Evangelical doctrinal emphasis and fervor to Quietism; others made the Quietist interpretation of the doctrine of the Inward Light an all-sufficient theology. Job Scott and Elias Hicks were of the latter type. David Sands, on the other hand, detected unsoundness in Hannah Barnard before anyone else. Stephen Grellet "labored with" Elias Hicks as early as 1808 because of suspected unsoundness on Scriptures and the atonement.[18] Thomas Shillitoe's orthodoxy precipitated the division in New York and Ohio yearly meetings and afterward he followed Elias Hicks in his travels, trying to counteract his alleged false teaching.

---

18 Grellet, *Life,* I, 142.

English Friends brought a new enthusiasm for Evangelical views to America and found groups in the large cities especially prepared to receive and listen to them. Thomas Shillitoe, Anna Braithwaite and her husband Isaac Braithwaite, Elizabeth Robson, William Forster, George and Anna Jones were outstanding among those who visited in America and zealously promulgated the new views. They were theologically sensitive, aggressively orthodox and on the look-out for doctrinal "unsoundness." They naturally came in contact with the city Friends first, who were naturally less conservative than the country Friends, and who therefore were among the first to accept the new doctrines. The "Evangelicals" thus came to coincide pretty much with the city Friends in contrast with those living in the country. The Society thus became a Leyden jar charged with passions of high potential, concentrated in two opposing groups. One consisted mainly of the country Friends, clinging to the phrases and practices of eighteenth-century Quietism, fearful of the new doctrines and the growing "worldliness" of city Friends, but having themselves imbibed a new revolutionary spirit of democracy and liberty and chafing under the autocratic authority of the elders. The other party, composed chiefly of the elders and their sympathizers in the cities, alarmed at the growing disregard of the discipline and especially fearful of any modes of doctrinal expression which seemed unsound by Evangelical tests, determined to suppress the new tendencies by more rigorous disciplinary measures at all costs.

Neither side understood the motives of the other nor sensed the real meaning of the new forces with which they were dealing. The "Evangelicals" ascribed the attitude of their opponents to mere obstinacy or desire to find a cloak for the irreligion of intellectual pride or moral license. They had no realization of the degree to which the love of freedom and democratic control had returned to the Society. On the other hand, the opponents of the elders thought the latter were animated solely by religious bigotry and the lust of power. They had no realization of the character of the new religious life and fervor which had come with the Evangelical movement; nor of the vital connection which its adherents felt between their new religious experiences and the Evangelical doctrines.

The Evangelical insistence on the fundamental importance of the "outward" facts of Jesus' life was strange to the Quietist tradition, according to which the essentials of religion were inward—the effort to silence the creature, to feel after the will of God for the existing situation, to be fully resigned to do his will; to relieve one's mind in meeting when a message arose, and so to find peace. They used the historical events of Scripture chiefly as symbols and illustrations of inward states and struggles, and found even in the gospel records little of value except what prompted or promised personal experience. Friends of this period had little to do with governmental affairs and thought little in legal or judicial terms. Justice, satisfaction, justification (acquittal), imputed righteousness and even forgiveness were terms which suggested little that was vital in their religious experience.

The Evangelicals, on the other hand, regarded the life, death and resurrection of Jesus as "transactions" by which the Son of God incarnate removed obstacles to forgiveness on the part of God by making "satisfaction" for their sins and so secured a status of imputed righteousness for the believer. To secure this status of "a sinner saved by grace," it was not only necessary to accept Christ as Lord, but to believe that salvation was brought about in this way. The first generation of Quaker Evangelicals had all had a profound adult experience of conversion, which aroused deep religious emotions of gratitude and devotion. Their creed was part of their experiences, and their emotions included not only Christ as Saviour, but the process by which he saved them as theologically defined. The Evangelical theology thus became to them a necessary part of saving faith and the only way given among men by which the gospel could be effectively proclaimed or be efficaciously accepted. To deny the full truth of this theology was to deny the Lord that bought them and be guilty of grossest infidelity.[19] This emotional element was something that the cooler, more rationalist temper of their opponents could never comprehend. Neither party knew the explosive quality of the new wine they were trying to hold in the old bottles; and neither party had the understanding, sympathy and patient love, which alone would have made it possible for them to get on together. It happened, therefore, that each of these opposite tendencies crystallized in about the same groups of people.

Thus the stage was set for a fierce struggle animated by religious passion and made tragic by class estrangement and personal misunderstanding. The ministry of Elias Hicks was the spark which set off the explosion; but some other incident, like the *Letters of Paul and Amicus,* could as easily have been the occasion of it.

About the close of the eighteenth century certain tendencies toward rational criticism of accepted doctrinal views aroused the fear of unsoundness among Friends. In 1797–1799 there occurred a considerable agitation in Ireland which resulted in a small separation, of which Abraham Shackleton was the leader. He was head of a school at Ballitore which had been in the family for three generations. He was a sensitive minister of the Quietist type and educated beyond the average. He became convinced that God would not have commanded certain atrocities in the Old Testament, since it would have been inconsistent with

---

19 See Forster, *Mem.,* II, 42, 43n. Speaking of the position of the Hicksites, Seebohm (the editor) says: "It was the foundation of the Christian faith—not the superstructure—which it was attempted to destroy." He admits that "on the question of worship and discipline, war, oaths, slavery and in some other particulars, very little difference was apparent." To the Evangelicals these latter were merely Quaker superstructure.

Christ's revelation of him. He could not believe that God could change or command immoral acts. He stood for freedom of belief, and for a more vital and inward religion than could be enforced by the discipline or adequately expressed in the Evangelical creed. His position came to the fore as a reaction from the extreme Evangelical attitude to the Scriptures in the preaching of David Sands, an American minister who spent some years in Ireland.[20] In 1797 Shackleton became involved in a controversy over "the Hebrew wars." The Irish Yearly Meeting of 1798 condemned the newly manifest tendency to weaken Friends' testimony to the authority of the Scriptures, and prescribed disownment for those who persisted in the spirit of speculation and unbelief.[21] Shackleton was supported by the more radical position of John Hancock, John Rogers, George Thompson, Ann Richardson and many other influential Friends. All these "disturbers" were ultimately disowned or withdrew from the Society.

The rationalistic tendency developed in widely divergent sections of Quakerdom. In Ireland it was aggravated by the influence of Hannah Barnard, a New York Friend, who had come into the Society from the Baptists and who travelled in Great Britain and Ireland with a minute from her yearly meeting. She had come to opinions much the same as Abraham Shackleton, but did not express them in such a way as to cause uneasiness during her service in Ireland, and the yearly meeting gave her a certificate of unity and approval on the completion of her work in May, 1800.

A few weeks later she applied in London for a minute to accompany Elizabeth Coggshall, another American minister, on a religious visit to the Continent. Objection to this was made by David Sands and Joseph Williams from Ire-

---

20 JLPQ, I, 292.

21 Rathbone, *Narrative,* pp. 52–54.

land on the ground that her teaching was at variance with that of Friends. In the subsequent proceedings she stated frankly her beliefs, showing that she shared the Irish separatists' views on the Old Testament wars and that she questioned the historical accuracy of some Scripture accounts of the supernatural. She distinguished sharply between a religious experience and belief in historic facts. Her attitude was mildly rationalistic but her criticisms were based on a keen sense of ethical values. Her case was carried up finally to London Yearly Meeting, where the advice of the lower meetings that she "desist from preaching and return home" was confirmed. On her return her case was carried from her home monthly meeting to the yearly meeting by which her disownment was confirmed. In the conduct of the case in her home yearly meeting there was a lamentable lack of condescension and charity on both sides.[22]

This case became a *cause célèbre*. It alarmed the Evangelicals who began to strengthen the defenses of the faith.[23] In 1801 Henry Tuke published a book of extracts from the early Quaker literature, called *The Faith of the People Called Quakers in Our Lord and Saviour Jesus Christ.* There is a doctrinal consciousness in the selection and setting of the extracts which is lacking in the original authors, and many of the religious phrases had come to have meanings for the Evangelicals which they lacked for early Friends. A more important work was the same author's *Principles of Religion, as Professed by the Society of Christians, usually called Quakers* (1805).

Much of it is an admirable account of the characteristic beliefs and ideals of Friends, but it is obviously written in a time of storm and controversy, and it aims to defend the faith at points where attack has been made, and it therefore leans strongly in the direction of orthodoxy. Tuke honestly be-

---

22 Thomas, *Hist.*, p. 120.

23 Hodgson, *Hist.*, I, 57, 67, 69.

lieved that his position was point for point the position of the first group of Friends . . . Tuke believes, no doubt, in the inner work of the Spirit, but he is really writing his book to stem a tide of thought which seems to him unorthodox, and he consequently raises Evangelical doctrines into unprecedented prominence. He is endeavouring to eliminate unsoundness, and this motive colours all his work.[24]

This work ran through many editions and was widely circulated so that it was found in almost every Quaker family.[25] It became for a time almost a standard expression of Quakerism.

Joseph Gurney Bevan, a very able and influential English Friend, printed a collection of extracts from the writings of early Friends to show that they were not Unitarians. He also published a booklet on *Thoughts on Reason and Revelation* (1805). The same year John Bevans, Jr., wrote *A Defense of the Christian Doctrines of the Society of Friends against the Charge of Socinianism.* Both of these were thoroughly Evangelical in their positions and avowedly contributions to controversy.[26]

In 1806 Philadelphia Yearly Meeting revised its discipline and introduced for the first time an article making it cause for disownment to "deny the divinity of our Lord and Saviour Jesus Christ, the immediate revelation of the Holy Spirit or the authenticity of the Scriptures." [27]

Efforts were begun at the same time to unite all the yearly meetings in the world or at least all the American yearly meetings in some central organization. "The two movements for evangelical orthodoxy and for union are especially significant with regard to the tendency of the Quaker groups at this time toward the formulation of an official declaration of faith. Hand in hand with the ortho-

24 JLPQ, I, 285, 286.

25 *Ibid.*, I, 287.

26 A similar work was published by Thomas Willis of New York in 1812 called *The Doctrine and Principle of the People Called Quakers Explained and Vindicated.*

27 *Discipline,* Phila., 1806.

dox current went an attempt to unify and combine the Society under one central body with a uniform discipline and set of beliefs."[28] The first effort in this direction came from the Philadelphia Yearly Meeting for Sufferings (1805). A similar proposition was made by Richard Phillips of London in 1811 to an American Friend. In Philadelphia, New York and Baltimore yearly meetings such a plan was proposed by a group of Friends and finally at Ohio Yearly Meeting in 1821 it was presented by William Forster of England. These plans met with the vigorous and successful opposition of all who feared the Evangelical program. These included both the conservatives who wished to preserve the traditional freedom of Quakerism from any doctrinal basis of membership, and those who wished freedom of theological thought in the new age.[29]

The "New Light" movement in New England during the first two decades of the nineteenth century was an extravagant and rather anarchistic form of Unitarianism. It attracted some adherents from among Friends and caused "New Lights" were finally disowned. A leader among them was Micah Ruggles, a convinced Friend who had previously considerable trouble in the Society.[30] A number of these belonged to several denominations. He was disowned by New Bedford Monthly Meeting in 1824, after he had caused great uneasiness among New York and Philadelphia Friends.[31] This, too, stimulated an Evangelical reaction. New England Yearly Meeting grew more and more cautious about publishing Job Scott's *Essays,* while in 1806 it recommended Tuke's *Principles of Religion* as an interpretation of Quakerism.

These tendencies toward an official orthodoxy thoroughly alarmed the non-Evangelical Friends, both conservative and liberal. They charged that the Society had departed

---

28 Mekeel, *Quakerism and a Creed,* p. 49.

29 See Mekeel, *op. cit.,* pp. 47–50 for the material in this paragraph.

30 Hodgson, *History,* I, chap. III.

31 Mekeel, *op. cit.,* p. 51.

from the ideals of the Founders; that it had lost its historical insight; and that the proceedings in the Barnard case signified an increasing tendency toward the "popish doctrine of implicit faith." [32] This party regarded the Inner Light as the final ground of personal doctrinal beliefs and girded themselves to preserve the original Quaker foundation principles as well as liberty of conscience and belief.

The first open clash came in 1823 in Philadelphia Yearly Meeting as a result of a series of articles which appeared in a Wilmington (Del.) paper, called the *Letters of Paul and Amicus,* Paul presenting a Presbyterian point of view and Amicus that of Friends. Some influential Friends thought Amicus did not correctly represent the Quaker position since he inclined too much to Elias Hicks' views,[33] and the Meeting for Sufferings appointed a committee to prepare a statement to vindcate the Quakers' orthodoxy. The committee brought in a strongly orthodox statement consisting of extracts from early Quaker writings, quoted with no designation of their authorship. This was adopted and signed officially by the clerk of the Meeting for Sufferings.

The non-Evangelicals feared that the doctrine of the Inner Light was to be nullified, while an "orthodox" declaration of faith was to be imposed on the yearly meeting. There was a stormy discussion at the ensuing yearly meeting when the minutes of the Meeting for Sufferings were read. The subject was finally disposed of by spreading on the minutes of the yearly meeting the minutes of the Meeting for Sufferings containing the proposed statement, but suspending any publication of it. In this way the Orthodox party got the statement in the yearly meeting minutes without official disavowal—a bit of sharp practice that widened the growing chasm between the parties. It only needed a magnetic leader to precipitate a separation.[34]

---

32 Mekeel, *op. cit.*, p. 46.
33 Hodgson, *Hist.*, I, 135.
34 *Ibid.*, I, 142.

III

The Modern Revival and Reconstruction 1827-1941

Period 1

Separations 1827-1861

Chapter 23

THE GREAT SEPARATION

The historical forces which worked in the Society of Friends during the half century after the Revolutionary War found expression in the character and work of four outstanding leaders, whose decisive action at critical junctures precipitated the separation of 1827 in Philadelphia Yearly Meeting and led to divisions in four other yearly meetings the following year. They were Elias Hicks, Samuel Bettle, John Comly, and Thomas Shillitoe.

Bettle was a Philadelphia merchant; Hicks a Long Island farmer; Comly was a Pennsylvania school teacher, and Thomas Shillitoe a London shoemaker. To characterize a man by an epithet is usually to caricature him; but it may help to understand these men in connection with what follows to remember Bettle as an elder, Hicks as a lover of liberty, Comly as a Quietist, and Shillitoe as a crusader. Both Hicks and Shillitoe were travelling ministers after the eighteenth-century pattern.

They were all conscientious men, sincerely devoted to the Christian ideal as held by Friends, and devout students of the Scriptures. They were all Quietist mystics, seeking God in the "silence of the creature," looking within for the divine leading, following Truth and doing God's will as light and strength were given them. Each deemed himself a guardian of a particular treasure in the Quaker patrimony: Bettle of authority, Hicks of truth, Comly of peace and Shillitoe of duty. They lost sight of the fact that love is the essence of Christianity; and considered something else more important than patience, forbearance, unity, mutual respect, coöperation and love.

Elias Hicks and Thomas Shillitoe were two of the most powerful preachers heard by American Friends in the first quarter of the nineteenth century.[1] Both possessed magnetic personalities, both brought new forms of thought and expression to the Quaker meeting-house galleries, and both travelled extensively and appealed to a public beyond the Society of Friends. Hicks reached the largest public, and his appeal was largely intellectual.

Elias Hicks (1748–1830), whose personality and teaching precipitated the controversy which led to the separation, was a younger contemporary of John Woolman and Job Scott, and like them he passed through early struggles on account of his love of "youthful diversions," yielded gradually to his convictions of right and finally yielded to a call to the ministry. He brought new intellectual and spiritual energy to the ministry, but it ran in the old channels. He travelled widely in America under special concerns with a minute from his home meeting, and strove carefully in meeting not to "outrun his Guide" and to attain inward peace. His preaching was concerned chiefly with the practical and philanthropical phases of Quakerism. Thus he lived and labored until he was past sixty-five years of age.

---

1 To these should be added Stephen Grellet as a third but he was not directly involved in the separation. He was the more cultured and charming personality. His interests and influence, especially in Europe, included all classes and social agencies, and he interested himself in new social reforms, as Hicks interested himself in the traditional Quaker philanthropic causes.

If he had died in 1815 he would have passed into history alongside Woolman and Scott as the third of a great trio of eighteenth-century itinerants.

It was in 1815 that the crisis came in Hicks' experience. Detained at home from meeting by a slight indisposition, he spent the time reading in Mosheim's *Ecclesiastical History of the Fifth Century* the story of the bitter struggles out of which the early creeds emerged, and the hatreds and persecutions they engendered. He saw there the first ugly fruit of the spirit of doctrinal intolerance—that same spirit which he thought he now detected entering in to destroy the peace and freedom of his beloved Society of Friends. From that hour he went forth to contend valiantly for the ancient Quaker freedom to follow the Inward Light and to believe only what Truth reveals. His attitude was essentially conservative. He represented the old ideals of Friends, except that under the influence of the new age he tried to rationalize the doctrine of the Inward Light. He became the champion of the Quietist methods and of freedom from the imposition by ecclesiastical authority of a doctrinal standard for Friends.[2]

He had a limited education but a logical mind. He liked to think things out to logical clearness. In purely logical thinking one's conclusions contain only what is already implicit in the premises and he got his premises from a quite limited experience. He felt the breath of a new age, but turned his quickened energy to the service of the old order. He was influenced to some extent by New England liberalism.[3] Deism and atheism he abhorred;[4] but the rationalistic method appealed to his logical mind as a protection from the attacks of Evangelicalism. The Evangeli-

---

2 See Hodgson, *Hist.*, I, pp. 221, 222.

3 He had read Priestly, *The Corruptions of Christianity* (Cf. Foster, *Report*, I, 112) and read and circulated among his neighbors copies of *The Celestial Magnet*, a periodical of Unitarian tendencies. Hodgson, *Hist.*, I, 72.

4 *Jour.*, pp. 70, 117.

cals stressed theology and he theologized in return. He attempted to vitalize the quiescent Quaker Quietism by rationalizing the doctrine of Inner Light, and in order to demonstrate the sole sufficiency of the Inward Guide and Saviour he thought it necessary to minimize the importance, as well as to deny the necessity of all outward helps and authority, such as church, Bible and the historic Christ.[5]

He owed a certain quickening of religious activity to contact with the Evangelical fervor. He was himself filled with a kind of missionary zeal; he often preached to non-Friends in Presbyterian, Baptist and Congregational churches, and in public halls, to non-Friends and to Negroes; but it was all done "as way opened," without organization or settled plan. Missionary and Bible societies, which were involved in the Evangelical program, although Friends had not yet taken them up, were to him an abomination.[6]

As early as 1808 Stephen Grellet had labored with Elias, because he felt that the latter had uttered sentiments "repugnant to the Christian religion."[7] In the next two decades the Evangelical movement spread rapidly among American Friends and grew more and more vigorous, aggressive, critical of doctrines and intolerant. In a manner quite unknown to previous Quakerism, it not only set up the Scriptures as an outward and final authority, but it tacitly identified its own doctrines with Scripture and allowed no other interpretation. It appeared to Elias Hicks that it sought to impose a doctrinal yoke on the Society and to use the authority of the elders to enforce the new orthodoxy.

A number of very earnest Evangelical ministers from England travelled extensively in America during the

[5] *Jour.*, p. 315. Cf. *ibid.*, p. 304.
[6] *The Quaker,* vol. III, p. 212. *Jour.*, p. 383.
[7] *Mem.* (Seebohm Ed.), I, 142.

decade 1818–1828, the most noteworthy of them being William Forster, George Withy, Isaac Stephenson, Elizabeth Robson, George and Ann Jones, Thomas Shillitoe and Anna Braithwaite, of whom the last four were the most active. These Friends were actuated by the zeal of new converts to defend and propagate their views, especially since they believed the Evangelical doctrines necessary to salvation.[8] Some of them followed Elias Hicks about during his last two preaching tours in Philadelphia Yearly Meeting, denouncing his doctrines in public. "The women Friends in particular, acting (it is needless to say) from a strong sense of duty, gave great offense to many by entering the men's meetings under religious concern and delivering long and impassioned addresses against 'infidelity.'"[9] Pamphlets and letters were published as the tension increased. A sharp controversy developed between Elias Hicks and Anna Braithwaite in New York Yearly Meeting. The latter had a talk with Elias and got a letter from him stating his views. Although it was written as a private letter, she published it together with very caustic comments, supposed to have been written by Joseph John Gurney. None of them seems to have made any genuine effort at reconciliation or mutual understanding.

The theology of Elias Hicks, although it was the occasion of conflict between himself and the Philadelphia elders, was not of itself important in Quaker history. It was never officially adopted by the division of Friends that came to be called, against their will, by his name[10] and few if any Friends would regard it as an adequate theology today; nevertheless some statement of his position is necessary in order to understand why it aroused such intense hostility.[11]

In the center of his theology was the old Quaker and

---

[8] Grubb, *Separations*, p. 17.
[9] *Ibid.*, pp. 31, 32.
[10] Grubb, *op. cit.*, p. 19.
[11] A good summary is given in JLPQ, I, 444–456.

Quietist doctrine of the Inward Light. He distinguished sharply between man's fallen nature and a portion of the divine life within him, which can operate effectively only "in the silence of all flesh." He held the same dualistic conception of human nature as the Evangelicals, although he expressed it in a different way. He believed strongly in the sufficiency of the Inward Divine Principle as a guide and savior of men.[12] His first theological principle was: God is Spirit. Consequently he held that all outward forms and helps are unnecessary and may even become hindrances to the religious life. He was, therefore, afraid of reliance on "the instrumentality of man"; the outward ministry and the Scriptures were to him useful but unnecessary to man's spiritual life; and the abuse of them greatly to be feared. To him education was religiously unnecessary; and *studied* preaching valueless. In this depreciation of education he came near the Evangelical position again. At times he so exalted the inner power and work of God in the soul and made man's dependence on it so absolute, that it almost amounted to a doctrine of election.[13]

While he valued the Bible highly as a source of spiritual knowledge and inspiration, he denied that it was an authoritative or final rule of faith or practice. He emphasized strongly continuous revelation. He was afraid of idolizing the Scriptures; and asserted that the literal and unspiritual use of them had done great harm; as, for example, when the Bible was made a warrant for slavery, war and religious intolerance. He believed in the divinity of Christ as one who was distinguished by the possession of a limitless measure of the Spirit. The historical life of Jesus had no great spiritual significance for him except as an example of a life wholly given over to following the Inward Guide; and he thought that the death of Christ as a historical

---

[12] *Jour.*, p. 304.
[13] JLPQ., I, 447.

event had no personal efficacy for the individual. He rejected the idea of the necessity of divine justice. The only "satisfaction" which God requires, he asserted, comes from the birth or creation of a new righteous self through the inworking of the Christ within.[14]

While Hicks believed in the fallen or "creaturely" nature of man, he rejected the idea of inherited guilt and the moral ruin of the race through Adam's sin. He believed that every new-born soul starts life morally clean and that all sin originates in self-will, just as Adam's sin originated. He spoke often of life as a "probationary scene."[15] In consonance with these views he did not believe in imputed righteousness. The only righteousness that ever saved any individual in the world, he said, is obedience to the manifestation of God's will within him.[16]

This theology shocked the Evangelical Friends very seriously. They took particular exception to his attitude in regard to the divinity of Christ, the inspiration of the Bible, and the atonement. To be sure, Hicks believed in all three, but with limitations and denials which to them amounted to infidelity. In his positions he did not go much beyond Woolman or Job Scott, but there had developed since their day a greater sensitiveness about theology among Friends. He was a little more logical in his thinking than his immediate predecessors, and while most of the men of his generation were somewhat hazy as to the relative place of the Bible and the Inner Light as sources of religious authority, he was neither hazy nor vacillating in his opinion. He held theology to be one of the nonessentials of the spiritual life. He had no disposition to make the Evangelicals conform to his doctrines nor to prevent them from preaching their own. He did claim, however, the right to explain Christianity in what seemed to

---

14 JLPQ, I, 455. *A Doctrinal Epistle,* p. 30.
15 *A Doctrinal Epistle,* pp. 17, 18.
16 *Ibid.,* pp. 10–12.

him a reasonable way; and it was largely by what he denied rather than by what he affirmed that he gave offense.

Rufus Jones comments on the situation:

> Nobody in the Society of Friends had adequately faced the implications and the difficulties involved in the doctrine of the Inner Light, and nobody on the other hand reached any true comprehension of the relation of historical revelation to the Light within the individual soul. Individual Friends used one or the other source of authority as suited their convenience or bent of mind. For a whole generation the Society had tacked, like a ship sailing against the wind, in a curious zig-zag, back and forth from Scripture to Inner Light and from Inner Light to Scripture.[17]

By 1827, however, the Evangelicals had ceased to vacillate as to the source of authority on one side and Elias Hicks on the other.

The first evidence of conflict between Elias Hicks and the Philadelphia elders was at the Pine Street meeting in Philadelphia in 1819, the occasion being far from theological. While he was visiting the women's meeting under a concern approved by the men's meeting, the latter adjourned and it was regarded by Elias' friends as a deliberate act of disrespect.[18]

It was chiefly as an official, as an elder and as clerk of Philadelphia Yearly Meeting, that Samuel Bettle had a part in the separation; but his actions as an official were the product of his character as a man. He was assistant clerk of the yearly meeting six years (1810–1816), and clerk for fourteen years (1816–1830). He was a strong character, quiet, determined, and persistent, accustomed to managing

---

17 JLPQ, I, 457.

18 Jonathan Evans, the prime mover in having the meeting adjourn, had been at one time an abstainer from the use of products of slave labor, but had gone back to the use of them and was much upset by Elias Hicks' strictures on the subject. Janney, *An Examination of the Causes which Led to the Separation of the Religious Society of Friends in America in 1827–28*, pp. 212, 213.

men. Conscientious, high-minded, careful of his inward peace and the integrity of his motives, he was ruled less by emotion than Comly or Shillitoe and less by reason than Hicks. As a business man he was accustomed to deal with men on the basis of business ethics and legal rights. In the Society the highest good seemed to him to be the maintenance of the old order by rigorous and impartial enforcement of the discipline. While he was thus contentedly conservative as to the discipline and organization of the Society, he had adopted the Evangelical doctrines. How far the new doctrines expressed a fresh spiritual experience, as they did with Rebecca Jones, Stephen Grellet or Thomas Shillitoe, it is impossible to say. More probably he simply accepted the current doctrines of influential Philadelphia Friends, such as Rebecca Jones, Thomas Scattergood, William Savery, Samuel Emlen and John Pemberton. Possibly he had read Henry Tuke's little manual, *The Faith of the People Called Quakers*.

With Bettle and his generation certain forms of doctrine came to be regarded as an essential part of "unsoundness" within the meaning of the discipline, and the elders set themselves to deal with "unsoundness" as the overseers dealt with outward infractions of the discipline. As in the Catholic church, heresy thus became rebellion against authority.

In 1822 Elias Hicks made a tour of the country meetings in Philadelphia Yearly Meeting down the Brandywine and up the Delaware. When he returned to Philadelphia the elders had received communications charging him with unsoundness. A group of them arranged for an interview with him regarding his reported utterances. Elias brought some of his friends with him to the meeting. This was a reasonable precaution in view of the very divergent impressions which may be honestly carried away from such an interview. The elders, however, insisted that the meeting be "select," that is, composed only of ministers and elders, who were charged by the discipline with dealing with unsoundness. Elias would not agree to the meeting without the presence of his friends and the attempt at a conference failed. In the correspondence that followed between the ten elders and Elias Hicks, he denied that the alleged utterances truly represented his beliefs, his words or the impression which most of his hearers had received, for they were quoted out of their context and otherwise garbled. It is doubtful, however, whether this interview represents the real watershed of the separation in Bettle's experience; nevertheless he had adopted a policy there and in the subsequent correspondence that was to lead to a tragedy which none of the parties yet desired or foresaw. Nearly thirty years afterward Bettle publicly stated that he believed that patient labor and suffering would have been better than division.[19] If so, the most promising moment for the exercise of patience and forbearance was the interview with Hicks in 1822.

Even after this incident, however, it was not too late for him to turn back. On two other critical occasions he faced the problem with fuller opportunity to foresee the outcome. In 1822 as a consequence of a newspaper controversy involving Friends' views, the Philadelphia Meeting for Sufferings adopted a thoroughly "Evangelical" statement of belief drawn from standard writings of Friends, and had an edition printed for public distribution.[20] When the minutes of the Meeting for Sufferings were read in the yearly meeting of 1823 a great storm arose, because the approval of the minutes would seem to make the document an official doctrinal statement of the yearly meeting. After long and exciting discussion extending through two sessions, Samuel Bettle as clerk finally made a suggestion of compromise which was accepted: "To avoid both diffi-

19 Hodgson, *Hist.*, II, 219, 220.
20 Foster, *Report*, II, 414–416.

culties by simply suspending the publication; not taking it off the minutes, and not circulating the pamphlets, but leaving the subject." [21]

In the sequel the opponents of the statement, who were largely country Friends, felt that they had been tricked again by the political finesse of Bettle and the other city elders; for when the minutes of the yearly meeting appeared, the statement appeared in the official minutes as part of an approved document. This gave a quasi-official standing to the Evangelical doctrines and a ground of official authority to the elders in their procedure against Elias Hicks and his sympathizers. It is not necessary to suspect Bettle of conscious trickery in his action. Nevertheless the normal procedure in face of such opposition to receiving the statement would have been to announce that there was not sufficient unity for the meeting to take action. Bettle was sincerely anxious to have the statement adopted and according to his own testimony in court at the Trenton trial he was accustomed to attach no weight to the opinions of the Friends who opposed its acceptance.[22] His action had further unfortunate consequences, for it led both parties further in the direction of seeking to gain advantage through disciplinary technicalities rather than by relying on fairness, patience and truth.

John Comly (1773–1850) of Byberry went to Westtown as a young teacher in 1801, when the school was but two years old. His description of the natural beauty of its location shows a spirit as rarely sensitive to outward beauty as it was to the inward harmonies of the spirit. After a few months there he married a fellow-teacher, and set up a private Friends school at Byberry, north of Philadelphia.[23] He was preëminently a Quietist mystic, with a soul as clear and as responsive to spiritual influences as the surface of a

---

21 Foster, *op. cit.*, I, 72.

22 *Ibid.*, I, 82.

23 *Jour.*, pp. 98, 132.

mountain lake to the breeze. He strove to keep it unruffled by outward circumstance or by the breath of evil desire, so that it might perfectly mirror the heavenly glory above. The early pages of his *Journal* are largely taken up with accounts of his feelings during meeting, with his efforts to attain inward collectedness and quietness of mind. At times he used the phrases of the current political and theological discussions, such as "the Great First Cause," "rational probability," and "inalienable rights," but they were little more than schoolmaster's jargon. He was probably one of the most scholarly Friends of the period; but in his religious life, it was not intellectual certitude which he sought, but rather the mystic's peace.

When the doctrinal controversies and struggles over the appointment of officials began to rage in the business meetings, and the vocal exercises of the meetings for worship were occupied by thinly disguised and intense theological debates, his soul was sore troubled. In such an atmosphere he could not keep the inner mirror unclouded. He could not make out the "accents of the Holy Ghost" amid the clamor. His religious experience was not of the Evangelical type, and he shrank from the Evangelical aggressiveness and intolerance. His city Friends soon marked his lack of sympathy, labeled him as "unsound," and avoided him. He felt very lonely amid the strife, which robbed him at once of the inner consolations of the meeting for worship and the outward solace of friendship. He records the critical points in his experience in the following revealing words:

Having thus viewed the awful state of Friends in the city and having seen the spreading of the same spirit in various parts of our Y.M., my mind had shared with others in deep exercise on account of these things, and became impressed with a religious concern to make a visit to the city, in order to mingle with Friends, and see and feel whether any opening might be present for active labour, in endeavouring to promote a reconciliation between the two contending parties. In accordance with this view and impression, I attended the quarterly meeting of ministers and elders held there in Second month, 1827, in which I had a full view of the nature of that spirit that was seeking to bear rule in the Society. I beheld also the confusion of languages among them, so that they could not understand one another's speech. As I sat silently observing the operations of the meeting, my heart melted in a feeling of brotherly compassion and pity toward Friends of both parties, and strong desires were raised in me that there might be a restoration of peace and harmony among them. . . .

The meeting not being able to get through its business till near four o'clock in the afternoon, occasioned a long sitting, trying to the patience but more so to the gentle feelings of Christian meekness and love.

Although this painful meeting afforded little prospect of a reconciliation, my mind was turned toward seeking for an opening to converse with some of the active ones in order to see and feel whether any door of hope remained for healing the awful breach. But some of them having long appeared to regard me with an eye of suspicious jealousy afforded no opportunity for such interview. Cold, distant, inhospitable, they passed by and left me to myself.[24]

My mind was opened to see, [he declares a little later,] that this contest would result in a separation of the two conflicting parts of the Society, as the only means of saving the whole from a total wreck; and the way and manner of this separation was clearly unfolded to my mental vision; that on the part of Friends it must be effected in the peaceable spirit of the non-resisting Lamb—first by ceasing from the spirit of contention and strife, and then uniting together in the support of the order and discipline of the Society of Friends, separate and apart from those who had introduced the difficulties, and who claimed to be the orthodox part of the Society.[25]

This then was to be the way out: "A quiet retreat from the scene of confusion." [26] It had the apparent simplicity of genius. He and other Friends together should quietly

[24] *Jour.*, pp. 306, 307.
[25] *Ibid.*, pp. 309, 310.
[26] *Ibid.*, pp. 310, 629.

abandon the meeting-houses, schools and other outward paraphernalia of the Society to the contenders, and themselves meet and rebuild in quietness the spiritual fellowship that had been lost. Early in 1827 John Comly proposed to his friends, who were chiefly sympathizers with Elias Hicks, that they withdraw from the yearly meeting; but they were not yet ready for such an extreme measure. They determined to make a last effort to beat the "Orthodox" (as the Evangelical party were now called) at their own game and seize control of the yearly meeting by electing a clerk from their own party. The discipline provided that the clerks should be nominated by the representatives from the quarterly meetings, but did not specify the number of representatives to be sent by each meeting, although custom had fixed an appropriate quota for each. The three sympathetic quarterly meetings sent about double the usual number to the yearly meeting, thus "packing" the nominating committee in their favor. The representatives met after the first session of the yearly meeting to nominate the clerks but were unable to agree and their meeting was prolonged until after the hour for the meeting to reconvene. It was the custom for the former clerks to serve until new ones were appointed; consequently Samuel Bettle resumed his place as clerk with John Comly as assistant clerk. By the simple device of holding the representatives in session until the hour for the next session came, the Orthodox secured a clerk of their own party.

This was the last straw for the Hicks party. Despairing of outmanoeuvering the Orthodox in disciplinary procedure, ignored by the clerk in making up the "sense" of the meeting, with the great bulwarks of official authority—the Select Meeting and the Meeting for Sufferings—in the hands of their opponents, they were faced with the alternative either to submit or secede. Even then a separation might have been avoided by a gesture of conciliation on the part of the Orthodox. If Samuel Bettle had promised to serve as clerk only until a new one could be regularly nominated; if the Orthodox members of the representative body had deferred to the majority for the sake of unity; or if the clerk had assured the other party that due weight would be given their voices in determining the will of the meeting, there might even at that late hour have been no separation. Such an attitude of consideration would have been safe for the Orthodox, because the other party was not seeking to impose a theology on them nor infringe their liberty of preaching, nor deny them the place which their numbers, wisdom and Christian character would give them in a Christian democracy. But "feelings averse to reconciliation" had been aroused. The sense of disciplinary rectitude was strong, and the elders could not believe that Friends would actually revolt.

The "Hicksite" group held conferences at Green Street Meetinghouse at night during the time of the yearly meeting, perfecting plans for the "quiet retreat," meanwhile taking part in the business of the yearly meeting. On the last day the yearly meeting appointed a committee to attend all the subordinate meetings with authority to assist and help them. Its last action was to appropriate money for helping North Carolina Friends remove free Negroes from the state.

After the close of the yearly meeting John Comly and his friends held a conference and issued an address, setting forth their case and principles.[27] It stated the fundamental principle of Quakerism as: "God alone is sovereign Lord of conscience." It asserted that a division existed in the yearly meeting over points of doctrine; that oppressive measures had been used and feelings aroused "averse to reconciliation," and proposed a "quiet retreat from the scene of confusion." They asserted that they had no new gospel or discipline to propose. In June another conference

[27] Comly, *Jour.*, pp. 627–629.

was held which issued a call for a yearly meeting in October "for Friends in unity with us" and invited both quarterly and monthly meetings to send representatives to it. This conference organized a Philadelphia Yearly Meeting and decided to meet regularly in April.[28]

There was a possibility that the separation in Philadelphia Yearly Meeting might have been localized there and not spread to other yearly meetings. It did not, in fact, lead to separations in New England, Virginia and North Carolina. Neither in New York nor Baltimore was the feeling so intense nor were the party lines so sharply drawn. That it did not stop with Philadelphia was due largely to the influence of Thomas Shillitoe (1754–1836), the fourth of the Friends chiefly responsible for the separation.[29] He was a convinced Friend, who brought a Church of England background, the Evangelical creed, and a fine missionary fevor into the service of a mystic devotion. He was almost as sensitive to spiritual atmosphere and visitations as John Comly. In "strippedness of the creature" he sought only to be true to the Inward Guide. He had a passion for lost souls and an interest in hardened sinners, and his preaching had something of the power and method of Whitefield. He kept as close, however, to the traditional Quaker methods as Hicks did; working only under a special concern and avoiding organized and long-planned evangelistic effort. When he came to America in 1826, he prayed after landing in New York that "quietness as a canopy in mercy" might "be the covering of his mind."[30] He kept

---

[28] Comly, *op. cit.*, pp. 630–636.

[29] The part of English Friends in causing the division in American Quakerism is variously estimated. Samuel M. Janney expressed the opinion that without the active interference of the earnest, if somewhat tactless English Evangelicals, already mentioned, the crisis might have passed without splitting the Society asunder, but this is by no means certain. *History of the Religious Society of Friends*, IV, 177, 178. But cf. Grubb, *op. cit.*, pp. 15, 50, 51.

[30] *Jour.*, II, 151.

in touch at first with both sides, and the "followers of Elias Hicks" entertained hopes at one time that he would espouse their cause. The decisive moment seems to have been during a visit to Jericho, Long Island, Elias Hicks' home town, where he was entertained in a Friend's house near Elias' home. While in Jericho he was visited by some of Hicks' friends, who urged him to call on them. At first he was inclined to acquiesce, but "after waiting where the divine counsellor is to be met with" he changed his mind. His *Journal* records the crucial experience:

> We took our dinner with G. Seaman; after which we proceeded to Jericho, and took up our abode this night with our kind friend Thos. Willis. In passing through the village of Jericho, E.H. was at his own door, he invited me into his own house to take up my abode. . . . I refused his offer in as handsome a manner as I well knew how. He then pressed me to make him a call. I was careful to make such a reply as would not make it binding upon me, although we had to pass his door on our way to the next meeting. I believe it was safest for me not to comply with his request.[31]

The result might possibly have been different if they had come together and discovered their spiritual oneness underneath the divergent outward forms of speech and thought. Soon after this, Shillitoe threw himself into the struggle on the Orthodox side and from that time he was the stormy petrel of the controversy. He conceived it his duty to follow Elias Hicks about, exposing his errors and denouncing his unsoundness with the fierce fervor of a crusader.

When New York Yearly Meeting assembled in 1828, he stretched a customary courtesy into a claim that his minute from London Yearly Meeting constituted him temporarily a full member of New York Yearly Meeting. Using this privilege, he objected to the presence of "disowned mem-

[31] *Jour.*, II, 154.

bers" (*i.e.*, members of the "Hicksite" party) from Philadelphia. At that time none but Friends and only those in regular standing were allowed to attend business meetings. This proposition to treat the Philadelphia visitors as non-Friends was rejected, but precipitated the division, the Orthodox withdrawing from the house. Thomas Shillitoe and Elias Hicks were both present at Ohio Yearly Meeting the same year, where the former's uncompromising attitude contributed to the final schism.[32]

Thus under the stimulus of the separation which occurred in Philadelphia Yearly Meeting in the spring of 1827, the conflicting tendencies produced divisions in four other yearly meetings the following year. There were violent scenes in New York and Ohio yearly meetings on account of the efforts of the contending parties to control the organization, involving even physical violence over the possession of clerks' desks and of the official records. In Baltimore and Indiana the division was more peaceable. In the former the Orthodox minority walked out quietly and reorganized in another place. In the latter the Hicksite minority seceded and set up a separate organization before the time of the regular yearly meeting. New England, Virginia and North Carolina yearly meetings were not divided and aligned themselves with the Orthodox. London and Dublin yearly meetings also "recognized" the Orthodox yearly meetings.

---

32 *Jour.*, II, 343–346.

CHAPTER 24

THE EFFECTS OF THE SEPARATION

THE third division of Quaker history, from 1827 to the present time, was dominated by the Evangelical creed and program. The first period (ending in 1861) resulted in the triumph of the Evangelical theology over Quietism in both doctrine and methods of religious work. The second period (which ended with the first World War), marked the triumph of Evangelicalism over Quietism in ministry and worship. This was followed in the third period by the struggle between the world outlook of Evangelicalism and modern Liberalism in science, philosophy and theology, with a revival of early Quaker mysticism. The whole third division was characterized by separations in the Society; but such separations lost their power to shake the Society to its foundations after 1857 when Philadelphia Yearly Meeting[1] ceased correspondence with other yearly meetings. The later Wilburite Separations (1877–1905) did not convulse Quakerdom as the Hicksite, Wilburite and Beaconite divisions had done.

As the separation of 1827–1828 marked the acceptance of the Evangelical theology on the part of the main body of American Friends, the Anti-slavery movement marked the beginning of the adoption of the Evangelical program as well. It signalized the first great step in the abandonment of the aloofness of the Society in America from official par-

[1] See below chap. 25, p. 355.

ticipation in the great reform movements, which Friends initiated or shared. This had already begun in England. As early as 1787 the members of the "Quaker Committee" had joined with a group of non-Friends "for effecting the Abolition of the Slave Trade." [2] In 1830 London Yearly Meeting in the General Epistle which was printed and circulated by the American yearly meetings,[3] said concerning the evils of slavery, intemperance and war, "We recommend to our members individually to unite with their fellow-countrymen in the measures now in progress for the removal of those evils." [4] Individual English Friends on their own initiative had already joined with non-Friends in Bible societies, prison reform, education and other good causes.[5]

After the separations of 1827–1828 the attention and energies of Friends were largely occupied for two decades with the readjustments made necessary by the divisions. The difficulty of finding distinguishing names for the American divisions of the Society was felt at once, since each "branch" claimed to be the true Society of Friends. The title "Orthodox" was applied to the "Evangelical" group with a certain appropriateness and acceptability since they laid great stress on their doctrinal soundness, but it was not adopted by them officially.[6] Their meetings adopted the device of publishing the names of "correspondents" to whom official documents should be addressed, to prevent them from going to meetings of the other branch claiming the same name. Some of them added to their official name the phrase "in unity with the ancient yearly meetings of Friends." [7] The Orthodox party made

---

2 Edgerton, *op. cit.*, pp. 19, 20.

3 *Ibid.*, p. 25.

4 *Loc. cit.*

5 See above chap. 20, pp. 259, 262, 263.

6 After the later separations the name "Orthodox" ceased to be altogether distinctive since both "Gurneyites" and "Wilburites" were orthodox.

7 Thomas, *Hist.*, p. 169.

a great deal of the fact that no yearly meeting as a whole went with the Hicksites.

Most commonly the other branch has been called "Hicksite," because Elias Hicks was the occasion of the separation and because he associated himself with them; but the name has not been acceptable to them, both because it is a party name while they claimed to be the original Society of Friends and because they never adopted his teaching.[8]

Law suits to determine the ownership of meeting property occurred in New Jersey (for Philadelphia Yearly Meeting), New York and Ohio—all instituted by the Orthodox. The Hicksites offered to divide the property on the basis of relative numbers, but the Orthodox regarded themselves as trustees of property left for the use of Friends and could not conscientiously surrender any of it to those whom they regarded as no longer Friends. The Chancery Court of New Jersey decided in favor of the Orthodox, on both legal and doctrinal grounds, although the Hicksites refused to reply on points of doctrine.[9] Later the State Legislature passed a bill providing for the division of the property in New Jersey. In Baltimore and New York yearly meetings and in the State of Pennsylvania the Hicksites generally remained in possession of the property where they were in the majority. Thus most of the country meeting-houses remained with them. In Philadelphia the bulk of the city property and the control of Westtown School, Tunesassa Indian School and Frankford Asylum remained

---

8 Since no set of names proposed is generally acceptable or appropriate, I have somewhat reluctantly adopted in this history, the usage of the U.S. census, and of the Thomas and Rowntree histories, calling the two branches "Orthodox" and "Hicksite." In the east the branches were very commonly designated according to the location of their meeting-houses in the large cities in New York, Orthodox and Hicksite being 20th St. and 15th St., respectively; in Philadelphia, Arch St. and Race St., respectively, and in Baltimore, Eutaw St. and Park Ave.

9 A very full report of the trial is given in Foster's *Report*.

in the hands of the Orthodox. The law suit in New York to determine ownership of the property was won by the Hicksites, who presented a fairly orthodox statement of doctrines; the one in Ohio by the Orthodox. These suits did much to deepen the division and accentuate the bitterness between the two branches. As a rule the Orthodox rigidly disowned the Hicksites, in order to vindicate their disciplinary position.

It is impossible to get exact statistics concerning the numerical strength of the two branches after the separations. In Philadelphia, where about two-thirds of the membership went with the Hicksites, there were approximately 16,000 Hicksites and 8,000 Orthodox. But in the city of Philadelphia the proportions were reversed, there being about 1,500 Hicksites and 3,000 Orthodox; which shows how largely it was a division between country and city. In New York the Hicksite party had approximately two-thirds of the membership; in Baltimore three-fourths; in Ohio about half. Only a small proportion of the members of Indiana Yearly Meeting withdrew, possibly not more than 1,500 altogether. The membership of the Hicksite yearly meetings at the time of the separation probably numbered between 35,000 and 45,000—by far the majority of the divided yearly meetings; but when the three undivided yearly meetings—New England, Virginia and North Carolina—are included with the Orthodox, the numbers of Orthodox and Hicksite Friends in America were about equal. Counting London and Dublin yearly meetings, the Orthodox groups had a decided preponderance of those who bore the name of Friends in the world.

On the whole, the Orthodox were the more promising group. The great majority of the official class—elders, overseers, ministers and members of the Meeting for Sufferings—were found in this branch. The city Friends, especially in Philadelphia, New York and Baltimore, constituted the more influential element among them and contributed a greater degree of education, culture and wealth. They were a positive and unified group. All who were undecided between the two contending parties or who refused to take sides or who were not decidedly orthodox in doctrine were rigidly disowned by the Orthodox. No one was allowed to "sit on the fence"—all who were not for them were against them. They were thus a fairly homogeneous, disciplined body, united by positive doctrinal beliefs, which carried with them by implication a working program and for the moment, at least, opened the way for progress. A teaching ministry was revived. *The Friend,* the first Quaker "church paper" in America, was established in Philadelphia just after the separation in the fall of 1827. They had Westtown School and inherited the awakening interest in education which led to the founding of Haverford College, shortly after the division (1833). There was a revival of literary activity among them. Thomas Evans published his *Exposition* of early Friends' views on the disputed points in Elias Hicks' teaching, and he and his brother William edited early Friends' writings in the *Friends' Library,* which ran to fourteen volumes. In 1829 the Orthodox yearly meetings sent representatives to a meeting in Philadelphia which prepared a *Testimony* &c—a very Evangelical statement which was adopted by all the yearly meetings represented.[10] They had the active support of the English Evangelicals, some of whom—notably John and Hannah C. Backhouse—did much to organize Bible classes and distribute Bibles among them. In 1830 a Bible Society was organized. The inherent intolerance of the Evangelical attitude toward intellectual progress, the conservatism of the elders and the rigidity of the discipline were destined, however, ultimately to neutralize these advantages to a great extent and to nullify much of the early promise of this branch.

---

10 JLPQ, I, 482.

The Hicksites, on the other hand, were a relatively heterogeneous group. Few of them shared Elias Hicks' doctrinal views. Probably most of them went with this branch chiefly as a protest against the arbitrary proceedings and theological intolerance of the Orthodox party. Many sided with them principally for social or family reasons. Many were simply disowned into this branch by the Orthodox. They were essentially a conservative group, except for the element of insurgency against the ancient authority of the elders. They shared the common Quaker traditions and practices in regard to meetings for worship and business, "dress and address," and philanthropic causes. At first they were even more conservative toward these traditions than the Orthodox. The doctrine of the Inward Light was held as Quietist Friends of the century previous had held it.

The first effect of the separation on them, however, at least in Philadelphia, seems to have been to cause a reaction in favor of more "orthodox" teaching. At all events, they addressed an Epistle to London Yearly Meeting in 1830, in which they protest that they hold *essentially* the same doctrines as they had always held, and that English Friends have misjudged them on *ex parte* testimony. They claim that the dissensions have not been caused by doctrinal differences so much as by the "exercise of an oppressive authority in the church." They also claim to accept the Scriptures with their record of Jesus Christ, and the fundamental principle of the light of Christ within, as God's gift for man's salvation, and all the blessed doctrines which grow from it as their root. They end by referring to their large majority over the other branch.[11]

They protested in their first published declaration that they had no new gospel to promulgate,[12] and their Philadelphia Yearly Meeting kept for a generation the old discipline which made it a disownable offense to deny "the

11 Thomas, *Hist.*, pp. 160–161.
12 Comly, *Jour.*, p. 629.

authenticity of the Holy Scriptures and the divinity of Christ." In the law suit over the possession of property in New York, the Hicksites submitted a statement of doctrine that was quite orthodox. There was a strong protest, however, against an orthodox reaction, which was led by Lucretia Mott. In the end freedom of doctrinal expression became the established policy. They held doctrines, not as essentials of Christian faith but as fruits of it. They were consequently very tolerant toward divergent statements of theological belief. The doctrine of the Inward Light, which was their one common theological belief, was construed generally in terms of individual responsibility and freedom of conscience and tended toward pure individualism.[13] They lacked a corporate discipline or common working program which would make progress and coöperation easy on any but traditional lines. They were united more consciously in many ways by what they did not believe than by what they did believe. They did not believe in arbitrary authority in the church; nor in the Evangelical theology, nor in organized religious or philanthropic activities. They were consequently nearly a generation behind the Orthodox in educational, literary and other new lines of corporate religious activity.[14] But their tolerant spirit has saved them further separation and from the violent struggles against organized conservatism and doctrinal intolerance which have befallen the Orthodox groups.

After the separation Friends were to remain for at least a century a small religious sect with its testimony weakened and its energies dissipated by division. The spectacle of its contentions and divisions weakened its prestige. For a generation, the energies that should have gone into the work of building up the kingdom of Christ had to be spent largely in the processes of revision and reconstruction

13 Hodgson, *Hist.*, I, 223, 224.

14 Their paper, *The Friends Intelligencer,* was founded in 1844 and Swarthmore College was opened in 1866.

which the divisions necessitated. The bitterness of the struggle tended to spiritual paralysis. The intense party feeling alienated neighbors, separated life-long friends and divided families.[15]

The separations led to a mutilated Quakerism. The Quaker heritage was divided between the branches, with the result that no group remained as a witness to the full-rounded Quaker gospel.[16] They divided up the literary heritage and religious emphasis. William Penn and Job Scott were popular with the Hicksites; Barclay and Woolman with the Orthodox. One stressed the mystical manifestation of Christ; the other the historic. The Inner Light came to be regarded by the Orthodox as a "Hicksite" expression; the phrase, the blood of Christ, became a badge of Orthodoxy.

The dismemberment of Quakerism went even deeper when the principle of separation had worked itself out in the Orthodox bodies in the conservative (Wilbur-Gurney) separations and the isolation of Philadelphia Yearly Meeting from the progressive yearly meetings. At the opening of the nineteenth century Quakerism had come to include three things: (1) the doctrine of the Inner Light as a principle of spiritual power and guidance in the individual; (2) a body of teachings and practices handed down from the Founders or developed during the ensuing century and finally embodied in the authoritative traditions and in the discipline of the Society; (3) a working organization for

[15] One reads with mixed feelings—comic and tragic struggling for dominance—of two Quaker brothers, partners in business but belonging to different branches, who would not speak to each other on First-day morning, if they happened to pass each other on the way to meeting, so great was the fear of seeming to condone one another's error!

[16] The Pennsylvania Dutchman who attempted to explain to a neighbor the commotion among their Quaker fellow-colonists was only wrong as to the basis of the partition. Without attempting his dialect his explanation ran thus: "They found out they couldn't agree, and so they agreed to disagree and divide up what they had. So the Orthodox took the theology and the Hicksites took the religion; and each got what he wanted."

the purpose of applying Christian principles and leadings to the concrete needs of the membership and of the world. In the various divisions of the Society each main group has retained and specially emphasized one of these elements of the larger Quaker heritage. The Hicksite branch stood chiefly on the first; to them nothing was essential in Quakerism except for each individual and group to follow faithfully the inner leading of Christ. Historical forms of Quakerism are interesting to them but not vital as such. Philadelphia Yearly Meeting Orthodox and the Conservative yearly meetings stressed the second element; they regarded the traditional beliefs and practices of the Society as more or less essential elements in Quakerism.[17]

After the separation of 1827–1828 each branch went its own way. Each developed its own religious vocabulary; cultivated different modes of thought and different lines of activity. In time each branch found religious fellowship with a different group of denominations. The Orthodox came more under the influence of the Evangelical churches. They used the Sunday school literature and borrowed the religious music of their neighbors. The Hicksites associated more with the liberal or non-creedal denominations. The result of these developments has been to make it more difficult for the two branches to understand or to coöperate with each other. In London Yearly Meeting the various types of Quakerism have remained united, worshipping together, serving on committees and transacting meeting business together. Consequently they understand each other and know how to coöperate in worship and religious work. But in America, when the two groups began to associate together in later generations, an interpreter was al-

[17] The later "Gurneyite" branches have laid great stress on the third element; it is the Society as a working body that is most important to them. If old methods of preaching, worship, and moral reform will not "work," they may be or must be changed. It is in accordance with this emphasis that many of their yearly meetings have substituted the name "Friends Church" for "Society of Friends."

most necessary at times to enable them to realize that they meant much the same thing by the different ways in which they expressed it.

The effects of the division were particularly felt in the country meetings. In many localities Friends barely had sufficient numbers and resources to minister to the needs of the community together. After the division neither group was strong enough to do this, and as the two resulting meetings were most frequently unequal in size, the weaker usually died out as a result of emigration to the west or into the cities.[18]

It happens occasionally in human history that periods of division and struggle are the seemingly unavoidable accompaniments of progress, when they are due to new ideas or new forces struggling for realization. In such cases as the Protestant Reformation or the Quaker movement in the seventeenth century, there is some compensation for the moral wastage of the struggle. If it bears much fruit, men are reconciled to the loss of the grain that falls into the ground and dies; but there is little compensation for the bitterness and lost opportunities of the separations just reviewed. The Evangelical influence was a sign of change, which ultimately led to new life and activity in the Society. It came, however, not as a victory of the Quaker interpretation of Christianity but rather as an abandonment of it in a great degree for an outside and essentially alien view. Its adherents had to their credit sincerity, tenacity of belief and partisan loyalty. But neither party in the controversy tapped afresh the "infinite ocean of victorious love" which George Fox found; neither party found again the high tension line of divine power which had furnished the amazing energy of the first Quaker movement.[19]

---

[18] Cf. Comly, *Jour.*, pp. 467–472.
[19] Cf. JLPQ, I, 484, 485.

CHAPTER 25

THE GURNEY INFLUENCE AMONG FRIENDS

THE Gurney family of Norwich, England, exercised a remarkable influence on the character and course of Quaker history. John Gurney, the father of Elizabeth Gurney Fry and Joseph John Gurney, and uncle of Hannah Chapman (Gurney) Backhouse, was a merchant and banker of Norwich who leased the neighboring estate of Earlham in 1786.[1] Although he was attached to the Society of Friends, he and his family were "gay" rather than "plain" Friends.[2] His family of eleven children were quite worldly, fond of

1 Although Earlham Hall remained in the hands of the Gurney family for over a century, they never actually owned it. See Lubbock, *Earlham*, p. 46.

2 In spite of the earnest exhortation of travelling ministers and the disciplinary efforts of monthly meetings, there were large numbers of members in England who did not conform to Friends' customs in "dress and address" and in other ways. When their lives were otherwise exemplary, they were not disowned. They attended the meetings for worship but were not usually admitted to business meetings nor appointed on committees nor chosen to serve as elders or overseers. Such Friends were called "gay" Friends. The term does not seem to have been used in America although the attitude existed. See Job Scott, *Jour.*, II, 357, 358. JLPQ, I, 427. The first use of the name that I have found is in Thos. Scattergood, *Jour.*, p. 286: "I have to tell some of the company that they were wearing linsey-woolsey garments, sowing their fields with diverse sorts of grain, and plowing with an ox and ass, etc., and my labor was close indeed. Today a Friend told me that there is a young man who is convinced, and comes to this meeting, whose mother threatened him much if he *thou'd* etc., which he believed it was his duty to do. She went to some of the 'gay' Friends belonging here to make her complaint, and said to them, she wished, if her son must go to the meeting that he might be such a Quaker as they were, who could attend meetings, and yet say *you* and use the world's language in other respects."

music and dancing, and of sports, literature, and society. The older girls were at one time quite inclined to skepticism as to religion; Rousseau's works being favorite reading.

One of two chief influences which brought the children to a strong religious interest was the friendship of an Anglican clergyman, Edward Edwards of Lynn, who was chiefly responsible for two of the sisters, Catherine and Richenda finally joining the Church of England and for bringing Joseph John into fellowship with two of the leaders of the "Low Church" group, who exercised a great Evangelical influence upon him. The other influence came through the family of their uncle Joseph Gurney of the Grove, who were more devoted Friends and attended Goats Lane Meeting, and at whose home they met William Savery and other travelling Friends, who were instrumental in Elizabeth Gurney's profound religious transformation.[3] Through the influence of this family and meeting, Joseph John also was gradually led to a Quaker "conversion."

After Margaret Fell, Elizabeth Gurney Fry, whose prison reform work has already been described,[4] was probably the most influential woman in Quaker history both within the Society and on the outside world. Her sister Hannah married T. Fowell Buxton, the great Anti-slavery leader, who was very sympathetic with Friends' views but finally decided not to join the Society. Buxton's sister married William Forster, the Quaker reformer and evangelist, and thus brought him into the Gurney circle, where he became an intimate friend of Joseph John Gurney and a helpful co-worker in Elizabeth Fry's reforms. A younger brother, Samuel Gurney (1786–1853), was a successful London banker and a Friends minister. He helped finance his sister

---

3 Hare, *The Gurneys of Earlham*, pp. 97–103.

4 Above, chap. 20, pp. 262, 263.

Elizabeth's prison reform work as well as many other reforms and served as treasurer of the British and Foreign Bible Society after 1843. He gave personal service and money during the Irish famine in 1849 and was one of the founders and friends of the Republic of Liberia.

Hannah Chapman (Gurney) Backhouse (1787–1850) was the daughter of Joseph Gurney of Norwich and thus a first cousin of the Gurneys of Earlham. In 1830 she began to travel among American Friends in the hope of helping to heal the breach between Hicksites and Orthodox Friends. The former gave her a hearing at first but remained unconvinced, so that her chief service was among the Orthodox. She spent much time in Pennsylvania and New England. She visited the Quaker frontiers from Canada to Carolina, endured great hardships from the intense cold and comfortless cabins of the Indiana and Ohio pioneers and from the very rough roads both in the west and in the Carolinas. Part of the time she was accompanied by her husband, Jonathan Backhouse, and for long periods her faithful companion was Eliza P. Kirkbride, who became later the third wife of J. J. Gurney. She had a growing concern to provide Friends with Bibles and to induce them to read and teach the Scriptures to their children. She devoted a good deal of time toward the end of her five years' stay in America to addressing meetings on the importance of Bible study, organizing Bible classes and First Day Schools, and introducing the Bible in Friends' Schools. Her work was especially fruitful in Indiana and New England. She prepared a booklet entitled *Scripture Questions for the Use of Schools* which was printed in Philadelphia in 1834. Her work aided materially the spiritual recovery and progress of Orthodox Friends.

By far the most influential of the Norwich Gurneys was Joseph John Gurney (1788–1846). After the founders of the Society, he was the most influential Quaker character, and did more to shape modern Quakerism than any other single person. He developed three fairly distinct characters. First of all, there was the gentleman and scholar. Though descended from both the Gurneys and Barclays, his father was only nominally a Friend. Joseph John Gurney was brought up, therefore, as a "gay" Quaker. He had at first the tastes and led the life of a young English gentleman. He was fond of outdoor sports and music and moved in high society. He had an unusual love for learning and literature. He received his early education at Norwich and Hingham; then he was sent to Oxford, where he was tutored by John Rogers, a classical scholar. While resident at Oxford, he gave some attention to the sciences—chemistry, geology, geometry and algebra; but he was especially proficient in the languages, and could read Latin, Greek, Hebrew, Aramaic, Arabic, Italian and German. After leaving Oxford he pursued his studies privately with great diligence. He read the Church Fathers extensively, made a careful study of the Greek New Testament, and worked through the Hebrew Old Testament. He developed considerable ability as a textual and literary critic. From his linguistic studies he passed to the study of the Bible, and then on to the study of theology. He was probably the greatest Biblical scholar among Friends since Barclay. Barclay's learning was more extensive in his own day, but Gurney's opportunities were greater. Gurney hesitated for a while between purely scholastic pursuits and religious studies, but finally passed from literature to theology.

Thus developed Gurney the theologian. His religious interests gradually swallowed up all others. He became more and more absorbed in reading and writing works on theology, in works of philanthropy and in preaching. He came early under the influence of a more definite theological system than was afforded by the Quakerism of the eighteenth century. It was partly through his Biblical interests and partly through his interest in the Anti-slavery movement and other reforms that Gurney was brought into contact with the Evangelicals. He and William Wilberforce were intimate friends and co-workers, both in the Anti-slavery movement and in the British and Foreign Bible Society. He helped establish the Norwich branch of the latter and was accustomed to entertain large companies of distinguished men and women at Earlham at the time of its annual meeting. At first he was not favorable to the Evangelical theology. He wrote in his diary:

> I believe I am prejudiced against the set of people who call themselves Evangelicals. . . . I differ from them in their favorite doctrine of the *Inefficacy* of good works, though my opinions may bear towards the same point. . . . As to prejudice, it is a sin, and I pray that I may be delivered from it. Pain I certainly have felt in the inclination of our family towards Calvinism and Calvinists. At the same time, I deeply feel that as long as the grand thing, practical Christianity, is kept in view by us all, we have no reason to be discontented at differing from one another on secondary points.[5]

The friendship between Joseph John Gurney and Charles Simeon, the leader of the Low Church School of the Anglican Church was quite strong, and he not only entertained Simeon in his home, but visited him at Cambridge.[6] This significant estimate of Simeon is found in one of his letters:

> The recollection of good old Simeon, whom I used to visit at King's College, is most hallowed in my mind. He was as truly "the saint" as almost anyone I have known, and he knew what it was to "gather into silence"—a lesson which the generality of the clergy are slow to learn. The Puseyism of the present day is a poor exchange for the strong, simple lives of Evangelical piety which characterized Simeon and the party in the Church of England which he led.

5 *Mem.*, I, 60.

6 *Ibid.*, I, 454–458. II, (frontispiece).

He was also much influenced by Henry Venn of Lynn, another Evangelical leader and later by Dr. Chalmers.[7] He was also a friend and co-worker of Bishop Bathhurst of Norwich. Next after these men and the Biblical commentators to which they naturally introduced him, Bishop Butler's *Analogy* exercised the greatest influence upon his religious thinking. He was introduced to the book by his sister, Catherine, who tells us that it had a great influence on his writings and that he embodied the gist of it in his *Portable Evidences*.[8] He was also much indebted to Paley's *Evidences* for materials and arguments.[9]

It was under such influences that Gurney's theology was formed. Its distinctive elements were those of the Evangelical Protestantism of his time. Its principal doctrines were the depravity of man as a result of the fall; the supreme outward authority of the Scriptures; the governmental theory of the atonement; justification as a distinct work from sanctification, and imputed righteousness.[10]

Gurney's Quakerism was the third and latest development in his many-sided character. While his own family was rather indifferent to Quakerism, his uncle Joseph's family exercised a strong influence over him. He often attended meeting with them where he often came under the influence of travelling Friends, both directly and through his sister, Elizabeth. At a critical period he was strongly influenced by Ann Burgess.[11] Points which he had in common with the Quakerism of that day, were his own love of introspection and his efforts at inwardness of religious life and experience. He became more and more devoted to the study of early Quaker literature. His religious

---

7 *Mem.*, I, 507–512.

8 *Mem.*, I, 48.

9 *A View of the Evidences of Christianity. Mem.*, I, 61, 250. Cf. JLPQ, I, 500.

10 *Mem.*, I, 102.

11 After her marriage, Ann Jones, *Mem.*, I, 87, 95.

life was a gradual growth under these influences. He writes:

> I was by no means insensible, in very early life, to religious considerations, being no stranger from the first opening of my mental faculties, to those various visitations of divine life which often draw the young life to its Creator and melt it into tenderness. If religion has indeed grown in me (as I humbly believe it has, although amidst innumerable back-slidings), it has pretty much kept pace with the growth of my natural faculties, for I cannot now recall any decided turning point in this matter, except that which afterwards brought me to "plain" Quakerism. Cases of this description are in my opinion in no degree at variance with the cardinal Christian doctrine of the necessity of conversion and of the new birth into righteousness.[12]

His tendency to self-examination he developed by means of a series of "nightly questions," a sort of brief edition of the queries:

> Have I this day been guarded in all my conversation, saying not one thing inconsistent with truth, purity or charity? Have I felt love towards my neighbor? Have I done my part towards my family? Have I been temperate in all respects, refrained from unlawful desires, habits and anxieties? Have I been diligent in business? Have I given full time to effectual study? Have I admitted any other fear than that of God? Have I passed through the day in deep humility, depending constantly upon and earnestly striving after divine assistance? And have I in everything acted, to the best of my knowledge, according to the will of God? Have I worshipped Him morning and evening? [13]

He was in the habit of devoting a period every three months to what he called "quarterly reviews" of his conduct along all lines. He was gradually drawn into greater sympathy with Friends, and finally was led to adopt "plain

[12] *Mem.*, I, 95–97.
[13] *Ibid.*, I, 51.

Quakerism." For those who grew up as "gay" Quakers, the adoption of the plain speech and dress served as a formal passing into active membership. When he had come to this resolution, he felt constrained to make some public declaration of his purpose. He went to a dinner party to which he was invited, entered the drawing room with his hat on, Quaker fashion, then put his hat in the cloakroom, and spent a very comfortable evening with the party. Afterwards he called on the Bishop of Norwich with hat on and in Quaker garb. After that his position was well understood, and he was invited to social functions no more except when the whole family was invited.[14] Finally, at the age of thirty, after he had for some time spoken occasionally in Friends meeting, he was acknowledged a minister.

The outstanding elements of Gurney's Quakerism were his conscientious scruples about his daily conduct, his love of silent worship, his earnest seeking for spiritual leading, and his active philanthropy. He found in the Friends meeting the source of spiritual power and service.

> The ministry of Friends affected me greatly and was often a means of comfort and strength. I never suffered myself to criticise it, but acted on the uniform principle of endeavoring to obtain from what I heard all the edification which it afforded. This is a principle which I would warmly recommend to my young Friends of today, for nothing can be more mischievous than for learners to turn teachers, and young hearers, critics. I am persuaded that it is often the means of drying up the waters of life in the soul, and sure I am that an exact method of weighing words and balancing doctrines in what we hear is a miserable exchange for tenderness of spirit and for the dews of Heaven.[15]

He took an active part in movements on behalf of slaves and prisoners and the American Indians, and for purifying municipal elections. Clarkson and Wilberforce found sub-

---

[14] *Mem.*, I, 95–127.
[15] *Ibid.*, I, 126.

stantial aid from Gurney's bank in carrying on their Anti-slavery agitation, and his sister, Elizabeth Fry, received much of her means for carrying on her work of prison reform from the quiet gifts of her brother. His interest in the Bible Society has been noticed. He took an active interest in education, especially in the Lancasterian schools and in First Day and Adult schools; and Ackworth received his personal attention and financial help. He was active in work for temperance and peace, for the abolition of capital punishment and for ameliorating the condition of the poor. All of this work is in accordance with his special interest in practical religion.

These three characters, the scholarly gentleman, the theologian, and the Quaker, were never quite fused together. He came to his ideals of scholarship and theology before he became a convert to "plain" Quakerism. It is typical of his somewhat divided character that in his daily program he carried on his Bible studies in the morning and his self-examination at night. He did not seem to get his theological thinking and his Quaker worship much nearer together than that. In one passage he speaks of the two in this fashion, implying that to him Quakerism was something simply superadded to the general Evangelical theology: "The Evangelical foundation, the spiritual superstructure—what a unity in the glorious whole. Who shall dare to mar it either by diminution or addition?"[16] In his most important works Gurney maintained the same distinction. His chief works were: *Observations on the Religious Peculiarities of the Society of Friends,* 1824;

---

[16] Forster, *Mem.,* II, 80. Gurney, *Mem.,* II, 177. He expressed his ideal of worship in these words:

"I own no priesthood, but the priesthood of Christ; no supper in worship, but in spiritual communion with him and his followers at his own table in his kingdom; no baptism, as an introduction to the hopes and citizenship of the Christian believer, but that of the Holy Ghost"; adding emphatically, "I heartily crave and pray that the blessed principle in me of light and life and love (even the perceptible operative influence of the Spirit of Christ), may consummate its victory." *Mem.,* I, 98.

Essays on the Evidences, Doctrines and Practical Operation of Christianity, 1825; *Hints on the Portable Evidence of Christianity*, 1832.[17] In his *Essays* he presents his Evangelical understanding of Scripture doctrine. In his *Observations* he presents the Quaker additions to it. He seems never to have combined the two into one system. It is characteristic that he presents the doctrine of the Universal Light as an *addendum* to a chapter on the grounds of religious union among mankind in the *Essays*. He distinguished sharply between the Universal Light and immediate revelation. He was Evangelical in theology; Quaker in feeling, manner of life and practice of worship. He put the Bible first as the authority for doctrine, but the Spirit first in the conduct of life and worship.[18]

These things aid in understanding the apparent contradictions in Gurney. He encouraged education, loved science, and acknowledged the rights of criticism, but in the acquisition of religious truth he believed all human learning valueless and the imagination of man wholly vain. He used his learning to reason out a system of theology in which the "analogy of nature" and "reasonable probability" played important parts, but beyond that he distrusted the human reason in matters religious. He considered reason sufficient for the stupendous task of proving the inviolable authority of Scripture, but he denied it any authoritative right in the interpretation and evaluation of Scripture. He expended large effort and means for the betterment of his fellowmen, but believed in the total depravity of human nature. The foremost thinker of the Society, he yet distrusted forethought in preaching or worship, and relied more and more on feeling and immediate impulse.[19] In him eighteenth-century Evangelical Ortho-

---

[17] The title is taken from Chalmer's *Reminiscences*, p. 8, where he calls the adaptation of Christian truth to a man's spiritual need "the portable evidence of Christianity."

[18] *Mem.*, I, 247.

[19] *Ibid.*, II, 112, 113, 126.

doxy and Quaker Quietism met. He shared the love of dogmatic authority of the one and the human love and spiritual fellowship of the other. As a manifestation of the one, he helped disown a Unitarian,[20] condemned the "Beaconites," and sympathized with rigid discipline against the Hicksites in America. In other matters he was broad and tolerant, working in the Bible Society and in philanthropic reforms with all sorts and conditions of men, visiting and having social fellowship with churchmen and dissenters, with philanthropists and reformers, of all creeds and of no creed alike.[21]

He also introduced the critical study of the Bible among Friends, although in this he was so far in advance of his time that this work had to wait until a generation had passed in mastering the elements of Biblical knowledge before it could receive attention. In his *Essays* he affirms that "the Scriptures, like any other literature, must be judged by the received rules of criticism and philology." [22] He introduced the principles and methods that make him the John the Baptist of modern Biblical scholarship among Friends.[23]

It was as a theologian that Gurney influenced most profoundly the course of Quaker thought and history. He sought to adjust the Quaker truth to the conditions of his own day and to state it in fresher, more vivid language, and in so doing gave his generation a new theology. He believed that he was only restating the doctrines of primitive Friends, and he was undoubtedly nearer in some matters to the early Friends than were the Quietists of his own

---

20 *Mem.*, I, 108.

21 He protested against the proposed exclusion of Unitarians from the Bible Society. *Ibid.*, I, 470–473.

22 *Essays*, Essay V (p. 135, Phila. Ed., 1856). Among his published works is a critical discussion according to the methods of the later higher criticism of the authorship of the Epistle to the Hebrews. According to the best knowledge of his time, he came to the conclusion that Paul was its author, but he would have followed the same method had it led him, as it has the modern world, to the conclusion that Paul did not write it.

23 *Mem.*, I, 442.

time. Yet it was inevitable that he should bring new ideas and the spirit of the early nineteenth century to the task.

The degree of new thought which Gurney introduced can be seen by comparing his *Essays* and *Observations* with Barclay's *Apology*. Barclay puts the Spirit first as the source of Christian knowledge; Gurney puts the Bible first as the source of doctrine. The difference in emphasis is seen in the order of topics in the *Essays* and in the *Apology*. Barclay's first chapter is on the sources of our religious knowledge; his second on immediate revelation, and his third on the Scriptures. Gurney's first chapter is on the probability of special divine revelation, and the next four are on the credibility and authority of the Scriptures. Barclay regards Christ's death as the effective historical manifestation of the same love and power of God that works for man's salvation through the universal and saving light. Gurney regards the cross of Christ as chiefly efficacious in removing legal obstacles on God's part to man's forgiveness. Barclay says that in justifying man, God first makes him righteous and then treats him as righteous. Gurney says that the righteousness of Christ is imputed to the believer, and that he is made righteous or sanctified by an afterwork of the Holy Spirit. Barclay teaches that conversion and spiritual enduement with power come when and as one yields to the Spirit that "lights every man coming into the world." Gurney believed that the Universal and Saving Light so differs, in degree at least, from the Holy Spirit as the guide of the converted man that they could not fairly be regarded as the same. The filling of the believer with the Holy Spirit he regarded as a sort of after-gift rather than a fuller incoming of the ever-present Spirit of God. Gurney also emphasized more than Barclay the evil of human nature as such. Gurney alone has a chapter on the devil, and assigns him an important place in the Christian scheme of thought.

In one respect at least Gurney radically changed the

basis of Quakerism. In his hands it became a system of doctrine quite divorced from experience; its final authority resting on something external instead of on an experience of the inward work of the Spirit, and the acceptance of a theological dogma being an essential element in saving faith. Thomas Shillitoe's discernment was correct, when he asserted that J. J. Gurney had "spread a linsey-woolsey garment over our members." [24]

Gurney's influence contributed greatly to a new humanism, and a fresh interest in education and Biblical scholarship and it intensified certain Evangelical tendencies that were already at work. It also led to many results that he did not approve, and produced contentions which he greatly deplored. In America he started unintentionally a movement somewhat like the Beaconite movement in England but one which was at once more extensive and less radical. The consequences of the tendencies which he started will appear in subsequent chapters.

---

[24] "I therefore declare, unequivocally, against the generality of the writings of J. J. Gurney, as being non-Quaker principles, not sound Quaker principles, but Episcopalian ones, . . . I declare the author is an Episcopalian, not a Quaker. . . . Episcopalian views were imbibed from his education and still remain with him. I love the man, for the work's sake, so far as it goes, but he has never . . . known the baptism of the Holy Ghost and of fire, to cleanse the floor of his heart from his Episcopalian notions. He has spread a linsey woolsey garment over our members; but in a future day it will be stripped off; it will be too short for them, as they will be without Jesus Christ the Lord." Cited in Hodgson, *Hist.*, I, 312, 313.

CHAPTER 26

THE "BEACONITE" CONTROVERSY AND THE "WILBURITE" SEPARATIONS

AFTER the Hicksite separations in America the zeal of the English Evangelicals was increased to guard against the spread of "Hicksism" to Britain. Ever since the "rationalism" of 1789–1801 Irish Friends were also on the watch for any fresh unsoundness.

The intensified Evangelical tendencies resulted in two developments of special importance. One of these was the "Beaconite" controversy in England and the other the Gurney influence and consequent "Wilburite" separations in America. The increasing emphasis on the authority of the Bible led to the formation of Bible classes in various centers. In Manchester, England, William Boulton, an elder, became the leader of a Bible class for the younger members of the meeting,[1] in which were taught extreme views of the final authority of the Bible, of which Isaac Crewdson (1780–1840), his brother-in-law and a prominent merchant became the chief exponent. A native of Kendal, he resided in or near Manchester from 1795–1844. He was a keen practical business man; a recorded minister and not at all mystical in his religious experience; intellectual in a superficial way and quite opinionated;—neither saint nor scholar

1 *The Friend* (London) 9th, mo. 1, 1870. Edward Ash, "The Beacon Controversy and the Yearly Meetings Committee of 1835–37."

in temperament.[2] He wrote a number of works on religious subjects.[3] He had come under the influence of "the powerful teaching and persuasion of a popular Calvinistic minister, presiding over a congregation of Dissenters in Manchester."[4] The development of his extreme Evangelical views of the Scriptures and his fear of "Hicksism" were intensified by a succession of Quaker ministers who visited the Manchester group 1830–1834.[5] Crewdson became convinced that the fundamental error of "Hicksism" was the doctrine of the Inner Light and the Quietist attitudes and principles. Accordingly he published in 1835 a brochure entitled *A Beacon to the Society of Friends &c.*[6] A second edition with some changes appeared within three months.[7] In his effort to avoid the errors of Elias Hicks he went to the opposite extreme and frankly repudiated the doctrine of the Inner Light and ridiculed the older Quietist expressions and vocabulary. "The great deception" of Hicksism, he says, "appears to have *originated* in the assumption that we are authorized to expect to be taught the true knowledge of God and of his salvation—our duty to him and to our fellowmen, *immediately* by the Spirit, inde-

---

2 His picture in Friend's Reference Library, Friends House, London gives a good idea of his character. See *The Gentleman's Magazine,* 1844, I, 668. Art. "Isaac Crewdson of Manchester."

3 *Religious Declensions &c.,* 1829 (Editor). *The Doctrine of the New Testament on Prayer,* 1831. *A Beacon to the Society of Friends &c.,* 1835. *A Defense of the Beacon,* 1836. *Water Baptism an Ordinance of Christ,* 1837. *The Trumpet Blows or an Appeal to the Society of Friends,* 1838. *Observations on the New Birth,* 1840.

4 *The British Friend,* 1870, p. 242n. Art. signed "D."

5 Prominent among them were Elizabeth Robins (frequently) Anna Braithwaite, George and Ann Jones, Jonathan and Hannah C. Backhouse; Stephen Grellet, John Wilbur, Charles Osborn and Elisha Bates from America; Luke Howard, Benjamin Seebohm and J. J. Gurney. See the MS in Friends Reference Library, London: *An Account of Friends in the Ministry Visiting or Attending Manchester Meeting,* 1818–1870.

6 The Collection of Joseph Bevan Braithwaite on the Beaconite Controversy in Friends Reference Library, London, contains most of the source materials.

7 In Braithwaite's copy in the above collection the changes are noted.

pendently of *his revelation* through the Scriptures;—an assumption which is unsupported by Scripture, contradicted by fact, and one which renders its votaries a prey to many false delusions."[8] And again, "In publishing these extracts in the hope that they may be a beacon to Friends, it is important to draw their attention to the pernicious theory before alluded to, *viz.*, that the revelation of the Spirit through the Scriptures is only a secondary rule—that the Spirit himself is a higher rule."[9]

Crewdson found supporters among the extreme Evangelicals such as Luke Howard, the able editor of *The Yorkshireman,* Isaac and Ann Braithwaite, John and Esther Wilkinson and Elisha Bates of Ohio. The publication of *A Beacon* precipitated a lively pamphlet controversy, both sides quoting Scripture and the writings of early Friends with equal confidence and indecisiveness. The anonymous *A Lamp for the Beacon &c.,* drew a deadly parallel between the positions of Crewdson and those taken by the opponents of early Friends. Thomas Hancock of Liverpool compiled an able pamphlet: *A Defense of the Doctrines of Immediate Revelation and Universal and Saving Light &c.* Henry Martin championed Crewdson's views in *Truth Vindicated,* to which J. J. Gurney replied (1836) in *Strictures on Truth Vindicated.*

The issue came before London Yearly Meeting in 1835, which finally appointed a committee of thirteen to help restore unity in Lancashire Quarterly Meeting. J. J. Gurney was a member of this committee and his part in the subsequent course of the controversy introduced the second great influence in promoting Quaker Evangelicalism; but before considering his contribution to the movement as a whole it is advisable to complete the immediate story of the Beaconite controversy. The committee of thirteen

---

[8] *A Beacon* &c., p. 6.
[9] *Ibid.*, p. 8.

bungled the matter from the start. After an extensive correspondence,[10] it recommended to Crewdson's monthly meeting, Hardshaw West, not to deal with him for doctrinal unsoundness, but that nevertheless he should not engage in public ministry and should not sit with the meetings of ministers and elders.[11]

These absurd and contradictory recommendations were due largely to the fact that the committee, as well as the yearly meeting, was divided on the issue involved. The sympathies of several prominent members of the committee were really with Crewdson, although they were somewhat shocked at the bold way he had put the case. Gurney had already written a personal letter to Crewdson in which he had approved certain features of the *Beacon* as "in accordance with the sentiments of every sound and enlightened Christian," and commended especially his treatment of the atonement and justification.[12]

The trouble lay primarily, not so much in the new ideas and personal conflicts involved, but in the lack of a settled basis of judgment as to what was Quakerly and an acknowledged principle of assimilation for new elements. It was proposed to the yearly meeting committee to test the *Beacon* by Barclay's *Apology,* but it decided unanimously not to do so but rather to try it by the Scriptures.[13] The real issue was not between Barclay and the Bible but between the traditional Quaker method of interpreting the Bible and the Evangelical method—between two traditional systems each seeking the mantle of Biblical authority to cover statements of its religious experience in terms of a particular *weltanschauung.* The living experiences behind

---

[10] The correspondence was published in two pamphlets: *The Whole Correspondence Between the Committee of the Y.M. and Isaac Crewdson,* and *A Few Particulars of the Correspondence.*

[11] Gurney, *Mem.*, p. 64.

[12] *The Whole Correspondence &c.*, p. 65.

[13] *The British Friend*, 1870, p. 280. *The Friend* (London), 1870, p. 208.

these two ways of interpreting the Scriptures were those of Fox and Wesley and their followers.

Crewdson refused to accept the committee's decision and resigned his membership in the monthly meeting in 1836. A small but influential section of the meeting seceded with him. They were joined by others from Kendal and Bristol making about three hundred who called themselves "Evangelical Friends." Most of them were led finally to practice the outward ordinances as a logical result of their acceptance of the literal authority of Scripture. A large part of them subsequently joined the Plymouth Brethren or Evangelical groups in the Anglican Church. The secession was important not on account of the numbers who separated, but on account of their standing and influence and because of the issues which it forced on the Society.

The yearly meeting of 1836 was a critical one, in that the struggle between the Quietist and Evangelical wings of the Society came to a crisis. The following request came up from Westmorland Quarterly Meeting:

> A difference of opinion having arisen in the Society as to the authority of holy Scripture in matters of faith and doctrine, this meeting requests the Yearly Meeting to take the subject into its serious consideration, and clearly to define what are, in its estimation, the authority, place and office of the holy Scriptures as the rule of faith and practice.[14]

In spite of an admonition in the epistle from Philadelphia "to enforce the discipline against persons who were disloyal to the fundamental principles of this Society" and oracular exhortations from many influential ministers (some of whom had been among the most vigorous opponents of Hicksism in America), J. J. Gurney carried the yearly meeting with him and secured the following pronouncement in the yearly meeting epistle, which was afterward incorporated in the discipline.

---

[14] JLPQ, I, 510.

It has ever been, and still is, the belief of the Society of Friends that the Holy Scriptures of the Old and New Testament were given by inspiration of God; that therefore the declarations contained in them rest on the authority of God Himself and there can be no appeal from them to any other authority whatsoever; that they are able to make us wise unto salvation through faith which is in Christ Jesus; being the appointed means of making known to us the blessed truths of Christianity; that they are the only divinely authorized record of the doctrines which we are bound as Christians to believe, and of the moral principles which are to regulate our actions; that no doctrine which is not contained in them can be required of any one to be believed as an article of faith; that whatsoever any man says or does which is contrary to the Scriptures, though under profession of the immediate guidance of the Spirit, must be reckoned and accounted a mere delusion.[15]

Much of this is taken from Barclay and other early Friends' writings but there are significant variations. The word "outward" is omitted from Barclay's statement that "there can be no appeal from them to any other outward authority whatsoever."[16] The idea that Christians are *bound to believe* any doctrines is a new one; and that in the Society of Friends any theological doctrines as such are *required* to be believed is revolutionary. As Rufus M. Jones aptly says, "This action was a complete triumph for the Evangelical wing of the Society and opened an extensive prospect of future service to Joseph John Gurney."[17]

Gurney tried to hold a middle ground in this controversy, teaching that the Bible was to be taken as a final authority in doctrine but not in the practices of worship. He adhered to the Quaker position on the ordinances on the ground of the authority of the Spirit. He was abused by both sides. The conservatives said he had sowed the seed

---

15 *London Epistles,* II, 272. Quoted in ***Christian Life and Thought*** &c., pp. 100–101.

16 *Apology,* Prop. III, § VI.

17 JLPQ, I, 510.

and then disowned the fruit; that "he laid the egg and Crewdson hatched it"; that he lacked the courage to go to the logical end of his teaching; and that he was too insidious and sly to declare openly the ends he aimed at, while Crewdson was blunt and outspoken. The Beaconites also felt that, logically, he should have gone with them and that he had acted inconsistently in condemning them.

The fact was, as Gurney pointed out to Crewdson, that the two men had started in their race from opposite points, had met and crossed on the road.[18] Gurney began as a classical and Biblical scholar, and his drift was steadily from the Evangelical insistence on the letter of Scripture toward Quaker Quietism and emphasis on the leading of the Spirit. It was only the one-sided development of this doctrine by Elias Hicks, resulting in the Hicksite separation in America, that prevented Gurney's going even farther in this direction. Crewdson, on the other hand, had been aroused from the Quaker Quietism, in which he had been brought up, by the new movement, and went to the logical end among the Evangelicals in the Church of England. Between the extremes of Hicksite, on the one hand and Beaconite, on the other, Gurney came to a stop. He records in his diary a conversation with a Friend:

> First, on the danger of conversation on the supposed unsoundness of others; on varying opinions; on American and *supposed* English Hicksism. Secondly, on the vast importance in our proclamation of orthodox doctrine, not to trench on the "anointing" or on those things which we have found experimentally to be truly precious. Earnestly do I desire that the evil, so much dreaded, and which I believe to be non-existent, may not be fretted into being.[19]

When Joseph John Gurney came to America he hoped that he might be able to win back the Hicksites to what

[18] *Mem.*, II, 25.
[19] *Ibid.*, II, 24.

he regarded as the safe middle ground. But he was ignored and repulsed by them. Even a large section of the Orthodox body opposed him and systematically worked up sentiment against him.

When in the United States, he associated with the scholars and statesmen of America in a way impossible to most of the Friends of that day. It is typical of his character that he visited the President of the United States and held religious service in the Senate chamber at the Capitol. He gave the rising generation of young Friends a new ideal of Quaker personality and character, released them in large measure from the paralyzing fear of "creaturely activity," gave a vigorous impetus to education, and especially promoted the study and teaching of the Bible.[20]

He came at a time when this service was especially needed. The Society in America had been desolated by the Hicksite separation. The young Friends had no uplifting interest or enthusiasm; their horizon was limited by ignorance both of the Bible and of the world, and they either rested apathetic under the bonds of the Society's ancient traditions or else sought vaguely for an opening for life and service outside the Society. To these he gave the vision of new possibilities. He illustrated in his own princely character the possibility of a new type of Quaker manhood and culture. He gave new subjects to think about and new movements to work for that enabled them to forget in a measure the old, petty strife. He aroused zeal for education. Not only did Earlham College get its name from his estate, but his influence made it and other Friends schools a possibility. Together with Jonathan and Hannah C. Backhouse, he promoted the study and reading of the Bible, so that Bible schools sprang up everywhere. The previous generation of Friends had been paralyzed by the fear that

[20] Hodgson says that the beginning of the evangelical trouble was when Joseph John Gurney tried to introduce Bible readings in Ackworth School. *Hist.*, I, 128. Cf. Gurney, *Mem.*, I, 175–183.

learning would destroy spirituality, that the Spirit would depart from a body that engaged in the systematic study of the Bible or in self-culture.

On the other hand, quite against his own desires, his influence started a movement in America somewhat like that of the Beaconites, but more extensive and less definite and radical. The Hicksite separation had started a reaction toward more emphasis on clear statement of doctrine and Bible study. The generation that felt this influence was headed away from the old Quaker forms toward the common beliefs and practices of Evangelical Protestantism, rather than coming from outside the Society toward a more definite Quakerism, as was the case with Gurney himself. The new elements which he introduced made contact with other denominations easier. The outgrowth was the dropping of many of the old "distinguishing views and practices" of Friends and the taking up of many beliefs and customs from the outside. Much of this was healthy and vitalizing to the Society. But the emphasis on the literal authority of the Scripture resulted here, as in England, in a large body being led on to the practice of the ordinances, especially water baptism. This caused many individuals to leave the Society and led at least one yearly meeting to the verge of breaking fellowship with the others. His emphasis on sanctification as a distinct religious experience subsequent to justification fostered in a measure the tendency that has lost the Society many members who have drifted out of it into various "holiness" movements. These tendencies to drift entirely away from the older Quakerism are due in large part, however, it is only just to state, to the fact that the Friends who followed his Evangelical influence to such extremes did not follow up Gurney's learning, love of education and emphasis on Biblical scholarship. Where the three influences he bequeathed the Society have been kept together, the Society has made the most healthful and substantial progress.

John Wilbur (1774–1856) was a New England Quaker of the Quietist type, deeply devoted to the doctrine of the Inner Life, which he construed in such a way as almost to amount to personal infallibility. He was fairly Evangelical in theology but stubbornly fearful of innovations which he attributed to "creaturely activity."

While on a visit to England in 1831–1833 he became the champion of the old ways of Quaker practice and thought, the leader of the solid opposition to new methods, and he denounced such "departures" as Bible Societies, Bible schools, Bible readings and lectures—everything that savored of preparation, premeditation or organization.

He regarded Joseph John Gurney as the most dangerous leader of these tendencies. He wrote a series of six letters to George Crossfield, in which he expressed these views and judgments, which the latter edited and published under the title: *Letters to a Friend on Some of the Primitive Doctrines of Christianity* (1832). This publication marked Wilbur as the fearless leader of the conservatives and the leading obstacle to the progress of the gospel in the mind of the Evangelicals.

When in 1837 Gurney requested a certificate liberating him for service in America, the yearly meeting of ministers and elders granted the certificate, although there was considerable vigorous opposition expressed. A special request was made that no word be allowed to reach American Friends of this opposition. Nevertheless a full account was sent to "concerned" Friends in Philadelphia.

Gurney was enthusiastically received by most American Friends but there was substantial opposition in Ohio and Philadelphia yearly meetings. John Wilbur felt it his duty to oppose Gurney and expose his errors by letters and in public and private talks.

The points on which he disagreed with Gurney were mainly practical. In theology he was in the main as much opposed to "Hicksism" and as thoroughly orthodox as Gurney himself. Wilbur, however, laid more stress on the Light Within against Gurney's emphasis on the Bible and the outward knowledge of Jesus' work; Gurney taught that justification precedes sanctification while Wilbur held that the two proceed together. Wilbur rejected the doctrine of imputed righteousness, objected to Gurney calling the first day of the week "the Christian Sabbath"; and objected also to lectures or courses of instruction on religious subjects and to systematic Bible study as creaturely activity. He resented Gurney's culture and social assurance as "worldly."[21] When Gurney came to New England Wilbur had an interview with him but got no satisfaction from him since Gurney defended all his published views.

His own monthly meeting sympathized with Wilbur's position but New England Yearly Meeting appointed a committee to deal with him. It found him contentious and obstinate; he stood on his rights under the discipline and went out of the way to make trouble. The ruling group in New England thereupon undertook to suppress Wilbur. They insisted that American Friends could not refuse to accept Gurney's credentials from London Yearly Meeting. Wilbur replied that Gurney had published his views in his writings to all the world and they were open to criticism. The yearly meeting finally appointed a committee to deal with him for "speaking against an approved minister." Both sides showed a lamentable lack of Christian love. His own monthly meeting refused to disown him at the request of the committee. Finally on the committee's motion the quarterly meeting laid down South Kingston, his monthly meeting, joining the membership to another meeting, which promptly disowned him. It was a high-handed proceeding and finally caused a separation in the yearly meeting in 1845. The separatists included about 500 out of a membership of 6,500 and were usually called "The Smaller

21 Wilbur, *Narrative and Exposition*, p. 35.

Body."[22] The Massachusetts courts decided in favor of "The Larger Body" in a lawsuit over the possession of property.[23] The separation, as usual occasioned a large crop of controversial literature.[24] Because of the question of correspondence it threatened to divide the other yearly meetings, for each "body" addressed epistles to all the other American yearly meetings. All of them except Ohio and Philadelphia promptly recognized "The Larger Body" as did London and Dublin.

In Ohio Yearly Meeting the question of correspondence with the New England "bodies" came up every year for nine years, when it finally led to a division over the question who should be clerk. Benjamin Hoyle, who had been the clerk for many years, belonged to the conservative section which wished to recognize "The Smaller Body" in New England. The "Gurneyites" tried to displace him but the representatives could not unite on any change, so that Hoyle continued as clerk from year to year. In 1854 the presence of T. B. Gould and other members of "The Smaller Body" in New England precipitated a sharp discussion as to their right to sit in the meeting. The "Gurneyite" party then made a very vigorous attempt to appoint Jonathan Binns as clerk, although they were greatly in the minority in the representatives. This resulted in a separation, one meeting being popularly called the "Hoyle" meeting and the other the "Binns" meeting, the "Wilburite" or "Hoyle" body being the larger.[25] A lawsuit over the possession of Mt. Pleasant Boarding School and other property was decided in 1874 in favor of the "Gurneyite" body.[26] Both of these meetings addressed epistles to the

---

22 JLPQ, I, 526.

23 See Bancroft. *Report in the Case of Earle vs. Wood and others*, Boston, 1855.

24 Thomas, *Hist.*, p. 148n.

25 JLPQ, I, 535.

26 Hodgson, *Hist.*, II, 263–280.

other yearly meetings and again there was danger of the separation spreading. London and Dublin and all the American yearly meetings except Philadelphia recognized the "Binns" meeting.[27] In 1849, 1851 and again in 1853 as the outgrowth of the New England and the Ohio separations, conferences were held in Baltimore to try to restore unity, but to no effect. The second conference exhorted Philadelphia and Ohio by name to recognize "The Larger Body" in New England.[28]

This second separation was particularly disastrous to Ohio Yearly Meeting. In the separation of 1828 it lost the liberal half of its membership and in the "Wilburite" division of 1854 it lost its large conservative element. Without the liberal leaven and the conservative balance wheel, it was peculiarly exposed to radical measures and liable to go to extremes, which tended to cut it off from sympathetic coöperation with other Friends. This makes its subsequent history a striking contrast with yearly meetings like London, Indiana and North Carolina which have never suffered from serious separations.

In Iowa there was Wilburite separation in Red Cedar Monthly Meeting in 1854. Later Wilburite Friends from Ohio settled along Coal Creek and at Whittier near Springville (about 1860). These three conservative monthly meetings were later organized into Hickory Grove Quarterly Meeting.[29]

Philadelphia Yearly Meeting had a strong minority of sympathizers with Gurney. They were centered about Haverford College and *The Friends Review*. In 1849 the Meeting for Sufferings reported the results of a careful investigation of the New England controversy.[30] Its con-

---

27 Thomas, *Hist.*, p. 152.

28 *Loc. cit.*

29 Jones, *Quakers of Iowa*, p. 158.

30 *A Report of the Meeting for Sufferings adopted by the yearly meeting of Friends held in Philadelphia in Relation to the Facts and Causes of the Division which occurred in New England yearly meeting in 1845.*

clusions were in effect that "the course taken by the smaller body was in the last resort revolutionary, though it was a revolution excused by the drastic methods of the majority."[31] The yearly meeting as a whole, however, sympathized with Wilbur's views rather than Gurney's.

The split in Ohio threatened to divide Philadelphia Yearly Meeting. At first it recognized the Hoyle meeting and the danger of a division was great. In 1856 Samuel Bettle, Jr., who had been clerk at the time of the separation in 1827, made a plea for unity, confessing the mistake and futility of the former separation and later proposed that no epistles be sent. This proposition was not accepted but Bettle's speech seems to have prevented further measures looking toward division. In 1857 the proposal to discontinue all correspondence failed. Finally, Israel P. Morris renewed a call made the previous year for Friends to remain behind at the close of the session and take definite action since the yearly meeting was by its correspondence with "separatists" cutting itself off from the main body of Friends.[32] A separation was saved by an agreement to suspend all correspondence for that year.[33] This compromise became the settled policy of the meeting through which its outward unity was preserved. The practice of Philadelphia Yearly Meeting, after it discontinued correspondence, was to receive members from both bodies into membership on certificate, but not to accept their ministers into membership as ministers, nor to read the minutes of traveling ministers nor to appoint meetings for them. The policy of doing nothing that would jeopardize the unity of the meeting has been the keynote of its subsequent history. This isolation of Philadelphia Yearly Meeting was tragic because it deprived the other Orthodox yearly meetings of its steadying conservative influence in the next period of great

---

31 JLPQ, I, 529.

32 Hodgson, *op. cit.*, II, 536.

33 *Min. of Phila. Yearly Meeting* for 1857. *The Friend,* XXX, 34.

change and also because it cut off the yearly meeting itself in large measure from the stimulus of liberal and progressive movements in London and the American yearly meetings.

In consequence of the tensions created in the Society by the spreading Gurney influences there were certain minor and sporadic conservative separations. In New York Yearly Meeting separations occurred in Scipio Quarter in 1848 and in Ferrisburg Quarter in 1853. In Baltimore Yearly Meeting a small group, which finally grew to include about a hundred, separated from Nottingham Quarter in 1854.[34]

When Philadelphia Yearly Meeting withdrew from correspondence with other yearly meetings, a few groups seceded in 1860 as a protest against continuing to exchange members by certificate with the "Gurneyite" meetings. A general meeting of these was established in 1861, which came finally to include four monthly meetings: Falsington and Philadelphia in Pennsylvania and Nottingham and Little Britain in Maryland. In 1867 Salem Monthly Meeting (Ohio) withdrew from Ohio Yearly Meeting (Wilburite) and joined the eastern General Meeting.[35] In 1863 "The Smaller Body" in New England lost a part of its members.

Some of these groups "recognized" one another by correspondence and otherwise. In the United States census of 1890 they were called "Primitive" Friends and their membership was given as 232.

---

[34] Hodgson, *Hist.*, II, chap. 25.

[35] *Ibid.*, II, 309, 310.

Chapter 27

THE ANTI-SLAVERY WORK OF FRIENDS

The great migration of Friends from the slave states into the Northwest Territory did not entirely relieve them of the problems of slavery. The issue followed them into their new homes. The passion for democracy which actuated the founders of the republic was antipathetic to slavery. Congress prohibited the slave trade after the year 1808 and it was anticipated that slavery would gradually die out. But the invention of the cotton gin (1793) made the cultivation of cotton profitable, especially on the large plantations which grew up after the removal of the Indians from the Gulf States (1832)[1] and slavery seemed necessary for it. Between 1820 and 1830 southern sentiment had definitely adopted slavery as its peculiar and sacred institution.[2] After the Missouri Compromise of 1820 slavery became a national issue. The "slave power" sought the continual extension of slave territory in order to preserve the balance of power in the Senate.

The free territory of the northwest offered asylum not only to Quakers seeking escape from a slave-holding society but also to fugitive slaves seeking freedom north of the Mason and Dixon Line as well as north of the Ohio river.

---

1 Siebert, *The Underground Railroad*, pp. 26, 308.

2 "In 1832 Professor Dew examined on behalf of Virginia the several plans offered from any quarter for discarding the 'peculiar institution' and found them all unfeasible. His weighty pamphlet persuaded a multitude that nothing could be done. Alert defense of 'southern rights' became the watchword everywhere." *Encycl. of the Soc. Sciences*, vol. xiv, p. 89.

These fugitives made slavery again a problem for Quaker consciences. The slave gangs and slave markets of the deep South modified the relatively easy-going family slave system of the border states. The fear of being "sold down the river," when a good master died or became financially embarrassed, intensified the efforts of runaway slaves to reach the free states and Canada. The War of 1812 had spread knowledge of Canada as a free country throughout the South.[3]

Friends were gradually involved in three anti-slavery movements: (1) the Underground Railroad; (2) the Colonization Society, and (3) the Anti-slavery movement proper which more and more became an Abolition movement. The divergent views of Friends about these movements led to a considerable separation in Indiana Yearly Meeting in 1842–1843 and to minor divisions elsewhere.

The Underground Railroad was an unorganized coöperation of humane people, chiefly in the free states, to aid runaway slaves.[4] The name was applied, of course, after the development of steam railroads in America[5] (between 1830 and 1840) but the effort to help fugitive slaves began much earlier.[6] It came ultimately to embrace thousands of persons, who gave their time and money freely to the effort to protect fugitives and get them safely to freedom in the North or Canada, often at the risk of property, person or even of life.

News of lands of freedom northward circulated among the slaves, especially of the border states, through Yankee traders, slaves who had accompanied owners on trips to the North, successful fugitives who returned for their families,

---

[3] Siebert, *op. cit.*, pp. 27, 28.

[4] But see *ibid.*, p. 68.

[5] On the name see *ibid.*, pp. 45, 46.

[6] Two letters of George Washington mention an association in Philadelphia to aid runaway slaves as early as 1786. See Spark, *Washington* IX, 158. Cited in Siebert, *op. cit.*, p. 33. Smedley records a definite beginning at Columbia, Pa. in 1804. *History of the Underground Railroad*, p. 26.

and other sources; and induced the more desperate or the more courageous to attempts for freedom. Information as to routes and stations across the Ohio or Potomac trickled through the same underground channels.

The "stations" of the Underground Railroad lay chiefly in territory settled by certain religious sects—Friends, Congregationalists from New England, Presbyterians, Covenanters and Methodists. Communities of free Negroes aided refugees, and in some cases immigrants from slave-holding states who had come north to escape slavery rendered valuable service. The "passengers" were sent on their way by foot, in wagons and carriages; by steamboats from Charleston, Norfolk and Washington to New England ports, and across the Great Lakes; later the steam railroads were used. The "agents" developed great ingenuity in disguising and hiding their protégés. The stories of hardships and cruelties told by the fugitive slaves contributed much to the growth of abolition sentiment among Friends.

The chief Quaker stations were Bangor and Salem, Iowa; Cincinnati and points north of it in eastern Indiana especially Newport, Ind., and western Ohio; Mt. Pleasant, Ohio; points in southeastern Pennsylvania and adjacent territory in Delaware and New Jersey; New York City; New Bedford, Boston, Salem, and Portland (Me.) in New England. The outstanding Friends in this work were Isaac T. Hopper of Philadelphia and later of New York, a Hicksite Friend, and Levi Coffin of Newport [7] and later of Cincinnati, whose outstanding service in the cause earned him the title "president of the Underground Railroad." [8] Both men were individualists working chiefly outside the Society of Friends; both took a great delight in defeating the efforts of slaveholders to recover their slaves; both were utterly fearless; both were moved by deep love for their fellow-

[7] Now Fountain City, Ind.

[8] *Rem.*, p. 190.

men, and neither allowed his hatred of slavery to lead him to hate the slaveholders. Isaac T. Hooper worked single-handed mostly, a true knight errant in behalf of fugitive slaves. He had a keen sense of humor and enjoyed the discomfiture of his adversaries, as a veritable Samson among the Philistines. In 1829 he moved to New York City and later became secretary of the Prison Association, caring for discharged prisoners.

Levi Coffin had more organizing ability and solidity of character. He won the confidence of his neighbors at Newport so that they aided his work and respected his business integrity. In 1847 he moved to Cincinnati as agent for the Free Labor Association to open a depot for goods made by free labor; but he spent a great part of his time and energy caring for the streams of fugitive slaves which came to that city by three or four converging routes. His work was so well done that, of the more than three thousand fugitives who passed through his hands, few if any were recovered by their owners.

The Underground Railroad was generally defended on the ground of the higher law, which with Friends has always taken precedence over all other laws. Jesus had commanded men to feed the hungry and clothe the naked, they asserted; Friends must above all else be faithful to the Inner Leading. In all other cases, however, Friends' disobedience to law or government for conscience' sake had been public and had been openly avowed, while the work of the Underground Railroad was done in secret. This was justified on the ground that secrecy was necessary for its success; that the secrecy was resorted to not to protect Friends but their protégés. One may question, in the light of history, whether it would not have been better for Friends to have avowed it publicly and taken the consequences when they found it obligatory to help fugitive slaves; or to have followed the example of Woolman, working in a kindly spirit to convert the slaveholders and induce them to let their slaves go free. This would not have been as hopeless as it seems from the bitter denunciations of the extremists on both sides. There were many slaveholders who felt the economic losses of slavery or its inhumanity or both. Many manumitted their slaves or moved north to escape the system. The records of Anti-slavery Friends disclose many openminded southern men who would have been glad to abandon slavery.[9] There were men in the southern churches who could have been enlisted in a moral crusade. The attacks of the Abolitionists and other anti-slavery leaders on the slaveholders as well as the system of slavery and the political rivalries involved in the Abolition movement nullified to a large extent these susceptible tendencies. The method of moral suasion used with loving patience and energized by the martyr spirit might have got rid of slavery without the Civil War. It would have been cheaper, spiritually and economically, to have followed the English method and have recompensed the slave owners.[10]

The American Colonization Society was organized in 1816 for the purpose of settling free Negroes in Africa, the West Indies and other places. Many anti-slavery advocates supported it in the hope that it would encourage private emancipation of slaves.[11] Later it was suspected by the more radical anti-slavery advocates of being a device on the part of the pro-slavery leaders to remove the free slaves from the country so that their presence would not be an incitement to slaves to seek freedom and also to forestall the Abolition

---

9 Cf. Pickard, *Life of Whittier,* I, 445, 446. Levi Coffin, *Rem.,* pp. 280–291.

10 Propositions of this kind were made by Whittier and others in 1861, but were unacceptable to the more radical Abolitionists as well as to the southern leaders. The suggested change of method came too late. Pickard, *op. cit.,* I, 433, 434.

11 Cartland, *Southern Heroes,* p. 52. Earle, *Life of Benjamin Lundy,* pp. 201–220.

movement. Anti-slavery Friends themselves were at first divided over the colonization plan.[12] Levi Coffin and Whittier both opposed it from the beginning of their anti-slavery work while Benjamin Lundy gave much time to it.

The opposition to slavery on the part of American Friends entered on a new stage in the early nineteenth century after slavery within the Society ceased. It now became opposition to slavery outside the Society, to slavery as an institution. The beginnings in the work of Lundy and Osborn have already been given. Friends began to be associated with anti-slavery reformers from other religious denominations, who gradually turned to political activities to accomplish their end.

Charles Osborn (1775–1850), a North Carolina Quaker who moved to Tennessee in early life, was a pioneer in the organized anti-slavery movement. During most of his adult life he was a Quietist minister, visiting meetings throughout Quakerdom after the eighteenth-century manner. He became convinced of the evil of slavery and, as early as 1814, began the formation of manumission societies among Friends and others. When the Colonization Society was organized he opposed it, insisting that the only Christian solution of the slavery problem was "immediate and unconditional emancipation." He removed to Mt. Pleasant, Ohio (1876), and began the publication of *The Philanthropist*.[13] Benjamin Lundy (1789–1839) of New Jersey settled near Mt. Pleasant, where he was aroused by the slave traffic on the Ohio river. In 1815 he organized an anti-slavery society called the "Union Humane Society." He wrote articles for *The Philanthropist* and afterwards worked with Osborn in his office. In 1819 he went to

---

[12] Edgerton, *History of the Anti-Slavery Separation in Indiana Yearly Meeting*, pp. 28, 29. The colonization movement was condemned by Indiana Yearly Meeting in 1836. *Ibid.*, pp. 34, 36. See Whittier's exposure of it in "Justice and Expediency" in his *Prose Works*.

[13] Osborn, *Jour.*, xi, xii.

St. Louis on business and remained there nearly two years, working to prevent Missouri from becoming a slave state. After he returned to Mt. Pleasant, he began the publication of *The Genius of Universal Emancipation.* Meanwhile Elihu Embree had begun the publication of *The Emancipator* at Jonesborough, Tenn. His death led Lundy to move to Tennessee and take over his press. He attended the Abolition convention in Philadelphia in 1823 and decided to move his paper to Baltimore. It was he who enlisted William Lloyd Garrison in the anti-slavery movement. He continued to publish the *Genius of Universal Emancipation* until his death in 1839.[14] He lost most of his papers, equipment and personal possessions when Pennsylvania Hall was burned by a mob in 1838. He made two voyages to Hayti; made three trips to Mexico and Texas in the interest of his colonization schemes, and went to Upper Canada twice to care for Negro colonists there. His interest in the Colonization Society (founded 1816) was threefold: to aid North Carolina Yearly Meeting to place the slaves which it held in a congenial place; to encourage slaveholders to emancipate their slaves; and to provide a refuge for free Negroes, who found it more and more difficult to maintain their liberty in the slaveholding and border states. North Carolina Yearly Meeting had become the legal owner of many Negroes, whom the state laws did not allow to be set free within the state.[15] In all these lines he had a measure of success, but with the growing tension of the Anti-slavery movement practically all Friends abandoned the Colonization scheme.[16] For a time free-labor associations, which attempted to make slavery unprofitable by refusing to use slave products, enlisted large numbers of Friends.[17]

---

14 See Earle, *Life of Benjamin Lundy* for details of his work.
15 Weeks, *Southern Quakers and Slavery,* pp. 224–231.
16 Cf. Levi Coffin, *Mem.,* 230, 231. *James and Lucretia Mott,* pp. 86–88.
17 Levi Coffin, *op. cit.,* chap. VIII.

The Society of Friends had been accustomed to confine their opposition to such evils as slavery chiefly to moral suasion, to appeals and petitions to governments, and to "passive resistance," although there had been a few sporadic attempts at organizations composed of Friends and non-Friends.[18] London Yearly Meeting had made an exception in the case of the Anti-slavery movement but American Friends were officially opposed to political methods and to "mixed associations."[19] Many of the leaders in the Anti-slavery movement among Friends, however, became impatient of the seeming apathy of the official leaders after 1830 and even suspected their motives. In the east many leading Friends were merchants and manufacturers whose chief markets were in the South;[20] many Friends had come to hold the common color prejudice of the society in which they lived; so that there was much apathy in regard to the historic testimony of Friends against slavery and most of the leaders were inclined not to press the issue until a more favorable time should come.[21]

The tension between the ardent Anti-slavery leaders and the leading Friends grew rapidly between 1830 and 1840 and finally produced an important division in Indiana Yearly Meeting and some smaller separations elsewhere. In 1842–1843 New York Yearly Meeting (H) disowned Isaac T. Hooper and two other Friends for activities in the Anti-slavery movement and the Underground Railroad. Lucretia Mott and others in Philadelphia Yearly Meeting narrowly escaped the same fate.

18 Hodgson, *Hist.*, II, 10–12. Edgerton, *The Anti-slavery Separation* &c., p. 25. In America an "Association for Promoting the Abolition of Slavery and the Relief of Free Negroes, unlawfully held in Bondage," composed of Friends and non-members (among the latter were Dr. Benjamin Rush, Judge Jay and Benjamin Franklin) was organized in Pennsylvania as early as 1774. Similar societies were organized in several other states.

19 See minute of advice in *Min. of Ind. Y. Mtg.*, 1841.

20 Child, *Life of Isaac T. Hooper*, pp. 387–398. *James and Lucretia Mott*, p. 201. See also Edgerton, *op. cit.*, pp. 26, 39.

21 *Life of Isaac T. Hooper*, p. 219. *James and Lucretia Mott*, p. 122.

The opposition to political action and mixed associations in the Anti-slavery cause led to a more extensive separation in Indiana Yearly Meeting (O) in 1842–1843. Daniel Puckett and Levi Coffin were prominent leaders of the radical anti-slavery wing and about 1839 Charles Osborn was converted to the Abolition cause. The leading Friends of the yearly meeting were generally satisfied with colonization or gradual emancipation as a solution of the slavery question and deprecated the uncompromising demand of the Abolitionists for "immediate and unconditional emancipation."[22]

Beginning in 1831 there were a series of insurrections and plots on the part of slaves in southern states to gain their freedom.[23] The South was thoroughly alarmed by these and adopted oppressive legislation against anti-slavery agitators and against persons educating Negroes or inciting or aiding them to escape. These things drew the line tighter between the Abolitionists and other Friends. The rise of the Abolition Party headed by Lovejoy, Garrison, Whittier and others was stimulated by this situation. Between 1835 and 1845 there were frequent outbreaks of mobs against Anti-slavery leaders. Garrison was mobbed in Boston in 1835, and Pennsylvania Hall the Anti-slavery headquarters in Philadelphia was burned in 1838, when the homes of Abolitionist leaders, including James and Lucretia Mott, were also threatened. Lovejoy was killed by a mob at Alton, Illinois, in 1837. The office of Birney's anti-slavery paper, *The Philanthropist,* in Cincinnati was wrecked in 1836 and again in 1841; and the "Scanlon Mob" threatened Abolitionists there in 1843.

In 1836 the State Anti-slavery Society of Indiana was organized. At that time the official yearly meeting seemed favorable to the Anti-slavery cause, but many influential

---

22 Osborn, *Jour.*, pp. 437–439.

23 See *Life of Lundy,* pp. 246, 247.

members were opposed to it. This opposition was strengthened by the violence of mobs and bitter attacks in the press and by the attitude of influential visiting Friends from the east and from England.[24] In 1840 Indiana Yearly Meeting for Sufferings warned Friends against participating in the Anti-slavery enterprise as well as that of colonization.[25] This position was sustained by the yearly meeting and an official movement to foster the use of free labor products was quashed.[26] Charles Osborn was urged by influential Friends to desist from his testimony against slavery. Levi Coffin's work for fugitive slaves was also viewed askance. The ostensible ground of opposition was that it was not the custom of Friends to join in mixed associations with others who were not accustomed to wait on God for guidance or to use political methods.[27] The yearly meeting advised against opening meeting-houses for Anti-slavery meetings (1841) and again warned against joining in the Anti-slavery enterprise as well as the work of the Colonization Society.[28] It condemned the circulation of an address to Friends in America by Joseph Sturge, written at the close of his American visit, in which he deprecated the lack of zeal in the Anti-slavery cause on the part of American Friends generally, because its publication had not first been approved by the Meeting for Sufferings. It also refused to sanction the publication of the *Free Labour Advocate and Anti-Slavery Chronicle*.[29]

In some cases the Anti-slavery advocates organized Anti-slavery societies composed of Friends only, but objection was made to these also. Their opponents asserted that the

---

24 Edgerton, *op. cit.*, p. 40.

25 *Ibid.*, p. 41.

26 *Ibid.*, p. 44.

27 *Ibid.*, pp. 38, 49. As to earlier practice in the Anti-slavery movement see Jos. Sturge, *Mem.*, pp. 221, 222. Edgerton, *op. cit.*, pp. 20, 23.

28 *Ibid.*, p. 41.

29 Started in 1847 at Newport, Ind., and edited by Henry H. Way and Benjamin Stanton, JLPQ, II, 588.

official business meetings were the proper places to promote such causes.[30] The leaders in those communities where Anti-slavery sentiment prevailed generally disregarded the advice of the yearly meeting. Consequently the yearly meeting of 1842 on the advice of the Meeting for Sufferings recommended that eight members of the latter body be replaced; [31] and that members of meetings refusing to conform to the advice of the yearly meeting be not appointed to offices or committees. A large committee from the yearly meeting and another from the select body were appointed to visit the subordinate meetings and enforce the order.[32] Charles Osborn asked in vain that the ground of his removal from the Meeting for Sufferings be put in the minutes.

At the close of the session a large number of Friends who were dissatisfied with these measures, remained in the meeting-house but were quickly ordered in the name of the trustees to vacate the premises.[33] They adjourned to meet next day at Newport, where after a long discussion they decided to wait to see whether the special committee would proceed against the Anti-slavery leaders. When it became evident that the edict was to be carried out,[34] a convention met the following February and after careful deliberation organized Indiana Yearly Meeting of Anti-slavery Friends. The Anti-slavery body consisted of four

---

30 Edgerton, *op. cit.*, p. 82.

31 The eight were Charles Osborn, Levi Coffin, Daniel Puckett, Thomas Frazier, Abel Roberts, Isam Puckett, Martha Wooton and Jonathan Hough. See Levi Coffin, *Mem.*, p. 231.

32 Charles Osborn, *Jour.*, p. 418.

33 Edgerton, *op. cit.*, pp. 24–26. These measures were made more offensive by the reception accorded Henry Clay, then a candidate for the presidency and secretary of the Colonization Society who came to Richmond during this yearly meeting. On Saturday he was presented with a petition with about 2,000 signatures, asking him to emancipate his slaves. This he refused to do, saying they were his legal property. The next day he was taken to the yearly meeting by Elijah Coffin, the clerk of the meeting at that time, given a prominent seat and otherwise honored.

34 Osborn, *op. cit.*, p. 420.

quarterly meetings, comprising ten monthly meetings with about 2,000 members. This was a rather small proportion of the 25,000 members belonging to Indiana Yearly Meeting at that time.[35] The new meeting issued a declaration of the reasons for their action; addressed an epistle to Anti-slavery Friends in Indiana Yearly Meeting, and epistles to the other yearly meetings, including London and Dublin. The Anti-slavery Yearly Meeting insisted that it "adopted no new doctrine, nor any new system of church government," and it claimed "to be in the strictest sense of the word a Society of Friends." [36] The separation and these ensuing statements gave rise to an extensive controversial literature, official and unofficial; but the new yearly meeting was never "recognized" by any existing yearly meeting.

Some of the English Friends were quite sympathetic with the separatists and *The British Friend* published their documents with favorable comment. In 1844 the Anti-slavery Yearly Meeting again addressed the Meeting for Sufferings and also individual members of London Yearly Meeting. The epistle was not read before the yearly meeting, which, however, appointed a commission consisting of William Forster, George Stacey, Josiah Forster and John Allen to visit the Anti-slavery Friends and present an address from the yearly meeting in the endeavor to heal the breach and produce reconciliation.

The commission mismanaged the affair from the start. They attended Indiana Yearly Meeting, which at their request appointed a committee to advise with them. The commission refused to meet with the Anti-slavery Friends in any official capacity and avoided even visiting with them as much as possible.[37] Their plan was to call together the Anti-slavery Friends, beginning with the most remote and weakest meetings in Iowa and on the Indiana fron-

[35] Hodgson, *Hist.*, II, 33.
[36] Edgerton, *op. cit.*, p. 75.
[37] *Ibid.*, p. 343.

tier,[38] read the minutes of their appointment and the address of London Yearly Meeting, and then urge them to abandon their separate meetings for worship and return to fellowship with their brethren. They declined to discuss what should be done about the meetings for discipline or to consider in any way the causes of the separation or the obstacles to reunion.[39] On the whole the commission made the situation worse.[40]

This separation had the effect of checking the harsh disciplinary proceedings in Indiana and other yearly meetings. The committee appointed to enforce the proscription of the Anti-slavery leaders ceased its work after the separation. The separatists pilloried the conservative leaders before the world as pro-slavery and drove them to greater zeal in their efforts for emancipation. The logic of events gradually forced them to take a different attitude toward the Abolition movement. As the original reasons for the separation gradually passed away, the majority of Friends regretted it and some of the newer leaders made overtures for reconciliation. The Anti-slavery Friends were given to understand unofficially that they would be welcomed if they would return. Charles F. Coffin, the son of Elijah Coffin who was clerk of Indiana Yearly Meeting at the time of the separation was especially active in the early Fifties, to bring the separation to an end.[41] Most of the Anti-slavery Friends gradually and quietly returned and were received without any acknowledgement of error; and in 1857 the remnant of the separated yearly meeting disbanded.[42]

The settlement of Friends in Iowa and Kansas contributed to the anti-slavery work of Friends in those states.

---

38 Edgerton, *op. cit.*, p. 332.

39 *Ibid.*, p. 334.

40 *Ibid.*, pp. 350, 351.

41 Johnson and Coffin, *Charles F. Coffin, &c.*, p. 105.

42 Edgerton, *op. cit.*, p. 46.

The settlement in southeastern Iowa began in 1835 and increased rapidly with the coming of Friends from eastern centers. Practically all groups were represented and there was in addition a settlement of Norwegian Friends. The Anti-slavery separation in Indiana found strong support in three meetings; there were stations of the Underground Railroad, which drew down the wrath of Missouri pro-slavery men; and John Brown found sympathizers and refugees among them. In 1863 Indiana Yearly Meeting to which most of the Iowa Friends belonged granted their request for a separate yearly meeting.

The settling of Kansas was bound up with the anti-slavery struggle. After the passage of the Kansas-Nebraska Bill (1854), there was a race between anti-slavery and pro-slavery elements to control the state. Quaker immigrants joined the ranks of those who made the state "free-soil." After the Civil War a second wave of Quaker emigrants left North Carolina chiefly for Indiana and Kansas and many young Friends joined the ranks of young men uprooted by the War seeking their fortunes in the prairie states. Friends shared the deprivations which followed in Kansas from drought, grasshoppers and the financial panic of 1873. In spite of this Friends held on and in 1872 Kansas Yearly Meeting was established.

In the years between 1842 and 1857 there were a number of separations, chiefly within the Hicksite branch of Friends, caused chiefly by the official attitude toward the Anti-slavery leaders. The separatists also objected to a strong organization in the Society and to the exercise of church discipline. As in the separation of 1827–28 the Meeting for Sufferings and the meetings of ministers and elders were particular objects of attack. The seceding groups favored a congregational polity and called themselves "Congregational" or "Progressive" Friends. The principal areas in which these separate organizations were formed were central and western New York, Ohio and

Michigan, with one each in Iowa, Indiana and Pennsylvania.[43] Their numbers were very small, and their one important ground of separate existence was their dissatisfaction with the attitude of the official Society on the slavery question. When this attitude changed to a more active interest in the Anti-slavery cause and especially after emancipation, they all disappeared except the meeting at Longwood, Penn., which kept up an association interested in various humanitarian reforms until 1940, when it formally disbanded.[44]

Two Friends deserve especial attention on account of their Anti-slavery activities: Lucretia Mott and John Greenleaf Whittier. Lucretia Coffin Mott (1793–1880) was the daughter of a prominent Nantucket Quaker family. At the old Nine Partners School (near Poughkeepsie, N. Y.) she became acquainted with James Mott, a young instructor there, and soon afterward they were married and settled in Philadelphia. When the separation of 1827 occurred they went reluctantly with the Hicksite party. She was a clear and independent thinker as well as a devout Friend. Some of the Evangelical doctrines were repugnant to her mind and the Evangelical intolerance repelled her.

The Anti-slavery cause soon enlisted the energies of her husband and herself and it remained until 1865 their chief concern. She was one of the founders of the Philadelphia Female Anti-Slavery Society (1833), because women were excluded from membership in the other Anti-slavery organizations. In 1837 the Anti-slavery forces split over methods to be pursued, the "new" society, including Whittier, devoting itself to constitutional methods and political action, but objecting to the admission of women delegates in the Anti-Slavery Society conventions. The original society under the lead of Garrison wished to admit women, favored

43 A list of these meetings as far as they are known, ten in all, is given by Allen C. Thomas in BFHA, Nov., 1920.

44 *Friends Intelligencer,* 8 mo. 31, 1940.

"moral suasion" only, and was willing to let the Constitution perish and the Union be dissolved, if need be, to secure "immediate and unconditional abolition." In 1840 Lucretia Mott and her husband went to England as delegates to the General Conference of the British and Foreign Anti-Slavery Society, from which, however, she and others of the American delegates were excluded because they were women. Here she met Elizabeth Cady Stanton and they pledged each other to the cause of the emancipation of women. James and Lucretia Mott were not officially recognized by Friends in England and Ireland because they were Hicksites, but they made many personal friends among the liberal and Anti-slavery Friends, contact with whom greatly encouraged them in their efforts to abolish slavery at home.[45] Along with other Anti-slavery workers in both branches of Friends her efforts were opposed by influential Hicksite Friends in New York and Philadelphia Yearly Meetings and she narrowly escaped being disowned at the time when other active Anti-slavery leaders were disowned in New York and Indiana Yearly Meetings.[46] In later years the opposition to her died down. Friends as a whole came over to the Abolition cause,[47] and enjoyed the reflected glory which her reputation brought the Society.[48] An account of her other philanthropic activities and the radical opinions which intensified the opposition to her will be given later.[49]

John Greenleaf Whittier (1807–1892) was a birthright Friend, a native of Massachusetts. His school education was meager, but he had an eager curiosity about men and

---

45 C. C. Burleigh, who succeeded Whittier as editor of *The Pennsylvania Freeman* asserted that "had Lucretia Mott been Orthodox (instead of a Hicksite Friend) she would have been admitted" to the Conference. Whittier did not think so. Pickard, *op. cit.*, I, 258.

46 Above, p. 364.

47 Pickard, *op. cit.*, I, 338.

48 *James and Lucretia Mott*, p. 461.

49 *Infra.*, chap. 29, pp. 395–397, 399, 400.

things and a remarkably retentive memory. Throughout his life he took an interest in politics and he had a rare gift of poetry. His interest in the Anti-slavery cause was aroused by Garrison. When the Anti-slavery movement entered on its new phase in 1832–1833, he dedicated his primary energies to it, making at the same time the great renunciation of his hopes of a political and literary career.[50]

In 1833 he challenged the Colonization program and came out for Abolition in a pamphlet entitled "Justice and Expediency." This beginning in the Anti-slavery work was made especially hard because of his political freindship for Henry Clay, who was the Whig Party leader and president of the American Colonization Society, and because the Colonization scheme had the support of many Friends and was popular in the churches.[51] The same year he was a delegate to the national Anti-Slavery Convention in Philadelphia in which Friends had a conspicuous part.[52]

Whittier was mobbed at various Anti-slavery meetings, especially those at which George Thompson, the English Anti-slavery advocate, was to speak. Meetings were broken up at Haverhill, Concord and Newburyport. He witnessed the Boston mob which threatened Garrison's life in 1838. His anti-slavery poems were perhaps his greatest contribution to the cause during these years.[53] He aided in the work of the Underground Railroad both in New York and Philadelphia. In 1838 he went to Philadelphia to aid Lundy with his paper *The National Inquirer.* Lundy retired in March, 1838, leaving Whittier as editor of *The Pennsylvania Freeman,* as it was henceforth called. He witnessed the burning of Pennsylvania Hall and barely saved a few papers from his office in it. The same year he at-

---

[50] Pickard, *op. cit.,* I, 125, 126, 131.

[51] *Ibid.,* I, 123, 139, 140.

[52] Of the sixty-two members thirty-one were Friends.

[53] Pickard gives a list of those written between 1833 and 1837. *Op. cit.,* I, 203.

tended the New England Anti-slavery Convention in Marlboro Hall, Boston, which was saved from a mob only by the vigorous action of the mayor.

The Pennsylvania Freeman was wholly devoted to the Anti-slavery cause. Whittier excluded political, religious or reform topics not directly bearing on it, because he felt that it was not right to use funds subscribed for an Anti-slavery paper for the discussion of alien topics. For similar reasons he objected to mixing the Anti-slavery cause with that of women's rights. He always opposed the use of physical force even on behalf of freedom.[54] He believed in political action under the constitution and in preserving the Union.

When the unfortunate division of the Anti-slavery forces came in 1837 Whittier went with the "New Society," not "having unity" with Garrison's insistence on committing the movement to women's rights, his attacks on the churches, his disavowal of political means and his indifference to the Union.[55]

In 1840 Whittier resigned his editorship of *The Pennsylvania Freeman* to go to the Anti-slavery Convention in London, but was prevented from attending by the ill health which so frequently incapacitated him throughout his life. Whittier felt a close comradeship with Joseph Sturge, when this staunch English Quaker Anti-slavery reformer visited America in 1841. He travelled with him and was especially chagrined that New England Yearly Meeting Friends refused him the use of meeting-houses for his lectures and Anti-slavery addresses.[56] He refrained from taking part in yearly meeting affairs for some years on account of it.[57] Whittier's poems continued up to the Civil War to be a mighty force in shaping northern senti-

---

54 Pickard, *op. cit.,* I, 230–231.

55 *Ibid.,* I, 207, 208, 235.

56 *Ibid.,* I, 269.

57 *Ibid.,* I, 548.

ment and crystallizing it in favor of Abolition. Of about three hundred poems written between 1832 and 1865 more than a third dealt with this question.[58] Other phases of Whittier's life and work will be dealt with later.

---

58 Pickard, *op. cit.*, I, 501.

Chapter 28

THE AWAKENING OF ENGLISH QUAKERISM

The periods of the third division of Quaker history in America were set off by two very definite events; the separation of 1827–1828 and the Civil War (1861); but in England these periods were not so definitely marked off. British Friends had begun officially to take an active part in public affairs with the anti-slavery issue; and individuals had, as has already been told, associated with non-Friends in efforts for various philanthropic reforms. It was natural, therefore, that the great economic and social changes of the Industrial Revolution should enlist them in the political, humanitarian and constitutional struggles, which these changes occasioned. The participation of Friends in the Anti-slavery movement which secured the abolition of slavery in the British Dominions (1833); the beginning of their participation in public life, signalized by the election of Joseph Pease to parliament (1832); the activities of Joseph Sturge and John Bright on behalf of parliamentary reform, and the Beaconite controversy (1835) were signs of the new era.

In England the end of the first period in modern Quaker history was indicated by the publication of John Stephenson Rowntree's *Quakerism, Past and Present* (1859), a study of the decline of the Society which startled English Friends into a consciousness of their actual state; by important changes in the discipline in 1859–1861 and by the rise of new religious concerns for the welfare of non-Friends, such as the adult schools and foreign missions.

The corresponding events in contemporary political and social history were largely the results of the Industrial Revolution and the rise to political power of the laboring and manufacturing classes, culminating in the Reform Bill (1832). In the religious world the most important events were: the repeal of the Corporation and Test Acts in 1828, which allowed Dissenters (including Friends) to hold public office; the Catholic Emancipation Bill (1829); the suppression of the Irish bishoprics (1833), and the beginning of the Tractarian movement. The influence of Wordsworth's poetry and of Coleridge's writings opened a fresh era in thought and literature. Together with the Romanticist mood of individualistic revolt, which passed its zenith with the passage of the Reform Bill, these mark the passing of the rationalistic era.

A different intellectual atmosphere was created by the passion for liberty and humanity of the writings of Byron, Shelley, Keats and Cowper. The philosophy of Kant and his successors produced a new constructive intellectual attitude, which Wordsworth and Coleridge popularized in England. They established the basis for a mystical faith that found its authority in the inward revelation of God and in personal spiritual experiences, and provided an escape from the intellectual presuppositions of Deism. This new attitude found expression in the Romantic School also, from the poems of Ossian at one end to Goethe's writings at the other. These influences tended to undermine the philosophical and theological presuppositions of Evangelicalism also, and stimulated a new interpretation of Christianity in the work of such distinguished preachers as Thomas Erskine, Macleod Campbell and later Frederick Denison Maurice. These movements belonged largely to the period before 1830, but as usual they reached Friends rather tardily.

The Industrial Revolution touched Friends more directly since a large part of the membership of the Society was brought into contact with the new conditions either as employers or reformers. The overcrowding, poverty, unrest and misery of the manufacturing centers and the injustices and exploitations due to the unbalanced distribution of economic opportunity and political power not only stirred men like Cobden, Kingsley and Carlyle but gradually changed the outlook, theology, practices and programs of the Society of Friends.

During this period Friends in England and America were bound together by the intervisitation of prominent ministers, some of whom made long and extensive religious journeys. In this way, especially, the philanthropic concerns of English Friends were kept before their American brethren. The visits and exceptional influence of Hannah C. and Jonathan Backhouse, of Joseph John Gurney and of Joseph Sturge have been described. Other valuable ministers were William Forster (1784–1854) whose three American visits were in 1820–1825, 1845–1846, and 1853–1854, John Pease, brother of Joseph Pease, whose American travels covered the years 1843–1845, and Benjamin Seebohm (1798–1871), the German Quaker historian and biographer whose visit to the United States lasted from 1846 to 1851. These three Friends visited almost all the centers and remote outposts of Orthodox Quakerism in America and Canada. They kept American Friends in touch with the causes to which British Friends were more and more devoted, the while they ministered to their personal and corporate life. Of American visitors to England Lindley Hoag and Eli and Sibyl Jones were probably the most influential. The work of the latter is narrated elsewhere.

The repeal of the Corporation and Test Acts in 1829 opened the way for Dissenters to enter public life and the Reform Bill of 1832 gave the Southern Division of Durham County a seat in Parliament to which his fellow-citizens elected Joseph Pease, a prominent Friend. In spite of the opposition of his family and of many other Friends, he consented to serve, was admitted to Parliament in 1833 and served until 1841. He was allowed to substitute an affirmation for the usual oath of office and was excused from addressing the speaker as "Sir" and from alluding to his colleagues as "the honorable members." He did not let political life destroy his interest in the Society of Friends, of which he became an elder and a recorded minister, nor prevent his active support of the Bible, School and Peace societies. He promoted schools among the mine workers and succeeded Joseph Sturge as president of the London Peace Society in 1860.

Of the leading Friends of this period, the four who were most influential in impressing Quaker ideals upon the world outside the Society were probably Joseph John Gurney, John Greenleaf Whittier, Joseph Sturge and John Bright. The work of the first two has already been discussed.

Rufus M. Jones regards Joseph Sturge (1793–1860) as "the consummate flower of Quakerism in the nineteenth century."[1] He was a friend and co-worker with Whittier in the Anti-slavery movement and supplemented the public work of John Bright. All three of these did notable work for Bible study, temperance, education, and peace. All entered public life. Whittier served but one term in the Massachusetts Assembly. Joseph Sturge was a candidate for Parliament twice, once to represent Nottingham and once Birmingham, but was defeated both times. His great public services were unofficial. All three suffered from opposition on the part of Quietist Friends because of their extensive participation in public affairs.

Joseph Sturge came under the influence of William Forster in 1812 and remained his close friend the rest of his life. He was a grain dealer but gave up handling barley

---

1 JLPQ, II, 803.

and malt when he realized the evils of intemperance. He was actively interested in the Reform Bill of 1832, in the abolition of slavery in 1833 and in the agitation for the repeal of the Corn Laws. He became one of the foremost leaders in doing away with the apprentice system which succeeded the abolition of slavery in the British colonies. He visited the West Indies, studied the system at first hand, and his report contributed largely to its abolition in 1838. He sponsored the Free Labour Movement to free the cotton industry from dependence on slave-grown cotton. In this he was joined by Bright who, as early as 1847, foresaw the danger involved in the complete dependence of the Lancashire cotton mills on slave-grown raw materials. Sturge at first favored the Evangelical Alliance, but was alienated by its narrow creed and its acceptance of members from churches which condoned slavery.

He was a leader in the agitation against the opium trade and opposed the Opium War against China (1840). His visit to America in 1841 was animated in part by the hope of improving relations between Great Britain and the United States, which had been disturbed by the Oregon question and the dispute over the Maine boundary. In 1850, in company with Elihu Burritt, he visited Prussia, Schleswig-Holstein and Denmark in an effort to secure the reference to arbitration of the issues between them and so to bring hostilities to an end. As one of a committee appointed by the London Meeting for Sufferings, he visited Czar Nicholas of Russia (1854) in an attempt to prevent the Crimean War. After the Crimean War he and Thomas Harvey distributed a relief fund raised chiefly among English Friends among the people of Finland, whose villages and shipping had been destroyed by the British fleet.[2]

He proposed a mission of conciliation to India after the Sepoy Rebellion, but the disturbed state of Indian affairs

---

[2] See Whittier's poem, "The Conquest of Finland."

at that time made the visit impracticable. He was one of the delegation which influenced Lord Clarendon to propose a protocol to the Congress of Paris (1856) in favor of arbitration for the settlement of international disputes.[3] He was elected president of the London Peace Society in 1848, the year before his death. He gave time and money to establish a reform school for juvenile criminals at Stoke Prior in Worcestershire. He was deeply concerned in extending the franchise to the working classes and in measures for improving their condition. In later life he took an active interest in a children's temperance organization, the Band of Hope, and in Sunday schools. He presented the first public park to the city of Birmingham.

Friends of this period made notable contributions to popular education, particularly of the neglected laboring classes. Some leaders of the Chartist movement, with whom Joseph Sturge was in contact about 1841, were interested in adult education. Friends had already opened such schools in Bristol and Nottingham. The latter, which had existed since 1798 under the care of Samuel Fox, came to Sturge's notice during the election contest of 1842. In 1845 he proposed to a group of younger Friends of Birmingham to open a First-day School for youths and young men at the rooms of the British School Society in Severn Street. It was a success from the start and older men came also. It was finally decided to hold the school from 7:30 to 9:30 Sunday mornings. Joseph Sturge provided the teachers with breakfast at 7 A.M. In spite of the many and even puerile objections of some of the conservative Friends[4] the school proved a godsend both to pupils and teachers.

A warm spirit of comradeship was developed, and, as the scholars grew in attainments, the school became more heartily democratic. Within a few years a well-established library and

---

[3] Richard, *Mem.*, pp. 496–502.

[4] See Hobhouse, *Joseph Sturge: His Life and Work,* pp. 169, 170.

savings bank had been added, and evening classes were held twice a week for arithmetic, grammar, and geography. In the annual report for 1859, the year of the founder's death, the number on the books of the school is given as 535. A Women's First-day School was started in 1848 and also proved a great blessing.[5]

A conference was held in Birmingham in 1847[6] at which the Friends First Day School Association was organized which guided the Adult School movement as it spread into other parts of Great Britain. In 1848 William White became a teacher in the Severn Street School, a position which he held for fifty-two years. He was one of the principal leaders in the development of the Adult School movement both in Birmingham and in the country at large. The later expansion of the Adult School movement and its influence on Friends belongs to another chapter.

John Bright (1811–1889) was the son of a Lancashire cotton spinner and a birthright Friend. Throughout his life he was a faithful attender of Friends' meetings, although he never "spoke in meeting." He was actively interested in the business meetings, both speaking to business and serving in official capacities. He observed Quaker ways until about middle life, when he dropped the "peculiarities." He grew more and more impatient with the isolation and conservatism of Quietist Friends and was especially indignant because his sister was disowned for marrying out of meeting.

He became one of the greatest liberal leaders in England during its great period of transition in the nineteenth century. His moral earnestness and eloquence made him an influential figure in English public life, both in the House of Commons and in popular assemblies. Next after William Penn he was the most powerful influence in apply-

---

5 Hobhouse, *op. cit.*, p. 170.
6 Rowntree & Binns, *The Adult School Movement*, pp. 15–17.

ing the Quaker ideals and principles to public life through political action. He and Richard Cobden carried the burden of the agitation for the repeal of the Corn Laws. He developed the technique of creating public sentiment and bringing it to bear upon Parliament and the government. His second great contribution to English life was his long struggle for enfranchising the laboring classes, which reached a successful issue in 1867. His public speeches helped educate the voteless workers so that they not only demanded the franchise but were prepared to use it intelligently. He was always a friend of the working classes and his political policies were dictated by faith in them and by a desire to enlarge their political power and their enjoyment of life.

He espoused the cause of the Irish and visited Ireland in 1849 and again in 1852. He championed measures for the economic improvement of the island, especially the Irish Land Act, the political enfranchisement of the Irish people and the disestablishment of the Irish Church. He opposed Gladstone's first Home Rule Bill, because he believed all members of the British kingdom should be represented in Parliament.[7]

Although not an absolute pacifist, Bright contributed greatly to the cause of European peace. He exposed the folly of the growing armaments of Europe.[8] He denounced Palmerston's policy of meddling in European quarrels, which led to the Crimean War, and exposed the inefficiency and folly of the conduct of the war. His influence was one of the forces which kept England from intervening on the side of the South in the American Civil War. He held the Lancashire operatives steady during the cotton famine;[9] helped prevent Palmerston from drawing Eng-

---

7 Trevelyan, *Life of John Bright,* pp. 457, 458.

8 *Ibid.,* p. 256.

9 It was at his suggestion that the North sent shiploads of flour to the Lancashire weavers.

land into war over the Trent affair through his influence in Parliament; he gave Lincoln's government, through his correspondence with Senator Charles Sumner, valuable advice as to the policy of America with regard to the blockade, emancipation, and the Alabama claims; and he aided in persuading the English government to prevent the sailing of the "iron-clad" commerce destroyers built at Birkenhead for the Confederacy. He attacked the policy of Palmerston of intermeddling with foreign affairs to maintain the balance of power.[10] He favored the armed suppression of the Sepoy revolt in India, but championed reforms in the Indian government and a change in the treatment of the natives. In 1861 he suggested to Gladstone a treaty with France providing for a limitation of naval armaments by mutual consent.[11] Bright believed that by its nature democracy would work for peace. He aided the government in keeping out of the Franco-Prussian War in 1870 and in settling the Alabama claims of the United States by arbitration.[12]

The Liberal Ministers, who had entered office with such reforming zeal at the end of 1868, were in 1872 nicknamed by Disraeli "a range of exhausted volcanoes," but meanwhile their lava had fairly covered the land below: they had disestablished the Irish Church, passed the Irish Land Act, set up—however imperfectly—national Education, abolished Purchase in the Army, opened the universities to dissenters, and established the ballot at elections. These changes, together with the earlier boons of Free Trade, Household Franchise in the towns, and the abolition of church-rates, and above all, the withdrawal of England from European entanglements, constituted a nearly complete adoption of Bright's programme.[13]

---

10 Trevelyan, *op. cit.*, p. 273.
11 *Ibid.*, pp. 292–293.
12 *Ibid.*, pp. 418, 419.
13 *Ibid.*, p. 415.

Bright fought the growing influence of the state Church after the revival of the Oxford movement. Locally in Rochdale he carried on a campaign against the collection of church rates and tithes; and he opposed the control of education by the Anglican Church. He worked for the disestablishment of the Church in Wales as well as in Ireland. He contributed much to the legal steps in 1851 and 1868 by which Dissenters were finally admitted to Oxford and Cambridge.

He was a lifelong champion of education, especially for the poorer classes. He was a friend of Ackworth School and a frequent visitor to the school. He finally secured the repeal of the paper taxes, so as to make cheap newspapers available to the poor. He would have no "taxes on knowledge." [14]

These leaders were supported by large and influential groups of Friends who were little by little emancipating the Society from the restraints and fears of Quietism and making Quakerism a vital force for social reform in the interests of justice, righteousness and peace. Their attitude toward the Society, however, differed radically from that of the "gay" friends, who dropped the "peculiarities" at the expense of their influence in the work of the Society and often because of indifference to its principles. Men like Bright, Joseph Pease and John Stephenson Rowntree were increasingly impatient of the "peculiarities" because they believed they were in large part the cause of the Society's inefficiency and its decline in numbers and influence.[15]

During this period Friends in England had become essentially a middle-class sect whose members were largely engaged in manufacture and trade, although there were still a good many country Friends engaged in agriculture, especially in Ireland, Wales and Yorkshire, and there were

---

14 Trevelyan, *op. cit.*, p. 212.

15 *Ibid.*, p. 173. Mills, *John Bright and the Quakers*, II, 7, 8, 13, 15. Rowntree, *Quakerism, Past and Present*, pp. 142–143.

some poorer Friends in the large cities. Quite a social gap existed between the extremes of these classes.[16] Many of the Quaker fortunes were made in commerce, banking and manufacturing. Curiously enough there were once a good many Friends in the brewing industry. "At the beginning of last century many innkeepers wore broad-brimmed hats; collarless coats were every whit as prominent among the brewers as among the bankers, or biscuit and chocolate manufacturers of a later day."[17] With the growth of temperance sentiment in this period, however, Friends gradually gave up "The Trade" for less anti-social occupations.

By the close of the period personal abstinence had become the rule rather than the exception among the leaders. J. J. Gurney, for example, signed the pledge as a "teetotaller" in 1845[18] and became associated with the work of "Father" Mathew. Although Bright was not always a total abstainer, he began his public speaking in the temperance cause, and in 1842 was president of the British Temperance League. He was the author of a temperance tract, *A Word with Serious People,* which had a wide circulation. The yearly meeting epistle of 1835 mentions "the dreadful evils which result to the community from intemperance and especially from the use of ardent spirits," and recommended Friends to abstain from the use of distilled spirits as a beverage.[19] In 1874 the yearly meeting seriously urged Friends still engaged in the liquor trade to give it up.

The Quakers had a great part in the development of English railways. Edward Pease, a Darlington wool merchant, was a devout Friend who vigorously opposed his own son's participation in politics; but the non-conformist habit of mind seems to make for originality and open-mindedness in many spheres of life besides religion. Ed-

---

16 Mills, *John Bright and the Quakers,* I, 405, 406.
17 *Ibid.,* I, 33.
18 *Memoirs,* II, 393.
19 Mills, *op. cit.,* II, 69.

ward Pease conceived the idea of running horse-drawn cars on iron rails to South Durham to give an outlet to the Darlington collieries and manufactured goods. George Stephenson proposed to build a steam engine to draw the cars. Pease had the daring to try the proposition and became "the father of railways." The Stockton and Darlington Railway was opened in 1825 and Edward Pease's sons helped in the great development of railways which followed, Joseph becoming treasurer of the first railway company. Friends were among the most influential promoters and managers of the English railway system. It was a Friend who determined the prevailing gauge of railroad tracks; another who invented the method of fastening the rails to the ties which is still in use in England; another who devised railway tickets and the machine for stamping them; and the originator of Bradshaw's time-tables was a Friend.[20]

The number of philanthropic enterprises and social and moral reforms in which practically all the Quaker leaders engaged in varying degrees is remarkable. In addition to those already mentioned there were plans for the education of free Negroes, the colonization of ex-slaves in Sierra Leone, the abolition of capital punishment, poor relief, and the rehabilitation of prisoners and criminals.

It has been asserted that the influence of the Wesleyan movement on the laboring classes during the latter part of the eighteenth century probably prevented a violent revolution in England at the time of the French Revolution. The Quaker influence was probably as great in enabling England to make the great democratic changes between 1830 and 1870 without a violent revolution and to weather peaceably the commotions caused in the rest of Europe by the second French Revolution (1848).

---

20 Beck, *The Friends: Who They Are and What They Have Done*, pp. 229–230.

During this period Friends made progress in providing for the better education of their own children. Samuel Tuke conceived the idea of schools for Friends equal to the English public schools. Outstanding leaders in York joined with him and established Bootham School for Boys in 1829 and Mount School for Girls in 1831. In the former year Joseph Rowntree, a member of the Ackworth School committee, took the lead in investigating the condition of education among adherents and attenders of Friends who were not members, the results of which led to the founding of Rawdon School in Yorkshire (1832). In 1837 Samuel Tuke and Joseph Rowntree led in the organization of the Friends Educational Society.

In 1848 Benjamin Flounders left a bequest of £40,000 for educational purposes, under which Flounders Institute for training young men as teachers was established adjoining Ackworth School, and rendered a valuable service in training teachers for the Society. In 1894 the Institute was moved to Leeds so as to have the benefit of Yorkshire College which was later incorporated in the University of Leeds (1904). The following English Friends schools not already mentioned were established during this period: Penketh School near Warrington, (1834); Ayton School (1841); [21] Sibford School in Oxfordshire (1842); and in Ireland there were Brookfield Agricultural College in County Antrim (1838) and Friends' Boarding School in Dublin (1840).

The influences which have been described in this chapter gradually loosened the hold of the disciplinary "peculiarities" upon the younger generation of Friends. In 1843 two Friends periodicals were established which were to exercise a great influence on the progress of the Society. *The Friend* was issued monthly until 1892 when it became a weekly.

---

[21] For a list of schools owned and managed by individual Friends or by groups of Friends at some time during the nineteenth century, see JLPQ, II, 706, 707.

It showed a "wider outlook and an enlarging sympathy" from the beginning. It fostered a missionary spirit and an international interest. *The British Friend*[22] was another sign of a new life in the Society, although more conservative in its attitude.[23]

In 1858 an anonymous offer of a prize for the best essay on the causes of the decline of the Society of Friends in Great Britain and Ireland "appeared in the public prints." The prize was awarded to John Stephenson Rowntree (1834–1907) for his work, *Quakerism: Past and Present.* His father Joseph Rowntree of York was actively interested in Quaker education especially in the founding and maintenance of Bootham and Mount Schools. He was deeply concerned from young manhood over the decline of Friends and in 1851 he urged his son, John Stephenson, to take an active interest in the Society. In 1854 the latter attended London Yearly Meeting and was disappointed in the discussion of the "state of society" because "no one grappled with the subject in a large and comprehensive manner." In 1856 he expressed alarm at the lack of vocal ministry shown by reports from quarterly meetings.

He welcomed, therefore, the opportunity to investigate the causes of the decline in the Society afforded by the prize offer in 1858. As a result of his studies, he estimated that there were in Great Britain and Ireland in 1680 about 66,000 Quakers or one to 130 of the population. Due to losses by emigration to America and other causes which he discussed, he estimated that in 1800 there were only about 32,000 Friends in these countries, or one to every 470 of the population. His estimates for 1856 were 14,530 members of London Yearly Meeting; 7,000 attenders not in

---

22 It was discontinued in 1912.

23 Other British Quaker periodical publications during this period were as follows: *The Yorkshireman,* edited by Luke Howard. Pontefract, 1833–1847; *The Irish Friend,* edited by William Bell Belfast, 1837–1842; and *The Inquirer* (A Beaconite publication), London, 1838–1840.

membership; and 4,000 members and attenders for Ireland, a total of 26,000 or one Friend to every 1,100 of the population.[24]

He considered the generally low tone of religion in England in the eighteenth century and the growing prosperity and worldliness of Friends as contributory causes of the decline. As the chief causes, however, he named the over-emphasis on silence and the disuse of the Bible in worship; the lack of adequate ministry due to the Quietist ideal of the ministry, the disparagement of intellectual qualifications, the repressions of the eldership, the limitations on the travelling ministry; the neglect of the gift of teaching; the serious lack of higher education throughout the eighteenth century and early nineteenth century, together with the distrust of the human reason and the Puritanic attitude toward music and the fine arts; and the ecclesiastical polity which was unsuited for widening the sphere of influence of Quakerism and "powerless as a proselytizing engine." The most important cause of the spiritual decline of the Society, in his opinion, was birthright membership; and he believed that disownment for paying tithes or marrying out of meeting caused the greatest loss in numbers. He estimated that in the first half of the nineteenth century, the Society disowned nearly one-third of all its members who got married—about four thousand persons in all.[25]

Within three years of the publication of this essay, which aroused great interest and much discussion, many of the changes which he advocated were made officially. In 1859 the disciplinary regulations were so changed as to permit the marriage of a Friend and non-Friend according to the manner of Friends. In 1860 the clause in the Queries regarding "plainness in speech, behaviour and apparel" was

---

24 *Quakerism, Past and Present,* pp. 68–88.
25 *Ibid.,* p. 183.

omitted. In 1861 a very important revision of the discipline was made, making numerous changes in the direction of more general participation in the yearly meeting and more democratic management of its affairs.[26]

---

[26] These changes led a small group of conservative Friends to withdraw from London Yearly Meeting between 1862 and 1869 and establish a "general meeting," which has been held at Fritchley since the latter date. Brayshaw, *The Quakers,* pp. 298–300.

Chapter 29

ACTIVITIES AND NEW TENDENCIES OF AMERICAN QUAKERISM

The first period (1827–1861) of the third division of American Quaker history was characterized by separations and was dominated by the slavery issue. Many other lines of philanthropic and educational work also engaged the interest and support of Friends. At the beginning of this period, however, the policy of isolation was emphasized by the leaders of American Friends, especially with regard to political, religious and philanthropic work. It became their settled policy not to form "mixed associations with the world's people" for any cause. The separation of 1827–1828 marked the abandonment of the Quietist theology,[1] but Quietism still reigned in religious work and worship. The leaders and travelling ministers were chary of general concerns or organized efforts. In their philanthropic efforts they were careful to proceed according to "immediate guidance." It was understood that all their plans were, like modern railroad schedules, "subject to change without notice." The latter part of this period witnessed the passing of Quietism in religious work.

In objecting to the anti-slavery leaders' work in "mixed associations," Indiana Yearly Meeting put it on the ground that the non-Friends "do not profess to wait for divine direction in such important concerns." [2] Over against this came to be set the ideal which Joseph Sturge advocated in

[1] This was true also for the Hicksites, who, while having no official theology, stopped with theological tolerance or went on to Liberalism.

[2] Edgerton, *op. cit.*, p. 49.

his address to American Friends, as he was finishing his visit to America (1841), "While I believe that the true disciple of Christ will be favored with the immediate guidance of the Holy Spirit, *whenever it is needful to direct his steps;* it appears to me especially important that, in matters of self-sacrifice, and conflicting with our worldly interest or reputation, we should guard against being deluded into a neglect of duty, *by waiting for this direct, divine, intimation, where the path of duty is obvious and clearly understood, and where testimonies are concerned, which we have long considered it our duty on all occasions to support.*"[3] Quietism in worship, however, lasted over into the next period. Even to Gurney "immediate" guidance in meetings for worship meant not merely direct and personal guidance by the divine Spirit but *extempore* guidance or leading *at the moment of action* to which Quietism tended more and more to confine it.

An estimate of the membership of the American Orthodox yearly meetings appearing in the *British Friend* in 1843 was as follows:[4] New England, 10,000; New York, 11,000; Philadelphia, 8,686; Baltimore, 800; Virginia, 500; North Carolina, 4,500; Ohio, 18,000; Indiana, 30,000.[5] It is more difficult to get a basis for estimating the membership of the Hicksite meetings. It seems probable that the numbers had not changed materially since 1830, when according to the Hicksites' claims their total membership was about 47,000 as follows: New York, 12,532;[6] Philadelphia, 18,485;[7] Baltimore, 4,000;[8] Ohio, 9,000;[9] and In-

[3] Edgerton, *op. cit.*, pp. 53, 54. Italics mine.

[4] The estimate was based on educational reports. See *The British Friend*, 1843, p. 117.

[5] Hodgson estimates that the Anti-slavery Friends of Indiana Yearly Meeting had 2,000 members against 25,000 for the "body" of the yearly meeting. Hodgson, *Hist.*, II, 31–33. Cf. Wm. Forster, *Mem.*, I, 366n.

[6] Estimate of John Barrow. Foster's *Report,* I, 263, 464.

[7] Estimate of Halliday Jackson, *Ibid.*, II, 176. Thomas Evans for the Orthodox allowed them 17, 153. *Ibid.*, II, 461, 495.

[8] Janney, *Hist.*, IV, 346.

[9] *Ibid.*, p. 306, JLPQ, I, 480.

diana, 3,000.[10] In 1840 James Mott claimed 80,000 for all the Hicksite Yearly Meetings but this seems entirely too large.[11] L. Maria Child gives the number about 1830 as "more than 70,000."[12]

In the separation of 1827–1828 Virginia and North Carolina Yearly Meetings were not divided. As a consequence the great stream of migration from the southern states into the Ohio Valley was composed of Orthodox Friends only. The Hicksites benefitted but little from the shifts in Quaker population. In 1834 Hicksite Friends in western New York were united with meetings in Canada to form Genesee Yearly Meeting.

During this period both branches of Friends continued in varying measure the traditional philanthropies. In addition to the anti-slavery cause, they engaged in work for the poor, the prisoners, the insane, and for free Negroes and the Indians. They promoted peace, temperance, and education. In addition to these causes, individual Friends worked for the rights of women, and opposed capital punishment and imprisonment for debt.[13] Friends were among the organizers and early supporters of the American Peace Society (1828) and of its constituent organizations, chiefly in Rhode Island, New York, Pennsylvania and Ohio.[14] John Griscom was the leading spirit in organizing the Society for the Prevention of Pauperism in New York City

---

10 Estimated. In 1890 Indiana and Illinois together had about 3,000. Allowing for growth in Illinois and decline in Indiana this seems fair. Cf. Thomas, *Hist.*, 4th ed., p. 227. See *Centennial of Whitewater Monthly Meeting* (Richmond, Ind., 1909), p. 73, where Eli Jay estimates the membership of Indiana Yearly Meeting in 1827 at 12,390 and in 1865 at 11,955 after Western (1858) and Iowa (1863) had been set off from it. Frances M. Robinson puts the membership of Indiana Yearly Meeting (H) in 1850, when statistics were first kept, at 1138. At this time it included part of Illinois Yearly Meeting which was set off in 1875. The estimated membership in 1840 given in the text is a liberal one.

11 *Life of James and Lucretia Mott,* p. 177.

12 *Isaac T. Hopper: A True Life,* p. 284.

13 See Whittier's The Prisoner for Debt.

14 Curti, *The American Peace Crusade 1815–1860,* pp. 9, 23, 33, 46, 49.

as well as one of the founders of the New York Historical Society. Whittier's early efforts were against slavery, intemperance and war.[15] The list of causes championed by Lucretia Mott is surprising:[16] they included the anti-slavery movement, woman's suffrage,[17] temperance,[18] peace,[19] the Anti-Sabbath Association[20] and the Free Religious Association.[21] She represented the extreme left wing of the Hicksite branch and carried on with fearless logic the revolt against external authority which was involved in the Hicksite separation. She undertook with remarkable independence to clear away all illogical theological doctrines, not because she was interested in theology, as such, but in the interest of religious liberty. She was associated with English liberals such as Harriet Martineau, as well as with the anti-slavery and women's rights leaders in America, and especially with the New England Unitarians—William Lloyd Garrison, Theodore Parker, Theodore Cuyler and William H. Furness. The basis of her fellowship with them was primarily a common interest in Abolition; but they also represented a revolt against outward theological and ecclesiastical authority in the interest of a religion of personal piety and philanthropy. Her anti-Sabbath attitude was not an attempt to secularize Sunday but an attempt to return to the early Quaker demand that every day be a holy day.[22] Her interest in women's rights was not a selfish interest in securing advantages for herself or her sex but to give women freedom and

---

15 Pickard, *op. cit.*, I, 57.

16 *James and Lucretia Mott,* pp. 100, 247–259, 304.

17 *Ibid.*, pp. 298–300.

18 *Ibid.*, pp. 247–250.

19 *Ibid.*, p. 282.

20 *Ibid.*, pp. 295–297.

21 *Ibid.*, pp. 369, 425.

22 *James and Lucretia Mott,* p. 297. The purpose of the Association was, as stated, "to advance the cause of true Christianity, to promote true and acceptable worship, and to inculcate strict moral and religious accountability in all the concerns of life, *on all days of the week alike.*"

political power for the betterment of mankind. These radical views alienated many of her fellow Quakers who might have approved her anti-slavery views. She learned in time, however, that much of the current liberalism was chiefly revolt against New England Calvinism and that she had unity with its negative aspects only. Her real religious interest was in the positive aspects of Quaker mysticism.

Friends began, early in the nineteenth century, to take a fresh interest in the evils of alcoholic intemperance. Nearly all the prominent anti-slavery leaders were also actively interested in the temperance movement.[23] The pioneer settlers west of the Alleghenies carried the "little brown whisky jug" with them and it became part of the standard equipment of the frontier home. Whisky was the common remedy for malaria, snakebite, and other "miseries." [24] It was furnished for all social gatherings—at elections, harvest time, log-rollings, funerals,[25] and weddings. Men would get drunk on these occasions or at the taverns and get into fights or go home and abuse their families. A good many succumbed to its habit-forming power, became "shiftless" and squandered their money. In the larger cities of the east the moral, social and economic evil effects of the use of alcohol manifested themselves on an increasing scale and the first efforts to curb intemperance arose there. The churches led in the movement as early as 1808. The American Society for the Promotion of Temperance was founded in Boston in 1826. It pledged its members to abstinence from strong "spirits" only. Father Mathews' temperance crusade in Ireland (1838–1842) influenced this country through the Irish immigrants after the potato famines in Ireland. Father

---

[23] For examples: Levi Coffin (*Rem.*, pp. 130, 278), Whittier (Pickard, *op. cit.*, I, 57), Lucretia Mott (*James and Lucretia Mott*, pp. 247–250). Cf. also Heath, *The Story of Lucy Stone: Pioneer*, p. 46.

[24] JLPQ, I, 372, 373.

[25] *Loc. cit.*

Mathews himself visited America in 1850. The Washingtonian and allied temperance movements flourished in America from 1840–1843; and the Order of Good Templars grew rapidly after their organization in 1851. Individual Friends joined in some of these movements but the yearly meetings did not join officially in such "mixed" societies until after the Civil War.

During this period protests against the use of alcohol among Friends became more common.[26] As early as 1811 White Water Monthly Meeting in Indiana requested the yearly meeting to caution its members against being concerned in the making or sale of alcoholic liquors.[27]

From this time Friends bore a steady official testimony against the excessive use of intoxicants and against the manufacture and sale of them. Reminders of this were early inserted in the Queries,[28] by most of the yearly meetings. Between 1825 and 1850 Friends generally discontinued the use of alcoholic liquors as a beverage on their tables or on social occasions. [29]

Friends continued an active interest in prison reform and were opposed to capital punishment. Many of their leaders, Lucretia Mott and Whittier especially, made efforts at times to have it abolished.[30] They maintained their testimony against war, especially against the use of force to

---

[26] Allen Jay's father, for example, a member of West Branch Quarter in western Ohio, was one of the first to refuse to furnish whisky at log-rollings. This must have been before 1825. There are cases on record in Indiana Yearly Meeting where the monthly meeting provided the whisky, so that a widow could get her grain harvested. *Autobiography of Allen Jay*, p. 16.

[27] JLPQ, I, 374.

[28] The query in the Philadelphia Discipline (O) of 1834 reads: "Are Friends careful to discourage the unnecessary distillation and use of spirituous liquors, and the frequenting of taverns; to avoid places of diversion, and to keep in true moderation and temperance on account of marriages, burials, and all other occasions?" (pp. 113, 114).

[29] *Memoirs of J. J. Gurney*, II, 138, Art. "Anthony, Susan Brownell," in *Dict. Am. Biog.* Levi Coffin, *Rem.*, p. 278.

[30] *Life of James and Lucretia Mott*, p. 264. Pickard, *op. cit.*, I, 292–293.

free slaves or the resort to warfare to abolish slavery.[31]

During this period Friends continued lines of work for the Indians already begun. After the separation of 1828 the Hicksite New York Yearly Meeting received the funds of the Indian Committee and continued the work among the Onondagas, which was later transferred to Cattaraugus where a school was opened among the Senecas in 1833. Friends were of great service in saving part of the lands of the Seneca nation from the Ogden Land Company, which had an option on the lands whenever the Indians should vacate them and which attempted to get possession of them by bribing their chiefs.[32] After their reservations at Allegheny and Cattaraugus were secured to them (1842) the Senecas decided not to emigrate to the West. Women Friends established a Female Manual Labor School at Cattaraugus to teach the Indian women the domestic arts of civilization. In 1849 the school was closed because it appeared that it had sufficiently served its purpose.

The work which Baltimore Yearly Meeting had begun among a part of the Shawnee tribe at Wapakaneta (near Lewistown, Ohio) was broken up during the War of 1812 but in 1815 members of the newly established Ohio Yearly Meeting took a share in the Shawnee work. They built a sawmill and grist mill at Wapakoneta and in 1822 a school was opened.[33] The agitation over the projected removal of the Indians west of the Mississippi river interferred with this work, so that the school was suspended several times, and the mission was closed when the last Senecas were removed in 1832.

In 1833 a deputation was sent by Indiana Yearly Meeting to visit the Senecas in their Kansas home where they were

---

31 Pickard, *op. cit.*, I, 231. See Whittier's poem, "Brown of Ossawatomie." Earle, *Life of Lundy*, p. 247.

32 Kelsey, *Friends and the Indians*, pp. 119–124.

33 After its establishment in 1821 Indiana Yearly Meeting also assisted in this work.

welcomed by their old protégés. Following this visit, Indiana, Ohio and Baltimore yearly meetings joined in establishing a school among the western tribes for literary and manual education and for teaching the Bible and the doctrines of Christianity. Other yearly meetings also contributed to this work. As a result of a visit of John D. Lang and Samuel Taylor, Jr., in 1842, New York and New England yearly meetings gave the mission substantial aid, but after 1850 the school declined. The Indians disagreed among themselves over the sale of a large part of their Kansas lands; an outbreak of cholera interrupted the school; and it suffered from a Missouri pro-slavery mob during the struggle over slavery after the passage of the Kansas-Nebraska Act (1854). It was kept up for several years, practically as a school for Indian orphans. In 1869, it was closed and the property sold. By that time most of the Shawnees had been removed to the Indian territory and incorporated with the Cherokee nation.[34]

It was natural that Quaker women should take the lead in the movement for women's rights. They had experience in taking part in public meetings and had been taught to believe in their equality with men in the church and before God. Of the four great women leaders of the suffrage movement: Lucretia Mott (1793–1880), Elizabeth Cady Stanton, Lucy Stone and Susan B. Anthony (1820–1906); the first and last were birthright Friends.

Lucretia Mott and Elizabeth Cady Stanton were delegates to the World Anti-slavery Conference in London in 1840. Mrs. Stanton became interested in women's rights first as a girl when she learned from her father, Judge Cady, the legal disabilities of women. It was 1848, however, before she and Lucretia Mott organized the first Women's Rights Convention at Seneca Falls, New York.[35] Here she

---

[34] See Kelsey, *op. cit.*, chaps. VI and VII for a fuller account of the Indian work of Friends in this period.

[35] Art. "Susan Brownell Anthony," *Encycl. Soc. Sciences.*

introduced a resolution for women's suffrage, although Lucretia Mott was not ready to approve it. Susan B. Anthony, a Hicksite Friend of Adams, Mass., was converted to the suffrage cause by Lucy Stone. She joined the Anti-slavery movement in 1856, after having been associated with Mrs. Stanton for five years. Friends generally were conservative about changing established customs and fearful of public agitation and association with non-Friends, so that these pioneer women found much opposition among them.

About 1800 a concern arose in Philadelphia Yearly Meeting for elementary education as a result of which elementary schools were established in nearly every monthly meeting of the yearly meeting. From this beginning monthly meeting elementary schools spread throughout Quakerdom.

On the frontier the schoolhouse appeared promptly beside the meeting-house and an effort was made to have a monthly meeting school in every community. Often these schools were "subscription schools"—private ventures where the teacher took the school for what he could make out of it.[36] The school rarely lasted more than three or four months a year. The log schoolhouse was poorly equipped with furniture; books were scarce and the teachers often young and inexperienced; but the schools became centers of literacy and educational inspiration. In the states of Ohio, Indiana, Iowa, Kansas, North Carolina and Tennessee the monthly meeting schools laid the foundation of the public school system or materially influenced its character.[37]

The influence of Roberts Vaux in Pennsylvania, John Griscom in New York and Barnabas C. Hobbs in Indiana in promoting general public education was especially out-

---

36 See Levi Coffin, *Rem.*, p. 87.

37 JLPQ, II, 685. Weeks, *op. cit.*, p. 302.

standing. Roberts Vaux (1786–1836) was one of the greatest contributors to popular education and the promotion of the sciences. He retired from business at thirty and devoted the remaining thirty years of his life to education and philanthropy.

> A devoted member of the Society of Friends, he gave not only of himself but practically all his time to the promotion of adult education, which was then beginning to be a problem as immigrants poured into the United States and the country was experiencing a great expansion, together with the necessity of making democracy work. . . . He had such a profound interest in our Philadelphia life that he took a leading part in the creation of a free public school system and was the first president of the board of controllers of the public schools of Philadelphia. He assisted in the organization of the Academy of Natural Sciences, the Linnaean Society, the Franklin Institute, the Athenaeum, the Historical Society of Pennsylvania, The Philadelphia Saving Fund Society and the Apprentices' Library. . . . He had a singularly interesting career although a short one. He helped to establish practically all of the important educational institutions of his day and was greatly admired in Philadelphia.[38]

In connection with the pioneer schools there was often a monthly meeting library, or in some cases a community library,[39] maintained by a local literary society. In many cases children of neighbors who were not Friends attended these schools. Many Friends' children on the frontier, on the other hand, had to go to schools kept by non-Friends for their schooling. In 1835 a summary of the educational

---

[38] Art. by Roland S. Morris, *The Friend,* Nov. 16, 1939. See McCadden, *Education in Pennsylvania, 1801–1835, and Its Debt to Roberts Vaux.*

[39] Levi Coffin formed such literary and library associations in North Carolina and later in Indiana. *Mem.*, pp. 70, 71, 88. See also Weeks, *op. cit.*, pp. 298, 299. *Autobiog. of Allen Jay,* p. 85. In 1830 Indiana Yearly Meeting appointed a committee to devise measures for establishing libraries of Friends' books within the limits of each monthly meeting. McDaniel, *The Contributions of the Society of Friends to Education in Indiana,* p. 129n.

reports of the quarterly meetings to North Carolina Yearly Meeting was as follows:

> The report of the Quarterly Meetings with respect to schools, the number of minors, the lack of Bibles in Friends families, etc., is as follows: 2391 under 21 yrs. of age, 644 of which are under 5 yrs. of age and 46 that are of sufficient age to be sent to school who are receiving no school learning. 45 schools to which Friends children go, but only 11 of which are taught by members of our society, 34 by those not in membership with us: all the schools in a mixed state and but 3 families without Bibles.[40]

The educational statistics of Indiana yearly meeting as reported for 1865 may serve as an example of the educational situation about the end of this period.

Number of children between 5 and 15	5,825
Number of children between 15 and 20	2,860
	8,685
Number of children taught in schools under the superintendence of Monthly Meetings' Committees	3,732
Number of children taught in schools not under such superintendence	3,365
Number of children growing up without school education	2
Number of schools not under the superintendence of Monthly Meetings' Committees, but taught by Friends	197
Number of Meetings without Friends' Schools; where such exist, they are generally on the Meeting-house premises	61
Number of First-day Scripture Schools under the care of Committees	138
Number of meetings without such schools	23

The average attendance at First-day Scripture Schools is supposed to be between three and four thousand.[41]

[40] Cited in Klain, *op. cit.*, p. 64.

[41] Cited in William Forster, *Mem.*, I, 366.

Following the Separation of 1827–1828 most of the older schools:—Westtown, Nine Partners, Moses Brown and William Penn Charter[42]—were retained by the Orthodox party. The Hicksites had only Fair Hill Boarding School at Sandy Spring, Md. (founded in 1819), Alexandria Boarding School, Va. (1824) and Wilmington School for Girls (1809). After the Separation the Hicksites began to establish other schools to take the place of those of which they had lost the use. The most important of these were Westchester Graded School, Pa. (1835); Sharon Female Seminary, Darby, Pa. (1838); Friends Academy, Richmond, Indiana (1844);[43] Friends Central School, Philadelphia, Pa. (1845); and Friends Seminary, New York City (1861).

The Conservative or Wilburite Friends of Ohio Yearly Meeting retained after the separation of 1854 the Friends Boarding School which was opened at Mt. Pleasant, in 1837; after the buildings were burned in 1876, the school was moved to Barnesville, Ohio, where it remains today.

Orthodox Friends carried on the interest in higher education which was just beginning at the time of the Separation of 1927–28. Among the pioneer schools in North Carolina was Belvidere Academy at Rich Square, (1835) where many of the Quaker leaders of North Carolina and the Northwest received their first training. In 1837 Friends' New Garden Boarding School began its career near Greensboro. The year following Union Normal Institute was established near High Point under the joint auspices of a group of Friends and Methodists. In 1857 Friendsville Academy was opened in eastern Tennessee and has done an important work in maintaining the rather isolated quarterly meeting there.

Among the Philadelphia (O) Yearly Meeting boarding schools and academies of this period were Clairmont

[42] These schools together with Haverford College furnished the leading teachers for Friends' schools of the south and west during this period.

[43] Reorganized and enlarged on a new location, 1867.

Boarding Academy near Frankford, the Friends' Select Schools (1828),[44] and Darby Friends' School (1854), later called Lansdowne Friends' School. Oak Grove Seminary at Vassalboro, Me., was opened by New England Friends in 1849.

Among Western Friends the following academies were founded before 1861: Raisin Valley Seminary, Mich. (1850); Farmers Institute, (near Lafayette, Ind.) (1850); Union High School, Westfield, Ind. (1861); Bloomingdale (Ind.) Academy, which was intended at first as an "agricultural manual labor school"[45] (1845); Salem Seminary, Ia. (1845); Friends Boarding School, Richmond, Ind. (1847).

Mention has been made of the founding of Haverford College in 1833 by Philadelphia Orthodox Friends.[46] Earlham College (1859) grew out of Friends Boarding School at Richmond, Ind., and owed much besides its name to the influence of J. J. Gurney. New Garden Boarding School did not become Guilford College until 1888. These schools drew educated men and women to the Quaker communities, furnished leaders to the frontier settlements and gave inspiration to the Quaker youth. They gradually added a much-needed intellectual element to Quaker leadership. It is difficult to imagine the continued existence of the Society in America without them. Its history would certainly have been sadly different without their influence. They were largely made possible by the self-sacrificing devotion of their teachers and officers who usually worked on meager and uncertain salaries, frequently refusing better positions, carrying on in the face of severe criticism, and giving of their spare time generously in lecturing and preaching among Friends away from the schools.

---

[44] These were really offshoots of Penn's public school. They were started by Samuel T. Griscom. JLPQ, II, 707.

[45] Brinton, *Quaker Education,* p. 107.

[46] Haverford is the only Friends college that is not co-educational.

These schools nearly all found it necessary to admit non-Friends in order to meet their financial obligations and through these students they exercised an influence on the ideals and practices of the world around them beyond any calculation.

The ideal of these schools always included religious teaching of the Bible and of Quaker principles, and the practice of worship "after the manner of Friends." In addition, the educational ideal continued to be that of a "religiously guarded education," which meant guarding the young people from early knowledge of or contact with the evils of the world. In most of them the Bible was read to the pupils daily and they attended the neighboring mid-week meeting.[47] The system proved fairly effective as a means of transmitting the Quaker ideal of life. It fell short of teaching men and women to do original thinking and in developing freely chosen virtue.

During this period a few Friends' periodicals were established. *The Friend* was, as already stated, founded in 1827 and remained the organ of Orthodox Quietism. In 1844 *The Friends' Intelligencer* (Phila.) became the organ of the Hicksite branch. In 1847 *The Friends Review* was started as the organ of the more liberal or "Gurneyite" wing of Philadelphia Yearly Meeting. Other periodicals were started during this period but none of them survived long or exercised much influence.[48]

Sunday schools began among Friends quite early. They were called Bible schools or First-day schools at first. In

---

47 See McDaniel, *The Contribution of the Society of Friends to Education in Indiana,* p. 131, Klain, *op. cit.*, p. 66.

48 The following American publications ran to more than two volumes:
The Friend or Advocate of Truth. Phila., 1828–1830 (Hicksite).
The Miscellaneous Repository. Edited by Elisha Bates. Mt. Pleasant, O. 1827–1836 (Orthodox).
Friends Miscellany. Edited by John and Isaac Comly, Phila., 1831–1839 (Hicksite).
The Non-Slaveholder (Phila.) 1846–1850, 1853–1854.

many of them the children had first to be taught to read in order that they might read the Bible.[49] At first the schools were conducted as a single class, young and old together. They simply read the Bible by turns or recited texts committed to memory, with little or no attempt at interpretation.

The first Sunday schools among American Friends appear to have been those started by Levi Coffin while a teacher at Deep River, N. C., in 1818 and at Honey Creek, Indiana, in 1826. Both were "mixed" schools.[50] Bible schools were encouraged by William Forster, who found them quite general in Ohio and Indiana in 1821,[51] and by John Pease, who visited among Friends in America in 1842. The work of Hannah C. Backhouse and J. J. Gurney during the years 1830–1838 in encouraging Bible societies, Bible study and Bible schools has already been recounted. In 1836 it was reported that in six of the auxiliaries of the Bible Association there were 4,253 Friends capable of reading who did not possess a copy of the Bible. It had 35 auxiliary associations. In 1850 the Association reported that since its establishment it had printed 22,350 copies of its reference Bible, beside 2,000 copies of a school Bible.

The experiences of this period prepared the way for the abandonment of many of the "peculiarities" or "testimonies" of the Society and the adoption of new programs and methods. The freedom of frontier life and the association of Friends with non-Friends in various religious and philanthropic activities and in schools, gradually undermined the traditional practices and prepared the way for the prevalence of Evangelical methods in the succeeding period.

---

49 In the old Blue River meeting-house, near Salem, Ind., as late as 1900 there were to be found copies of Webster's blue-backed spelling book, which were said to have been secured as long ago as the oldest members could remember for use in the Bible schools.

50 *Mem.*, pp. 71, 72, 88.

51 William Forster, *Mem.*, I, 330.

Many of the travelling ministers continued to hold meetings in Baptist and Methodist meeting-houses during this period, as their predecessors had been accustomed to do. In Virginia and the Carolinas the Methodists absorbed many of their Quaker neighbors into their membership.[52] Young Friends especially began to attend "revival" meetings in the neighboring churches.[53] Even in Philadelphia Yearly Meeting (O) reports from the quarterly meetings that some Friends were attending other churches, led the meeting to send down minutes warning against "hireling ministers" in 1854 and 1856.[54]

---

52 Weeks gives this as one cause of the disappearance of many meetings. *Op. cit.*, pp. 291–295.

53 Allen Jay told the author a story regarding Eleazer Bales, one of the charter ministers of Western Yearly Meeting. He visited a monthly meeting where they were just disowning a young woman "for getting religion in a Methodist meeting." She was an admirable character; Friends had nothing against her except this violation of the testimony against a "hireling" ministry. Eleazer arose and said solemnly: "Friends, I think things have come to a pretty pass in Western Yearly Meeting when we have to disown a young woman for getting religion." She was not disowned. Cf. also William Forster, *Mem.*, II, 138.

54 See *Minutes of Philadelphia Yearly Meeting* in loco.

Period II

Reconstruction
1861-1914

Chapter 30

FRIENDS IN THE CIVIL WAR AND FREEDMEN'S AID

The War between the States made a definite break in the history of American Quakerism. The Society was forced out of its official isolation both because of its pacifist attitude and by its relief work. The war dragged many of the young men from their home communities and compelled them to reëxamine their inherited Quaker traditions, the pacifist tradition in particular. It brought many Friends a fresh baptism of suffering for their principles; and committed the Society, both in England and the United States, to help the Negro freedmen and to aid in the religious and educational reconstruction of parts of the South.

The Civil War, which brought about the emancipation of the slaves, brought an end to the Underground Railroad and the struggle for Abolition;[1] but these ends were achieved by warlike methods which Friends abhorred. President Lincoln stated their dilemma as he saw it in his letter to Eliza P. Gurney:

---

1 Levi Coffin, *Rem.*, p. 712.

> Your people—the Friends—have had, and are having a very great trial. On principle and faith, opposed to both war and oppression, they can only practically oppose oppression by war. In this hard dilemma, some have chosen one horn and some the other. For those appealing to me on conscientious grounds, I have done, and shall do, the best I could and can, in my own conscience, under my oath to the laws.[2]

Friends did not acknowledge war, however, as the only practicable way to oppose and abolish slavery; although their neighbors charged them bitterly with having helped bring on the war by their anti-slavery work and then refusing to aid in finishing it. President Lincoln and his cabinet were on the whole sympathetic with Friends' position.[3] In 1863 a conference was held in Baltimore attended by delegates from New England, New York, Baltimore, Ohio, Indiana, and Western yearly meetings, which appointed a committee consisting of Francis T. King, Charles F. Coffin and Samuel Boyd Tobey, which went to Washington and interviewed President Lincoln and members of his cabinet. Negotiations with the government continued after the conference adjourned and greatly influenced the terms of the draft law and the treatment of conscientious objectors.[4] When Congress passed the draft act, it provided exemption for Friends on the payment of $300 per person, the money to be used for hospital service and other non-military purposes, which was satisfactory to most Friends although a few refused to accept even this exemption.

Officially the Society stood firm on its peace testimony. Whittier spoke for Friends as a whole when he affirmed, "The levelled gun, the battle-brand, we may not take." [5]

---

[2] The letter is given in facsimile in BFHA, XXVIII (1939), No. 2.

[3] His cabinet was sometimes called "The Quaker Cabinet." Lincoln's great grandfather, Mordecai Lincoln, was a Pennsylvania Quaker. His own grandfather was disowned for "marrying out." See Cartland, *Southern Heroes*, p. 129.

[4] See *Charles F. Coffin: Quaker Poineer*, pp. 119–123.

[5] Anniversary Poem.

Many of the young men, however, did not share the traditional peace views of the Society and enlisted or acquiesced in the draft, although the proportion of the whole membership doing so was quite small.[6] In the Orthodox yearly meetings the young men who served in the army were either disowned or made to acknowledge their error. The Hicksite young men who served in the Union army were not dealt with or disowned as a rule. This left in active membership a group powerfully swayed by political interests and loyalties and very lightly bound by the peace traditions of the Society, a number of whom have been prominently occupied with public affairs and very jealous of any action by Friends which would seem to be inconsistent with political loyalty.

In North Carolina, Tennessee and Virginia the sufferings of Friends were greater than in the northern states. Friends were fewer and less influential, the needs of the Confederacy for men and materials were more desperate and the territories where Friends lived where ravaged by armies of both sides. It was estimated that Friends in Hopewell Quarter in the upper Shenandoah Valley were robbed of more than $40,000 worth of property by both armies. In lower Virginia a partial list of losses reported totals more than $11,000.[7]

Largely through the efforts of John B. Crenshaw, Isham Cox, John Carter, Allen U. Tomlinson and Nereus Mendenhall, the Confederate Draft Act of 1862 allowed those who were Friends at that date to be exempted on furnishing a substitute or on the payment of $500 or the performance of hospital service. Since this tax was for military purposes, North Carolina Yearly Meeting advised against paying it; but left the matter to the individual conscience.[8]

---

[6] JLPQ, II, 736, 737.

[7] Cartland, *op. cit.*, pp. 366, 367. On conditions in North Carolina see chap. XVIII, "Conditions in Carolina at the Close of the Civil War," by Mary Mendenhall Hobbs, in the *Autobiography of Allen Jay*.

[8] Cartland, *op. cit.*, pp. 139, 140.

Many paid the exemption fee; others emigrated through the old routes of the Underground Railroad to the Northwest;[9] a number of young men "hid out" to escape the draft and were hunted assiduously by the "Home Guards," who even tortured their parents or wives to make them betray their hiding places. Many who refused to pay the exemption fee, refused to perform military service when taken to camp and endured great sufferings for their steadfastness.[10] The greatest sufferers were the many convinced Friends who joined after the outbreak of the war and could claim no exemption under the Draft Act. None of these was executed for their refusal to bear arms, although many were threatened with death. Some of them were compelled to go through battles, yet none was killed. Several were imprisoned in the military prisons and a number died from exposure, disease or ill-treatment in camp, in prison or in the hospitals.

Friends responded to the appeal of human suffering during the Civil War by caring for the prisoners, the sick and the wounded. Elizabeth L. Comstock was very active in visiting hospitals and prisons to administer material relief and spiritual consolation. She was given an omnibus pass by President Lincoln to all Union hospitals; and later a pass to the prison camps in Virginia was granted her by Secretary of War Stanton.[11] Early in the war Eliza P. Gurney, Elizabeth F. Comstock and other Friends visited President Lincoln to pray with him and to encourage him to emancipate the slaves. He seemed to value their concern and encouragement.[12]

Even before the Emancipation Proclamation the slaves began to follow the Union armies and to throng the Union camps. These "contrabands" were a natural concern of

---

9 Cartland, *op. cit.*, Chaps. XIX, XXI.

10 For detailed accounts see *Ibid.*, chaps. X–XX.

11 *Life of Elizabeth L. Comstock*, pp. 109–202.

12 Cartland, *op. cit.*, pp. 132–138.

Friends, and different yearly meetings appointed committees to help them. The refugees near Fortress Monroe, where General Benjamin F. Butler first ignored the Fugitive Slave Law and treated them as "contraband of war" in 1861, came under the care of the "Women's Aid" of Philadelphia Yearly Meeting in 1862.

This "Women's Aid Committee" was promptly asked to coöperate with the National Freedmen's Relief Association.

The Emancipation Proclamation thrust upon the nation the task of taking care of three million destitute, untaught and dependent ex-slaves. The humane principles and anti-slavery activities of Friends gave them a large share in this task. Whittier wrote:

For fields of duty, opening wide,
  Where all our powers
Are tasked the eager steps to guide
Of millions on a path untried:
  The Slave is Ours!

Ours by traditions dear and old,
  Which make the race
Our wards to cherish and uphold,
And cast their freedom in the mould
  Of Christian grace.[13]

Young Friends especially threw themselves into this work. Among the leaders were Levi Coffin, Samuel R. Shipley, Elizabeth L. Comstock, Sarah F. Smiley, Elkanah and Irena Beard, Timothy Nicholson, Lizzie Bond, Yardley Warner and a host of others. They were inspired and encouraged by the prophetic fervor of Eli and Sibyl Jones, by the preaching of English anti-slavery leaders, who visited America, prominent among whom were Josiah and William Forster, John Pease, and John Hodgkin,[14] and by Whittier's poems.

---

13 Anniversary Poem.

14 JLPQ, II, 598.

As the greatness of the need became evident, associations of Friends were formed in different yearly meetings to "relieve the wants, to provide for the instruction and to protect the rights of the Freedmen."[15] Philadelphia Friends became interested in the groups of freedmen around Washington and in southeastern Virginia from Yorktown to Norfolk. They helped them plant gardens and build cabins on government grants of land, furnished garments and opened stores to supply necessaries of life at cost. Schools were opened near Yorktown with thirteen teachers; at Williamsburg with two and in Washington with six. At these schools more than 2,000 freedmen received instruction during the first two years of the work.[16]

With the assistance of the government the Philadelphia Association furnished seed and livestock, and provided instruction in farming. By 1868 the work of the Association had extended into southern Virginia, North Carolina and Tennessee. In 1865 Nereus Mendenhall of North Carolina Yearly Meeting was made superintendent of schools for Negroes in that state with nine teachers under him.

> At the period of climax in the work of the Philadelphia Association, which was reached in 1870, it maintained and managed forty-seven schools, with no less than six thousand coloured people in attendance, under sixty-seven teachers. Those who could earn the money to pay in part for their schooling were charged a small tuition fee; the main supply of funds, however, came in through the liberal contributions of Friends at home and abroad, which, in 1870, had amounted to $253,415.[17]

Men and women Friends of New York Yearly Meeting began similar work in the Norfolk area and near Alexandria in 1862. In 1863, under the direction of Sarah F.

---

15 JLPQ, II, 600.

16 *Friends Review*, XVIII, 698, 707.

17 JLPQ, II, 603.

Smiley, they began a system of industrial and elementary schools centering around Richmond and extending as far south as Tampa, Florida. By 1889 it was reported that New York Friends had spent $149,251 in this work. New England Friends began work in and about Washington in 1864, their chief efforts being to provide cheap and adequate housing for the freedmen. In 1875 they turned over their schools in Washington to Howard University and took charge of Maryville, Tenn., Normal School for training Negro teachers. In 1865 Friends and others in Baltimore formed the "Baltimore Association for the Moral and Educational Improvement of the Coloured People," which established within two years a normal school and four industrial schools in Baltimore and over seventy schools in the Maryland counties.[18]

Contemporary with these efforts in the eastern states, western Friends attacked the problem of the freedmen. In 1862 and again in 1863, Levi Coffin made a trip of investigation down the Mississippi river. His reports led to great efforts for the refugee slaves and freedmen. The Western Freedmen's Aid Commission was organized, of which he was the general agent and in which Friends were the most prominent leaders. Indiana Yearly Meeting appointed a Committee on Contraband Relief with Timothy Nicholson as secretary, and Joseph Dickinson as receiving and shipping agent. The work of providing clothes was organized in the local meetings, and Cincinnati became the shipping center.

After the fall of Vicksburg in 1863 there were great concentrations of freedmen ten miles north of Vicksburg near Young's Point, and there were other concentrations near Helena and Little Rock, Arkansas. Elkanah and Irena Beard and Lizzie Bond of Indiana Yearly Meeting went to Young's Point to relieve the destitution of the Freed-

---

18 JLPQ, II, 605, 606.

men, to organize their camps and to establish schools. By December, 1863, they had three schools established with about 300 pupils.[19] The relief headquarters were moved later to a place about two miles from Vicksburg where the government gave a tract of land to establish a Freedmen's Home and Orphanage. About a thousand Negroes were supplied with seed and farming implements on this plantation.

At the request of General Buford, Elkanah Beard visited Helena, Arkansas, where the army turned over some barracks and later erected buildings for the establishment of a school for orphans. This grew into Southland College, which was kept up by Indiana Yearly Meeting until 1925.[20] Other more or less permanent schools were established and maintained by Friends. New York Yearly Meeting maintained the Industrial School at High Point, N. C., until 1923, when it was taken over by the city and incorporated into the public school system.

The Hicksite Friends have had an active share in the work for the freedmen and still maintain a normal and industrial school at Aiken, S. C., named Schofield School in honor of Martha Schofield, its real founder. They also established a school at Mt. Pleasant, S. C. In 1869 the Philadelphia Association took an interest in a school established at Christiansburg, Va., by Captain Charles S. Schaeffer. In 1884–1886 the Association raised a large sum to build and equip this school; and later it provided an extensive farm to make it a large agricultural and industrial school. A great number of educational and philanthropic institutions were established in Philadelphia to care for the Negroes who crowded into that city, most of which are still in existence.[21]

---

19 JLPQ, II, 607.

20 A Negro monthly meeting was established in the Southland community, the only one in the United States, but since Friends gave up the college the meeting has gone down.

21 For a list of these see JLPQ, II, 614.

A notable work was done by Friends in New York City through the New York Coloured Mission, founded in 1865 on West 13th Street. Augustus Taber was superintendent for many years and the varied activities of the mission were of great benefit to the surrounding district. In 1917 the mission was moved to a new site in Harlem at 130th Street. Another important work of Friends in New York is the Coloured Orphan Asylum. Originally started in 1836, it was burned out by a mob during the draft riots and rebuilt in 1863.

In 1864 Levi Coffin went to England on behalf of the Freedmen's Aid Commission. He was given a cordial hearing not only by Friends but by other English philanthropists, and in eight months collected over $100,000 for the cause.[22] The London Freedmen's Aid Society was organized to help with the work of American relief. In 1865 English Friends organized the Central Committee of the Society of Friends for the Relief of the Emancipated Slaves in America. Other local committees were formed, notably the Birmingham and Midlands Committee, which coöperated with the London Society and in 1866 the existing societies were consolidated into the National Freedmen's Aid Union of Great Britain and Ireland. At that time £86,000 had had been raised for the cause.

In their work for the ex-slaves the Friends had the satisfaction of working with the national government (instead of against it as in the Underground Railroad). Their aid was welcomed and even solicited by the army, the authorities in Washington and the Freedmen's Bureau. At the close of the war the care of the ex-slaves was taken over to a large extent by the Freedmen's Bureau of the federal government which undertook to provide for their physical needs; to protect their rights and liberty and to settle them as free citizens. Friends gradually withdrew from physical

---

22 *Rem.*, p. 704.

relief as the government took charge and concentrated on educational work.

The harsh reconstruction measures, the often tactless activities of the Freedmen's Bureau and the exploitation and dispossession of the former ruling caste in the South by the "carpetbaggers" and "scalawags," finally provoked the violent proceedings of the Ku Klux Klan and similar organizations, who terrorized Yankees and Negroes alike. A few Friends' school-teachers were driven out of the South by them along with the "carpetbaggers."[23]

One result of this reaction was a great exodus of freedmen to Kansas, which rumor represented to them as a land of refuge. In 1879 and 1880 about 70,000 of them arrived in that state in great destitution. The young state was in no position to care for them in a desperately cold winter and on top of a plague of grasshoppers. Elizabeth L. Comstock, Laura S. Haviland and John M. Watson coöperated heroically with Governor St. John in the effort to care for these refugees. They raised funds and supplies from Friends both in America and England; visited the refugees in their barracks and organized schools. They got many of them settled out on the land and persuaded Iowa, Nebraska and Illinois to take and care for large numbers of the refugees. The abatement of the terror in the South, largely due to the changed policy of the federal government, and the spread of information among the southern Negroes of the true situation in Kansas checked the migration in 1881.[24]

At the close of the Civil War North Carolina Friends were in a desperate condition. Many of their young men had gone west or died in camp or prison or were broken in health.

---

[23] See Tourgee, *A Fool's Errand.*

[24] See *Life and Letters of Elizabeth L. Comstock,* chaps. XIX–XXI. The gratitude of the refugees to Elizabeth Comstock and Laura S. Haviland found expression in the large number of babies named "Cornstalk" and "Heavenly." *Ibid.,* pp. 375, 429.

They had had little opportunity for schooling. Their resources had been taxed to pay draft exemption fees; their Confederate money became worthless; their livestock and crops had been taken or destroyed by the foragers of both Johnston's and Sherman's armies.[25] New Garden Boarding School had been kept open and out of debt but its equipment was poor.[26]

Most of the North Carolina Friends had relatives in the northern states where farmers had prospered during the war. Many of them felt that it would be best to follow their people. Addison C. Coffin, a nephew of Levi Coffin, shared this view and organized "excursions" to Indiana and others. In the year 1866 he helped about 5000 people to go to the Northwest from southern Virginia and North Carolina.[27] Many of these were Friends, and Addison Coffin believed that southern Friends as a whole should emigrate to the Northwest.

The continued existence and subsequent recovery and growth of North Carolina Yearly Meeting was chiefly due to the work of Francis T. King of Baltimore who took a different view of the situation and after a survey of the field, advised Friends to remain in North Carolina.[28] His attention was called, early in 1865, to the plight of North Carolina Friends, by a group of about fifty whose homes had been ruined by Johnston's and Sherman's armies and who had been given permission to go to Friends in the Northwest but were stranded in Baltimore. Local Friends relieved their pressing necessities and sent them on their way. They then sent a shipload of provisions and farming

---

25 *Autobiog. of Allen Jay,* chap. XVIII.

26 See Gilbert, *Guilford: A Quaker College,* chap. III. Thomas, *Hist.,* pp. 188, 189.

27 *Life and Travels of Addison C. Coffin,* p. 139. Most of these were families of Confederate prisoners who remained in the North and of Quaker immigrants. Others were people emigrating to the prairie states to get a new start after the devastations of the war. *Ibid.,* chap. IV.

28 *Autobiog. of Allen Jay,* pp. 162, 163, 174.

tools to North Carolina and helped about 450 other Quaker emigrants westward. They then organized The Baltimore Association of Friends to Assist and Advise with Friends in the Southern States. Francis T. King was the president and leading spirit. The Association secured Joseph Moore to be principal of New Garden Boarding School and to supervise the organization and reëstablishment of Friends schools and Sunday schools.[29] He was ably assisted by John Scott, Richard M. Janney and Sarah M. Smiley. In 1869, after three years' service, Joseph Moore was called to the presidency of Earlham College.

The Association then secured Allen Jay to be superintendent of their work. He settled near Springfield (at Bush Hill, now Archdale) in the fall of 1868. With the hearty coöperation of North Carolina Friends he set about the threefold program of the Association. It repaired the buildings and equipment of the boarding school, established monthly meeting schools and Sunday schools wherever possible, and distributed books and other literature. A normal school for teachers which had already been started by Joseph Moore was held each year. Non-Friends were admitted to all these schools. They exercised a great influence in providing teachers for the public school system of the state and stimulating its development.[30]

The Association purchased and operated a model farm near Springfield to improve the economic status of Friends. It introduced better breeds of livestock and better farm implements. It demonstrated the best known methods of soil restoration and cultivation, such as rotation and diversification of crops; it notably increased the fertility and productiveness of farm lands in Alamance, Guilford and Randolph counties to this day.

A revival broke out in 1874 at Trinity College near

---

[29] *Autobiog. of Allen Jay*, pp. 178–181.
[30] *Ibid.*, p. 225. See also Klain, *op. cit.*, *passim.*

Springfield, in which Friends joined. This spread through the yearly meeting under Allen Jay's inspiring preaching and careful supervision and led to a great influx of new members. In all this work Dr. Nereus Mendenhall and Delphina E. Mendenhall were Allen Jay's invaluable assistants.

In 1873 the educational work was turned over to the yearly meeting which asked Allen Jay to continue in charge one more year. In 1891 the Baltimore Association closed up its work, having spent a total of $138,300 on the rehabilitation of North Carolina Quakerism, about $50,000 of which was supplied by English and Irish Friends.[31]

The number of Friends in North Carolina Yearly Meeting at the close of the Civil War is difficult to obtain. In 1861, on the basis of yearly meeting reports on another subject, there were probably about 2000 members. The membership increased by 1865, in spite of losses by emigration. The example of Friends during the war had attracted the favorable attention of their neighbors. In 1883 it was estimated that the membership had grown from 2,200 in 1866 to 5,641; the number of meeting-houses from 28 to 52; that there were 42 Friends' schools, that 1300 children of other denominations attended them; and that there were 700 Friends in the quarterly meeting in East Tennessee.[32] The yearly meeting has had a steady growth since the Civil War, without the aid of immigration, chiefly through large families, schools and revival work.

---

[31] *Autobiog. of Allen Jay,* p. 224.
[32] *Ibid.,* pp. 172-174.

Chapter 31

THE GREAT REVIVAL

There was a spirit of religious awakening in many widely separated places in the United States just before the Civil War. There were rather remarkable revival meetings in New York, Philadelphia and in other cities in 1858 and in Indianapolis in 1857–1858. The peak of Charles J. Finney's revival was in the decade 1850–1860. This awakening was checked by the Civil War but broke out again in the late 1860's. There was a renewal of revival activities in Indianapolis in 1865–1866. Finney's movement was still strong between 1865 and 1870. In 1870 Dwight L. Moody and Ira D. Sankey began their great evangelistic campaigns.

Similar tendencies had been working in the Society of Friends before 1860. The ground had been prepared by the ministry of English visitors such as Robert Lindsey, William Forster and John Pease. These Friends visited almost all of American Quakerism and were very vigorous in their preaching. Of especial importance was the ministry of Eli and Sybil Jones of Maine, who visited a large part of American Quakerism. Sybil Jones was a preacher of great power and was distinguished by her direct appeal to her hearers for a personal religious decision.[1]

---

1 Hay believes that the development of higher education among Friends was an important influence in preparing for the revival. He calls attention to the fact that 18 educational institutions were started between 1830 and 1870 including four colleges and nine high schools. See Hay, Alex. H., *The Pastoral System Among Friends.* Unpublished M.A. thesis. Haverford Col., 1938.

There were almost simultaneous manifestations of religious fervor and activity among Friends in different sections of the country. In the winter of 1859 there were profound stirrings of religious interest among the students in Farmer's Institute near Lafayette, Indiana, under the ministry and personal influence of Jeremiah A. Grinnell and Allen Jay. At the beginning the young people met for social gatherings which usually ended with "a religious occasion." [2] There were similar manifestations at various places in eastern Indiana. Groups of interested Friends began to hold "social meetings" at private homes and also meetings for Bible reading.[3] There was a group of very influential Friends in Cincinnati who came into contact with the famous Bethel Mission Sunday School in 1858 and were drawn into coöperation with the work of other denominations.

A remarkable development of the movement occurred at Indiana Yearly Meeting in 1860, when Sybil Jones was in attendance. Two visiting Friends, Lindley M. Hoag of Iowa and Rebecca T. Updegraph of Ohio Yearly Meeting requested the appointment of an evening meeting for youth. Their request was seconded by Sybil Jones and other Friends, many of whom were from the Cincinnati meeting.[4] The older attenders were requested to keep silent. It proved to be a very remarkable meeting and lasted until nearly midnight with an almost continuous succession of prayers and public testimonies. After the close of the yearly meeting Sybil Jones asked to meet with all who had taken part in the meeting. About 150 met with her at the home of Charles F. and Rhoda M. Coffin.[5] A some-

---

[2] *Autobiog. of Allen Jay,* p. 81.

[3] Woodard, *Sketches of a Life of 75,* p. 19.

[4] *Charles F. Coffin, Quaker Pioneer,* pp. 115, 116.

[5] For many years afterward the local leaders of this movement continued to meet regularly at the Coffin home. *Ibid.,* pp. 116, 117.

what similar though less vigorous manifestation occurred the same year in Ohio Yearly Meeting.[6]

As was the case in the church at large, these movements were checked by the outbreak of the Civil War. The new religious interest of young Friends went largely into the struggle to maintain their peace testimony. Toward the end of the War and after its close relief and reconstruction and educational work among the ex-slaves gave practical expression to the younger generation's new religious enthusiasm and dedication.

After the Civil War the revival movement reappeared. In Earlham College during the year 1866–1867 there was a very remarkable religious awakening among the students and faculty.[7] In the spring of 1865 "The Christian Vigilance Band" was organized at Center Grove Academy near Oskaloosa, Iowa, and four years later a similar band was formed at Whittier College at Salem, Iowa, with remarkable manifestations of religious interest.[8] Neighborhood meetings began to be held in private houses for Bible and tract reading and then for prayer and testimonies in widely separated sections of the Society. These meetings were transferred to the meeting-houses little by little.[9] In 1867 Indiana Yearly Meeting appointed a Committee on General Meetings. Under its supervision series of meetings were held in various centers quite after the fashion of the youth's meeting in 1860. The preaching was *extempore* without pre-arrangement and great care was taken that the meetings should be orderly. The example of Indiana Yearly Meeting was followed within a relatively short period by most of the other orthodox American yearly

---

6 *Friends Review,* xiv, 105.

7 See the Report of the President in *Minutes of Indiana Yearly Meeting,* 1866. Dougan Clark had preached the Baccalaureate Sermon there the spring of 1866.

8 Jones, Louis T., *op. cit.,* p. 98.

9 *Rem. of Nathan and Esther Frame,* pp. 50, 57.

meetings. In 1871–1872 a number of general meetings were held in New York Yearly Meeting. The movement extended to Kansas in 1873 just after the setting up of the yearly meeting. Gradually local meetings arranged for special series of meetings instead of waiting for the initiative of yearly meeting committees.

The revival movement rapidly developed a group of enthusiastic young leaders. Most of them had very deep and revolutionary adult religious experiences which were not connected with the traditional quietist methods or the "peculiarities." Practically all of them were converted or powerfully moved by outside influences. Sybil Jones was greatly helped and instructed by a Methodist minister of Augusta (Me.) and had a strong love for the Methodists.[10] Charles F. Coffin (1823–1916) was converted in connection with the visit and ministry of J. J. Gurney.[11] John Henry Douglas (1832–1919), who was perhaps the most vigorous and influential of the revival leaders, was a native of Maine, a birthright Friend and educated at Friends' schools. He had come, consciously or unconsciously, under vigorously Evangelical influences and, at nineteen, was converted during a storm at sea.[12] In 1866 he visited the British Isles and the Continent of Europe and was particularly attracted to Father Spitler's training school for missionaries.[13] He settled in Ohio in 1853 and was recorded a minister five years later. His brother, Robert W. Douglas, was a powerful minister and closely associated with him in much of his earlier work.

David B. Updegraff (1830–1894), although a birthright Friend, was the most radical of the group. His family lived

---

10 Eli and Sybil Jones, *Life*, p. 30.

11 *Charles F. Coffin*, p. 102.

12 He does not name these influences in any records available but the fear of "wild-fire" on the part of ministers and elders who were his associates both in Maine and Ohio shows that such movements existed in his environment.

13 See MSS. statement of his wife. Copies are in the libraries of Haverford and other Friends' colleges.

at Mt. Pleasant, O., and were intimate with Charles G. Finney. He was converted in a Methodist revival when thirty years old.[14] Nathan T. Frame and his wife Esther Gordon Frame (d. 1920) came to Friends from the Methodists, largely because the latter would not allow a woman to preach.[15] Dougan Clark's father was for three years a Methodist minister before he became a Friend and married Asenath Hunt, daughter of Nathan Hunt of North Carolina.[16] Dougan (1828–1896) was a classmate of David B. Updegraff at Haverford.[17] Among the outstanding leaders, Allen Jay (1831–1910) and Luke Woodard (1832–1925) seem to have been the only ones to be converted wholly under influences already at work within the Society.[18]

Other prominent evangelists and leaders in the movement were Luther B. Gordon, brother of Esther Gordon Frame, Daniel Hill, John Y. Hoover, Asahel Hussey, William P. Pinkham, Calvin W. Pritchard, Elwood C. Siler, Amos Kenworthy, Elwood Scott, Caroline C. Talbot, Esther Tuttle (who married Calvin W. Pritchard), William Wetherald, Isom P. Wooten, and Rufus P. King. Hannah Whitall Smith (1832–1911) was converted in a noonday meeting in Philadelphia in 1858 and came under the influence of the Plymouth Brethren.[19] Luther Gordon and

---

[14] JLPQ, II, 899; Clark, *Life of David B. Updegraff,* pp. 11, 17–19. Elisha Bates of Mt. Pleasant had gone over to the Methodists a generation earlier (1823).

[15] *Rem. of Nathan and Esther Frame,* pp. 32–42. Esther's mother came of a Quaker family and Esther had attended a Friends school. *Ibid.,* p. 30.

[16] Weeks, *Southern Quakers and Slavery,* p. 301n.

[17] JLPQ, I, 899.

[18] *Sketches of a Life of 75. Autobiog. of Allen Jay,* p. 81. Allen's evangelistic work proper, however, began in conjunction with the Methodists at Trinity and High Point, N. C. *Ibid.,* pp. 205–210. He coöperated at first in order to conserve the new life and interest which the revival aroused in young Friends. *Ibid.,* pp. 205–210.

[19] See *The Unselfishness of God,* p. 179. Although she left Friends, Quaker mysticism had a profound influence upon her thought. Her book, *The Christian's Secret of a Happy Life,* had an enormous influence, chiefly outside the Society. She and her husband, Robert Pearsall Smith, were

Esther Tuttle came to Friends from other denominations. Rufus P. King joined the Methodists during the Civil War. He became a pacifist after being drafted in the Confederate army and after various trials finally escaped to Indiana where he came under the influence of Friends and became one of their powerful ministers. *The Gospel Expositor* was started in 1883 at Columbus, Ohio, by Dougan Clark, editor, Asahel Hussey and William G. Hubbard. It was merged later with *The Christian Worker.*

William P. Pinkham and Dougan Clark were the theologians of the movement.[20] In 1871 *The Friends Review* took a position hostile to the pastoral system; whereupon *The Christian Worker* was started in Chicago as the organ of the revival movement, with Calvin C. Pritchard as editor.

Two of the earliest manifestations of religious enthusiasm came in 1867 at Bangor, Iowa, and at Walnut Ridge, Indiana. In that year two ministers, Stacey Bevan and John S. Bond, held meetings at Bear Creek Meeting near Bangor. In this meeting according to Stacey Bevan's account:

> . . . many hearts were reached and all broken up, which was followed by sighs and sobs and prayers, confessions and great joy for sins pardoned and burdens rolled off, and precious fellowship of the redeemed. But alas, some of the dear old Friends mistook this outbreak of the power of God for excitement and wild fire and tried to close the meeting, but we kept cool and held the strings, and closed the meeting orderly.[21]

The meetings at Walnut Ridge were even more radical in their departure from the traditional methods of Friends. A group of earnest members of the meeting began to meet in private houses for Scripture reading. It grew into a

---

influential evangelists both in the United States and England. Their period of greatest popularity was 1873–1874.

[20] Their principal books were Pinkham, *The Lamb of God,* and Clark, *The Offices of the Holy Spirit.*

[21] Cited in Jones, *Quakers of Iowa,* p. 164.

Sunday evening meeting held in the meeting-house to pray for a revival in that community. The interest spread to the regular meetings for worship and there resulted violent manifestations of religious emotion in praying, testimony, shouting and singing. Many of the older members and even elders and overseers attended and a number of them professed conversion. Here for the first time among Friends a "mourner's bench" was arranged, where "seekers" could come for prayer. The more conservative Friends were frightened and shocked by these happenings.[22]

The new methods spread almost at once to many places and within a few years the revival became general in the Orthodox "Gurneyite" meetings. Under their influence silence in the meetings for worship was superseded by public testimony and prayer; young people took part; and the Bible was more frequently read in them. The young and eager leaders of the revival movement were vigorously opposed to the older quietist methods which they regarded as the cause of the static and unspiritual condition of the Society. Many of the older customs, such as the plain speech and dress, the emphasis on silence in worship, the habit of rising during prayer, the wearing of men's hats in meetings, the "plain" names of the days of the week and the month and marriages after the order of Friends were generally discontinued within the decade. Other new methods were imported by the revivalists. Singing was introduced because many of the leaders coming from other denominations felt that there could not be a revival without singing,[23] and after some years of hesitation musical instruments were brought into the meeting-houses also. Other practices which became general in the revival meet-

---

[22] A story current at the time says that Calvin Wasson, a minister from Western Yearly Meeting, finally got the floor in one of these meetings and exclaimed, "Solomon says there is nothing new under the sun; but Solomon never was at Walnut Ridge."

[23] *Rem. of Nathan and Esther Frame, op. cit.*, pp. 52, 122.

ings were "mourner's benches,"[24] working in the congregation with penitents, exhortations to public profession of conversion, and public testimonies to definite religious experiences.

There were frequent manifestations of religious enthusiasm in Iowa and Kansas in the decade beginning in 1870. In 1874 a revival "broke out" in Cotton Wood Quarter, Kansas, under the leadership of Mary H. Rogers, following which a wave of such revivals spread over the yearly meeting. In Iowa at the close of Bear Creek Quarterly Meeting in 1877 a revival was held in the meeting-house by Benjamin B. Hyatt and Isom P. Wooten, who were recognized leaders of the revival movement. After a few days a call was made "for all those who wish to forsake sin and lead a different life to come to the front seats."[25] At once a score came forward amid great confusion, some stepping over the backs of the benches in their haste. Some who did not come forward became the center of praying groups in their seats. While some were praying others cried aloud and, interspersed with personal pleadings, an occasional stanza of a hymn was sung. "To those who all along had been displeased with the revival methods, such a scene in their quiet meeting-house was simply intolerable; and in utter astonishment and consternation they arose and abruptly left the meeting."[26] The revival closed the following day with a continuous five-hour session of intense emotion. This so outraged the feelings of conservative members that it precipitated a separation later that year.

As the revival movement spread the meetings attracted many non-Friends and, in the course of time, union meetings with other denominations were held. In these union meetings Allen Jay, David B. Updegraff and Nathan and

---

24 David B. Updegraff was the first to introduce the "altar of prayer" among Friends as a regular feature of revival meetings. See *Life,* p. 43.

25 Jones, *op. cit.,* p. 165.

26 *Ibid.,* p. 166.

Esther Frame were perhaps the most conspicuous and influential evangelists. Because of the novelty of women preachers, some of the Quaker women who were preachers of great power were in great demand in many non-Quaker churches and communities. Among these were Elizabeth L. Comstock, Laura S. Haviland, Sybil Jones, Sarah Smith and Caroline C. Talbot. They exercised a great influence in extending the effects of the revival beyond the Society and in some degree the influence of Quaker convictions such as the equality of women with men in the church, women's ministry, peace, and worship without the sacraments.

These changes in doctrine and practice were not uniformly acceptable to Friends and there was a considerable conservative element which resisted them vigorously from the beginning. In many sections conservatives held official positions, many of them naturally being elders. Their opposition proved quite ineffective, as the younger generation in their enthusiasm brushed the elders aside, took charge of the meetings, and often replaced the conservative officials by their own sympathizers. The revival at Bangor, Iowa, which provoked a separation in Iowa Yearly Meeting in 1877 has been mentioned. The number of separatists here was not very large, at first only three monthly meetings being affected. In the fall of that year Iowa Yearly Meeting of Conservative Friends was organized. In 1879 the separation spread to Springdale and West Branch neighborhoods. In 1884 a new conservative quarterly meeting was organized, afterward known as West Branch Quarterly Meeting. The number of members of this conservative yearly meeting is difficult to ascertain. There was a similar separation in Kansas in 1879. In that year about thirty-five leaders of the revival from other yearly meetings attended the yearly meeting and took practical control of its exercises. After the yearly meeting closed they visited the local meetings, spreading their new methods and message. This resulted in a small conservative separation chiefly in Cotton Wood Quarterly Meeting which formed a conservative yearly meeting.

A similar separation occurred in Western Yearly Meeting in 1877. As early as 1867 the revival leaders were holding evening prayer meetings in private houses in Plainfield during the yearly meeting. There was official opposition to this, but by 1877 the practice had increased until almost every other house in the village had a prayer meeting of fifteen or twenty people. These were often held until after midnight with singing, loud praying, public testimonies and shouting. Allen Jay comments on the situation as follows:

> Until the revival era night meetings were almost unknown among Friends. They never occurred except when a traveling minister was present and had one appointed. But the liberty and spiritual life which Friends always had in theory, and in some measure in practice, would not long submit to this rigidness. Perhaps we were too determined in declaring that we would hold meetings where and when we pleased, while the Conservatives were just as determined to prevent them. The spirit of controversy was raised and indulged in by both sides, until it culminated in a separation at Plainfield, in 1877.[27]

Western Yearly Meeting endorsed the revival movement that year by appointing a Committee on General Meetings and refusing to discipline the revival leaders, and in consequence the conservatives walked out and organized a yearly meeting at Sugar Grove near Plainfield. In 1881 there was a small conservative separation in Canada Yearly Meeting.

There were lawsuits in Western Yearly Meeting and in Canada over the possession of meeting property which were both decided against the Conservatives. Gradually these four new Conservative yearly meetings were recognized by

---

[27] *Autobiog. of Allen Jay,* p. 112.

the older "Wilburite" bodies by means of correspondence and visiting ministers, so that New England (1845), Ohio (1854), Iowa and Western (1877), Kansas (1879) and Canada (1881) yearly meetings formed a definite group which is usually called Conservative Friends. In 1904 after the adoption of the Uniform Discipline by North Carolina Yearly Meeting there was a small secession in the northeastern counties of the state, which formed another recognized Conservative yearly meeting.[28] In 1878 London Yearly Meeting sent a deputation to the United States to assist Friends of Western Yearly Meeting in particular in their tried condition. The members of the deputation were J. Bevan Braithwaite, J. J. Dymond and Richard Littleboy. Their influence was chiefly with the moderate evangelistic Friends; they were too "Gurneyite" in sympathies to suit the Conservatives; and too quietist to suit the radical revivalists.[29]

The Conservative bodies suffered a steady decline in numbers. Naturally they consisted of the older members and the losses have been heavy by death and through the falling away of their young folks who often associated with "Gurneyite" young Friends or went to school with "the world's people." They cling to the traditions, forms and testimonies of ancient Friends, but few, if any, of their young people wear the plain dress any more. In recent years they have begun to hold their young people to a larger extent especially in Ohio and North Carolina. This is largely due to the influence of their boarding school at Barnesville, Ohio. In 1890 the United States census gave their membership as 4,329, about half of whom belonged to Ohio Yearly Meeting.[30]

---

28 Thomas, *Hist.*, 5th Ed., pp. 209–211.

29 Cf. Stanley Pumphrey, *Mem.*, p. 206. *J. Bevan Braithwaite: A Friend of the Nineteenth Century*, pp. 244, 245.

30 Thomas, *op. cit.*, p. 226. He estimates the membership of the seven yearly meetings in 1919 at 3,600 and in 1926 at 2,966.

The Great Revival influenced the character of Quakerism in many ways. It brought new life and interest to the Society. Membership was no longer a mere inheritance nor Quakerism simply a tradition for most members. Freedom in the meeting for worship was restored and there was more general and vital sharing in the vocal exercises. Business meetings became more democratic and separate business meetings for men and women were abolished. It aided in disencumbering the Society from meaningless traditions and practices. By means of it large numbers of converts were gathered in, which caused a rapid growth membership in some sections of the Society. It led to the expansion of the organized work of Friends in such fields as peace, temperance and foreign missions. It stimulated changes in the organization of the Society to take care of its new membership and fields of work. The separations which resulted from the radical changes it produced took from the Society conservative elements which were needed as a balance wheel. In consequence sections of the Society suffered from unrestrained radicalism and lost much of their contact with its past history, literature and fundamental principles.

Between 1870 and 1890 the growth of the membership in some yearly meetings was marvelous. Exact figures are difficult to obtain. In 1875 Stanley Pumphrey estimates the membership of the American yearly meetings as follows:

> With regard to the numerical strength of the different yearly meetings on the American continent, Indiana stands first, with 18,000 members (in round numbers); Western second, with 12,000; Iowa third, with 9,000; Philadelphia and North Carolina have 5,000 each; New England, Kansas, Ohio and New York, 4,000, more or less; Canada has 1,600 and Baltimore about 600 only; giving a total membership of about 67,000.
>
> The Wilbur Friends, as they are called for distinction, are chiefly to be found in Eastern Ohio, though there is one good-sized quarterly meeting in Iowa, and a small remnant of the

800 who separated in New England, numbering altogether about 4000. The recent separatists in Western, Iowa, and Kansas yearly meetings are about 1000. The followers of Elias Hicks claim 28,000 members, of whom one half belong to Philadelphia, where they are a large and influential body, half the remainder belong to Baltimore and New York, and the rest to their four very small yearly meetings, which include western New York and Canada, Ohio, Indiana, and Illinois. The whole number of persons therefore, who claim to be Friends in America is just about 100,000.[31]

The attached tables will give an idea of the growth in membership of the Orthodox "Gurneyite" yearly meetings during the revival period. The growth in numbers continued until near the end of the century, but after 1900 the membership remained stationary or declined, except for yearly meetings fed by immigration, as those on the Pacific coast or having an increase from a large birthrate, as North Carolina. The influence of the revival may be fairly judged by its influence on Indiana and Iowa Yearly Meetings, since they were the great "mother" yearly meetings. Indiana set off Western, Iowa, Kansas and Wilmington; Iowa set off Oregon, California and Nebraska.[32] The members added to Indiana Yearly Meeting by "convincement" during the revival period are shown as follows: 1872, 440; 1874, 1,120; 1879, 520; 1886, 1,174; 1904, 460.[33]

In Iowa the evangelistic committee was appointed in 1883. John Henry Douglas served as superintendent 1886–1870. Persons "converted, renewed or sanctified" were reported as follows: 1884, 2,200; 1885, 1,310; 1886, 1,888. During the years 1887–1890, there were 7,430 conversions reported and 2,595 additions to membership. The numbers declined after 1890.[34]

---

31 Newman, *Memories of Stanley Pumphrey*, pp. 113–114.

32 Technically Nebraska was established by the Five Year Meeting, but its membership was subtracted from Iowa.

33 Hay, *op. cit.*

34 See Jones, *op. cit.*, pp. 99, 100.

ESTIMATED MEMBERSHIP OF ORTHODOX YEARLY MEETINGS

	1843	1873	1896	1900	1904	1930
New England (1662)	10,000	4,000	4,502	4,503	4,415	3,674
Baltimore (1672)	800	600	1,125	1,214	1,155	1,182
Philadelphia (1681)	8,686	5,000	4,450	4,468	4,441	4,717
New York (1695)	11,000	4,000	3,757	3,756	3,339	3,400
North Carolina (1698) ..	4,500	5,000	5,454	5,456	5,619	10,373
Ohio (1813)	18,000	4,000	5,009	5,773	5,577	5,232
Indiana (1821)	30,000	18,000	19,510	20,144	20,049	16,155
Western (1858) **		12,000	15,091	15,868	14,347	13,166
Iowa (1863) **		9,000	11,124	10,865	11,135	7,941
Canada (1867) *		1,600	1,034	1,030	1,112	987
Kansas (1872) **		4,000	10,848	10,869	11,094	9,467
Wilmington (1892) ** ...			5,207	6,089	6,291	5,368
Oregon (1893) ***			1,566	1,553	1,635	3,208
California (1895) ***			1,359	1,510	2,046	5,507
Nebraska (1908) ***						2,422
Virginia (1672)	500	(Laid down and remnants joined to Baltimore in 1845)				
Totals	83,486	67,200	86,027	93,098	92,255	92,799

* Set off from New York.
** Set off from Indiana.
*** Set off from Iowa.

CHAPTER 32

FRIENDS' FOREIGN MISSIONS

THE travelling ministers of the early nineteenth century kept pretty close to Quaker territory. If they preached to non-Friends, it was chiefly to those who came to meeting or lived in Quaker neighborhoods. A few Friends, such as Elizabeth Fry, William Allen, Stephen Grellet and William Forster, visited European capitals chiefly in the interest of prison reform, religious education or the abolition of the slave trade.

The transition to regular foreign missionary work began about 1840. It had been prepared for in a measure by the acceptance of the Evangelical point of view. Foreign missions as well as religious education were part of the Evangelical program. The quietist aversion to planned and organized religious activities, however, as well as the objection to a "hireling ministry" delayed organized missions among Friends.

In 1833 Daniel Wheeler (1771–1840), who had already resided a long time in Russia, where he engaged in reclamation work for the Czar, went on a long voyage to the South Seas.[1] He visited missionaries and their native converts in the South Sea islands from Tasmania to the Sandwich Islands. In 1830 James Backhouse (1794–1869) went on a religious visit to Australia and the Australasian islands with a special concern for the convicts of the penal colonies.

---

1 *Memoirs of Daniel Wheeler,* chaps. 13–34.

He spent ten years there and then accompanied Daniel Wheeler to Norfolk Island, where he remained; while Wheeler and his son visited Hawaii and then returned home, making an extensive religious visit among American Quakers on the way. Robert Lindsey and his wife visited Friends in the far west of America and extended their concern to Hawaii, Australia and New Zealand in 1852–1856. Stanley Pumphrey (1837–1881), J. J. Neave and Walter Robson went on a similar mission to Australia, New Zealand and the South Sea islands between 1860 and 1870. Isaac Sharp (1806–1897) visited missionary stations, chiefly of the Moravians, in Iceland, Greenland and Labrador in 1846; in Africa and around the world, 1891–1894; and in Mexico and Syria, 1894–1895.

All of these English Friends traveled on individual concerns to comfort missionaries and the native Christians and to deepen the spirituality of their work, without any attempt at permanent or organized missionary work. They gained first-hand knowledge of missionaries and their methods, saw their unselfish devotion and witnessed the transforming power of the gospel. Their experiences prepared the way for regular foreign missions among Friends, as work for the Indians and freedmen had prepared the way for organized home missions.

Eli (1807–1891) and Sybil Jones (1808–1873), of New England, began their foreign work in a similar way. In 1857 they went on an extended visit to the newly established republic of Liberia. There they became definitely interested in foreign missionary work.[2] In 1867 they made a religious visit to Syria and Palestine.

While in the neighborhood of Jerusalem they visited Ramallah. There was a boys' school in this place, and here they were met by a young woman who asked that she might be helped to teach a girls' school. Eli Jones asked her if she could teach, to

---

[2] Jones, *Eli and Sybil Jones,* pp. 62, 63, 65.

which she answered, yes. After consideration it was decided to take some of the money which had been entrusted to them, to start this young woman—Miriam—in the work of educating the girls of the neighborhood. On returning to England at the end of their visit, and reporting what they had done at Ramallah, it was at once accepted by the English Friends, and the little school thus begun was adopted and liberally supported [3] [This was in 1869].

During their travels in Syria they met with Theophilus Waldmeier, a Swiss Protestant, who had been previously engaged in missionary work in Abyssinia for ten years. He was attracted by their message, joined Friends, and started a mission school and ultimately a hospital for the insane at Brummana in the Lebanons near Beirut. Eli and Sybil Jones induced New England Friends to support this work. In 1876 and again in 1882 Eli Jones returned to Palestine in the interest of the work of these missions to help start a Friends' meeting and boys' school at Brummana and a girls' training-home at Ramallah.[4] In 1888 American Friends assumed the care of the Ramallah mission and turned over the work at Brummana to the English Friends' Syrian Mission.[5]

Since 1830 voices had been heard among English Friends urging religious work among other races. The anti-slavery cause strengthened this interest, especially in Liberia and in other African missions. A number of Friends travelling in the ministry had extensive contacts with missionaries and their work. The Sepoy Rebellion in India (1857) and the establishment of the Indian empire greatly disturbed certain Friends and aroused an interest in the Indians.[6]

In 1859 George Richardson, then in his eighty-sixth year, who had come under the influence of Carey through his

---

3 *Life of Eli and Sibyl Jones,* pp. 192, 193.

4 *Ibid.,* pp. 292–294.

5 Hodgkin, *Friends Beyond the Seas,* pp. 83, 84.

6 *Ibid.,* pp. 37–40.

co-worker, Dr. Marshman,[7] began writing a series of vigorous letters urging Friends to begin missionary work among the heathen and to organize a society for that purpose. Other influential Friends took up the cause and in 1860 a conference was held at Ackworth to consider the whole subject and bring it to the attention of the yearly meeting, which considered the subject at length in 1860 and 1861, and finally approved the principle of organized missions in spite of misgivings and objections. Missionary sentiment among Friends was quickened by letters from travelling Friends; and some Friends began privately to contribute to the missions of other bodies in Syria, Africa and India.[8] It was not until 1865, however, that through the vigorous efforts of Henry Stanley Newman and J. S. Sewell a Provisional Committee on Foreign Gospel Service was formed,[9] having before it knowledge of openings in India, Italy and Madagascar.[10] In 1866 Rachel Metcalfe went to India with the support of the Committee; and in 1867 J. S. Sewell with Louis and Sarah Street from America went out to Madagascar. Rachel Metcalfe worked under the London Missionary Society in Benares until 1870, when the arrival of Elkanah and Irena Beard from America made it possible to establish a work of their own at Hoshangabad and Bhopal and although the American helpers had to retire within a short time on account of ill health, the mission has been maintained ever since by English Friends.

When it became evident that the Meeting for Sufferings would not undertake the management of foreign missionary work, the Provisional Committee was transformed into a permanent organization called the Friends Foreign Mission Association (1870) which, however, did not take over the Syrian work until 1887.

---

7 *The Friend,* 1892, p. 254 (cited in Hodgkin, *op. cit.,* p. 43n).
8 Hodgkin, *op. cit.,* pp. 50, 80.
9 *Ibid.,* p. 55.
10 *Ibid.,* p. 56.

The mission field in Madagascar was fully opened in 1869 when with the accession of Ranavalona II idolatry was publicly renounced and Christianity favored. Friends were first called into this field by the London Missionary Society; and when J. S. Sewell and Louis and Sarah Street arrived they felt it necessary to work in close connection with the London Society. The territory was divided and Friends were assigned a district extending west and southwest from Tananarive, the capital. They carried on evangelistic work and established schools for boys and girls at the capital. Additional workers came out in 1871, a printing press was set up, and by the next year there were fifty-nine congregations and some 15,000 worshippers in the Friends' district.[11]

American Friends were not only involved in the beginnings of the missionary work of English Friends; but they soon developed missions of their own also. In 1870 a Foreign Missionary Society was formed among Indiana Yearly Meeting Friends. In 1871 Samuel A. Purdy[12] came to Indiana Yearly Meeting on the invitation of the Society, which sent him to Mexico to begin Friends' missionary work there. He settled in Matamoros and began work in three ways: through church, school and literature. He set up a printing press, which had a wide influence in Spanish-speaking countries, especially through the periodical *El Ramo de Olivo* and a series of school textbooks. He later moved to Victoria in Tamaulipas (1887) and afterward opened a mission at Gomez Farias in San Luis Potosi. The work grew in spite of irregular support from the home field and difficulties due to the climate, epidemics and other sicknesses, and the opposition of the priests. Schools for boys and girls were established and churches built in Matamoros and Victoria. In 1893 Irving and Anna Kelsey came to the field and in 1895 Samuel Purdy retired. Western

11 Hodgkin, *op. cit.*, pp. 75–77.

12 See Purdy, *Life of Samuel Purdy*.

Yearly Meeting aided in the Indiana Mexican work until 1889 when it established a station in Matehuala, which embraced a mission school and a printing press. Stations were later established at Cedral and Catorce Real in the same state.

In 1869 a missionary association had been organized among Iowa Friends, but its activities were confined at first to home missions. In 1877 Stanley Pumphrey and John F. Hansen urged Iowa Yearly Meeting to take up foreign missionary work, which was one occasion of the conservative separation there that year.[13] In 1881 Evi Sharpless went to Jamaica in company with William Marshall with a minute for service. He labored for a while with Protestant missionaries already at work on the Island, but in 1883 began an independent work. Iowa Yearly Meeting was led by William Marshall's report, when he returned home, to sponsor the work; and Jesse and Elizabeth Townsend were sent out to take it over. Other workers who went out for the Jamaica mission were Gilbert L. Farr and Arthur H. Swift in 1893. After the latter's death in 1909, his widow, H. Alma Swift, carried on the work. All departments of the yearly meeting threw themselves into its support and by 1914 there were seven stations with a combined native membership of 1,360 members.[14]

The pioneer work in foreign missions was in most cases done unofficially by the women's missionary societies which were organized in course of time in all the yearly meetings. They are one more evidence of outside influences in the Society. Since women had a place in the organized Society, as they did not have in other churches, separate and unofficial women's missionary societies were an anomaly among Friends. They did get the work started, however, in most cases before the yearly meeting as a whole was ready.

---

13 Newman, *Memories of Stanley Pumphrey*, p. 235.

14 Jones, *op. cit.*, p. 237.

In the early stages of the foreign mission work each yearly meeting chose its own field, often because some member had a concern for this particular field. In 1902 the situation was as follows:

> New England had Syria for its field; New York had Mexico; Philadelphia, through its Foreign Missionary Association, which at first was composed only of women and was entirely dissociated officially from the yearly meeting, had Japan, in which Baltimore and Canada had joined; Ohio had China and India; Indiana and Western had Mexico; Iowa took Jamaica, and Kansas took Alaska as its field, in which at a later time Oregon and California joined.[15]

One of the greatest influences in fostering the early stages of this work, especially in America, was the ministry of Stanley Pumphrey (1837–1879), who came to America in 1875 with Allen Jay who was returning from a visit to Great Britain and Norway. He was a preacher of power, with a rich spiritual experience and broad sympathies. His early religious life had been quickened by a discerning Methodist minister; he had shared in the Irish revival in 1859–1860. He had been helped by contacts with Benjamin Seebohm, Elizabeth L. Comstock and Dwight L. Moody. His interest in missionary work had been stimulated by acquaintance with Theophilus Waldemeier and by coöperation with the Moravians. He was greatly interested in the American Indians and freedmen. He sympathized more fully with American revivals than most English visiting Friends; helped "hold" one "protracted" meeting in Western Yearly Meeting[16] and realized the need for support of certain types of ministry.[17] He urged Friends to engage in foreign missions and was the first to advocate a united missionary board for American Friends.[18] He proposed

15 JLPQ, II, 912.
16 *Memories of Stanley Pumphrey*, pp. 253, 254.
17 *Ibid.*, pp. 246, 247.
18 *Ibid.*, p. 259.

such a board at Indiana and Ohio yearly meetings in 1877.[19] His plan was in advance of American sentiment; but the need for it became more evident as the work developed. There were overlapping interests; conflicts between women's societies and yearly meeting committees; and competition between different fields for support. The proposition for a united board of missions was revived at the first Quinquennial Conference in 1892 and the organization of the American Friends Board of Foreign Missions was accomplished in 1894. It had at first, however, no administrative duties but only advisory and educational functions. It served chiefly as a bureau of information and a medium of communication between Friends and the missionary boards of other denominations.

After the Spanish-American War, Cuba became a concern to American churches. Two independent religious congregations were found in Habana province who were essentially Friends, the results of literature from the Quaker presses in Mexico. Since each yearly meeting was already fully engaged in its special field, the American Friends Board undertook the direction and development of sections assigned to Friends at Banes, Holguin and Gibara, in addition to the meetings in Habana province.[20]

Three young friends, Arthur C. Chilson, Edgar T. Hole and Willis R. Hotchkiss, became interested in a new type of industrial mission in equatorial Africa. Such a mission seemed practical to many Friends and in 1902 the Friends' Africa Industrial Mission was organized and began work among the Kavirondo tribe in British East Africa.[21] This added a fourth competing missionary organization, soliciting funds in most yearly meetings, and stimulated the demand for the consolidation of these various agencies. When the Five Years Meeting was established in 1902 the

---

19 *Memories of Stanley Pumphrey*, pp. 249, 259.

20 *Min. of Five Years Meeting*, 1907, p. 61.

21 Now Kenya Colony.

American Friends Board became its official board of missions.[22] It proved so efficient and the advantages of unified management of the scattered work of a small denomination became so evident that by 1912 the management of practically all of the missionary work of American Friends had been placed in its hands except that of Canada, Philadelphia and Ohio.

The foreign mission work of both English and American Friends developed under the traditions of the travelling ministry—the work in each field beginning as a definite individual concern. There was little Quaker experience to go by. American Friends were guided somewhat by their experience in the relief and educational work with the freedmen and American Indians. Many English Friends had travelled in the missionary fields of other churches and had come in close contact or association with their work. The methods of educational and publishing work of foreign missions of other churches created little difficulty for Friends. They were chiefly held back from adopting their methods of religious organization by the quietist antipathy to planned and organized work and fear of a "hireling ministry."

In 1907 Charles E. Tebbetts became secretary of the American Friends Board of Foreign Missions. He attempted to organize and systematize the mission work of American Friends on the lines marked out by the best experience of other denominations and especially by the Edinburgh Missionary Conference of 1910. During the five years of his secretaryship, he made the missionary work the best organized and best supported united work of American Orthodox Quakerism.[23]

The later development of the foreign mission work of

---

[22] In 1906 a conference was held at Richmond, Ind., which drew up a plan for the administration of the different missions by the American Friends Board of Foreign Missions. *Min. of the Five Years Meeting*, 1907, p. 63.

[23] See *Min. Five Years Mtg.*, 1912, pp. 33–48.

English Friends has consisted largely in the intensive development of fields entered in the pioneer stage.[24] The newer fields are (1) at Bhopal in India where a work was opened among a Moslem population in 1890; (2) among the mixed races in Ceylon in 1896–1897; and (3) on Pemba Island where among the newly emancipated slaves an industrial mission was established in 1897.

The work in India was modified by the necessities of relief during the famines of 1895 and 1896. Orphanages and schools were established to care for destitute children in which vocational training was given. Relief work on reservoirs, bridges and roads was provided and grants were made to farmers to enable them to put in their crops.

The work in Madagascar was predominantly educational with publications as an important factor. When the French conquered Madagascar (1894–1897), the mission work was seriously threatened. On six months' notice the government required all schools to be conducted in French. The mission suspended its schools, rushed its teachers to the capital for an intensive six months' course and met the requirement!

The work of the Syrian Mission also has been characterized chiefly by its educational work. Fresh stations have been opened at Ras-el-Metyn, Beit Meri and Abadeyah. In 1896 Theophilus Waldemeier retired from the mission to found the Lebanon Hospital for Mental Diseases at Asfurîyeh near Bayrut.

About the beginning of the twentieth-century English Friends began the reorganization of their work according to definite policies. Shortly after the Syrian Mission was amalgamated with the work of the F.F.M.A., a deputation was sent out to survey the whole work in Syria (1901). It reorganized the educational work, provided the church

---

[24] For the information regarding the later work of English Friends the author is indebted almost wholly to Hodgkin, *op. cit.*, chaps. V and VI.

with a new constitution (discipline) and strengthened the staff. The church suffered from the hopes and disappointments of the Lebanon peoples in the Turkish revolution of 1908 but the educational work expanded through the Lebanons between 1902 and 1914; and the church grew in self-reliance.

The Madagascar Mission had always been carried on in close coöperation with the work of other churches. In 1913 the three leading missionary societies sent out a joint deputation to organize the field. They surveyed the situation, divided the field so as to avoid overlapping, coördinated their educational work, and took measures especially calculated to develop an independent Malagasy church.

The Friends' work in China began in 1884 when Henrietta Green was sent out for work in Szechwan province. Robert J. Davidson and his wife followed in 1886 but it was not until 1890 that they were established in Chungking. They opened schools, hospitals and dispensaries, and preaching stations. The Boxer uprising in 1900 necessitated the abandonment of the field. In 1899 a conference of the missionaries in the three western provinces resulted in an Advisory Board for West China and a close coördination of the publishing and educational work. In 1906 a Union Normal Training School was established at Chengtu from which the West China Union University developed under the joint auspices of the American Baptists and Methodists, the Canadian Methodists and the Friends. The Friends' Mission has helped establish the Y.M.C.A. in Chengtu and the Friends International Institute in Chungking. The work throughout Szechwan province has had a great influence in improving conditions and there has grown up a united native church largely autonomous and self-supporting.

During the period 1900–1917, the greatest problems which English Friends had to face in the home field were the relation of the F.F.M.A. to the yearly meeting, the difficulties of adequately staffing a rapidly expanding work, which suffered frequent losses of personnel due to unhealthy climate, abnormal living conditions, overwork or illness; and the problems of financing the growing missions. These involved problems of missionary organization and education and the deepening of the spiritual life of the home field.[25] Gradually the yearly meeting came to feel an official responsibility for the work until the Meeting for Sufferings itself established the work in Pemba Island (1898).[26] In 1896 an important conference on the whole problem of its foreign mission work was held at Darlington by the yearly meeting. There was also a growing coöperation with the missionary leaders of the Protestant world, culminating in its response to an invitation to join in the Edinburgh World Missionary Conference of 1910. The establishment of a Home for Missionaries' Children (1897) and of Kingsmead Hostel at Selly Oak for the training of missionaries in 1906 marked important stages in the improvement of the missionary personnel.

Henry T. Hodgkin gives the following summary of the missionary enterprise of English Friends in 1916:

> Today we see the Society of Friends, small though it be, grappling with great problems in China, in India, in Madagascar, in Constantinople and Syria, in Pemba and Ceylon. Its missionaries number upwards of 120. They are working among populations certainly not less than one hundred times as large as the entire membership of the Society in Great Britain and Ireland. Most of the people are in areas where no other Protestant mission is working, and a very large proportion would have no means of hearing the Gospel if it were not proclaimed by Friends. The Christian community already gathered together is almost one-fifth of the home membership, and, if the number of adherents be added, the total is nearly as large as that of the members and attenders of London Yearly Meeting.

---

25 Hodgkin, *op. cit.*, pp. 142, 143.

26 *Ibid.*, chap. VI.

In seeking to provide for the education of this large community, over 200 teachers are engaged in teaching some 7,000 scholars in about 120 schools. Something like 20,000 patients are being treated annually in hospitals and dispensaries. In order to maintain this widespread work, gifts, reaching an average of upwards of £1 for every man, woman, and child in the Society at home, were received last year.

The variety of the work is not less striking than its extent. Preaching by the spoken and written word, and by the lives of missionaries and native Christians, everywhere takes precedence. In meeting-houses and chapels, in the market and bazaar, camping among the villages, visiting in the zenanas, in Sakalava huts, in prisons and in yamens, to rich and poor alike the good news is made known. By training the people for simple handicrafts, by teaching them to till the land, by gathering the women together to sew, by preparing students as doctors and teachers—many are being fitted to take their place as useful Christian citizens in their different countries. The prejudiced official is having his eyes opened, the cramped mind of the girl-wife is being enlarged, the ex-slave is being uplifted, the worn body is being set free from pain and disease, the child is being led out into new worlds of knowledge, the sin-bound soul is being redeemed.[27]

The experiences of the First World War and the post-war relief and reconstruction work brought about great changes in the interests of the new generation of Friends. The adult schools, home and foreign missions, temperance and similar reforms did not grip them as they had the Friends of the preceding half century. They were more interested in problems of the social order, international relations, post-war relief, and goodwill centers over the world. In order to meet this situation the Friends Foreign Mission Association was merged in 1927 with the Friends Emergency and War Victims Relief in the Friends Service Council, and the whole foreign service was viewed and dealt with as a whole. This involved considerable changes

[27] *Op. cit.*, p. 239.

in the personnel and in the objectives of the young people volunteering for the foreign work, whether in the older mission fields or the newer goodwill centers.

The foreign missionary work of American Friends continued in the same fields after the First World War, but suffered great retrenchments after the depression of 1929, both in personnel and expenditures. On account of differences in methods and ideals it has not been possible to merge the work of the American Friends Board of Foreign Missions with that of the American Friends Service Committee; but in 1927 the Boards of Home and Foreign Missions of the Five Years Meeting were merged.

In 1911 as part of a general redistribution of mission fields the Alaskan mission on Douglas Island, was given over to the Presbyterian Board on condition that the members should not be required to be baptized as a condition of continued membership.[28] On the other hand, California Friends undertook a mission in Guatemala. After Oregon Yearly Meeting withdrew from the Five Years Meeting, it established missions at La Paz and Amacari in Bolivia. In 1940 Kansas Yearly Meeting established an independent work in the Belgian Congo, West Africa.

A tabular statement showing the present foreign missionary work of Friends with statistics of schools, membership and workers may be found in *The Handbook of the Religious Society of Friends,* 1941.

---

[28] Kelsey, *op. cit.*, p. 253. California Friends still keep up a school at Kotzebue Sound, Alaska. *Ibid.*, pp. 253–256.

CHAPTER 33

MODERN DEVELOPMENTS IN EDUCATION

IN THIS chapter the important new features and developments of Quaker education during the whole period from 1861 to 1941 will be treated, since the changes between 1917 and 1941 are not of sufficient importance to justify a separate chapter. Educational work among the Indians, Negroes and in connection with foreign missionary work is treated in the chapters dealing with these subjects.

The characteristic and most important phrases of Quaker education in America during this period were (1) the discontinuance of elementary schools, except among eastern Friends; (2) the rise and decline of the academies in the middle and far west; and (3) the growth of the Quaker Colleges.

In this period the monthly meeting schools were generally still pioneer efforts at education in the western and southern states where Friends settled and where public schools were not yet well established. The children of non-Friends were admitted to practically all of them. They contributed to the general intelligence of their communities and stimulated the desire for greater educational facilities. Friends were as a rule leaders in the development of public schools in their communities.[1] As the public school systems

[1] Friends preferred their own schools because they could provide religious instruction according to their own ideals but the only opposition to the public schools, as such, seems to have been due to an early Indiana statute providing that fines and sums paid for exemption from military service should be "applied to the support of county seminaries." McDaniel, *op. cit.*, p. 129n.

developed, Friends' schools were generally displaced by them or absorbed in them.[2] The first step was usually the granting of subsidies to the Friends' schools from public funds, which were often used to provide for longer school terms. When the communities became able and willing to provide public schools, Friends often sold, leased or donated their school buildings for public use; but in many cases they continued for a time to provide teachers and constitute part or all of the local school committees.[3]

The Quaker schools exercised a profound influence on the development of the public school systems especially in Pennsylvania, North Carolina, Ohio, Indiana, Michigan, Wisconsin, Iowa and Kansas. In Indiana, Barnabas C. Hobbs, the first president of Earlham College, was State Superintendent of Public Instruction from 1868 to 1871.[4] Western and southern Friends gave up their elementary schools chiefly because of the heavy financial burden entailed by keeping up their own schools in addition to paying public school taxes and because the changes in doctrine and practice following the Great Revival lessened greatly their conviction of the need of separate Quaker schools.

In Philadelphia, Baltimore and, to some extent, in New York Friends of both branches still maintain their separate schools. Philadelphia Friends of both branches especially have a fine system of elementary schools in addition to their academies. Brinton lists thirteen belonging to the two Phil-

---

[2] This process has been carefully traced for the yearly meeting schools in North Carolina by Zora Klain, *Quaker Contributions to Education in North Carolina;* and for Indiana by McDaniel, *The Contribution of the Society of Friends to Educaton in Indiana* (Indianapolis, 1939), chap. VI. See also Jones, *The Quakers of Iowa,* p. 247.

[3] Klain, *op. cit.,* pp. 146, 147, 175, 197, 205, 269, 273, 274. *Proceedings of a Conference on Education.* Phila., 1880, p. 19. For New England see Klain, *Educational Activities of New England Quakers,* pp. 25, 26, 33, 58, 59. For Indiana, see McDaniel, *op. cit.,* chap. III.

[4] JLPQ, II, 698.

adelphia yearly meetings. There are five under control of the Conservative yearly meetings in Ohio and Iowa.[5]

In 1893 George School was founded by John M. George who left the greater part of his estate (about $750,000) to Philadelphia Yearly Meeting (H) to found and maintain a boarding school for the education of members of the Society of Friends and others. It is beautifully situated on a large farm near Newton, Pa. It is coeducational and is conducted along liberal and progressive lines. Only a minority of the students are Friends. Among Hicksite Friends it has exercised an influence corresponding to that of Westtown among the Orthodox.

This period witnessed the flowering and decline of the Quaker academies, especially in the middle and far west. Most of the strong quarterly meetings in Ohio, Indiana, Iowa, Kansas, Oregon and California established and maintained academies. They arose gradually and naturally from the monthly meeting schools. Often they were due to an unusually gifted or enthusiastic teacher who offered advanced courses and created a demand for an academy. Often it came from the "concern" of individuals or of an educational committee.[6] Between 1860 and 1900 at least fifty were established,[7] including those which afterward became colleges.[8] McDaniel lists twenty-four in Indiana. These academies provided indispensable centers for propagating and conserving Quakerism in the course of its west-

[5] Brinton, *Quaker Education in Theory and Practice,* pp. 41, 42.

[6] McDaniel, *op. cit.,* pp. 174, 175.

[7] JLPQ, II, 708, 709 for a partial list. In addition to those listed there, Klain (*Quaker Contributions to Education in North Carolina*) names the following academies in North Carolina: Summerfield High School, 1873–1889; Sylvan Academy, 1871–1912; Woodland Academy, 1876–1916; Blue Ridge Academy, 1912–1922; Augusta Academy, 1898–1905. In 1926 Lincoln School for Girls was established in Providence, R. I., leaving Moses Brown as a school for boys.

[8] These were New Garden (1837), Friends Boarding School at Richmond, Ind. (1847); Whittier (1888) and Friends Pacific (1885).

ward spread and brought educated leaders into their communities. Attendance at midweek meetings was required. They attracted travelling ministers and provided public lectures on Quaker subjects. With few exceptions they were coeducational.

As public high schools were established in the middle and far west, these academies found it increasingly difficult to secure endowments, equipment and patronage sufficient to sustain them. The same influences that led to the discontinuance of the Quaker elementary schools led later to the gradual abandonment of the academies or the merging of them with the public high schools.[9] A number of them were converted into Bible training schools.

At the close of the War between the States there were two Quaker colleges in the United States—Haverford and Earlham. The next forty years witnessed the founding of Swarthmore College (Hicksite) 1864, Swarthmore, Pa.; Wilmington (1871), Wilmington, O.; Penn (1873),[10] Oskaloosa, Ia.; Guilford (1888) near Greensboro, N. C.; Whittier (1901), Whittier, Calif.; Pacific College (1891), Newberg, Oregon; Friends University (1898), Wichita, Kan.,[11] and Nebraska Central (1899), Central City, Neb.

Canadian Friends (O) have had a single educational institution, Pickering College, which has had a checkered career and was never a college in the American sense. It was established 1878 at Pickering, Ont.; closed for lack of support in 1885; reopened in 1892 under the principalship

---

9 McDaniel, *op. cit.*, chap. VI.

10 Salem (Ia.) Academy was founded in 1845 and expanded into Whittier College in 1868 but financial disasters and fire led to its discontinuance in 1873. In 1917 Penn College was removed to a fine new set of buildings in the outskirts of Oskaloosa. Poor crops and the depression prevented the payment of many of the subscriptions to the debt thus incurred and in 1933 the college went into bankruptcy. It was reorganized and continued as William Penn College, leasing the plant from the bondholders.

11 The building of Garfield University at Wichita, Kans., was purchased and given to Kansas Yearly Meeting by James M. Davis who insisted that it be called Friends University.

of William P. and Ella Rogers Firth; burned in 1905; rebuilt at New Market in 1908; loaned to the government as a hospital for shell-shocked soldiers in 1916; and reopened as a school for boys in 1927.[12]

By 1900 all existing Friends' colleges had discontinued their preparatory departments and gradually conformed their curricula to the standards set by the state and other standardizing agencies, chiefly because a large percentage of their students became school teachers[13] which put them under the necessity of competing with the standard colleges. In all of these Quaker colleges the majority of the students and in many of them the majority of the faculty are not Friends.[14] All of them except Haverford are coeducational; practically all adhere closely to the ideal of a small college, with a liberal arts curriculum, but most of them offer training in music; and all of them offer courses in Biblical and other religious subjects.

Four of these colleges are under the direct control of yearly meetings: Earlham,[15] Wilmington, Friends University, and Nebraska Central. The others are each managed by a self-perpetuating board of trustees, in many cases nominated in whole or in part by the yearly meeting. New England, New York and Baltimore orthodox yearly meetings have no Friends college in their limits or under their control. The Hicksite yearly meetings join in supporting Swarthmore College. A table of present endowments, faculties, enrollment, &c., is appended to this chapter.

The colleges of Friends were founded and maintained at a very great sacrifice both on the part of Friends who have given them financial support, and by the personal

---

12 Dorland, *Quakers in Canada,* pp. 303–307.

13 In most states graduates of standard colleges have distinct advantages in securing certificates to teach in the public schools.

14 Brinton estimates the proportion of Quaker students in all the colleges at 18% which seems too low. *Quaker Education,* p. 50.

15 Earlham is under the joint control of Indiana and Western Yearly Meeting.

devotion of the men and women who have constituted their faculties.[16] They have had a continuous succession of able teachers who have served for meager pay, purely for the love of the work. This spirit of devotion to the church and to the cause of education has left its impress upon the traditions of the schools and the character of the pupils; and it constitutes one of their greatest assets. All the colleges have regard to Christian character as well as to scholarship in the choice of the faculty.

These colleges have exercised a great influence on the history of the Society in America. Both the faculties and alumni have supplied invaluable leadership in both educational and religious work. They have in varying degrees been centers of progressive influences. Many of the yearly meetings are held on the college campus or in the college town. An unusually large percentage of Guilford and Earlham students have become school teachers; most of them in the public schools or in colleges and universities not controlled by Friends. Penn and Earlham have supplied a large proportion of American Quaker foreign missionaries. It is hard to standardize the colleges of Friends according to the size of the endowment and the income of the college. Many of them are able, on account of the sacrifices of the faculty, to provide a grade of instruction that could not be secured by much larger incomes; and to provide, as well, positive moral and spiritual influences, which have been of inestimable value as preparation for spiritual and religious work.[17]

Three American educational institutions of an original

---

[16] In the two decades after 1890 many of the western colleges and Guilford were deeply indebted to the efficient and devoted services of Allen Jay in raising money for debts, buildings and endowment.

[17] Swarthmore College pioneered in introducing the "honors system" in American undergraduate instruction in America. Whittier College reorganized its curriculum to correlate its instruction more closely with the life interests of students. *Report of Commission IV,* for Friends World Conference 1937.

and progressive character owe their origin to men who were either Friends or were brought up in the Society and owed much of their independent point of view to Quaker influences. In 1868 Ezra Cornell (1807–1874) gave a half million dollars to found Cornell University on condition that the state of New York devote to the university the income from the sale of 990,000 acres of land granted the state by the Federal government for school purposes. The University was to put an emphasis on scientific research and technical skill new in American education. In 1873 Johns Hopkins of Baltimore gave eight million dollars to found a hospital and a university devoted to advanced study and research. At his death he bequeathed ten million more to these institutions.[18] Under President Gilman, Johns Hopkins University became a pioneer in graduate education and scientific research in the United States. In 1880 Joseph W. Taylor of Burlington, N. J., who had previously initiated a project at Bryn Mawr, Pa., for a college for the higher education of women, bequeathed his estate of more than a million dollars to a board of Quaker trustees for this purpose. A large part of the Friends' Educational Conference of 1880 was devoted to the discussion of plans for the new college by experts in the educational field. Bryn Mawr College was opened in 1885. It has long since ceased to be in any special sense a Quaker college, although the trustees have always been Friends.[19] Under the presidency of M. Carey Thomas of Baltimore it developed into one of the leading women's institutions in the country, her ideal being to make it the feminine counterpart of Johns Hopkins University rather than a female companion for Haverford College.

---

[18] Johns Hopkins had been disowned for the sale of liquor as part of his wholesale grocery business in the South. He continued to attend meeting, however, and named Friends as trustees of the hospital and university.

[19] At present the alumnae nominate five of the trustees.

Friends have had a share in three other unusually important educational ventures. In 1907 Anna T. Jeannes, a member of Philadelphia Yearly Meeting (H) gave a fund of one million dollars to promote the education of rural Negroes. The trustees of this Rural Negro Fund have administered it largely in coöperation with the Peabody, Slater and Phelps-Stokes Funds and the General Education Board to improve Negro schools in the southern states by giving salaries for Negro teachers and supervisors and for the improvement of school houses and courses of study.

In 1917 on the death of T. Wistar Brown of Philadelphia Yearly Meeting (O) it was revealed that he had given the treasurer of Haverford College $450,000 to establish a graduate school of religion at Haverford open to both men and women. After the school was organized it met with difficulties both from the lack of students and from the prejudice of Haverford alumni against women students on the campus. Finally in 1927 by an agreement with the heirs of Wistar T. Brown the school was discontinued and the income of the fund used for aid for candidates for the A.M. degree, studying at Haverford or at Pendle Hill.[20]

The Quaker influence in the founding of Duke University was important but not so definite as in the cases just described. About 1838 Union Normal Institute was started (near High Point, N. C.) by Friends and Methodists together for the training of teachers. Braxton Craven, under whose leadership it became Trinity College, was brought up in a Friends family and had studied at the newly established Friends Boarding School at New Garden. Benjamin N. and James B. Duke came under Quaker influences when they attended New Garden Boarding School. There were three Friends among the trustees to whom James B. Duke entrusted the administration of the endowment under which it became Duke University. President William Pres-

---

[20] *The Quaker*, II, 14 (10th mo. 14, 1921).

ton Few, who planned and organized the university, was descended from a Pennsylvania Quaker family.

American Friends have made very little provision for the training of ministers and religious workers. Woolman School, Swarthmore, Pa., was established in 1915 by Hicksite Friends on the model of Woodbrooke Settlement in England and reorganized in 1917 with a board of trustees composed of Friends of both branches, when the author became its director. It was discontinued in 1927 but in 1930 it was succeeded by Pendle Hill, a residence school for graduate religious study, of which Dr. Henry T. Hodgkin of England became director. It is a small community of persons engaged in the study of religious and social problems, endeavoring to lead the kind of life which supplies the answer to current social problems.[21]

After the First World War efforts were made to establish a graduate theological school in the Five Years Meeting for the higher training of ministers, but it proved impossible to secure adequate funds or to agree on the location and type of such a school. Young Friends, looking to the ministry, have continued to go for training beyond the biblical departments of Friends' colleges chiefly to the University of Chicago Divinity School, Boston University School of Theology and Hartford Theological Seminary. There was a period in which Quaker students went to Hartford more than to any other school. At one time they constituted its second largest denominational group of students and there were three Friends in its faculty.[22]

Friends in England have made no great changes in their educational set-up since the establishment of Woodbrooke

21 Pendle Hill conducts no examinations and grants no certificates nor degrees. Work done there, however, may under certain conditions lead to a Master's Degree at Haverford College.

22 By years the number of Friends in attendance was: 1911–1912, 6; 1912–1913, 5; 1913–1914, 10; 1914–1915, 10; 1915–1916, 7; 1916–1917, 9; 1917–1918, 16; 1918–1919, 7; 1919–1920, 5. Since 1920 the number has declined.

Settlement. They have no institutions for higher education comparable to the Quaker colleges in America. The proportion of youth in England who receive college education is smaller than in the United States. Since the admission of Dissenters to Oxford and Cambridge in 1871 and the founding of new universities, the relatively few young Friends wishing advanced education go to them. At the University of Manchester, Dalton Hall was provided in 1876 as a hall of residence for Quaker students.[23]

The English Friends' schools, however, are as a rule more thorough and develop a greater interest in literature and general culture than the Quaker academies and public high schools in America. English Friends as a class have enjoyed greater leisure, more extensive private libraries and devote themselves to serious study more than American Friends. The most important of their schools are Ackworth, Bootham, (York); The Mount (York); Saffron-Walden Leighton Park (Reading); Sidcot, Sibford, Wigton, and Ayton. Irish Friends have Newtown (Eire) and Lisbourne (N. Ireland).

The post-war depression led to efforts to eliminate some of their weaker schools or consolidate them and to raise their standards. In this the Central Education Board formed first in 1881 and reorganized as the Central Education Committee in 1902 has been efficiently active. William Edward Forster, who was born a Friend and educated in Friends schools although he was no longer a member of the Society, was chiefly responsible for the Education Act of 1870 which established universal compulsory elementary education in Great Britain. London Yearly Meetings set up a fund in 1936 to aid parents needing help to educate their children in Friends schools.

Members of the Society of Friends and men and women brought up in the Society have made distinguished con-

---

[23] For many years John William Graham was its head.

tributions to the natural sciences. Ruth Fry estimates that "judging by the statistics between 1851 and 1900 a Quaker or man of Quaker descent had forty-six times more chance of election as a Fellow of the Royal Society than his fellow countrymen." [24] This disproportionate interest in the natural sciences was partly due to the fact that Friends were shut out from many of the activities which were open to non-Friends. A considerable proportion of the Society in England during this period were of the well-to-do class with considerable leisure. Relaxations and recreations were few which the meeting would approve, so that an astonishing number of Friends devoted themselves to the study of nature or the pursuit of the natural sciences. This tendency was reinforced by the unconventional attitude toward the world which the Quaker non-conformity fostered. Their religious beliefs not only did not inhibit scientific research but the Quaker conception of the immanence of God in the world and in man gave religious stimulus to the study of the natural sciences.

Among the eminent scientists who were influenced by Quaker breeding and education within the period after 1800 may be mentioned Francis Galton (1822–1911), founder of the science of eugenics; Sir Edward Burnett Tylor (1832–1917), the pioneer of scientific anthropology; Silvanus P. Thompson (1851–1917), noted physicist; William Pengelly (1812–1894), British geological investigator; Sir Arthur Eddington (1882–   ), a leading English astronomer and physicist; Joseph 1st Baron Lister (1827–1912), discoverer of the value of antiseptics in surgery.

Social science leaders of the twentieth century include Sir George Newman, builder of the medical service in public elementary schools and B. Seebohm Rowntree, a leading authority on social welfare in industry.

---

[24] *Quaker Ways,* p. 206. She gives a list of those elected Fellows of the Royal Society between 1663 and 1915 on pp. 214–215. Twenty-one of these belong in the period 1863–1915.

Several English Friends have made valuable contribution to Quaker history and to liberal theology: notably William C. Braithwaite, A. Neave Brayshaw, Edward Grubb, William E. Wilson and Herbert G. Wood. J. Rendel Harris (1852–1941) was for a half a century one of the leading English New Testament scholars. The Quaker contribution to the world's literature and ideals is considerable, both directly and indirectly. Quaker ideas profoundly influenced Emerson and Gandhi, Benjamin Franklin and John Fiske. Among American men of letters Walt Whitman's mother was a Quaker and his father an admirer of Elias Hicks; Charles Brockden Brown, "the father of the American novel," and James Fenimore Cooper grew up in Quaker families; William Dean Howells had a Quaker father. Although Howells' father later joined the Swedenborgians, he remained strongly influenced by Quaker ideals. In England, Thomas Hodgkin, the historian, was the author of the eight-volume history of *Italy and Her Invaders.* Among the post-war German converts to the Society, Dr. Gerhart von Schulze-Gävernitz was a member of the Commission on Intellectual Coöperation of the League of Nations, and Alfons Paquet a widely known writer and dramatist.

American Friends have produced a large number of Biblical scholars and teachers in proportion to their numbers. President Thomas Chase of Haverford was a member of the New Testament company of the American Committee for the Revision of the Bible (1881–1884). Henry J. Cadbury of Harvard is one of the present committee to revise the American Standard Revised Version. Of special note for their contributions to Biblical scholarship are George A. Barton, of Bryn Mawr and Pennsylvania University, Elihu Grant of Haverford and Paul Haupt of Johns Hopkins.

Among educational administrators of Quaker upbringing may be mentioned: Walter A. Jessup, formerly president of the State University of Iowa and now president of the Carnegie Corporation and Robert L. Kelly, for many years Secretary of the Council of Church Boards of Education and of the Association of American Colleges. Rufus M. Jones' researches and numerous writings have done more than those of any other American writer to popularize mystical Christianity.[25]

A List of Friends Colleges

College and Location	President	Date of Founding and Charter	Number of Faculty	Number of Students	Endowment	Value of buildings, grounds, equipment
Haverford Haverford, Pa.	Felix Morley	1833 1856	50	336	$4,375,815	$4,356,000
Swarthmore Swarthmore, Pa.	John W. Nason	1864	100	750	$7,894,642	$4,399,101
Guilford Guilford College, N. C.	Clyde A. Milner	1837 1888	36	425	$649,413	$498,952
Wilmington Wilmington, Ohio	S. Arthur Watson	1871	24	300	$325,000	$400,000
Earlham Richmond, Ind.	William C. Dennis	1847 1859	40	450	$1,260,635	$817,577
William Penn Oscaloosa, Iowa	H. Edwin McGrew	1873	22	325	$26,000	$400,000
Friends Univ. Wichita, Kansas	W. Albert Young	1898	38	460	$538,000	$450,000
Nebraska Central Central City, Neb.	Ora W. Carrell	1899	8	90	$50,000	$140,000
Whittier Whittier, Calif.	W. O. Mendenhall	1888 1901	51	702	$887,000	$420,000
Pacific Newberg, Ore.	Levi T. Pennington	1885 1891	16	100	$265,831	$87,808

25 For a list of Friends Schools throughout the world see *Handbook of the Religious Society of Friends, 1941*, pp. 96–99.

CHAPTER 34

INDIAN WORK AND OTHER ACTIVITIES OF FRIENDS

THE two decades after 1850 were critical in the relationship of the United States government to the Indians. Most of the tribes had been moved west of the Mississippi. "Then came the movement to the Oregon country, the mad rush of the 'forty-niners' to the gold fields of California, and the building of the first trans-continental railway. The Indian saw the buffalo and other game everywhere recklessly slain or driven from the prairies; and everywhere encroachments were being made on his hunting grounds. At last, thousands of the tribesmen of the plains arose in a desperate and final attempt to stay the advance of the white men."[1]

The Indian wars proved extremely costly in men and money and many officers and military leaders despaired of settling the Indian question in this fashion. By 1867 some statesmen were suggesting that milder methods might be more effective; and in that year a joint committee of Iowa, Indiana, Western and Ohio yearly meetings was formed to consider means of dealing with the Indian problems. It secured the active assistance of Baltimore, New York and New England yearly meetings. The next year this committee urged upon the government "that in the appointment of officers and agents to have charge of their interests care should be taken to select men of unquestioned integrity

[1] Jones, *Quakers of Iowa*, p. 205.

and purity of character."[2] Shortly after this the committee secured an audience with the President-elect, General Grant. His answer to their insistence upon the appointment of religious men to deal with the Indians was, "Gentlemen, your advice is good. I accept it. Now give me the names of some Friends for Indian agents and I will appoint them. If you can make Quakers out of the Indians it will take the fight out of them. Let us have peace."[3]

His formal proposition to Friends to undertake the supervision of the Indian agencies was issued on February 15, 1869 and was elaborated in his first message to Congress as follows:

> I have attempted a new policy toward these wards of the nation. . . . The Society of Friends is well known as having succeeded in living in peace with the Indians in the early settlement of Pennsylvania, while their white neighbors of other sects in other sections were constantly embroiled. They are also known for their opposition to all strife, violence, and war, and are generally noted for their strict integrity and fair dealings. These considerations induced me to give the management of a few reservations of Indians to them and to throw the burden of the selection of agents upon the Society itself. The result has proven most satisfactory.[4]

In consultation with Friends the government decided to divide the Indian reservations into three parts. The civilized tribes in the eastern part of the Indian territory were in the main given over to the care of other religious denominations. The Hicksite Friends had the Northern Superintendency, chiefly in the State of Nebraska, of which Samuel M. Janney was made superintendent. To Orthodox Friends who had meantime organized the Associated Executive Committee of Friends on Indian Affairs (1869), was given the Central Superintendency, embracing the Indians

[2] Kelsey, *Friends and the Indians,* p. 166.
[3] Cited in Jones, *op. cit.,* p. 207.
[4] Cited in Kelsey, *op. cit.,* p. 170.

in the rest of the Indian territory and in the State of Kansas. Dr. William Nicholson served as general agent and spent most of his time visiting the various agencies as the representative of the Associated Committee, by which he was paid and to which he frequently reported.[5]

Among the Indians in this area were some of the most hostile and savage tribes. Friends undertook this work for the Indians avowedly as a missionary enterprise and found it a very serious and varied undertaking. They had to quiet and pacify some of the wilder tribes of the southwest agencies, often with danger to their lives from them as well as from flooded rivers and quicksands. Often they had to settle quarrels among the Indians themselves. Their difficulties were aggravated by lawless whites who encroached upon the hunting grounds and by the delays and corruption of the Federal departments. "Aside from the routine duties of distributing rations and annuities, instructing the Indians in agriculture and the various modes of civilized life, and counseling them in their great and petty difficulties, one of the all-important tasks of the Agents was to oversee the establishment of the system of government schools." [6]

The work of the seven Hicksite yearly meetings in the Northern Superintendency was similar in character although not so difficult. The agents distributed the government supplies, allotted lands, adjusted difficulties, promoted schools, encouraged agriculture and held religious meetings. They were greatly aided by the visits of eastern Friends from time to time and especially by a delegation of ministers in 1869.[7]

The Friends of both branches who undertook these re-

---

[5] His diary was published in the *Kansas Historical Quarterly*, Vol. III, Nos. 3 & 4 (Aug. & Nov. 1934) under the title "A Tour of Indian Agencies in Kansas and the Indian Territory in 1870."

[6] Kelsey, *op. cit.*, p. 175.

[7] *Ibid.*, p. 190.

sponsibilities were mostly farmers or small business men and had, as a rule, little experience with administrative work. Some of them had had experience in the work of the Freedmen's Aid and a few had served as Indian agents or on peace missions under President Lincoln. They had, however, in their favor, the traditional respect of the Indians for the "people of Onas," a firm faith in the peaceable gospel and an unselfish sense of mission in the attempt to win the cooperation and love of their savage charges. They were assisted by a large number of Friends' ministers who visited the agencies from time to time under a religious concern; they helped to bolster up the morale of the agents, and to reassure the Indians that there were many "pale faces" who were interested in their welfare. Among the Friends from abroad who visited the Central Superintendency were Stanley Pumphrey,[8] Isaac Sharp[9] and Henry Stanley Newman.

At one time the Orthodox Friends had in this service "a superintendent of Indian Affairs, eight Agents, and eighty-five other members acting as employees under the government" in the Indian service. "The accounts of all of the agents nominated by Friends were honorably settled" when they withdrew.[10] In every case where suits were brought against them in the United States courts Friends were honorably acquitted and the cost of the suits thrown upon the government.[11]

This method of dealing with the Indian problem was distinctly a policy of President Grant. His successor, President Hayes, was not favorable to it and on his inauguration in 1879 the authorities in Washington began to close up the Quaker agencies. However, Friends remained in charge

---

[8] *Memories of Stanley Pumphrey,* chap. 17.

[9] *An Apostle of the 19th Century,* pp. 251–252.

[10] Thomas, *Hist.,* p. 182.

[11] Report of the Committee on Indian Affairs, 1886. See *Min. Baltimore Yearly Meeting,* 1886, p. 39.

of several of them as late as 1885 when the official relationship of Friends to the Indian work finally came to an end. By that time the Indians were settled in their reservations and had developed their farms and established their boundaries. They had become, in a measure, reconciled to a government whose agents dealt with them honestly and justly. Schools had been established for their children and many of the leaders had been converted to Christianity. Kelsey sums up the results of Grant's peace policies as follows: "On the whole the effort was crowned with a fine success. The Indians, many of them wild and warlike, or filthy and debased, made remarkable progress toward civilization, especially in the early years when Friends were unhampered by adverse political influences. The establishment of a school system, the instruction in agriculture, the training of the Indian women in domestic arts, the teaching by precept and example of the benign principles of Christianity—these were the outstanding features, and these wrought the prime successes of the work of Friends. And before all, and above all, the 'Peace Policy' brought peace."[12]

Although Friends withdrew from official connection with the administration of the Department of the Interior the Associated Committee continued an unofficial missionary work among the Indians which has been kept up to the present time. This work gradually became established in two permanent centers. The first was among the Pawnees and the other in the Quapaw agency. In 1881 a monthly meeting of Friends was organized among the Indians, consisting of four preparative meetings. In the Central District the missionary work was under the special care of New York Yearly Meeting until 1884 when it was transferred to the care of the Associated Committee. Among the Kickapoo Indians a monthly meeting was established in 1884 and a

---

12 *Op. cit.*, p. 199.

meeting-house built the following year. The results of this work, which was partly educational and partly evangelistic, were in many respects very notable. Some of the fiercest of the leaders of the tribes were converted and became good Quakers. The most noteworthy cases were among the Modoc Indians, who after a war of great ferocity were conquered in the lava beds in Oregon and brought as prisoners to the Quapaw agencies. One of their leaders was Frank Modoc, who was called "Steamboat Frank." Through the influence of his daughter who had been at a Friends school he became converted and travelled among Friends as a minister.

"The general lines of missionary effort to be followed by Friends in the Oklahoma field had been clearly laid in 1885 when the official work under the government was relinquished. The chief element in all activities was to be the preaching of the gospel message and the building up of mission churches among the Indians. The missionaries were also to lay great emphasis upon house to house visitation, comforting and helping the needy in every possible way, material and spiritual."[13] As a result of the rapidly expanding work carried on among the Indians from 1885–1894 the four monthly meetings were organized into Grand River Quarterly Meeting which included a fifth monthly meeting in Kansas. The four monthly meetings in the Indian and Oklahoma territories comprised thirteen preparative meetings, twenty-three meetings for worship and several out-stations where meetings were occasionally held. The Indian membership of these meetings was 426 among whom were fifteen Bible classes with an enrollment of 807.

A notable result of this mission work was the large number of white settlers who joined the meetings. After the opening of the Indian territory to settlers a great many of them were reached by the missionaries and in 1894 there

---

13 Kelsey, *op. cit.*, p. 210.

were 576 white members as against 426 Indians. All these meetings belong to Kansas Yearly Meeting.

From 1881 to 1892 Friends conducted a boarding school for Indian children at Cherokee on the Cherokee reservation in western North Carolina and carried on religious work among them.[14] Under President Hoover's administration Friends' influence was strengthened in the management of Indian affairs. In 1929 Charles J. Rhoads was appointed as commissioner of Indian affairs and J. Henry Scattergood as assistant commissioner, both members of Philadelphia Yearly Meeting (O).

In 1851 Josiah White, founder of the Lehigh Coal and Navigation Company, willed to Indiana Yearly Meeting $40,000 to establish manual training schools in Indiana and Iowa where poor children, white, colored, and Indian, might receive a religious education in accordance with the teaching of Friends. The Iowa school near Salem was taken over by Iowa Yearly Meeting in 1864 and has had a checkered career, being hampered by an unfavorable location, by debt and fire. For ten years it was leased to the state as a reform school; for a few years it served as an Indian school; for a brief period the income from the farm was used to pay tuition of students at other schools; after 1911 the school was conducted along the lines laid down by Josiah White. In 1913 there were twenty-eight children at the Institute;[15] in 1930 the number had declined to eight. A disastrous fire at this time led to the gradual disposal of its rather unfavorable site. It has purchased a new location near New Providence and is building new buildings.

The White's Indiana Manual Labor Institute was established near Wabash in 1850 where it has had a steady growth. To the original endowment $37,000 was added by Josiah White's daughters and $20,000 later by Mary Emily

---

14 Kelsey, *op. cit.*, pp. 241–245.

15 Jones, *Quakers of Iowa*, pp. 215–231. *Min. Iowa Yearly Meeting*, 1930, p. 7.

Smith. It has served Indians, Negroes and whites. At present it cares for orphans and for delinquent children who are wards of the county and juvenile courts. From 1915 to 1935 attendance averaged 200 children or more. Since then additions to the buildings have enabled it to care for about 500.[16]

In 1883 Albert K. Smiley organized the Lake Mohonk Conference on the Indians and other Dependent Peoples which was held annually until 1913 at his splendid estate and summer hotel in the Catskills, New York. It enlisted the thought and assistance of leaders in politics, religion and philanthropy and powerfully aided in protecting the Indians and shaping a more humane policy toward them on the part of the government. He and his brother, Daniel, after him, were members of the U. S. Board of Indian Commissioners for nearly forty years.[17]

In the period following the War between the States the main bodies of Friends both in England and America have joined in organized movements in the Protestant world for philanthropy, education, reform and Christian unity. This coöperation has reacted upon the organization and methods of a large part of the Society. In many lines Friends simply adopted in their own work the types of organization and methods of their Protestant neighbors. In many meetings a large part of the meeting activities came to be carried on by organizations and committees that were extra-disciplinary and borrowed, such as the Women's Auxiliary or Ladies' Aid Society, the Men's Social Union, the Adult Bible Class, the Christian Endeavor Society, the local Pastors' Alliance or Ministerial Association, and the city Federation of Churches.

Many methods of Friends foreign missionary work, both

---

16 *Min. Ind. Yearly Meeting,* 1915, p. 59. *Ibid.,* 1936, p. 19. McDaniel, *op. cit.,* pp. 165, 166.

17 Kelsey, *op. cit.,* pp. 257, 258. Cf. *Am. Dict. Nat. Biog.* and *Who's Who in America* in loco.

on the field and at home, were adapted from the experience of other denominations or from the ideals of the interdenominational missionary movement.[18] Separate women's missionary societies were hardly a purely Quaker development. The recent trend has been toward merging men's and women's meetings completely; but the Women's Missionary Union of Friends in America has maintained its separate existence and been recognized by the Five Years Meeting, largely for the sake of interdenominational fellowship with the women's foreign missionary associations of other churches.[19]

Friends Bible schools, as the "First day" or Sunday schools are generally called officially in the "pastoral" yearly meetings, have generally used the International Lessons; and for the most part joined fully in the local, state and international Sunday school conventions. They have used "lesson helps" and other literature put out by undenominational publishing houses or the Friends "quarterlies," published jointly with two or three other small denominations.[20] The chief difference was in the substitution of other lessons for those on the ordinances, and of course a special cover for *The Friends Quarterly*. Yearly meeting Bible School conferences have been an annual feature of the work in many yearly meetings. Western seems to have led the way with its Bible School Institutes in 1877

---

18 The "every member canvass" and the "envelope system" of contributions are examples.

19 Since its organization in 1885, it has done good service promoting missionary interest through its local societies and the publication of *The Friends Missionary Advocate*. See *Friends Missionary Advocate*, 1931, p. 351.

20 *The Friends Quarterly* was first published by Willett Dorland; and later by P. W. Raidabaugh in Chicago and afterward in Plainfield, Ind. as The Publishing Association of Friends, from about 1882 to 1912, when he discontinued it to make way for the *Penn Series* of Bible School publications put out jointly by the new Bible School Board and Board of Publications of the Five Years Meeting. In recent years the *Penn Quarterly* also has been published jointly with other denominations, chiefly for financial reasons. (*Semi-Centennial Anniversary of Western Y.M.*, p. 194).

and its Assembly in 1887. Indiana organized one in 1882. Kansas organized a Biblical Institute in 1893 and North Carolina in 1894.[21]

These interdenominational connections have contributed to breadth of outlook but they have made it difficult for Friends to put proper emphasis on their distinctive principles. The desire to maintain working relations with the International Sunday School movement has prevented Orthodox Friends in America from pioneering in better methods of religious education, as they did earlier in other fields of education. The Hicksite First-day School Committee, on the other hand, has produced an independent series of lessons and lesson helps intended primarily for Friends.

Among English and Irish Friends the Sunday School has had a less important role. It is confined largely to quite young children. The interdenominational Pleasant Sunday Afternoon, the adult schools, and young people's organizations have carried on part of the work done by the Bible schools among American Friends.

Friends' chief temperance work has been done in connection with interdenominational organizations, and the speakers at the temperance sessions of the American yearly meetings have been quite regularly prominent workers in the Women's Christian Temperance Union, the Anti-Saloon League, or the Prohibition Party.

The Men's Conference of the Five Years Meeting in 1915 was a helpful movement, productive of permanent good, but the impulse to such a conference seemed to come from the Laymen's Missionary Movement, the Men and Religion Forward Movement, and the notable conference of Methodist laymen in 1914, rather than from any distinct function provided for in Quaker ideals and polity

---

21 *Min. Kansas Yearly Meeting,* 1894, p. 76. *Min. N.C. Yearly Meeting,* 1897, p. 43. *Semi-Centen. Anniversary Western Y.M.,* pp. 193, 194.

for men and laymen as groups distinct from women and ministers.

The Christian Endeavor movement, organized in 1881, soon attracted the attention of young Friends. The first Quaker Society seems to have been organized in 1887 at Minneapolis, Minn.[22] The movement spread rapidly among Friends during the next two decades and furnished the methods and organization by which the Young Friends Movement in the "pastoral" yearly meetings developed. The Friends Christian Endeavor Union was at one time part of the World Christian Endeavor organization. Since the First World War it has given way to the Young Friends Movement in most yearly meetings.

When Friends began to use singing in public worship they borrowed the hymns of their neighbors; at first the *Gospel Hymns* of Moody and Sankey and then various collections intended for revivals, Sunday schools and young people's societies. In 1907 a committee of the Five Years Meeting adopted as the *Friends Hymnal* a rather colorless publication of a New York publishing house with the omission of the hymns for communion services.[23] When the Hicksite young people began to sing at social and informal religious gatherings, they naturally used song books of liberal or non-creedal churches. In England Friends have largely used *The Fellowship Hymn Book*. This was compiled mainly for use in adult schools and in the Society is used chiefly for programmed evening meetings and by various young people's organizations.[24]

Friends continued through this period to furnish leaders in many reforms and philanthropies. In 1877 Barnabas C. Hobbs was "liberated" by Western Yearly Meeting to lecture on international peace and arbitration in Europe; he

[22] See *American Friend*, 1900, p. 231.

[23] *Min. Five Years Meeting*, 1907, pp. 121, 122.

[24] The non-pastoral groups do not use hymns in the regular meetings for worship.

presented a memorial on this subject to the Czar and Kaiser, and addressed the Pan-American Congress.[25]

Timothy Nicholson of Indiana Yearly Meeting may be taken as an outstanding representative of American Evangelical Quakerism at its best. He combined its evangelistic zeal and devotion to philanthropy with the inward sensitiveness of Quietism:

"I have ever since a child had that thought about our Heavenly Father that makes His presence real: 'Thou God seest me,' " he once said. "I was trained to have faith in God and His promises. I was trained to try to do His will, and that is the only thing that comes up when anything presents itself to me; it is not what somebody will say about it, it is not what somebody will think about it: 'Is it the thing to do?' And if this seems clear to me, He has kindly given me grace to move right on, do the best I can and leave the result to Him." [26]

He was actively identified with almost the whole round of contemporary Quaker philanthropic and religious concerns, serving preferably as promoter and organized rather than as a public speaker or advocate. In addition to activities mentioned later, he was superintendent and teacher of his Sunday school, and also a member of the International Sunday School Committee; chairman for years of Indiana Yearly Meeting Book and Tract Committee; an ardent worker for local option in Richmond, and first president of the Indiana Anti-Saloon League. He was a trustee of the Indiana State Normal School and an active member of the board of trustees of Earlham College. He was the first secretary of the Friends Educational Conference. He was one of the initiators of the Richmond Conference of 1887 and of the organization of the Five Years Meeting. He was clerk of Indiana Yearly Meeting for many years, and was regularly a delegate to the Five Years Meet-

[25] *Semi-Cent. Anniversary of Western Yearly Meeting,* p. 147.

[26] *Testimonial in Honor of Timothy Nicholson,* p. 61.

ing where he served once as chairman of the business committee. He was devoted to the cause of peace, especially in the effort to protect conscientious objectors and have Friends exempt from military conscription.[27]

The forerunner of *The Messenger of Peace,* which became the organ of The Peace Association of Friends in America upon its organization, was published first at New Vienna, Ohio, by Daniel Hill.

In 1895 Albert K. Smiley (1828–1912) organized the Lake Mohonk Conference on International Arbitration, which was held each year until 1916. It brought together influential men and women from all walks of life who were interested in international affairs and exerted a great influence on public opinion and policies in America. Benjamin F. Trueblood (1847–1916) served as secretary of the American Peace Society and editor of its organ *The Advocate of Peace* from 1892–1915. In 1903 the Committee on Legislation of the newly organized Five Years Meeting, chiefly through the efforts of its chairman, Timothy Nicholson, secured a provision in the new national militia bill exempting conscientious objectors on religious grounds.[28] Jane Addams, who was born of Quaker parentage, had a notable part in peace work from 1914 when she went on Ford's "Peace Ship" until her death. She was president from 1915 to 1919 of the American branch of the Women's International League for Peace and Freedom and of the International organization from 1915 to 1935. She and Alice Paul were also valiant leaders in the movement for woman's suffrage. Hannah Clothier Hull was president of the American branch of the Women's International League from 1924 to 1939.

In 1919 Frederick J. Libby, one of the able converts to Friends during the First World War, organized the

---

27 Cf. Woodward, *Timothy Nicholson: Master Quaker.*

28 *Min Five Years Meeting,* 1907, pp. 66–73.

National Council for the Prevention of War, a federation of a large number of national organizations. The work of the peace section of the American Friends Service Committee, especially under the leadership of E. Raymond Wilson and Ray Newton, in organizing student peace caravans, work camps for conscientious objectors, institutes of international relations and the Emergency Peace Campaign of 1935–1936 is treated in Chapter 37.

A large part of the work of American Friends for temperance has been done through such organizations as the Women's Christian Temperance Union, the Anti-saloon League and the Prohibition Party. Hannah J. Bailey was for a time president of the national W.C.T.U. and Friends furnished a number of state presidents, among whom were Mary J. Weaver, Hannah W. Smith, Mary Whitall Thomas, Mary C. Woody, Sarah J. Hoge, Margaret Hillis and Esther Pugh.[29] S. Edgar Nicholson (1862–1936) was the author of the first Indiana local option law (1895) and served as a state or national secretary of the Anti-saloon League from 1898 to 1927. The evangelists and travelling ministers of the revival period all used their influence in favor of personal temperance and against the liquor traffic. The temperance work of English Friends has been more in the direction of moderation and total abstinence and they have been less interested in political measures against "the Trade." J. W. Harvey Theobold (1863–1940) was from 1907 until his death secretary of the Friends Temperance Union. The Band of Hope was originated by an English Friend, Sarah Hotham, in 1837.[30]

Friends continued their interest and leadership in prison reform in this period. Timothy Nicholson was for nineteen

---

29 *Am. Friend,* 1899, p. 256. Elizabeth T. Stanley, although not a member of the Society was closely associated with Friends by marriage and in various Quaker activities. She was vice-president of the Indiana W.C.T.U. for twenty years and president for twenty-one years.

30 Fry, *Quaker Ways,* p. 191.

years a member of the Indiana State Board of Charities. He was the author of the state indeterminate sentence and parole law. Once he served as president of the National Association of Charities and Corrections. Albert H. Votaw was for a long period secretary of the Pennsylvania Prison Society. James Wood was one of the founders and a member of the Board of Managers of the New York State Prison for Women at Bedford from 1900 to 1918. Among the women Friends who have been active in prison reform and work for prisoners were Drusilla Wilson, Elizabeth L. Comstock, Laura C. Haviland and Sarah Smith.[31] Thomas Mott Osborne, who reformed the Auburn and Sing Sing prisons in New York had a Quaker background; he was the grand nephew of Lucretia Mott.

Friends have supported and furnished leaders to many other reform movements. It was a Friend who started the children's fresh air mission.[32] O. Edward Janney was president of the American Purity Alliance beginning in 1900; he was one of the organizers of the National Vigilance Committee (1906); and was appointed by President Taft as the official delegate to the International White Slave Conference at Lisbon (1910). James Wood was president of the American Bible Society, 1912–1919.

A number of homes for aged Friends have been established and maintained among Hicksite Friends. In Philadelphia Yearly Meeting there are eight of these under the management of the quarterly meetings.[33] Shortly before her death, Anna T. Jeannes (1832–1907) established the Joseph Jeannes Fund to aid these homes and she also left a legacy for infirmary services for the inmates of them.

---

31 In 1887 the Bertha Ballard Home for girls was established in Indianapolis by an association of Quaker women and in 1890 the Hadley Industrial Home was established largely through the instrumentality of Friends. (*Semi-Centennial Anniversary of Western Yearly Meeting*. pp. 214, 215.)

32 Thomas, *Hist.*, 6th Ed., p. 185.

33 There was formerly another at Plainfield, N. J.

There are similar Friends Homes under the care of other yearly meetings in New York, Baltimore, Waynesville, Ohio, and Richmond, Ind. Anna Jeannes also bequeathed the residue of her estate which amounted to about a million and a half dollars to found a hospital for the treatment of cancer and allied diseases, in accordance with which the Jeannes Hospital, thus provided for, was established at Fox Chase near Philadelphia and opened in 1928.[34] Mrs. Russell Sage, who established the Russell Sage Foundation, had a many-sided Quaker inheritance.[35]

Carl Heath, a London Friend, was for ten years secretary of the federation of British peace societies known as The National Peace Council. He later took charge of the international service of English Friends and remained secretary of it until his retirement in 1934. He is still active with other Friends in movements for peace and particularly for freedom for India.

English Friends also have long expressed an active interest in penal reform. This was notably stimulated by the imprisonment of many Friends as conscientious objectors to war service 1916–1919. They are particularly interested in the abolition of capital punishment.

These pioneers and leaders in modern philanthropies and reforms were not solitary figures. They were products and representatives of profound convictions and sustained activities within the Society of Friends. Behind them is the succession of concerned Friends who served on committees of monthly, quarterly and yearly meetings or worked quietly and faithfully to promote Bible schools, peace, temperance, prison reform and other good causes.[36]

[34] *Friends Intelligencer,* XCVIII, 183, 184.

[35] Holder, *The Quakers in England and America,* chap. XIV.

[36] In addition to the relatively few wealthy Quaker philanthropists in America who have endowed educational and other philanthropic institutions, there have been thousands of Friends who have given relatively small sums and left small legacies for such purposes. Almost every yearly meeting has funds accumulated in these ways, the aggregate good accomplished by means of them being impossible to record.

American Friends have not been as prominent in political life as have English Friends. Just before the outbreak of the First World War there were eight Quakers in Parliament. It was only after the Civil War that American Friends or men of Quaker training began to take an active part in public life. There have been a few Quaker state governors: Herbert S. Hadley of Missouri (1909–1913); Walter R. Stubbs of Kansas (1909–1913) and Arthur Capper (1915–1919); William C. Sproul of Pennsylvania (1919–1923), and Frank White of North Dakota (1901–1905). Paul M. Pearson was governor of the Virgin Islands, 1931–1935. Joseph G. Cannon, who for many years was speaker of the national House of Representatives, was a birthright member and named for Joseph John Gurney. Joseph Moore Dixon was United States senator from Montana 1907–1913. Attorney General A. Mitchell Palmer in the Wilson Administration (1919–1921) was a member of Philadelphia Yearly Meeting (H). Senator Arthur Capper of Kansas (since 1919) and Senator Burton K. Wheeler of Montana (since 1923) were of Quaker extraction.

Herbert Hoover (b. 1874) had a distinguished career as head of the Belgian Relief Commission during the First World War and then served as Food Administrator under President Wilson. He was director of the American Relief Administration following the war, and of the European Children's Fund. He served as secretary of commerce under Presidents Harding and Coolidge and was elected president in 1928. He had the distinction of being the only Quaker to become the responsible head of a great nation.

American Friends have taken relatively little interest in social problems. The majority of them are still rural and the development of the problems of capitalist society has been relatively late in America as a whole. The Five Years Meeting of 1912 established a board of social service but it was relatively inactive and was discontinued in 1922. The two Philadelphia yearly meetings have had coöperating committees dealing with problems of the social order in recent decades. Following the First World War this committee sponsored some very fruitful investigations into problems of employment and labor by a group of Quaker business men and employers.

English Friends naturally began to wrestle with social problems much earlier than American Friends because the industrial revolution developed earlier in England and a larger proportion of London Yearly Meeting was of the employing class. The British Conference of Quaker Employers has met three times at ten-year intervals, beginning in 1908 and has done useful work in trying to formulate a Christian standard in business management and in exchanging experience gained in trying to operate such a standard.[37] The post-war generation of English young Friends were keenly and often radically interested in questions of the social order. In 1915 London Yearly Meeting appointed a Committee on War and the Social Order, which prepared a social creed usually known as the Eight Points which was adopted by the yearly meeting in 1918 as the foundation of a true social order.[38] In 1928 the committee was revised and called the Industrial and Social Order Council.[39]

This is perhaps the most suitable place in this history to mention certain important contributions to social welfare and industrial progress by Quaker business firms. Friends, especially in England, have engaged in business very extensively, largely for the same reasons that led them to turn to the natural sciences, partly because the church, the armed forces and, to a large extent, state service generally were closed or unwelcome to them. They have carried on business enterprises with distinguishd success on the whole and have also contributed through them to social progress

37 *The Survey*, XLI, 8 (Nov. 23, 1918).

38 Graham, *The Faith of a Quaker*, pp. 319–324.

39 Brayshaw, *The Quakers*, p. 327.

and the common welfare. Friends played a distinguished part "in the introduction of fixed prices, the marking of merchandise in plain figures, the smelting of iron ore by coke or peat instead of charcoal, the establishment of garden cities, and other industrial innovations."[40] Many Quaker family names have long been associated with important industries and businesses, such as the Gurneys, Barclays and Lloyds with banking; the Frys, Rowntrees and Cadburys with cocoa; Allen and Henbury with medicines; Clark with boots and shoes; and Reckitt with starch. In many cases Friends abandoned lucrative businesses, such as brewing and distilling, for conscience' sake. In others they gave to the public the benefit of inventions, such as non-poisonous matches.[41]

Rather typical of the many-sided interests of many English Quaker industrialists of the later nineteenth century was Joseph Storrs Fry (1826–1913), a cocoa manufacturer of Bristol. He was devoted to the Society of Friends, a great business man and philanthropist. He conducted a devotional service every morning in the factory for his employees until after he was eighty and he distributed large sums among his work-people. He was a pioneer in promoting education among Friends and a life-long worker on behalf of schools and Sunday schools. He was clerk of London Yearly Meeting for fifteen years (1870–1875, 1881–1889).[42]

There were many prosperous and successful British Friends who kept their simple ways and devout life along with their wealth; but there was in the later periods of Quakerism as in the early eighteenth century the inevitable "conflict between worldly success and Quaker simplicity."

---

40 *The Friends Intelligencer,* XCVII, 755.

41 *Loc. cit.* Cf. Fry, *Quaker Ways,* chap. 13. Emden, *Quakers in Commerce,* p. 17.

42 *Dict. Nat. Biog. Twentieth Cent. Supplement,* 1912–1921.

Wealth, as can be generally observed in commercial countries, very seldom remains long in the same family. With comfort, enterprise stops; and looking through the history of quite a number of Quaker houses it can be discerned that after a few generations they parted either with wealth or Quakerism. "A carriage and pair," as the perspicacious Henry Tuke Mennell once remarked, "does not long continue to drive to a Meeting House." [43]

---

[43] Emden, *op. cit.*, p. 231.

Chapter 35

CHANGES IN DOCTRINE AND ORGANIZATION

The revival movement led inevitably to changes in practice, in doctrine, in organization and in the relation of Friends to their environment. The yearly meetings organized the revival work by appointing committees on evangelistic work to succeed the committees on general meetings. To the duty of organizing and financing the revivals the responsibility of church extension and pastoral work was soon added. The tendency was toward centralization; the yearly meeting committees and superintendents grew in power. In Iowa Yearly Meeting John Henry Douglas was Superintendent of Evangelistic and Pastoral Work from 1886 to 1890. He and his committee accomplished an enormous amount of work with a relatively small financial outlay. The territory of the yearly meeting extended from Wisconsin to Oregon, from the Mississippi river through Denver to southern California. The population of the west was growing rapidly and the need of religious organization was pressing. The yearly meeting conferred on him and his committee authority to organize and establish monthly meetings and to receive members into membership.[1]

1 *Min. Iowa Yearly Meeting,* 1890, pp. 6, 7. Report of The Pastoral and Evangelical Committee. In 1881 ministers had already been granted authority to organize missions and report their members to the monthly meeting. *Min.,* 1881, p. 19. This was an extreme case but it shows how near the yearly meeting superintendent came to exercising episcopal functions.

So many of the converts were not birthright Friends or were inexperienced in new methods and fields of work that it appeared necessary to provide the new meetings with leadership, especially with a teaching ministry and pastoral care.[2] In places there were whole meetings with only a few birthright members. Often converts in a series of meetings would join Friends merely because the preacher was a Quaker and they had no other denominational preferences.

The pastoral arrangement—it has never become a system—began chiefly in two ways: (1) after a revival, members of the local meeting would ask the minister to stay for a year or so in order to conserve and organize the results of the work; or (2) a minister might be invited to come and live in a community having the official status of a resident minister only, so that the meeting would have the benefit of his ministry.[3] Some means by which he could make a living for himself was provided,[4] or as was often the case, a few members would form an unofficial committee and solicit funds for his support.

Both these methods were at first unofficial; and it sometimes happened that a few members would take it upon themselves to invite a minister not aceptable to the rest of the meeting. It became desirable therefore to have the choice approved by the meeting and the invitation made

---

[2] *Memories of Stanley Pumphrey,* pp. 242, 243. He was particularly impressed with the need of teaching ministry. John Wilhelm Rowntree was convinced of the failure of the old type of ministry in America. *Present Day Papers,* Vol. II, "A Plan for a Settlement for Religious Study," pp. 12, 13.

[3] Luke Woodard claims to have been the first pastor. Cf. *Friends Intelligencer,* Third mo. 19, 1938, p. 197. *Sketches of a Life of 75,* pp. 77. Hay, *op. cit.,* pp. 74–77.

[4] Nathan Frame was provided with a school at Chester, Ind. (*Rem.,* pp. 65, 103). Dr. Dougan Clark was given an appointment as physician to an Orphanage in Cincinnati. Levi Mills established himself as a lawyer in Wilmington, Ohio.

official.[5] As the demand for pastors increased the assistance of the yearly meeting evangelistic committee was sought both in securing them and in supervising their work. In Indiana Yearly Meeting the discipline was revised in 1878 and references to a hireling ministry omitted. Iowa made the same change in 1886.[6] The yearly and quarterly meeting evangelistic committees thus gradually became also pastoral committees.

In the older polity of the Society the care of the ministry and of the religious interests of the membership was in the hands of the "Select Body" or meeting of ministers and elders. In many meetings the overseers also sat with this body. It seemed logical that it should have the responsibility for the choice and oversight of the work of the pastor. The final approval of a "call" and of the financial arrangements fell to the monthly meeting.[7]

The pastoral system was not adopted by a number of eastern yearly meetings during the period of the Revival proper and even then never by all their meetings. These were New England, New York and Baltimore. A few important meetings in Indiana and North Carolina were very slow in seeking pastors. Of course, there were no pastors in Philadelphia (O), nor in any of the Hicksite or Conservative yearly meetings. In recent years it has become common to distinguish these groups, as "pastoral" and "non-pastoral" Friends. British Friends are also "non-pastoral."

The Uniform Discipline of the Five Years Meeting provided that the pastoral committee of the monthly meeting (which naturally came to consist of a single congregation)

---

[5] Occasionally a pastor was arranged for in order to "protect" the meeting from fanatical preaching or unacceptable visiting ministers. In a few cases it was the conservative element in a meeting which wanted a pastor for such reasons. See Hay, *op. cit.*, p. 41.

[6] Jones, *Quakers of Iowa,* p. 106.

[7] For the most part the pastor's salary was not added to the meeting assessment or "stock," but was raised by voluntary subscription.

should consist of the ministers, elders and overseers of the meeting and such other persons as the monthly meeting might appoint to serve with them. In many places the Sunday school superintendent, the president of the Christian Endeavor Society, the president of the Missionary Society or of the Ladies' Aid, or all of them, were appointed on the pastoral committee.

As it became common the pastoral system produced new tendencies in the Society. It diminished the influence of women's ministry notably, since relatively few women were chosen as pastors; it reduced the opportunities for resident ministers and members to take vocal part in the worship. It tended to make every meeting having a pastor a monthly meeting. The older ideal of a meeting for worship was a group small enough so that the members would feel that there was time and opportunity for each person to take part in the vocal exercises. The pastoral arrangement requires a meeting large enough to be able to provide for the pastor's living.

The meeting for worship underwent great changes after the revival. A new spirit of democracy asserted itself in the business meetings by abolishing separate business meetings for women and giving them equal voice with men. In consequence most of the meeting-houses were remodelled. The partition was taken out and the gallery was replaced by a pulpit and platform. The newer meeting-houses show a great variety of ecclesiastical and "chapel" architecture. There was a more frequent participation in the vocal exercises "outside the gallery" and more regular preaching.

At first the pastor had only the official status of a resident minister. Gradually, and usually with the tacit consent and even encouragement of the meeting, he assumed functions which Protestant ministers exercise in public worship; the pastor "timed the meeting" in place of the head elder; he felt the obligation to preach regularly and the meeting came to expect it; the elders no longer "faced the meeting." There were often periods of silence but the worship became more and more like that of "low-church" Protestant bodies, without the sacraments or a fixed order of service, but with a fairly definite program established by custom.[8]

The westward migrations had largely spent themselves by 1890. Oregon (1893) and California (1895) yearly meetings grew out of the continued migration of Friends to the Pacific coast states. Later some new Friends meetings were established between 1890 and 1915 in the plains states next the Rocky Mountains, especially in Texas, Colorado, Nebraska and South Dakota. Nebraska Yearly Meeting was set up by the Five Years Meeting in 1908.

The decades between 1880 and 1910 witnessed the growth of great urban centers at the expense of the rural population. Friends were chiefly a rural people, especially in the Middle West, where they were most numerous, and suffered heavy losses in the migration to the cities, in which the small denominations are always chief losers. There was usually but one Quaker meeting in a large city, if any. It often required considerable effort for most of the resident Friends to get to it. Methodist, Presbyterian, Baptist and Congregational churches were easily accessible in every suburb and they usually welcomed Friends and their children by letter with no insistence on baptism or communion. Many of the young Friends of that generation who had dropped the distinguishing practices of Friends, had not found a deeper basis of loyalty. They could find the same type of doctrine and worship to which they were

---

[8] On these changes Cf. Jones, *op. cit.*, p. 110. "At the present time a strong tendency toward formality in the religious services prevails; when the given hour arrives the minister ascends the pulpit, a hymn is announced, the organ or piano begins to play, the choir sings, the scriptures are read, prayer is offered, the sermon prepared for the occasion is delivered, another hymn is sung, the benediction is pronounced, and the service ends—a service which is in strange contrast with the simple, silent meetings which universally prevailed among the Friends in former days." Cf. *ibid.*, pp. 111, 112. *Rem. of Nathan and Esther Frame,* pp. 426, 427. *The Friend,* LXIV, 349.

accustomed in many Protestant churches. The Christian Endeavor movement rising during this period attracted young Friends and saved many of them to the Society by its pledge of denominational loyalty. Gradually it merged into a young Friends movement and reëstablished contact with their heritage of history and literature.

Ohio Yearly Meeting (O) has suffered more severely from separations than any other, because it has been more evenly divided each time. In 1828 about half its membership went with the Hicksites, by which it lost its more liberal and thoughtful membership. Again in 1854, the Wilburite Separation cost it the larger conservative section which was most devoted to the Quaker traditions. Orderly progress in a religious body is surest where new tendencies and proposed changes are subjected to free criticism and required to justify themselves to those conservatives who have a strong sense of "the good the past hath had." In large yearly meetings like London and Indiana which have not suffered serious divisions, the blending of many temperaments, tendencies and points of view has better assured well considered and consistent progress, and promoted tolerance, comprehension, and coöperation among them. On the contrary the separations took out of Ohio Yearly Meeting those most liberal in thought and conservative in practice. The Great Revival found in the Gurneyite remnant of the yearly meeting a fertile field, where in addition to the usual revival features and Evangelical emphasis on justification, it developed, under the leadership of David Updegraff (1830–1894), an extreme "Holiness" doctrine, as well as the other features of the "Fourfold Gospel"—faith healing and the imminent Second Coming of Christ.[9]

Beginning with the teaching of Gurney and nourished by Methodist and other Evangelical influences in the Great Revival, a new attitude toward the Bible had developed

[9] JLPQ, II, 926.

among Friends. In many places the belief in the outward authority of the Bible had supplanted the older view of Scripture, with neither respect for Quaker tradition nor historical insight to keep them from bondage to the letter. It has always been difficult for Friends, who hold this view in the midst of other Christians who practice the ordinances, to resist the contention that the ordinances are obligatory, because plainly commanded in the New Testament.[10] David Updegraff and his followers began to teach the Scriptural obligation to practice the ordinances, especially water baptism and David himself was baptized by the minister of the Berean Church in Philadelphia.[11] The movement was strongest in Ohio Yearly Meeting, where about 1890 it was estimated that perhaps half the members had been baptized; but it had numerous adherents in North Carolina and Iowa. Many of the influential leaders of the later revival movement, such as Esther Tuttle Pritchard and Dougan Clark, shared the Updegraff attitude toward baptism.[12]

In 1885 Ohio Yearly Meeting refused to make it a disciplinary matter for a minister to participate in or advocate the necessity of the outward ordinances.[13] This deviation from one of the historical "testimonies" of the Society alarmed the other Orthodox yearly meetings. Many of them in succession adopted strong statements the following year.[14] London reaffirmed its historical position.

[10] This had been the case with the Beaconites and other Evangelicals in England. In 1836 Elisha Bates of Ohio had been baptized in England and later resigned his membership in Ohio Yearly Meeting. Hodgson, *op. cit.*, I, 255. Clark, *Life*, p. 102.

[11] *Ibid.*, chap. XII. The date is not given. It must have been about 1884. *The Friend*, LVIX, 38 (9th mo. 5, 1885).

[12] In 1893 Dougan Clark attended Ohio Yearly Meeting and was baptized. *The American Friend*, I, 246.

[13] *Min.*, 1884, p. 23.

[14] The Indiana minute read: "We believe it inconsistent for anyone to be acknowledged or retained in the position of a minister or elder among us who continues to participate in or teach the necessity of the outward rite of baptism or the supper," *Min.*, 1886, p. 52.

The condition of American Quakerism in the latter half of the decade from 1880 to 1890 was beyond question seriously grave and acute. All fixed habits and customs were unsettled. There were many cross currents of thought and practice. Meetings were divided in attitude towards the innovations. The old brakes no longer held, and the speed of the progressive movement threatened to bring on an irreparable catastrophe.[15]

To meet this situation and bring to bear the convictions of the whole body of Friends upon these problems, Indiana Yearly Meeting in 1886 proposed a conference of representatives from all yearly meetings in correspondence with London, which met in Richmond, Indiana, in 1887.[16] London and Dublin yearly meetings sent delegates, and some Friends of Gurneyite sympathies from Philadelphia were present unofficially.

The conference decided to issue a declaration of faith chiefly for the purpose of defining afresh the attitude of the Society on the points at issue. A committee consisting of twelve members was appointed to draft the declaration, but it was largely the work of J. Bevan Braithwaite of London, Dr. James E. Rhoads of Philadelphia, and Dr. James Carey Thomas, of Baltimore. Allen Jay gives the following description of the actual process of preparing the Declaration:

The committee met, and different ones were appointed to prepare certain sections of the declaration, but the greater portion of it was prepared by our late dear friend, Joseph Bevan Braithwaite, of London yearly meeting. . . . When he left home, thinking that something of the kind might claim the attention of the conference, he put in with his baggage several books and manuscripts that were prepared by the earlier writers among Friends and had not been changed by Friends of more recent date in this country or anywhere else. His remark was:

---

[15] JLPQ, II, 930.

[16] Western Yearly Meeting had proposed such a conference in 1870 and again in 1875. *Min.*, 1870, p. 23; 1875, p. 9.

"We want the original Quakerism free from the influence and thought of some of our Friends who have imbibed some of the spirit and practice of other denominations or have been influenced by their environments." Our dear friend worked early and late when not in the conference. . . . Before it was presented to the conference it was gone over carefully, Joseph Bevan Braithwaite sitting at the desk reading carefully what had been written, Dr. James E. Rhoads, of Philadelphia, looking over the quotations from Friends' writings to see that they were correctly quoted, and Dr. James Carey Thomas, of Baltimore watching the Scripture quotations to see that there were no mistakes made there.[17]

The Declaration was adopted as presented by the committee with but slight changes. Judging from the personnel of the committee and from the way it was prepared, it should be a conservative statement of English and American Gurneyism. The conference directed that it should be a "restatement of our Christian belief" prepared "from the established disciplines and declarations of faith of the different yearly meetings."

As to the Declaration in general, Thomas gives the following estimate of it, which seems impartial and just.

The "Declaration" consisted largely of extracts from standard writings, and is too diffuse and general in its statements to be regarded as a rigid creed; nevertheless, it much more nearly approaches one than any of the Declarations that have preceded it. It conforms much more nearly to the standards of ordinary evangelical denominations. As might have been expected from the fact that baptism and the Supper were the questions then at issue, the space occupied in the consideration of these topics is disproportionately large. While it acknowledges the distinguishing views of Friends of the universality of the operation of the Spirit of Christ, it tends to pass them over. It states the Quaker doctrine of peace, and against oaths, etc., clearly and well; states in guarded language

---

[17] *Autobiog. of Allen Jay,* pp. 361–362.

the doctrines of future rewards and punishments; and reaffirms the deity of Christ and salvation through him. The "Declaration" met with strong apposition in England, and London yearly meeting took no action on the document except to place it on its Minutes as part of the report of its committee. New England and Ohio took essentially the same position as London. Dublin, New York and Baltimore gave a general approval of it without adopting it. The other (Orthodox) yearly meetings in the United States adopted it.[18]

At the Richmond Conference Dr. William Nicholson of Kansas had proposed a "conference of yearly meetings with certain delegated powers and to meet at stated intervals" but no definite action was taken about it.[19] In 1897 a small conference at Oskaloosa, Iowa, decided to call another general conference which accordingly met in Indianapolis the following year, at which only the Orthodox American yearly meetings were represented. The conference adopted certain features of William Nicholson's proposal in 1887; representation was on the basis of five delegates from each yearly meeting with one additional delegate for each thousand members or major fraction of one thousand, which became the established rule for succeeding conferences. He had proposed meetings every three years but Allen Jay suggested every five years, which became the established interval. These quinquennial conferences continued until they were merged into the Five Years Meeting in 1902. They had a vital conservative and unifying influence on

---

18 *Hist.*, p. 199. The Declaration did not satisfy the more radical elements of the Society. In Ohio the "Waterites," as the party favoring the ordinances was called, aided by the "second definite experience" holiness group, the pre-millenarians, and the ultraevangelicals were able to prevent its adoption. It was printed, however, and circulated by order of the yearly meeting. The Declaration, however, aided by other influences caused the "Waterite" movement gradually to decline. Among these influences one of the most important was that of Walter and Emma B. Malone through the Cleveland Bible Institute. At the present time the whole movement to the ordinances is practically forgotten.

19 For his whole proposal see the *Proceedings*, pp. 263–269.

American Orthodox Quakerism. They constituted milestones along the way by which the non-Quaker tendencies of the Evangelical and Revival movements were assimilated and neutralized by bringing the common judgment and testimony of Friends to bear more effectively in dealing with local and individual deviations from Quaker principles.

The conference of 1892 was most vitally concerned with the question of the ministry. The pastoral arrangement with its implications for polity and worship was strongly advocated; but the conference reaffirmed the fundamental Quaker ideas of worship and the ministry, though not with the decisiveness that marked the Richmond Declaration on the ordinances. This was due partly to the absence of English and Irish representatives from this conference, and partly to the lack of any better arrangement to meet the urgent need of leadership and a teaching ministry. Since then there has been a slow reaction against the extreme tendency toward a ruling "one-man" pastorate.

At the Indianapolis Conference of 1892 the question of a uniform discipline for the Orthodox yearly meetings was presented by Francis W. Thomas of Indiana Yearly Meeting, but no action was taken. Timothy Nicholson had been active in promoting these conferences and in working for a closer organized unity among Friends. The Indianapolis Conference of 1897 received requests from four yearly meetings [20] for the establishment of a conference with delegated powers and binding authority. Rufus M. Jones, who had become editor of the *American Friend* [21] in 1894 and professor of philosophy in Haverford College, advocated a conference with legislative authority and Edmund Stanley of Kansas Yearly Meeting championed one uniform discipline for all the yearly meetings. After full discussion the conference endorsed both ideas in principle and ap-

20 Wilmington, Indiana, Western and Kansas.

21 It succeeded *The Friends Review* and *The Christian Worker.*

pointed a committee of two representatives from each yearly meeting represented to draw up a plan for a closer union and to prepare a draft of a uniform discipline.[22] The actual work was done chiefly by James Wood and Rufus M. Jones.[23]

The draft, as approved by the large committee, was submitted to the yearly meetings in 1900, proposing that if sufficient yearly meetings adopted it, the Quinquennial Conference of 1902 should become the first Five Years Meeting. The proposed Discipline added the Five Years Meeting with certain delegated powers to the historic organization of the Society. It departed from the traditional order in that it is a delegated body, while all other business meetings (monthly, quarterly and yearly) are in theory gatherings of the whole membership. It allowed each member yearly meeting five delegates, and one additional for each thousand members or major fraction of one thousand. It adopted the plan of pooling the travelling expenses of delegates so as to make the place of holding it financially indifferent. A second departure from previous Quaker practice was the substitution of an associate membership for children of Friends in place of birthright membership.

Under the old order the monthly meeting of Ministry and Oversight[24] was charged with the responsibility for the pastoral care of the membership. As a concession to the "pastoral" meetings this meeting was designated as the pastoral committee of the local congregation, and given power to secure the special service of a minister as its agent to aid in the discharge of its responsibilities, where the meeting desired such a pastor. The discipline seems to assume that a meeting with a pastor should become a monthly meeting by itself.[25]

---

22 See the *Proceedings of the Quinquennial Conference,* 1897.

23 Jones, *The Trail of Life in the Middle Years,* p. 110.

24 Composed of elders and overseers.

25 *Uniform Discipline,* chap. XIV.

In regard to doctrinal beliefs the discipline contained a section on "Essential Truths" in which the Quaker position was stated in simple terms with a strong Evangelical flavor, at the close of which the statement was added, as a concession to the extreme Evangelicals of the West: [26]

> For more explicit and extended statements of belief, reference is made to those officially put forth at various times, especially to the letter of George Fox to the Governor of Barbardos in 1671, and to the Declaration of Faith issued by the Richmond Conference in 1887.[27]

The Discipline was adopted in order by New England, New York, Indiana, Kansas, California, Wilmington, Western, Baltimore, Iowa, Oregon and Canada.[28] The first Five Years Meeting organized by creating the following new boards: Evangelistic and Church Extension, Education, Legislation, Condition and Welfare of the Negroes and adopting the inter-yearly meeting organizations that were already going concerns—the American Friends Board of Foreign Missions (1894), the Associated Executive Committee on Indian Affairs (1869) and the Peace Association of Friends in America (1867). A series of educational conferences held approximately every five years since 1877 furnished the practical basis for the Board on Education. It took a great deal of time for these boards, especially the new ones, to find their work and establish themselves in the plans and confidence of Friends. One or two of the new boards represented interests which it was believed Friends should have rather than actual interests.[29]

---

26 Jones, *The Trail of Life in the Middle Years,* pp. 111–113.

27 *Uniform Discipline,* p. 39.

28 Canada adopted the Discipline in 1900 but rescinded its action the next year on the ground that it did not suit their conditions. In 1907, however, it joined the Five Years Meeting again. Ohio rejected the Discipline because its doctrinal statements were not definite enough. Philadelphia did not even consider it.

29 Thomas, *op. cit.,* pp. 219, 220.

At the next Five Years Meeting held in 1907 in Richmond, Indiana, California and Western yearly meetings requested that the Discipline be changed so as to restore birthright membership, but the change was never approved by the requisite number of yearly meetings. The meeting was much agitated by the question of modern Biblical scholarship and progressive religious thought. It voted to join the Federal Council of Churches of Christ in America. It authorized the setting up of Nebraska Yearly Meeting in 1908.

The meeting of 1912, held at Indianapolis, established a Board of Publications, assumed the ownership and management of *The American Friend,* with S. Edgar Nicholson as editor, and established boards of Social Service, Bible Schools and Young Friends Activities, and a central office in Richmond, Indiana, with a general secretary.

The organization of the Five Years Meeting completed the unification of the "Gurneyite" section of American Quakerism (except Ohio Yearly Meeting), thus partially realizing an ideal proposed by Philadelphia Yearly Meeting in 1683 for a central representative meeting of American Friends, but which was found impossible at that time on account of distance and difficulty of traveling.

After the Civil War there was a development of very liberal tendencies in theology among Hicksite Friends and of useful activities in connection with the abolition of slavery and in coöperation with President Grant's Indian policy. To the five Hicksite yearly meetings at the time of the separation—New York, Philadelphia, Baltimore, Ohio and Indiana two others have been added: Genesee Yearly Meeting (1834), which comprises Friends in western New York and in Canada, and Illinois Yearly Meeting (1875), which embraces Friends in northern Illinois and southern Indiana. These seven yearly meetings had in 1930 about 18,000 members, more than one-half belonging to Philadelphia Yearly Meeting. Ohio and Genesee were both very small, having about 500 members each.[30]

Following the profound stirrings of the Civil War, new methods of work and new interests began to grow up in this branch of Friends. Swarthmore College was founded in 1866. First Day schools were established gradually, and in 1868 the first of the Biennial First Day School Conferences was held by interested members from the seven yearly meetings. In 1882, the Friends' Union for Philanthropic Labor was organized and thereafter met with the First Day School Conference. It gradually included the subject of prison reform as well as work for Negroes and Indians in its programs. In 1896 the Educational Conference was added to the other two, and in 1900 these three were combined into the Friends General Conference, which first met in 1902. The Committee for the Advancement of Friends' Principles was organized at that time as a department of the General Conference. The biennial Friends' General Conference thus came to embrace the four departments: First Day Schools, Philanthropic Labor, Education, and the Advancement of Friends' Principles. In the same year the Young Friends' Association was organized and recognized as a department of the Conference. The Committee for the Advancement of Friends' Principles has an office with a general secretary in Philadelphia, which serves many other departments of the Conference also. The General Conference has no legislative power but the Central Executive Committee and the general secretary have a great influence in shaping and coördinating the activities of this branch of Friends. The General Conference corresponds in a general way to the Quinquennial Conferences of the Orthodox branch that grew into the Five Years

---

30 Ohio Yearly Meeting has ceased to hold its annual meetings and only preserves a legal existence through a representative committee of twenty-two members. *Handbook of the Religious Society of Friends,* Phila., 1941, p. 14.

Meeting. They were rather similar developments; but the Hicksites, true to their more individualistic tendencies, have merely a conference instead of a super-yearly meeting. After the First World War there was a movement to promote a more general participation in the meetings for worship, following a similar movement among English Friends. The recording of ministers was discontinued and the meeting of ministers and elders became the meeting for ministry and counsel, for the oversight of the spiritual welfare of the membership.

Philadelphia Yearly Meeting (O) has been more conservative than the yearly meetings of the Five Years Meeting. The preservation of the unity of the yearly meeting has been the key-note of its policy down to the present time. This means that in official matters and methods of religious work, the yearly meeting progress has been very slow, the meeting proceeding no more rapidly than the whole membership were ready to go. The members are careful of official propriety and very tender of individual religious concerns. At the same time the more progressive element has carried on activities through unofficial organizations on behalf of freedmen and Indians, and for the promotion of First Day schools, foreign missions, peace, temperance and other philanthropic causes. In the decade before the First World War there were practically two yearly meetings. The official sessions, held at Arch Street meeting-house were very conservative in methods, keeping close to the traditional lines. Between sessions at the South Twelfth Street meeting-house, the various unofficial organizations held their annual meetings. To a large extent the same Friends participated in both but with considerable variation in the leaders, and there was coöperation in arranging the program so that the two sets of sessions during yearly meeting week would not conflict.

The Philadelphia (O) Young Friends Committee which was organized in 1915 was the outgrowth of the Young

Men's Institute (1879) which grew into the Friends Institute, and the Young Women's Auxiliary (1911). Their work was carried on largely through "tea meetings," study groups, round tables and conferences.

In the decade before the First World War the Philadelphia Young Friends Movement came into gradual coöperation with English Young Friends and with the Young Friends Movement of the Five Years Meeting. There was also a considerable amount of coöperation with the Hicksite young friends. The pastoral question and the use of music in meetings for worship were the greatest obstacles on their part to close affiliation with the Five Years Meeting.

A movement in England to make the meetings for worship more democratic resulted in the discontinuance of the practice of recording ministers and the abolition of the meetings of ministers and elders. In place of them the regular business meetings of the Society were charged with the duty of reviewing periodically the state of the ministry and the religious life of the meeting. Separate meetings for men and women were discontinued in 1896. In 1907 the Morning Meeting was merged with the Meeting for Sufferings, which took over its functions of care for travelling ministers from abroad or going abroad and also the supervision of Friends literature.

In London and in many American yearly meetings "junior yearly meetings" are held for the children; they serve to interest the younger members in attending yearly meeting and to train them in the activities and methods of business meetings.[31]

---

[31] *Report of Com. IV, Friends World Conference, 1937,* p. 29.

Chapter 36

LIBERALISM AND REACTION AMONG FRIENDS

The liberal movement among Friends was largely, at first, a reaction from the Evangelical theology and the Quietist attitude of hostility to philosophy and science. In America it was also a rebound from the extremes of the revival theology. In both countries, but especially in England where it developed first, it was stimulated by intellectual movements in the church at large and by the new spirit of the age. Scientific speculation was provoked by the new discoveries and theories in the natural sciences, especially the new geology and the Darwinian doctrine of evolution. New approaches to philosophical and theological problems were provided by the quickened historical sense of the age and by the social and political changes following the Industrial Revolution. Friends were made more susceptible to these influences by long contacts with liberal thinkers in many social and political reforms. They were also more open to influences from outside the Society at the time when the abandonment of the traditional peculiarities let down many of the old barriers against the world.

Friends were particularly influenced by a number of religious writers and liberal preachers of England and Scotland and by the writings of Kingsley, Maurice, Browning and Tennyson. The later writings of John Greenleaf Whittier were among the earliest of the liberal forces within the Society. He had gained a large public through his anti-slavery efforts, and his poems exerted an influence far beyond the Society of Friends. His poetry has furnished at least twenty hymns in use in English-speaking churches. Whittier remained to the end of his life a member of the Society in spite of the fact that its conservatism in regard to his anti-slavery work and the suspicions of the Evangelical wing of the Society that he was doctrinally "unsound" made him very uncomfortable at times. He was devoted to Friends' mystical worship and found in it not only the main spring of his philanthropic devotion but the source of his

"Hate of tyranny intense and hearty in its vehemence."

Partly as a result of his association with New England liberals and partly from the urge of his "swelling and vehement heart" when he contemplated human pain and sorrow, he outgrew the limits of the Evangelical theology. For one thing, like Joel Bean, he could not limit the love of God; and for another, the Evangelical doctrine of the atonement seemed to him too limited and too artificial. Nevertheless in the discussion of religious subjects he preferred for the most part the old Evangelical terms, enriching and spiritualizing them from his own deep experience and his wide outlook.

In England the liberal movement was most directly the result of the work of Friends in the adult schools and other educational efforts for the religious training of the working classes. In their efforts to teach the Bible and Christian principles, the teachers came to realize their own need of fuller knowledge. This stimulated Biblical and religious studies among them.[1] The adult schools brought new blood as well as new interests into the Society. Local meetings were recruited from the more sympathetic and responsive members of the adult schools and many new

---

1 Rowntree, *Man's Relation to God,* pp. 17–19.

meetings were established. Between 1864 and 1900 the membership of the London Yearly Meeting increased from 13,761 to 17,153.[2]

This growth in numbers chiefly from the adult schools, corresponds to the accessions in America from the Great Revival. English Friends did not take the members of the adult schools into membership *en masse,* however, as sections of American Quakerism did the converts in the Great Revival. In 1900 English Friends had under their care about 45,000 adult school pupils;[3] but most of them never became members of the Society. After about 1915 the adult schools became an independent, undenominational influence and Friends lost their main opportunity with them. On the other hand, those who joined the Society joined only after very careful sifting and indoctrination. The problem of pastoral care was solved largely by voluntary and often systematic visitation by leisured Friends and partly by systematic care through the Home Mission Committee, which was organized in 1882.[4]

As a result of these influences Friends developed a liberal attitude toward religious education which was taken up and carried on by a group of scholarly and enthusiastic young leaders. In 1889 there appeared a set of liberal essays upon religious subjects by members of the Church of England entitled *Lux Mundi,* which created a great sensation in the religious world. In 1884 a similar book entitled *A Reasonable Faith* had been published by three young Friends and provoked widespread discussion. Among the older Biblical scholars in the Society was Joseph Bevan Braithwaite. He was an ardent Biblical and patristic scholar but thoroughly Evangelical in his theology.

---

2 *The American Friend,* 1900, pp. 1240–1241. John Stephenson Rowntree: "London Yearly Meeting during 250 Years."

3 Hobley and Mercer, *The Adult School Movement,* p. 16.

4 Brayshaw, *Quakers,* p. 311.

J. Rendel Harris was a keen New Testament scholar and showed a remarkable mixture of Evangelical and liberal in his religious thinking. Among the younger leaders were Caroline E. Stephen, whose *Quaker Strongholds* (1890) powerfully re-enforced the movement for "rational mysticism"; A. Neave Brayshaw, William Charles Braithwaite, Edward Grubb, John William Graham and Joshua Rowntree.

The leader of this group was John Wilhelm Rowntree of York. With great enthusiasm he threw himself into the task of modernizing the Society of Friends. He was devoted to the methods of historical and critical study, but believed in the mystical worship of Friends and in a voluntary ministry. His writings and lectures did much to fix the attitude of his generation toward modern religious scholarship and the reorganization of the Society of Friends. In 1897 he and Rufus M. Jones, editor of *The American Friend,* planned a series of Quaker historical works. He was to write a history of the Society of Friends and Rufus a history of mysticism. The early death of the former in 1905 thwarted this project, but Rufus Jones, in collaboration with William Charles Braithwaite and other Friends, completed the histories according to a modified plan. Yorkshire Quarterly Meeting formed a committee called the *Yorkshire 1905 Committee* to carry on the movement inaugurated by John Wilhelm Rowntree. It was the pioneer of quarterly meeting extension committees.

In 1895 a conference was called at Manchester by the Home Mission Committee with the authorization of the yearly meeting, to consider the problems raised by the liberal movement in general, and particularly the question of the ministry. A number of summer schools were held in England and Ireland, the first one at Scarborough in 1897, for the purpose of popularizing the results of modern Biblical and religious scholarship.

In 1899 John Wilhelm Rowntree published in *Present*

Day Papers a plan for a permanent settlement for religious study which attracted wide attention.[5] The idea found realization in the Woodbrooke Settlement for Religious and Social Study opened in 1903. George Cadbury gave his house and grounds, "Woodbrooke," at Selly Oak near Birmingham for the project. Dr. J. Rendel Harris became its first director of studies and reinforced it by his scholarship and personal piety. The plan was a combination of school and social settlement. It never attracted great numbers of British young Friends, but it became a powerful center of liberal religious influences. It drew students from many other countries, notably Holland, Scandinavia and America. It brought together a group of Quaker or near-Quaker scholars, whose writings and lectures stimulated the revival of Quaker mysticism, sustained the new scholarship, both in Great Britain and Ireland, and furnished a meeting place for young people from various lands and branches of the Society.

In the course of time the original Woodbrooke became the nucleus of a group of schools: Westhill for training Sunday school and home mission workers; Fircroft for working men and Kingsmead for training workers in the foreign mission field. These "Selly Oak Colleges" were affiliated with one another for the exchange of lecturers and courses, and finally coördinated with the University of Birmingham so that credit could be received on work done in them toward university degrees.[6]

In America the liberal movement came as a gradual reaction from the doctrinal extremes and intolerance of Evangelicalism. The Great Revival did not obliterate all traces of Quaker traditions in the revised Society, in spite

---

5 Vol. II (1899) "The Problem of a Free Ministry," September; "A Plan for a Quaker Settlement," December.

6 Religious schools of other denominations have been attracted to the Woodbrooke vicinity so that there are now eight schools in the Selly Oak group.

of the repeated declaration of the evangelists that they "cared more for the Gospel than for Quakerism." There remained the literary heritage of early Quakerism; connections with other kinds of Friends, especially in Great Britain, and the consciousness of other types of Quakerism with whom they had fewer contacts, such as the Philadelphia Orthodox, Conservative and Hicksite yearly meetings; the testimonies for peace, women's ministry, a non-sacerdotal ministry and non-sacramental worship, the equality of men and women in the church; and faith in inward spiritual guidance. The history of the Society from 1881 onwards is an account of a slow reaction toward the original Quaker basis of life and worship. In the post-revival period, however, the Evangelical tendencies went to great extremes of doctrine and intolerance before the reaction set in.

Early in the development of the Revival movement came the Holiness modification of the Evangelical theology. Its acceptance was facilitated by the earlier emphasis on the atonement and the forgiveness of sin as the essence of salvation. A large part of the converts were adults with a strong sense of sin who felt most keenly the need of forgiveness. Afterward, however, many felt the need of spiritual power to save them from a life of sinning. The holiness theology supplied this need in a second experience of sanctification. The chief leader in this movement was David B. Updegraff of Ohio. He insisted upon a definite distinction in Christian doctrine and experience between justification and sanctification. He was an enthusiastic and powerful preacher and he was the chief influence by which the Holiness movement was brought into the Society. In the course of a few years it spread through most of the area affected by the revival movement. It became customary for the Evangelists to call not only for professions of conversion but of sanctification or "the second blessing" also. The yearly meeting statistics of a great many yearly meetings in reporting the results of their evangelistic work recorded not only "conversions" and "accessions" but also "sanctifications." This doctrine found its fullest theological expression in the writings and teachings of William P. Pinkham and Dougan Clark. Their theology was chiefly a popular form of Arminianism which had already been domesticated in the Society during the previous century by the Evangelicals and later by J. J. Gurney. Its special features were adopted chiefly from the Methodists.[7]

The Great Revival marked the culminating stage of Methodist influence on the Quaker movement. In the middle of the eighteenth century the Methodist revival affected Friends profoundly but the new religious interest turned to perfecting the discipline. At the beginning of the nineteenth century the Evangelical theology came into the Society at first chiefly through association with Church of England Evangelicals in educational and philanthropic work and afterward through a group of ministers who were converts from Evangelical Protestant Churches. The Revival was the occasion of further steps in the direction of Methodism, in which its holiness theology, revival methods, type of worship and pastoral ministry were largely incorporated into the polity of "Pastoral Friends."[8]

The Evangelical movement had always a degree of theological intolerance in it, because it connected the Christian life and experience inseparably with the Evangelical doctrines. The Revival was characterized by this dogmatic spirit in an intensified form. The emotional stress of revival preaching was not conducive to the detached attitude which liberal theology demands. The great issues

---

7 In 1884 when Dougan Clark was appointed head of the newly established Biblical Department of Earlham College, he used as a textbook of theology, Fields' *Handbook of Christian Theology,* written by an Australian Methodist. The reference books were mostly Methodist, including Steele on *Perfect Love* with a sprinkling of the writings of such authors as F. B. Myers of the Keswick movement and Dwight L. Moody.

8 Cf. *The Friend* (Phila.), 1871, pp. 119, 120. 1873, pp. 240, 247, 272.

of eternal life and death with which the evangelists dealt were to them too serious for doubt or for tolerance of dissent. About these matters both preacher and hearers must have positive assurance. The Scriptures and their interpreters, the church and its ministers must speak with authority.

In the absence of clear pronouncements in the Bible or satisfactory and incontrovertible *dicta* in Quaker authorities, the evangelists took it upon themselves not only to define sound doctrine but to pronounce judgment on the soundness of fellow ministers and teachers. The disciplines prescribed an official procedure for trying cases of suspected heresy, but the Revival had broken down the discipline and the Revival leaders distrusted many of the elders, who constituted the meetings to which the discipline referred such cases. It was enough for the accepted teachers to pass the word around that such and such a Friend was unsound in doctrine or that his teaching was "tainted with Hicksism." This attitude was one influence which retarded the development of a liberal movement among American Friends.

The Richmond *Declaration of Faith* was the beginning of an attempt to restore official standards of doctrinal soundness. In 1879 Ohio Yearly Meeting had expressly repudiated the doctrine of the Inner Light.

> We do not believe that there is any principle or quality in the soul of man, innate or otherwise, which, even though rightly used, will ever save a single soul; but that it pleased God by the foolishness of preaching to save them that believed; and the Holy Spirit is sent to convince the ungodly of sin, who, upon repentance towards God, and faith in Jesus Christ who died for us, are justified by His blood; and we repudiate the so-called doctrine of the inner light, or the gift of a portion of the Holy Spirit in the soul of every man, as dangerous, unsound, and unscriptural.[9]

---

[9] Cited in Grubb, *Separations,* p. 111.

In 1885 San José Monthly Meeting in California was laid down by Honeycreek Quarter (Iowa) on the ground that "the governing part of that monthly meeting is not sound in the doctrines of the Christian religion." [10] In 1890 Iowa Yearly Meeting revised its Discipline, inserting in it a list of questions for all nominees for ministers and elders to answer. Some of these questions represented crude and extreme theological positions. Taking advantage of these questions Honeycreek Quarter in 1892–93 dealt with Joel and Hannah Bean of San José for alleged unsoundness, and when they did not give satisfactory answers to the questions submitted, they were disowned.[11] These events shocked and alarmed the more conservative Friends not only in Philadelphia and London yearly meetings but also in many of the American Gurneyite yearly meetings.[12]

In 1884 a Biblical Department was established in Earlham College under the direction of Dr. Dougan Clark. He taught an extreme Holiness theology using largely textbooks of Perfectionist Methodist theologians. In 1892 Walter and Emma B. Malone founded the Cleveland Bible Institute which exercised a great influence among Friends since it became the chief distributing center of the "fourfold gospel" type of theology. Together with other Bible training schools of a similar type it promoted a very strong ultra-Evangelical influence in the Society for two decades.[13]

---

10 Mekeel, *Friends and a Creed,* p. 89.

11 Together with other sympathetic Friends they afterward organized the College Park Association of Friends which was the pioneer of a number of independent meetings, chiefly composed of Friends liberal in theology and devoted to "silent" worship in the midst of Evangelical and "pastoral" yearly meetings.

12 Honeycreek Monthly Meeting rescinded its action in 1899 and restored Joel and Hannah Bean to membership.

13 Other similar training schools managed by Friends were the Union Bible Institute, Westfield, Indiana; the Huntington Park Training School, Los Angeles, Cal.; Friends Kansas Central Bible Training School, Haviland, Kan.; Greenleaf Seminary, Greenleaf, Idaho. They were strongly supported by similar institutions not managed by Friends such as the Knapp School, Cincinnati; and the Moody Bible Institute, Chicago.

In 1893 Rufus M. Jones became Professor of Philosophy in Haverford College and editor of *The Friends Review* which the following year was combined with *The Christian Worker* of Chicago and called *The American Friend.* He was ably supported by a group of liberal Friends[14] and proposed to make the new paper the organ not of a party or sect but of a liberal Quakerism. His emphasis was upon the religion of inward experience; upon the realities of the Christian faith rather than any theological formulation of them, and especially upon the first-hand experience of God. The paper was committed to the search for truth without theological limits or sectarian reservations and undertook to promote the cause of Christianity in all its phases.[15] From this time *The American Friend* exercised a quiet and definite liberalizing influence among Friends. In 1897 Rufus Jones visited England and formed a lasting friendship with John Wilhelm Rowntree. He was instrumental in bringing the latter to America in 1898–1900 where he powerfully reinforced the liberal movement, especially by his visits to Quaker colleges and his lectures in the Haverford Summer School.

In 1895 the author was appointed Professor of Biblical Literature at Earlham College to revive the Biblical Department which had suffered a severe set-back through the defection of Dougan Clark. Changes in courses and textbooks were made in accordance with modern scholarship on the one hand and the promotion of vital religious experience on the other. In 1897 the first Earlham Bible Institute was organized largely through the efforts of Allen Jay and Joseph John Mills, then president of Earlham College and the author, who acted as secretary. The Insti-

---

[14] The group included President Isaac Sharpless of Haverford College, James Wood, President James A. Rhoads of Bryn Mawr College, John B. Garrett, Dr. James Carey Thomas and Dr. Richard H. Thomas, both of Baltimore, David Scull, T. Wistar Brown, Joshua L. Baily of Philadelphia.

[15] Jones, *The Trail of Life in the Middle Years,* chap. IV.

tute, lasting about ten days, was held each summer for twelve years with the coöperation of Indiana, Western and Wilmington yearly meetings. The lecturers were leading Friends and liberal scholars and leaders of other denominations. They exercised a liberalizing and at the same time unifying influence which was an important factor in preventing a threatened division in these yearly meetings.

In 1900, as a result of the efforts of Rufus M. Jones, George A. Barton of Bryn Mawr College and Richard H. Thomas of Baltimore, a summer school of religion was held at Haverford College with a staff of lecturers thoroughly committed to the methods and results of Biblical criticism and modern religious thought. This marked an epoch in the attiude of the leaders of the eastern yearly meetings. Succeeding schools were held approximately every two years until these summer schools were merged with summer assemblies which had been held by the progressive leaders of the Hicksite Friends at George School. They contributed materially to the formation of a common type of thought among the leaders of both branches in the East. The last of these schools was held at Haverford, 1923.

Period III

Quakerism after the First World War
1914-1941

CHAPTER 37

FRIENDS RELIEF AND RECONSTRUCTION WORK[1]

IN MANY important respects the First World War marks the beginning of a new period in the history of the Society of Friends both in England and America. The war found some Friends hesitant in their attitude toward it and the issues which it raised and the traditional Quaker testimony against all war held the loyalty of members with varying degrees of power.

With regard to participation in the war, three distinct groups emerged. One adhered from conviction to the historic Quaker opposition to all war as incompatible with their Christian discipleship. From this group many young Friends went before the English tribunals and to the American cantonments as conscientious objectors. Some of these refused to accept any imposed alternative to military service. Others of them felt free to accept a variety of alternative services of a beneficent character. A second group retained their opposition to war generally, but felt that an

[1] For fuller accounts of this work see Fry, *A Quaker Adventure;* Jones, R. M., *A Service of Love in Wartime;* Graham, *Conscription and Conscience;* Jones, M. H., *Swords Into Ploughshares;* and Jones, Lester M., *Quakers in Action.*

exception should be made of this particular war, because of the moral issues involved and the "righteous" aims of the Allied nations. Many of them were led to support the war under the belief that it was "a war to end war" and afforded the only practicable way to make sure of the triumph of peace, justice and democracy. Both these groups were agreed that the Society should not change its corporate attitude toward war; and thanks to the intense convictions and spiritual leadership of the first group, and the acquiescence of the second, all the Society's official pronouncements reaffirmed the historic testimony of Friends against war.[2]

The third group frankly renounced the pacifist tradition. This group was strongest among Hicksite Friends, because of their greater individualism and their previous tolerant attitude toward their members who took part in the War between the States, and in some parts of the Five Years Meeting where new elements brought in during the Great Revival had not been thoroughly indoctrinated with Friends' peace principles. The second and third groups created no serious disciplinary problems in America, such as arose at the close of the War between the States. Their meetings generally respected their patriotism and sincerity, and allowed them to remain in membership unless they voluntarily resigned.

The problems created by this World War were faced by English Friends for three years before America entered it. An influential section took the absolutist pacifist position and so maintained the testimony of the Society. The Meeting for Sufferings promptly issued a clear statement to the world of the Society's religious peace position which attracted wide attention.[3] Friends aided in the struggle to maintain freedom of speech and the press. During the war

---

2 In America Swarthmore was the only one of the colleges under Quaker control to allow a students army training corps to be established in it.

3 Graham, *Conscription and Conscience*, pp. 115, 156.

the Friends' premises at Devonshire House were often the only place available for liberal and pacifist meetings. A number of official or semi-official committees and other organizations were formed to give expression to the positive elements of Quaker pacifism or to care for its pacifist members. Friends Emergency Committee undertook to help those enemy aliens who were interned or imprisoned in Great Britain, and their distressed dependents.[4]

In the early days of the war the Fellowship of Reconciliation was organized in England to provide social and religious support for pacifists on religious grounds in all churches. Dr. Henry T. Hodgkin and other Friends were among the pioneers in the organization. Later it spread to America and was of great value in giving support to Christian pacifists who were ostracized or driven from their churches.

A group of young Friends who wanted to give their services in the care of the wounded in the field without enlisting in the army, formed the Friends Ambulance Unit which served throughout the war. The unit was organized by Philip J. Noel Baker and his friends, and the buildings at Jordans were used as a training center. It was never officially sponsored by the Society, being managed by an independent council of Friends. Not all members were Friends but the coming of conscription limited its enrolment to conscientious objectors. Its assistance was accepted and valued by the Belgian, French, and later the British military authorities.

> Hospitals were set up, hundreds of motor ambulances brought over and dressing stations manned at the front. . . . The first expedition consisted of 43 men and eight cars. At the end there were 600 men working abroad and £138,000 were spent. The Unit ran a dozen hospitals, made 27,000

[4] See Fry, *A Quaker Adventure*, pp. 300, 301. The Friends Emergency Committee was merged with the War Victims Relief Committee in 1919 under the name, Friends Emergency and War Victims Relief Committee.

inoculations against typhoid in Belgium, fed and clothed refugees and began lacemaking and other industries. It distributed milk and purified water, and managed three recreation huts at Dunkirk. It carried 33,000 men home in its two hospital ships; the motor convoys carried over 260,000 sick and wounded; and the four ambulance trains ever moving behind the British lines conveyed over half a million patients. It was all done voluntarily without pay.[5]

When the draft acts were passed in 1916, Parliament made provision for the exemption of conscientious objectors to military service, but the administration of the acts was put in charge of local tribunals in which prejudice and the influence of the military representative were strong and whose membership was selected with little or no regard for judicial ability. They nullified the government's intention to give absolute exemption to men who could not conscientiously accept conditions from the state for non-participation in war. Nearly all of these, and many others who would have accepted civilian alternative work, were refused the exemption to which they were entitled and when handed over to the army were imprisoned for disobedience to military orders. Some six thousand men were imprisoned, about fifteen hundred of them repeatedly for repeated refusals to perform military service.[6]

The total number of members or attenders at meetings of the Society of Friends of whose imprisonment particulars are known was 279. Of these 142 were Absolutists. . . .The relative smallness of the number of Quaker objectors is partly due to the smallness of the total number of the Society, to the fact that they were better treated by the Tribunals, that many of them before conscription came in had entered upon relief work abroad, and that 32% of the available young men in the Society entered the Forces.[7]

---

5 Graham, *op. cit.*, pp. 158–159. For a full account see Tatham and Miles, *History of the Friends Ambulance Unit.*

6 See Graham, *op. cit.*, p. 352.

7 *Ibid.*, p. 348.

Friends acted in support of their conscientious objectors in prison through the Service Committee and gave substantial support to the No Conscription Fellowship, the national body which stood by conscientious objectors of all persuasions, most of whom had no other corporate encouragement.

In the autumn of 1914 the Meeting for Sufferings set up the War Victims Relief Committee to organize and direct work abroad on behalf of refugees and other civilian victims of the war. When, over a year later, conscription was enforced, it was able by the scale of its operations, chiefly in France at that time, to provide service for a large number of young Friends and other pacifists. This development was destined to have a very important influence on the spirit and organization of the Society and to lead to worldwide services of constructive Christian love.

A regulation issued by the government in 1917 provided for a censorship of all publications dealing with the war or the making of peace. The Meeting for Sufferings informed the government and the press that it would not relinquish its right and duty to publish the truth without submission to the censor. Three officers of the Friends Service Committee were prosecuted for publishing "A Challenge to Militarism." The chairman, Harrison Barrow, a Birmingham City Councillor, and Arthur Watts, joint-secretary, were sentenced to six months imprisonment. The other joint-secretary, Edith Ellis, was fined £100 and 50 guineas costs and was imprisoned three months for refusing payment.

When the Germans invaded Belgium in 1914 a great number of Belgian refugees escaped into Holland, where the Dutch government cared for them as best it could, although of necessity its provision for the one-half million uninvited guests had to be meager. English Friends through the War Victims Relief undertook to assist in providing more fully for the wants and in alleviating the condition of the destitute Belgian refugees. They also assisted in removing some of these refugees to England where they could be better cared for; and at the close of the war they aided in the repatriation of many of them until the Belgian government could assume the full responsibility for them.[8]

The care of refugees in France and the reconstruction of devastated areas was begun under the War Victims Relief in all the main lines along which the work was carried on during and after the war both by the English and American Friends. The Quaker red and black double star already used in the Franco-Prussian War in 1871 was adopted as a symbol of the work.[9]

When America entered the War, Friends had been somewhat prepared to face the decisions which it necessitated, by the experiences of their British co-religionists. On the other hand, the American government adopted a selective draft at the beginning of hostilities so that American Friends had to face the problems of compulsory military service at once. Some few suffered mistreatment in the cantonments, although there was little persecution of Quaker conscientious objectors in the United States compared to what English Friends suffered. Only thirteen American Friends were sentenced to military prisons. It was the convinced pacifists who took the lead in the financing and management of the work of the American Friends Service Committee and supplied most of the personnel of its workers. The fact that they continued to volunteer for such service after the war closed removed to a large extent from the public mind the suspicion that young men Friends took the attitude of conscientious objectors because they were slackers or draft-dodgers.

It is impossible to secure full or accurate statistics to show in what proportions American Friends of the various

---

8 Fry, *op. cit.*, chaps. XIII–XV.

9 *Ibid.*, p. xv.

branches assumed the attitudes mentioned above. The best information obtainable for the Five Years Meeting and Ohio Yearly Meeting (O) indicated that a large number of Friends ministers sanctioned and supported the war, as did a large proportion of the membership. In some cases meetings purchased Liberty Bonds. The volume of money contributed by "Pastoral" Friends to the Red Cross, Y.M.C.A., and similar "drives" was apparently (no statistics are available) much in excess of that contributed by them to the American Friends Service Committee. The yearly meetings belonging to the Five Years Meeting comprise in their membership about three-fourths of the Friends in America. Up to the beginning of 1919, there was contributed to the work of the American Friends Service Committee from all sources $909,731.33. Most of this came from Friends, the membership of the Five Years Meeting furnishing $130,-326.78, or a little less than 15% of the total.[10]

The total number of American Friends, men and women, in reconstruction service (to January 1, 1919), was 251. To these should be added about fifty furloughed by the draft boards for farm work. There is no means of knowing how many served in the army, the Y.M.C.A. or under the Red Cross. In many cases young Friends known to have conscientious scruples against war were given deferred classification or exempted for farm work by their draft boards. For these reasons it is difficult to estimate the number of young Friends who took the full C.O. position.

[10] Full statistics are lacking as to the attitude of the young Friends of the Five Years' Meeting and Ohio (O) toward military service. An attempt to secure statistics from the monthly meetings brought replies from meetings representing only about 27% of the membership. *Conclusions drawn from them must be taken with reserve.* Nevertheless, the general showing cannot be ignored. These reports would indicate (*if the proportions hold for the meetings not reporting,* which is not at all certain) that of the young men drafted or liable to the draft possibly 350 stood against any service under military direction as straight out C.O.'s; about 600 accepted some form of non-combatant service, and about 2300 went into combatant service.

The "non-pastoral" yearly meetings and the students and alumni of Quaker schools furnished a larger proportion of C.O.'s than other groups. The Young Friends movement and the Quaker academies and colleges (along with other influences) had at the outbreak of the war produced a group of young Friends who held the Society's peace principles from conviction as well as tradition.

The organization of the American Friends Service Committee in 1917 followed shortly after the United States entered the World War. Its activities and influence proved to be epoch-making in the history of American Quakerism. It was composed at first of members of Philadelphia (O), the Hicksite Yearly Meetings and the Five Years Meeting. Later it came to include official representatives from practically all the American yearly meetings. It devoted itself to care of the Quaker C.O.'s in the cantonments, to gathering funds and clothing for the work in France and to training the workers for service abroad when at last the government defined non-combatant service which conscientious objectors might undertake and allowed the Quaker contingents to be furloughed for service in France under the civilian American Red Cross.

During the summer of 1917 a group of one hundred Quaker young men, who took the conscientious objector attitude, underwent training at Haverford College under the auspices of the American Friends Service Committee, as the first unit for reconstruction and relief work in France. Rufus M. Jones was made chairman of the committee and except for a short interval, he has held that position since. The success of the committee has been largely due to his devotion, energy and spiritual vision. The three secretaries of the committee, who furnished the indispensable executive ability and personal enthusiasm, were Vincent D. Nicholson, Wilbur K. Thomas and Clarence E. Pickett.

The relief and reconstruction work of the committee was

accomplished in spite of the great difficulties of securing permits and transportation in wartime France with which the project was confronted and it was carried out in coöperation with English Friends War Victims Relief Committee which was already at work in France. Their experience and organization were invaluable for the new American workers and soon the two "adventures" were united.[11] The workers were distributed to the various centers and each group, or *equipe,* was largely self-directing. The work was mostly hard and monotonous and accommodations and food were primitive and often inadequate. On the whole the workers maintained a fine devo- ı and coöperation. The joint enterprise contributed greatly to a spirit of understanding fellowship between various groups of American Friends as well as between the American and British workers.[12] A. Ruth Fry summarizes the adventure thus:

> Beginning with a party of thirty-three pioneers who went out, animated with a deep desire to help, but inevitably uncertain how that help could best be given, this organization developed beyond expectation. In 1918-19 there were more than five hundred English and Am[illegible]ican men and women, trained and untrained, in as many as forty-five centres, ministering to the extraordinarily varied needs of a population who had lost practically everything by war, and were endeavoring to piece together their broken lives. Before they left, this group of volunteers was providing houses, food, clothing, furniture, agricultural implements and agricultural work; small stock, such as sheep, goats, poultry, rabbits, bees, as well as medical care of the civil population, both in their homes and in institutions.

---

11 The central offices were at 20 South Twelfth Street, Philadelphia; Devonshire House, London; and the Hotel Britannique, 20 Avenue Victoria, Paris. A list of the various *equipes* is given in Jones, *A Service of Love in Wartime,* pp. 283, 284, and complete lists of the English and American workers are given in Ap. A; and the names of the English workers are in the Appendix to Fry, *op. cit.*

12 Fry, *op. cit.,* pp. 141–143. Jones, *op. cit.,* pp. 77, 78.

In order to accomplish this, they had also to have an elaborate organization for equipping the workers. These had to be fed, clothed and housed, so that there was a sort of republic on communal lines established, where all the ordinary needs of daily life were provided in return for voluntary service. For it must be remembered that both workers and inhabitants were living in a country denuded of the ordinary conveniences of civilization. In particular, transport was almost lacking and a fleet of motor-cars had to deal with the movements of workers and the goods for reconstruction.[13]

The work of relief and reconstruction which the Quaker units accomplished during the war years in France was of a very great variety. A maternity hospital was established at Châlons-sur-Marne which was of incalculable value to the refugees and local population. At the close of the war it was rebuilt. endowed and left as a permanent memory of the service. Sawmills were established at Dôle in the Vôsges mountains and at Ornans for producing lumber to build two-room demountable houses for the temporary housing of the inhabitants in the ruined villages. Since the French government promised to rebuild these villages, the peasantry were reluctant to allow the sites of their ruined homes to be cleared off until the damages were assessed, so it was usually necessary to set up the temporary houses in open spaces near the villages, or on cleared spots on the city lots. The units provided bedding, clothes and furniture for the refugees and for repatriated prisoners and exiles from the occupied territory and coming home through Switzerland. Homes were provided for refugee children as well as schools and recreation. The hospitals and medical service provided were of extraordinary value; the units found it necessary to supply agricultural tools, seeds, and plant trees to enable the returning peasantry to cultivate their fields and become self-supporting at the earliest possible moment.

---

[13] Fry. *op. cit.,* pp. 1, 2.

The work accomplished falls into four main divisions, which must be dealt with separately: Building, Agricultural, Medical, and Relief, a term which covers a multitude of activities, and which, as the most general, shall be treated first. It was carried out principally in the Departments of Somme, Aisne, Ardennes, Marne, Meuse and Aube, with lesser activities in Paris, Calvados, Seine-et-Marne, Meurthe-et-Moselle, Jura, Doubs and Haute Savoie, though this does not exhaust the list of districts where help was given. Five hundred and eighty-eight English and five hundred and seventy American workers took part in it, of whom eight died whilst serving in France. It lasted from November, 1914 to May, 1920. The money spent on it is practically impossible to compute; it included £392,357 1s. 7d. received in London, $2,057,985 received in America, besides very large grants from the American Red Cross (including goods to the amount of one million francs). Further, large gifts of clothing were received and forwarded by the London and Philadelphia committees, and in ways far too numerous to mention our workers administered the funds of other societies and of the French Government, so that a rough guess might put the total amount administered by the Mission as nearly one million pounds.[14]

In the work in France the American Friends Service Committee had the coöperation of the Menonites of the Old Order in America and of some members of the Church of the Brethren. Nearly sixty of their young people served under the Service Committee and they contributed more than two hundred thousand dollars to the work.

The effects of the work of the American Friends Service Committee were felt at home as well as in France. It enlisted Friends of all branches in the work. Local committees and sewing societies were organized in almost all the meetings in America which contributed to the support of the work. The storeroom in Philadelphia received and distributed knit goods, second-hand clothing, and new mate-

---

[14] Fry, *op. cit.*, pp. 1, 2.

rials at an average rate of 50 packages and 3,200 garments per week.[15]

In January, 1919, Friends were given the task of the rehabilitation of the Verdun area. In addition to the former departments of work coöperative stores were organized which furnished the returning peasants with tools, furniture and livestock. The sales up to July, 1919, amounted to more than 800,000 francs. Friends bought several military "dumps" of all sorts of material and supplies, which the American army in France no longer needed. They not only secured from them cheaply needed materials for the work of reconstruction, but from the sale of these materials elsewhere were able to add to the capital relief funds.[16] After the armistice the labor of some six hundred German prisoners of war, whose release was long delayed, was put at the disposal of Friends by the French army. Working beside Friends many of these depressed, homesick men found new encouragement. Friends were not allowed to pay them wages, but such compulsory labor was contrary to Quaker principles. Besides feeding them, they kept careful account of their labors. Three of the relief workers were sent to Germany as soon as it was accessible and spent the winter of 1919–20 distributing wages, photographs and messages to the families of the prisoners scattered over Germany.[17]

After the armistice, the relief and reconstruction in Europe was greatly extended. The French government finally took over the work of reconstruction and the care of its war victims in northern France, but English and American Friends extended their work into other war-ravaged countries. The post-war settlement dismembered the Austrian Empire leaving German Austria a poverty-stricken remnant, with one-third of its population in

15 Jones, *A Service of Love in War Time,* p. 81.
16 *Ibid.,* pp. 231–234.
17 *Ibid.,* pp. 234, 235.

Vienna, cut off by nationalistic hate and customs-barriers from Hungary, Yugoslavia and Czechoslavia from which the capital had in times past drawn its chief food supplies. Friends established a center in Vienna and did a valuable work in feeding students and destitute members of the middle class and in promoting projects for better housing. An important work was done in assisting Serbian refugees who had fled to the Adriatic from the first Austrian drive (1915). Their lot was relieved during their exile in Corsica and Corfu and later help was given at the time of their repatriation. In Poland the Quaker units helped stamp out the typhus plague, fed destitute peasants who were cut off from Russia by the post-war settlement and provided work-animals, seed and food in the resettling of refugees on the land. Two members of the mission died from typhus fever.

In the German and Austrian drive of 1915 great numbers of Poles and Russians were driven out of Bessarabia and White Russia, many of whom settled in the lower Volga Valley. Friends began relief among these refugees in Russia in 1916. During the years 1921–1922 a terrible drought ruined the harvest in the Volga basin which produced accute famine. The war had seriously impaired the railroad systems of Russia so that it was very difficult to get food stuffs into the region even where they were available. Friends undertook relief work among the refugees in Samara province and afterwards opened a center in Moscow which also had suffered from a serious food shortage. When the American Relief Administration was organized under the direction of Herbert Hoover, Friends workers in Russia assisted it in the distribution of food, but in spite of the utmost endeavors of this and other relief organizations in England and of the League of Nations, it is estimated that at least two million people died of starvation and diseases of undernourishment in the Volga basin. Here again many of the workers contracted typhus fever from which two of them died. Anti-malaria work extended under Friends care into Siberia as late as 1923. Friends continued the work in Russia with Moscow as a center, especially for the restocking of the peasants' farms and the care of orphan children until the Soviet government relieved them of further opportunities.

During the First World War when the Allies occupied Salonika, some of the French African troops brought the germs of black malaria to that area. This spread with fatal results to the Greek settlers who subsequently came from Asia Minor in the exchange of populations between Turkey and Greece. Friends established a center at Salonika for the work of malaria prevention in the old Turkish villages and the new settlements of surrounding areas, which was carried on in coöperation with the Near East Relief and the League of Nations.[18]

At the close of the war the German civilian population was seriously undernourished because the chief food supplies had been reserved for the army. By the terms of the Armistice the Germans were to be allowed to import food while the peace treaty was being negotiated, but the French government, in spite of the efforts of Herbert Hoover, prevented the admission of food stuffs for seven months.[19] After the signing of the Treaty of Versailles, Friends, who went to Germany to examine conditions, discovered that a whole generation of German children were suffering from undernourishment. With the assistance of Herbert Hoover and the American Red Cross, and later with the moral backing of General Allen of the American Army of Occupation, Friends undertook to supervise a child-feeding program in Germany. The funds were largely supplied by the German government, the American government, the Save the Children Fund, and American citizens of German

---

[18] In 1936 Harry and Rebecca Timbres undertook anti-malaria work under the Soviet government in the Marieskii Republic with the encouragement of the A.F.S.C. See Timbres, *We Didn't Ask Utopia.*

[19] See Brooks, *America and Germany,* chaps. II, III.

ancestry. The Friends undertook to provide the cost of administration so that all contributions were delivered in Germany without diminution. During the years 1920–1921 between one and two million German children received supplementary feeding and medical supplies which saved them from rickets, tuberculosis and other diseases of under-nourishment. All together there was expended under the English and American Friends organizations some twenty million dollars in the German child-feeding.

As these pressing emergencies in Europe passed away Friends turned their attention to other services. In 1925 the American Friends Service Committee was reorganized and its work continued under four definite sections: (1) The European section to continue coöperation with English Friends and keep up the European contacts and goodwill centers; (2) The Interracial Service Section; (3) The Peace Section and (4) The Home Service Section for relief and rehabilitation work in the United States. The Committee has done rehabilitation work among the striking and unemployed miners in Pennsylvania and West Virginia, has organized Summer Peace Caravans and Institutes of International Relations and promoted the Emergency Peace Campaign in 1936–1937.

In England the War Victims' Relief Committee was dissolved in 1923 and the winding up of its work was left to the Council for International Service, which had been set up by London Yearly Meeting in 1919 to carry on the spiritual work of Friends on the continent of Europe. In 1927 this Council was merged with the Friends Foreign Mission Association in a new body, the Friends Service Council, which since then has had charge of the missionary and international work of English and Irish Friends overseas. In collaboration with the American Friends Service Committee they have maintained international centers and goodwill embassies in many parts of the world.

In the course of the Civil War in Spain 1935–1939

appeals were made to Friends to organize relief for children and refugees on both sides of the conflict. The American Friends Service Committee and the Friends Service Council carried on the distribution of this relief by funds contributed mostly by non-Friends; and later they extended their care to Spanish refugees in southern France in collaboration with the International Commission for Refugees.

After the Jewish "purge" in Germany in 1933 and the conquest of Poland in 1939, the American Friends Service Committee got permission to distribute aid to the victims of these atrocities without distinction of nationality, race, or religion. After the conquest of Austria the Vienna Center and the office of the Friends Service Council in London were particularly active in enabling persecuted Austrian Jews and intellectuals to migrate to friendly countries. The centers in Berlin, Paris and Vienna remained open and active after the beginning of the Nazi conquests until 1941.

When the Low Countries and France were overrun by the German armies in 1940, Premier Reynaud of France appealed to the Service Committee for aid in caring for the millions of Dutch, Belgian and French refugees in unoccupied France. In coöperation with the American Red Cross, the Service Committee has carried on this work as far as possible under the handicaps of lack of shipping and difficulties of foreign exchange.

As a result of the foreign services of Friends during and after the First World War a number of new yearly meetings have sprung up in various countries and small groups already in existence have been greatly strengthened. In consequence of these services and the foreign missionary work of American and British Friends, there are now yearly meetings or groups of Friends or international centers in the following countries: Alaska, Belgian Congo, Bolivia, China, Cuba, Denmark, France, Germany, Guatemala,

Holland, Honduras, India, Jamaica, Japan, Kenya, Madagascar, Mexico, Norway, Palestine, Pemba and Syria. A table showing the distribution and membership of the Society throughout the world in 1940 is appended.

ESTIMATED NUMBER OF FRIENDS IN WORLD 1940 [20]

Great Britain and Ireland		
London Yearly Meeting	19,673	
Dublin Yearly Meeting	2,044	
Fritchley General Meeting	60	
Scotland, General Meeting for Scotland (1935)	347	
		22,124
North America [21]		
Alaska (Quarterly Meeting)	1,727	
Baltimore (FYM)	1,162	
Baltimore (GC)	2,166	
California (FYM)	6,038	
Canada (FYM)	723	
Canada (C)	160	
Genesee (GC)	389	
Western Canada (Ind.)	41	
College Park Association (Ind.)	75	
Illinois (GC)	350	
Indiana (FYM)	15,860	
Indiana (GC)	575	
Iowa (FYM)	7,802	
Iowa (C)	950	
Kansas (Ind.)	8,903	
Nebraska (FYM)	2,235	
New England (FYM)	3,335	
New England (C)	113	
New York (FYM)	3,673	
New York (GC)	2,789	
North Carolina (FYM)	11,799	
North Carolina (C)	500	
Ohio (Ind.)	6,160	
Ohio (C)	1,200	

[20] Statistics taken from the *Handbook of the Religious Society of Friends, 1941*.

[21] FYM, Five Years Meeting; GC, General Conference (H); C, Conservative; Ind., Independent.

Ohio (GC)	22	
Oregon (Ind.)	3,252	
Pacific Coast Association[22]		
Philadelphia-Arch St. (Ind.)	4,865	
Philadelphia-Race St. (GC)	10,712	
Western (FYM)	12,618	
Western (C)	175	
Wilmington (FYM)	5,145	
New and United Meetings[23]	576	
		116,090
Other American Countries		
Bolivia (no report)		
Cuba (Yearly Meeting)	483	
Guatemala (Annual Conference)	4,340	
Honduras (Annual Conference)	1,068	
Jamaica (Yearly Meeting)	1,097	
Mexico (Annual Conference)	184	
		7,172
Europe		
Denmark (Yearly Meeting)	35	
Holland (Netherlands Yearly Meeting)	60	
France (Yearly Meeting of Friends in France)	115	
Germany (German Yearly Meeting)	273	
Norway (Yearly Meeting)	80	
Sweden (Yearly Meeting)	38	
Switzerland (General Meeting)	26	
		627
Asia		
China: (Eastern Group)	837	
China: (West Szechwan Yearly Meeting)	400	
India: (Mid-India Yearly Meeting)	201	
Japan Yearly Meeting	750	
Palestine and Syria Yearly Meeting	150	
		2,338

[22] The Pacific Coast Association membership overlaps that of other bodies.

[23] The membership of the independent and united particular meetings overlaps in part that of other bodies. Their total membership is reported as 576, exclusive of those belonging also to other bodies.

Africa		
Kenya (Eastern Group)	7,500	
Madagascar (Imerina Sakalava Yearly Meeting)	6,700	
Pemba (Half-Yearly Meeting)	100	
South Africa (General Meeting for South Africa)	128	
		14,428
Other Countries and Colonial Dependencies		
Australia (General Meeting)	633	
New Zealand (General Meeting)	299	
		932
Total		25,497
Grand total for the world		163,135

CHAPTER 38

THE PROBLEM OF UNITY IN THE SOCIETY OF FRIENDS

EARLY in the twentieth century there appeared signs of growing unity between the various divisions of the Society of Friends in America. The historic lines of division between Orthodox, Hicksite and Conservative Friends no longer corresponded to real differences in the Society. Wide-open doors for service appeared in the modern world, which Friends could enter effectively only as a united Society, and American Friends found it impossible to explain satisfactorily to new groups of Friends in Europe and other parts of the world why they remained divided. The First World War created common problems and common opportunities for service for all branches of the Society which greatly quickened the consciousness of unity. Changing conditions made the problem of unity easier. A hundred years after the separation of 1827 the process of reunion was well under way. Friends were influenced by the growing spirit of Christian unity in the church at large; and the issues which resulted in the separation of 1827–1928 were dead issues. The struggle for democracy in the Society had been won. The elders, so far from oppressing anyone, had come to be mere figureheads in most meetings. In the "pastoral" yearly meetings the chief power had passed into the hands of the ministers. The young Friends no longer had a grievance and in all but a few yearly meetings, country Friends predominated in the membership and had the controlling voice in the meeting, if they chose to exercise it. The theology of Elias Hicks was never endorsed even by the branch of the Society that is called by his name. There was practically none among those who called themselves Friends who would find in Elias Hicks' system of theology an adequate statement of his religious beliefs. On the other hand, no Orthodox bodies would accept the declaration adopted by the Philadelphia Meeting for Sufferings in 1823 as a sufficient statement of their doctrinal beliefs. A comparison of this statement with those of the new disciplines of London and Philadelphia yearly meetings or even with the Richmond Declaration of Faith (1887) shows how thoroughly the theologies of the original controversy had been outgrown. The issues of the later separations were almost equally obsolete.

The historical divisions in American Quakerism no longer corresponded to the vital differences in the Society. In most of the communities where members of two branches had lived side by side since the separations, one could not tell with any certainty the position of a Friend on any live Quaker issue by noting the meeting which he attended, especially if the young folks had attended the same schools. The real differences were between "pastoral" and "non-pastoral" Friends, between theological conservatives and liberals, and between socially progressive and socially conservative Friends.[1]

As for theology there were "fundamentalists" and

[1] At first glance one might believe that the division between "pastoral" and "non-pastoral" does correspond to the old divisions; that the "Gurneyite" or Five Years Meeting yearly meetings are pastoral and that the Conservative "Wilburite" and Hicksite are non-pastoral. But the Philadelphia Orthodox is most closely associated with the Hicksite yearly meetings. New York (O) is officially pastoral, but Twentieth Street Meeting in New York City and Croton Valley meeting are non-pastoral. Baltimore Yearly Meeting (O) is officially non-pastoral, but several of its meetings have pastors. There are many members of the Five Years Meeting scattered over the country who are by preference non-pastoral and the Young Friends Movement in that body has been accused of leaning that way. Most of the "independent" meetings are non-pastoral. On the other hand, there are Hicksite Friends who are frankly pastoral in their preferences and several of their meetings have secretaries whose functions are hardly distinguishable from those of many pastors.

"modernists" among Friends as in other denominations and, as with them, the line of division between them cut right across the historic divisions; and moreover, as in other denominations, the fundamentalists or liberals in different branches were closer to each other theologically than were the conservatives and liberals within the same branch. The same was true of attitudes toward the social applications of Christianity. A Friend's attitude toward war, industrial democracy, interracial relations or any such social problem was not indicated by the "branch" to which he belonged.

There were other conditions that augured well for the prospect of reunion. Young Friends of the present generation in all branches receive practically the same general education, whether in the public schools or in Friends' schools. They have the same modern outlook on life, talk the same religious language and are interested in the same problems. Through the study of Friends' history they have recovered much of the undivided Quaker heritage.

In England Friends holding to the diverse tendencies, which led to separation in America, had remained together within one yearly meeting. They knew from experience how possible it is for different groups to remain in one organization and to work and worship together. English visitors in recent years found points of sympathetic contact in more than one American branch and refused to be limited by division fences. Young English Friends, in particular, were the means of bringing about joint meetings of American young Friends from different branches and thus exerted a strong influence toward mutual acquaintance and coöperation.

In 1910 the first Young Friends' Conference in America was held at Winona Lake, Indiana. Afterwards it was transferred to Cedar Lake, Indiana, and then to Earlham College. From the outset it was comprehensive. Young Friends from Ohio Yearly Meeting (O) as well as from all types and sections of the Five Years Meeting were included; English and Philadelphia (O) young Friends were invited; and at last Hicksite young Friends were welcomed. Emphasis was put from the start on the study of Quaker history and principles, on spiritual life and experience, and on a wide range of practical activities. The conference was a great force in deepening Quaker loyalty and promoting mutual understanding and coöperation in American Quakerdom.

Under these favoring conditions an actual unity of spirit and organization came into being among American Friends and between Friends on both sides of the Atlantic. Common study, work and worship enabled them to understand one another and to adjust themselves to one another's ideas and methods. The forms of association and coöperation that developed may be grouped under four heads, although they are not separated by any hard and fast lines and they were more or less contemporaneous in their development. There was, first, the unofficial association of members of the different branches in study and work—at tea meetings, in joint lectureships, pilgrimages, Quaker "tramps," summer camps and summer schools. Some of the summer schools were at first simply attended by members of both branches, but afterwards they were jointly managed. Such were the Haverford summer school, the summer schools held at Swarthmore College and at George School; the summer terms of Woolman School; the Young Friends' Conference held first at Winona Lake, and later at various places including Oskaloosa, Iowa; the Eastern Young Friends' Conference held at Westtown, George School and Guilford College; and such joint enterprises as the Whittier Guest House and Woolman School. The Whittier Guest House (1911–1914) at Hampton Falls, N. H., the Haverford Graduate School and Westtown School have all served in some measure as Quaker melting pots, although the latter was only recently opened to the children of Hicksite Friends.[2]

[2] See below, p. 535. Westtown School began to admit a limited number of children who were not members of the Society in 1921. *The Friend,* XCIV, 481.

The second group included joint celebrations, mostly official, of centennials or other notable anniversaries of Quaker meetings or meeting-houses. These began with the joint celebration in 1895 of the two hundredth anniversary of the establishment of New York Yearly Meeting. The centennial celebrations of the setting up of Ohio (1912) and Indiana (1921) yearly meetings were less notably joint occasions; but the observance of the two hundred fiftieth anniversary of Baltimore Yearly Meeting (1922) was in spirit very thoroughly a family reunion. Among the individual meetings that celebrated centennials jointly are Waynesville, Ohio, Whitewater, Ind., Goose Creek, Va., Sandy Spring, Md., and Wilmington, Del. The many joint celebrations of the bicentennial of the birth of John Woolman in 1920 and of the tercentennial of the birth of George Fox in 1924 served the same end.

The third class included the coöperation, mostly official, of Friends of different "branches" in peace and relief work. The Associated Executive Committee on Indian Affairs has united the work of Philadelphia (O), Ohio (O) and some of the yearly meetings that now constitute the Five Years Meeting on behalf of the Indians of the old Indian Territory since the days of President Grant's Quaker Indian agencies. A joint Friends Peace Conference was held in Philadelphia in 1901. The two New York yearly meetings had a joint peace committee before the outbreak of the First World War. This joint committee had been enlarged to include fourteen yearly meetings of different branches by 1915, and in that year it sponsored a Friends Peace Conference at Winona Lake, Ind. The two Philadelphia Yearly Meetings have had a joint peace committee since 1917 and their committees on the social order have coöperated closely in their work. The London All-Friends' Conference (1920) and the Young Friends' Conference at Old Jordans the same year gathered Friends from all parts of the world to reconsider Friends' peace testimony in the light of the First World War.

The greatest of these coöperating agencies for peace and relief work has been the American Friends Service Committee. Not only did it draw practically all branches into coöperation in work of reconstruction and relief in post-war Europe, but it brought young Friends from all groups into association with one another on a new basis.

Coöperation was gradually extended to include official recognition and united effort in the regular activities of the Society. The two New York Yearly Meetings have a joint committee on closer coöperation. In 1917 they held a joint session to receive and consider the report of their joint peace committee. In 1924 they held three yearly meeting sessions jointly in celebration of the tercentenary of the birth of George Fox and they held an entire yearly meeting together in 1928 as a gesture of reconciliation and regret for what happened in 1828.

Since the separation of 1827 the question of official correspondence has been regarded as crucial. To exchange epistles with a yearly meeting was to recognize it as sound in doctrine, correct in its action, and a genuine member of the true Society of Friends. In 1921 London Yearly Meeting abandoned its ancient discrimination between recognized and unrecognized yearly meetings in America and addressed one epistle "to all who bear the name of Friends." Gradually epistles came to be exchanged on occasion between particular Hicksite and Orthodox yearly meetings, and Philadelphia (O) began to exchange occasional epistles not only with the Conservative and Orthodox yearly meetings but with the Hicksite also. This general resumption of the practice of correspondence was helped by the new and struggling yearly meetings, which have been the fruit of Friends missionary and relief work. They began sending epistles to those who bear the name of Friends regardless of the ancient divisions, and thus added to the common interests of all groups.

In the two New York yearly meetings there is a joint organization of Young Friends which reports to both yearly meetings and a similar organization in Baltimore, has a secretary supported by appropriations from the treasuries of both yearly meetings.

In 1926 Philadelphia Yearly Meeting (O), took action to recognize the Hicksite Yearly Meeting as a yearly meeting of Friends by receiving members from them by certificate and opening Westtown School to their children. This action was heartily reciprocated by the Hicksite Yearly Meeting, so that their relations are now much the same as those between any two "independent" yearly meetings of the same branch, such as Ohio and Kansas (O). As far as official relations are concerned the policy of recognition and coöperation is now accepted "in principle" by the three yearly meetings—New York, Philadelphia and Baltimore—in which the first separations occurred and the only ones in which there are considerable numbers of both branches. In recent years the branches of each of these yearly meetings have regularly held some of their annual sessions jointly.

To the fourth group belong those cases where meetings of different branches have begun to worship together again. At Hopewell, Va., the Orthodox and Hicksite meetings worshipped in the same house on opposite sides of the closed partition for almost a century. Then the meeting-house had to be repaired, and the partition was left out. The meetings at Pelham, Canada, Waynesville, Ohio, Chester, Concordville and Birmingham, Pa., were among the earliest to unite in their worship. At Wilmington, Del., the mid-week meetings only were at first held together. At Sandy Spring, Md., the two branches met together every other week; at Woodbury, N. J., once a month. At London Grove, Pa., and Moorestown, N. J., the Friends' Schools were consolidated under one management.[3] In several places the First-day schools were united, and in many other

[3] The Moorestown schools were united in 1920. The activities of the two meetings are all carried on jointly except the meetings for worship and business. There are occasional joint monthly meetings.

places occasional joint meetings for worship were held, as in Germantown, Pa., and at Westbury, N. Y. Such manifestations of unity in worship have developed with great rapidity in the last quarter of a century.

In many Eastern cities and universities "independent" meetings have come into existence, composed of members belonging to different branches of the Society. Some of the early examples of such were at Buffalo and Cornell University, N. Y., Cambridge, Mass., Montclair and New Brunswick, N. J., State College, Pittsburgh and Chestnut Hill, Pa. These meetings made the problem of unity acute. The members did not, as a rule, want to sever official connection with the work of their own branch of Friends. It did not seem courteous to compel new members, who had no interest in the Society's divisions, to choose between its meaningless branches. Some of these mixed meetings solved the problem by incorporating as independent monthly meetings; others were content to remain as unofficial meetings; in both cases the members retained an absentee membership in their own branch. A few joined the yearly meeting to which the majority belonged and in the territory of which they were situated. In New York Yearly Meeting a plan was adopted by which such joint meetings may belong to both yearly meetings reporting to both and their members being reckoned as full members of both.[4] There were in 1935 about fifty-eight such united and independent meetings in the United States.[5] In 1940 the number had increased to seventy.

In 1935 the Friends Fellowship Council was organized by the American Friends Service Committee to care for

---

[4] In New York and Philadelphia there are cases where persons hold membership in the local monthly meeting of both branches.

[5] See the lists in the *Handbook of the Religious Society of Friends,* 1935 and 1941. Many of these are seasonal or otherwise unstable groups, at winter resorts or at universities. Others are groups which prefer "silent" meetings although situated near Friends of the "pastoral" type.

these independent and united meetings, with authority to set up monthly meetings where connection with an established yearly meeting was not practicable.

The steadfast attitude of Friends during the first and second World Wars, their work of relief, reconstruction and rehabilitation, their peace activities and provision for conscientious objectors secured the sympathetic interest and coöperation of many non-Friends, some of whom coveted fellowship with Friends, but were prevented from joining the Society because of geographical isolation or because they had important positions or opportunities in other denominations. For the benefit of these the Wider Quaker Fellowship was organized in 1935 under the Friends Fellowship Council. In 1941 the membership grew to about 1900.

After a little more than a century of separation in America, unity is acknowledged in principle, and coöperation prevails in a large measure in practice, where these conditions are most important, *i.e.,* where members of two of the largest branches of Friends are situated close together. It is significant and promising of future progress toward unity, that progress has been most rapid where the two bodies know each other best. The real difficulty today is with the large body of Orthodox Friends in the middle and far West, who do not know Hicksite Friends except through an ancient and distorted tradition, and where the Evangelical fear of unsoundness still operates to a considerable extent as a barrier to reunion.

On the other side of the picture there developed after the First World War some centrifugal tendencies toward disunity and division. These are chiefly due to the recrudescence of Evangelical and other fundamentalist types of theology. *The Evangelical Friend,* which was established in 1905 at Cleveland, Ohio, as the organ of this tendency, made vigorous onslaughts on the alleged unsoundness of *The American Friend;* it voiced the demand that all "unsoundness" be removed from the ministry and all "modern thought" rooted out of the colleges.[6] Requests were received from Kansas, Western and California Yearly Meetings by the Five Years Meeting of 1912 for a decision whether George Fox's Letter and the Richmond Declaration of Faith were corporate parts of the Uniform Discipline. These requests were prompted by a growing fear of doctrinal unsoundness on the part of the Evangelicals. Many of the yearly meetings had adopted the Discipline with the express understanding that these documents were part of the disciplinary statement of the beliefs of Friends. The Five Years Meeting adopted the following interpretation: "These documents are historic statements of belief, approved by the Five Years Meeting in 1902, as expressed in the clause of the Discipline referred to and approved again at this time, 1912, but they are not to be regarded as constituting a creed."[7]

The Five Years Meeting at this time took over the management of the *American Friend.* It was to be published in Richmond, Ind., and S. Edgar Nicholson was chosen editor to succeed Rufus M. Jones, who turned over his interest in the paper to the Five Years Meeting. By agreement the *Evangelical Friend* was to be discontinued as a weekly periodical. These measures allayed Evangelical discontent at the time and before long the attention of Friends was turned to problems created by the First World War.

The Young Friends movement which was officially recognized as a department of the Five Years Meeting[8] in 1912 became one of the most effective and promising agencies for

---

[6] About this time an effort was made in Ohio Yearly Meeting to establish a college whose motto should be "Holiness to the Lord" and in which the teaching should be free from all taint of modern error. *Min.*, 1902, pp. 8, 17. See *Evangelical Friend,* II (1906), p. 802; III (1907), pp. 1, 2, 36, 817.

[7] *Min.*, 1912, p. 49.

[8] *Ibid.*, pp. 59–76.

the restoration of a definite and distinctive Quaker consciousness. The beginnings of the movement were in Friends' connection with the Christian Endeavor movement, which turned them toward the study of Quaker principles and history, by the pledge of denominational loyalty which the Christian Endeavor exacts. This reaction toward our historical position has been greatly aided by contacts with the young Friends' leaders in England and the eastern "non-pastoral" yearly meetings.[9]

In the period following the First World War tendencies toward coöperation in movements for church unity continued to receive the support of both English and American Friends. The Five Years Meeting had already joined the Federal Council of Churches of Christ in America in 1907. Although London Yearly Meeting has not joined the National Council of Evangelical Free Churches, Friends meetings in many localities are associated and two Friends have been national presidents of it. English Friends were also active in the post-war "Copec" conference.

Friends representing the Five Years Meeting, Philadelphia (O), and London and Dublin yearly meetings were active in the Ecumenical Movement, beginning with the Edinburgh Foreign Missionary Conference (1910), from which it took its rise; and these bodies were officially represented at the Stockholm (1925) and Oxford (1937) Conferences on "Life and Work" and at the Lausanne (1927) and Edinburgh (1937) Conferences on "Faith and Order." Friends and several other smaller denominations were represented by the author at the Utrecht Advisory Conference (1938) which prepared the constitution for the proposed World Council of Churches.

In all denominations the World War stimulated premillenarian and Adventist types of thought tremendously,

---

[9] See especially the report of the Commission on Young People's Activities, *Min.*, 1912, pp. 180–205.

and Friends shared in these movements. This was manifested especially by an increase in the number and activity of the training schools which are centers of this type of Quakerism or which are patronized by Friends. Haviland Academy (Kan.) and Greenleaf Academy (Idaho) were transformed into religious "training schools"; and after the World War the Union Bible Seminary (Westfield, Ind.) greatly enlarged its influence. There were extensive changes in the personnel of the faculty at the Cleveland Bible Institute. *The Friends' Minister,* published at the Union Bible Seminary (Westfield, Ind.), increased its circulation among Friends in the middle West, and though it changed its name to *The Gospel Minister,* it remained in effect a successor to the *Evangelical Friend,*[10] as the organ of the ultra-Evangelical wing of Quakerism.

There was a period of quiescence after the effort at the Five Years Meeting of 1912 to incorporate the Richmond Declaration of Faith in the Uniform Discipline as a standard of doctrine; but about 1920 a concerted demand was made for a revision of the minute of 1912 by omitting the phrase "but they are not to be regarded as constituting a creed." Attacks were made in print and in public speech on certain Friends' educational institutions, on leaders of the Five Years Meeting, and the Forward Movement, as well as on the American Friends Service Committee, the London All-Friends Conference and all tendencies toward coöperation and union with other branches of the Society. In 1920 a powerful movement to have Oregon Yearly Meeting secede from the Five Years Meeting barely failed. The same year Indiana Yearly Meeting was induced to appoint a committee (to which members from Western were later added) to investigate the soundness of the teaching at Earlham College. There were also threats of

---

10 In 1927 *The Evangelical Friend* was revived, as the official organ of Ohio Yearly Meeting, and is now published monthly at Damascus, O.

investigations of the soundness of *The American Friend* and of the heads of several of the departments of the Five Years Meeting. As a concession to the Evangelical group in the interest of unity, the Five Years Meeting of 1922 omitted the offending phrase in the minute of 1912.

In 1925 Oregon Yearly Meeting withdrew its financial support of the boards of the Five Years Meeting because it would not remove certain secretaries regarded as "unsound." In 1926 it formally withdrew from the Five Years Meeting. In 1937 Kansas Yearly Meeting withdrew from support of the work of The American Friends Board of Foreign Missions because the latter accepted missionary candidates who were regarded as not sound by the yearly meeting board of missions, and the yearly meeting withdrew from the Five Years Meeting in 1937.[11] These yearly meetings have undertaken independent missionary work; Kansas in the Belgian Congo in Africa, and Oregon in Bolivia. These withdrawals, however, have caused no great disturbance in the Society. Epistles continue to be sent by the yearly meetings belonging to Five Years Meeting to these yearly meetings, whose status is therefore analogous to that of Ohio (O).[12]

These setbacks to the movements toward unity are apparently only temporary. There were large and influential elements and leaders in both yearly meetings opposed to secession from the Five Years Meeting. These elements are, judging from the course of events in yearly meetings further east, likely to grow in influence. They comprise the young Friends, the educational leaders and those most interested in the revival of the historic Friends' ideals.

Since the First World War there have been tendencies to co-ordinate the purposes and programs of the Society on a

---

11 *Min. Five Years Meeting,* 1927.

12 In 1926 a group of Evangelicals separated from Western Yearly Meeting in Indiana and established Central Yearly Meeting. It reported 829 members for 1940. See *Handbook,* 1941, p. 66.

world-wide scale. In 1920 there was held in London an All-Friends Conference, promoted largely by British Friends, the purpose of which was to reconsider the historic testimony of Friends in the light of the war experiences and the post-war problems. Various topics were studied by commissions appointed in advance and the conference based its proceedings on their reports.[13] The discussions covered a wider range than the original purpose of the conference indicated.[14] It was the most representative conference of Friends since the Richmond Conference of 1887. In connection with it a Young Friends Conference was held at Old Jordans and many of the delegates attended a conference at Keble College, Oxford, on the application of Christianity to the social order.

In 1929 an All-American Friends Conference was held under the auspices of the American Friends Service Committee at Penn College. It was originally intended to be held at Friends University but owing to vigorous opposition on the part of Kansas Evangelicals to inviting Hicksite representatives, the place of meeting was changed. Some English Friends were present unofficially.[15] The chief value of the conference lay in the mitigation of prejudice through personal acquaintance and frank discussion, especially between Evangelical and Hicksite Friends on one side and pastoral and non-pastoral Friends on the other.

The post-war years were a period of great changes in methods, outlook and activities in all branches of Friends. The international centers which were established in various parts of the world as a result of Friends' foreign service, superadded to the results of Friends' foreign missionary work created a world-wide Quakerism. J. Passmore Elkin-

---

[13] *Handbook,* 1941, p. 33.

[14] An important event during the conference was the purchase by the American delegates of the original MS of George Fox's *Journal* for the Friends Library, then at Devonshire House, London.

[15] See the published *Proceedings.*

ton of Philadelphia Yearly Meeting who comes of a Quaker family of wide interests and who has travelled extensively among Friends,[16] conceived the idea of a world conference of Friends, which was held at Swarthmore and Haverford colleges in September 1937 under the auspices of the American Friends Service Committee. Much of the success of the plan to secure world-wide representation was due to the faithful work of his wife, Anna Griscom Elkinton, chairman of the committee of arrangements, and of Leslie D. Shaffer, its secretary. The studies and reports of preparatory commissions provided the principal topics for the discussions, and the committee of arrangements prepared a valuable *Handbook of the Religious Society of Friends* in advance.[17] All branches of Friends were represented by appointed or by unofficial representatives. The presence of representatives from so many races and nations brought a vivid realization that Quakerism was no longer merely an Anglo-Saxon sect but a world-wide movement. The conference decided to establish a Friends World Committee for Consultation as a means for more effective coöperation of Friends in all parts of the world as need might arise.[18] The Conference also recommended the establishment of a Quaker goodwill center in Shanghai, China.

The Five Years Meeting of 1940 met under the shadow of the Second World War abroad and of peace-time conscription at home. There was a fine spirit of unity. Few English fraternal delegates were present on account of the war-blockade, but there was a large fraternal delegation

---

16 His grandfather was Joseph S. Elkinton, the leader in settling the Russian Doukhobours in Kansas and Canada. His father, Joseph Elkinton, travelled widely in the ministry and died in England. His aunt, Mary E. Nitobe was the wife of Inazo Nitobe, a Japanese Quaker and a member of the Secretariat of the League of Nations.

17 *Handbook of the Religious Society of Friends,* Philadelphia, 1935.

18 The Committee has promoted better mutual understanding. It was represented at the establishment of Jamaica Yearly Meeting, 1941, and undertook the preparation of the 1941 *Handbook.*

from Kansas and from Philadelphia (O). Individuals and delegates with minutes from meetings in Oregon and in the Friends General Conference were welcomed and given the privilege of the floor without discrimination or protest. It reaffirmed Friends' ancient peace testimony, approved measures to care for American conscientious objectors and for relief work in Europe, and authorized the establishment of Jamaica Yearly Meeting in 1941.

After the Nazi government of Germany began its persecution of Jews and liberals, the Quaker centers in Europe were able to render valuable service in aiding refugees to escape from Germany, Austria and other conquered and occupied countries. The Friends Service Council in London and the American Friends Service Committee aided great numbers of refugees to obtain visas, passage money, and positions in other lands.

The outbreak of the Second World War in 1939 found English Friends better prepared for the emergencies it created than in 1914. The Friends Service Council was still functioning and other organizations were easily revived, among them the Friends Ambulance Unit. The draft laws were more considerate of pacifist consciences than in 1916, and the tribunals were more favorable in administering the law. Young Friends divided about as in the First World War; some were given absolute or conditional exemption; a few refused to accept the decision of the tribunals and went to prison; a number accepted non-combatant or combatant military service.

When the United States adopted the Selective Service Act of 1940, it provided for exemption from military service for conscientious objectors because of religious belief or training, on condition that they perform service of national importance under civilian direction. The American Friends Service Committee, acting with other religious organizations, secured approval of the Director of the Selective Service for civilian public service camps for those who would not accept even non-combatant service under military control. These camps provided for work on projects set by the National Forestry or Park Services and also for the study of the implications of Christianity for citizenship, especially in its constructive aspects.

BIBLIOGRAPHY AND SYMBOLS

B.

Bancroft, George, *Report in the Case of Earl vs Wood and others,* Boston, 1855.

Barclay, A. R., *Collection of Letters, etc. in Friends Library,* London, 1841.

Barclay, *Apology* — Barclay, Robert, *An Apology for the True Christian Divinity* (no place), 1678.

————, *Truth Triumphant through the Spiritual Warfare, etc., of Robert Barclay,* 3 vols., London, 1717–1718.

Barclay, *Inner Life* — Barclay, Robert (the younger), *The Inner Life of the Religious Societies of the Commonwealth.* London, 1876.

Beck, William, *The Friends: Who They Are and What They Have Done.* London, 1893.

Beck, William and Ball, T. F., *The London Friends' Meetings,* London, 1869.

Besse, *Sufferings* — Besse, Joseph, *A Collection of the Sufferings of the People Called Quakers from 1650–1689.* 2 vols., London, 1753.

Bishop, George, *New England Judged by the Spirit of the Lord,* London, 1661.

Bowden, *History* — Bowden, James, *History of the Society of Friends in America.* 2 vols. London, 1850–54.

Brailsford, Mabel R., *A Quaker from Cromwell's Army: James Nayler,* N. Y., 1927.

Braithwaite, Joseph Bevan, *Joseph Bevan Braithwaite, A Friend of the Nineteenth Century,* by his children, London, 1909.

————, *Memoirs of Joseph John Gurney, etc.,* 2 vols., Philadelphia, 1854.

BBQ — Braithwaite, William C., *The Beginnings of Quakerism,* London, 1912.

BSPQ — ————, *The Second Period of Quakerism,* London, 1919.

Brayshaw, A. Neave, *The Quakers: Their Story and Message,* London, 3d ed., 1938.

Brayshaw, *Personality* — ————, *The Personality of George Fox,* London, 1933.

Brinton, *Quaker Education* — Brinton, Howard H., *Quaker Education in Theory and Practice,* Wallingford, Pennsylvania, 1940.

Brookes, George S., *Friend Anthony Benezet,* Philadelphia, 1937.

Brooks, Sydney, *America and Germany,* New York, 1925.

Bunyan, John, *Complete Works of John Bunyan,* edited by George Offor. 3 vols., London, 1862.

Burnyeat, *Journal* — Burnyeat, John, *The Truth Exalted,* London, 1691.

Burrough, *Works* — Burrough, Edward, *The Memorable Works, etc., of Edward Burrough,* London, 1672.

C.

Cartland, F. G., *Southern Heroes; or Friends in War Times,* Cambridge, 1895.

Child, L. M., *Isaac T. Hopper: A True Life,* Boston, 1853.

Clark, Dougan, *Life of David B. Updegraff,* Cincinnati, 1895.

————, *The Offices of the Holy Spirit,* Philadelphia, 1879.

Coffin, Addison, *Life and Travels of Addison Coffin,* Cleveland, 1897.

Coffin, Levi, *Reminiscences of Levi Coffin,* Cincinnati, 1876.

London *Epistles* — *A Collection of the Epistles from the Yearly Meeting of Friends in London, etc.,* Baltimore, 1806.

Comly, *Journal* — Comly, John, *Journal of the Life and Religious Labors of John Comly,* Philadelphia, 1853.

Comstock, Elizabeth L., *Life and Letters of Elizabeth L. Comstock,* compiled by her sister, C. Hare, Philadelphia, 1895.

Crewdson, Isaac, *Religious Declensions, etc.,* Manchester, 1829.

————, *The Doctrine of the New Testament on Prayer,* London, 1831.

————, *A Beacon to the Society of Friends,* London, 1836.

————, *A Defense of the Beacon,* London, 1836.

————, *Water Baptism, an Ordinance of Christ,* London, 1837.

————, *The Trumpet Blows or an Appeal to Society of Friends,* London, 1838.

————, *Observations on the New Birth,* Manchester, 1840.

Croese, Gerard, *The General History of the Quakers, etc.,* London, 1696.

Crosfield, George, *Memoirs of Samuel Fothergill,* Liverpool, 1843.

Curti, M. E., *The American Peace Crusade, 1815–1860,* Durham, N. C., 1929.

D.

Davies, Richard, *An Account of the Convincement of Richard Davies,* London, 1794.

Dewees, Watson, *History of Westtown Boarding School 1799–1899,* Philadelphia, 1899.

Dorland, Arthur G., *History of the Society of Friends (Quakers) in Canada,* Toronto, 1927.

E.

Earle, Thomas, *Life of Benjamin Lundy,* Philadelphia, 1847.

Edgerton, Walter, *History of the Anti-Slavery Separation in Indiana Yearly Meeting,* Cincinnati, 1856.

Edmundson, William, *A Journal of the Life, etc., of William Edmundson,* London, 1774.

Edwards, Thomas, *The First and Second Part of Gongraena, etc.,* London, 1646.

Ellwood, *Life* — Ellwood, Thomas, *A History of Thomas Ellwood, etc.,* London, 1886.

————, *Rogero-Mastix: A Rod for William Rogers in Return for his Riming Scourge, etc.,* 1685.

Emden, Paul H., *Quakers in Commerce,* London, 1940.

Emmott, Elizabeth Braithwaite, *A Short History of Quakerism (Earlier periods),* N. Y., 1923.

Evans, *Exposition* — Evans, Thomas, *Exposition of the Faith of the Society of Friends.* Philadelphia, 1827.

F.

Fox, Margaret Fell, *A Brief Collection etc. Relating to the Life and Services etc. of Margaret Fell Fox,* London, 1710.

FPT — *First Publishers of Truth,* edited by Norman Penney, London, 1907.

Fogelklou, Emilia, *James Nayler: the Rebel Saint,* London, 1931.

Forster, William, *Memoirs of William Forster,* edited by Benjamin Seebohm, 2 vols., London, 1865.

Foster, *Report* — Foster, Jeremiah H., *An Authentic Report of the Testimony in a Cause of Issue in the Court of Chancery of the State of New Jersey, etc.,* 2 vols., Philadelphia, 1831.

Fox, *Epistles* — Fox, George, *A Collection of Many Epistles, etc., of George Fox,* London, 1698.

Bicent. Journal — ————, *A Journal or Historical Account of the Life, etc., of George Fox,* Bicentenary edition, London, 1891.

Camb. Journal ————, *The Journal of George Fox,* edited by Norman Penney from the MSS., 2 vols., Cambridge, 1911.

Short Journal ————, *The Short Journal and Itinerary Journal of George Fox,* edited by Norman Penney, Cambridge, 1925.

GTD ————, *Gospel Truth Demonstrated, in a collection of Doctrinal Books, etc.,* London, 1706.

Frame, Nathan T., and Esther G., *Reminiscences of Nathan T. and Esther G. Frame,* Cleveland, 1907.

Friends Library *Friends Library,* edited by William and Thomas Evans, 14 vols., Philadelphia, 1837–1850.

Fry, Anna Ruth, *A Quaker Adventure: the Story of Nine Years Relief and Reconstruction,* London, 1926.

G.

Gilbert, Dorothy Lloyd, *Guilford, A Quaker College,* Greensboro, N. C., 1937.

Graham, John William, *Conscription and Conscience,* London, 1922.

Green, J. R., *History of the English People,* 4 vols., London, 1878.

Grellet, *Memoirs* Grellet, Stephen, *Memoirs of the Life and Gospel Labors of Stephen Grellet,* edited by Benjamin Seebohm, Philadelphia, 1860.

Grubb, Edward, *The Historic and the Inward Christ,* London, 1914.

————, *Separations, Their Causes and Effects,* London, 1914.

Gummere, Amelia, M., *The Quaker: A Study in Costume,* Philadelphia, 1901.

————, *The Journal and Essays of John Woolman,* London, 1922.

Gurney, *Essays* Gurney, J. J., *Essays on the Evidences, Doctrines and Practical Operation of Christianity,* Philadelphia, 1840.

H.

Hallowell, A. D., *Life and Letters of James and Lucretia Mott,* New York, 1884.

Hallowell, Richard P., *The Quaker Invasion of Massachusetts,* New York, 1887.

Handbook of the Religious Society of Friends, Philadelphia, 1935 and 1941.

Hare, Augustus J. C., *The Gurneys of Earlham,* New York, 1895.

Harvey, T. Edmond, *The Rise of the Quakers,* London, 1905.

Hay, Alexander H., *The Pastoral System among Friends,* Haverford College, 1938. (M. A. thesis, unpublished.)

Heath, E. Margaret, *The Story of Lucy Stone: Pioneer,* London, 1935.

Hicks, Edward, *Memoirs of the Life and Religious Labors of Edward Hicks,* Philadelphia, 1851.

Hicks, Elias, *A Doctrinal Epistle,* New York, 1834.

Hicks, *Journal* ————, *Journal of the Life and Religious Labors of Elias Hicks,* Philadelphia, 1828.

————, *The Quaker,* 4 vols., Philadelphia, 1827–28.

Hobhouse, Stephen Henry, *Joseph Sturge, His Life and Work,* London, 1919.

Hobley, E. F., and Mercer, T. W., *The Adult School Movement,* London, 1910.

Hodgkin, Henry T., *Friends Beyond the Seas,* London, 1916.

Hodgkin, Thomas, *George Fox,* New York, 1896.

Hodgson, *History* Hodgson, William, *The Society of Friends in the Nineteenth Century: A Historical View of the Successive Convulsions and Schisms therein during the Period,* 2 vols., Philadelphia, 1876.

Howgill, *Works* Howgill, Francis, *Dawnings of the Gospel Day, etc.,* London, 1672.

Hull, W. I., *William Penn and the Dutch Quaker Migration to Pennsylvania,* Swarthmore, 1935.

————, *Willem Sewel of Amsterdam, etc.,* Swarthmore, 1933.

J.

Janney, Samuel M., *History of the Religious Society of Friends, from its Rise to the Year 1828,* Philadelphia, 1859–68.

————, *The Life of William Penn, with Selections from his Correspondence and Autobiography,* Philadelphia, 1852.

————, *An Examination of the Causes which Led to the Separation of the Religious Society of Friends in America, 1827–28,* Philadelphia, 1868.

Jay, Allen, *Autobiography of Allen Jay,* Philadelphia, 1910.

Johnson, Mrs. Mary (Coffin) and Coffin, P. B., *Charles F. Coffin, A Quaker Pioneer,* Richmond, Indiana, 1923.

Jones, Lester M., *Quakers in Action,* New York, 1929.

Jones, Louis T., *Quakers of Iowa,* Iowa City, 1914.

Jones, Mary H., *Swords into Ploughshares; an Account of the American Friends Service Committee, 1917–1937,* New York, 1937.

Jones, Rufus M., *A Dynamic Faith,* Philadelphia, 1902.

————, *Eli and Sybil Jones: Their Life and Work,* Philadelphia, 1889.

————, *George Fox, an Autobiography,* Philadelphia, 1903.

JLPQ ————, *The Later Periods of Quakerism,* 2 vols., London, 1921.

JQAC ————, Sharpless, Isaac, and Gummere, Amelia M., *The Quakers in the American Colonies,* London, 1911.

———, *A Service of Love in Wartime,* New York, 1920.

———, *The Trail of Life in the Middle Years,* New York, 1934.

———, *Studies in Mystical Religion,* London, 1923.

———, *Spiritual Reformers in the 16th and 17th Centuries,* London, 1914.

K.

Kelsey, Rayner W., *Friends and the Indians, 1655 to 1917,* Philadelphia, 1917.

Kersey, Jesse, *A Treatise on Fundamental Doctrines of the Christian Religion,* Concord, Pennsylvania, 1818.

Klain, Zora, *Educational Activities of New England Quakers,* Philadelphia, 1928.

———, *Quaker Contributions to Education in North Carolina,* Philadelphia, 1924.

Knight, F. A., *A History of Sidcot School,* London, 1908.

L.

Leslie, Charles, *The Snake in the Grass,* London, 1696.

———, *A Second Scourge for George Whitehead, or a Switch for the Snake,* London, 1702.

Lossing, John Benson, *History of England,* New York, 1871.

Lubbock, Percy, *Earlham,* London, 1930.

M.

Macaulay, Thomas B., *The History of England from the Accession of James II,* 5 vols., New York, 1879.

McCadden, Joseph J., *Education in Pennsylvania, 1801–1835, and its Debt to Roberts Vaux,* Philadelphia, 1937.

McDaniel, E. H., *The Contribution of the Society of Friends to Education in Indiana,* Indianapolis, 1939.

Mekeel, Arthur Jacob, *Quakerism and a Creed,* Philadelphia, 1936.

Mills, Joseph Travis, *John Bright and the Quakers,* London, 1935.

Milton, John, *Prose Works of John Milton, with a Life of the Author,* edited by Charles Symons, 2 vols., London, 1806.

N.

Nayler, *Works* — Nayler, James, *A Collection of Sundry Books, etc., by James Nayler,* London, 1716.

Neill, Edward D., *Virginia Carolorum,* Albany, 1886.

Newman, Henry Stanley, *Memories of Stanley Pumphrey,* New York, 1883.

O.

Oldmixon, John, *History of England during the Reigns of the Royal House of Stuart,* London, 1730.

Osborn *Jour.* — Osborn, Charles, *Journal of that Faithful Servant of Christ, Charles Osborn,* Cincinnati, 1854.

P.

Paley, William, *A View of the Evidences of Christianity,* New York, 1814.

Pickard, Samuel Thomas, *Life and Letters of John Greenleaf Whittier,* 2 vols., New York, 1894.

Pinkham, William P., *The Lamb of God,* Cleveland, 1899.

Priestley, Joseph, *A History of the Corruptions of Christianity,* Rutt ed., London, 1818.

Q.

Quaker Biographies, edited by the Book Committee of Philadelphia Yearly Meeting, 10 vols., Philadelphia, 1909.

R.

Richard, Henry, *Memoirs of Joseph Sturge,* London, 1864.

Richardson, Caroline Francis, *English Preachers and Preaching, 1640–1670,* New York, 1928.

Robinson, Charles H., *History of Christian Missions,* New York, 1915.

Robinson, William, *Friends of a Half Century, etc.,* London, 1891.

Rowntree, John Stephenson, *Quakerism Past and Present,* London, 1859.

Rowntree, J. W., and Binns, Henry, *The History of the Adult School Movement,* London, 1903.

Rowntree, J. W., *Man's Relation to God,* Philadelphia, 1919.

——— *Present Day Papers,* 4 vols., York, 1898–1904.

Scattergood, Thomas, *Journal of the Life and Religious Labors of Thomas Scattergood,* Philadelphia, N.D.

S.

Scott, Job, *Journal of the Life, Travels, and Gospel Labors of Job Scott,* New York, 1798.

Semi-Centennial Anniversary of Western Yearly Meeting of Friends Church, Plainfield, Ind. 1908.

Sewell, *History* — Sewell, William, *A History of the Rise, Increase and Progress of the Christian People Called Quakers,* 2 vols., London, 1725.

Siebert, W. H., *The Underground Railroad,* Washington, 1896.

Sippel, Theodor, *Werdendes Quäkertum,* Stuttgart, 1937.

Smith, Hannah Whitall, *The Unselfishness of God, and How I Discovered It; A Spiritual Autobiography,* New York, 1903.

Smith, *Catalogue* — Smith, Joseph, *A Descriptive Catalogue of Friends' Books,* 2 vols., London, 1867.

————, *Bibliotheca Anti-Quakeriana or A Catalogue of Books Adverse to the Society of Friends, etc.,* London, 1873.

Smith, Patrick, *A Preservative against Quakerism,* London, 1732.

T.

Tallack, William, *George Fox, the Friends and the Early Baptists,* London, 1868.

Tatham, Meaburn, and Miles, J. E., *Friends Ambulance Unit, 1914–1919: A Record,* London, 1920.

Thistlewaite, W., *Lectures on the Rise and Progress of Friends,* London, 1865.

Thomas, *History* — Thomas, Allen C., and Thomas, Richard Henry, *A History of Friends in America,* 8th edition, Philadelphia, 1930.

Thomas, A. B., *The Story of Baltimore Yearly Meeting from 1672–1938,* Baltimore, 1938.

Timbres, Rebecca Janney, *We Didn't Ask Utopia, a Quaker Family in Soviet Russia,* New York, 1939.

Timothy Nicholson, Testimonial in Honor of, Richmond, Ind., 1908.

Tourgee, Albion W., *A Fool's Errand, by One of the Fools,* New York, 1879.

Traill, Henry Duff, *Social England,* 6 vols., London, 1901–04.

Trevelyan, George Macaulay, *England Under the Stuarts,* 17th ed., New York, 1938.

————, *Life of John Bright,* New York, 1913.

W.

Weeks, Stephen B., *Southern Quakers and Slavery,* Baltimore, 1896.

Wheeler, Daniel, *Memoirs of the Life and Gospel Labors of Daniel Wheeler,* London, 1842.

Whitehead, George, *The Christian Progress of George Whitehead, etc.,* London, 1725.

Whiting, John, *Persecution Exposed,* London, 1715.

Whitney, Janet Payne, *Elizabeth Fry; Quaker Heroine,* Boston, 1936.

Whittier, John Greenleaf, *Writings of John Greenleaf Whittier,* Cambridge Press, 1888, 7 vols.

Wilbur, John, *A Narrative and Exposition of the Late Proceedings of New England Yearly Meeting,* New York, 1845.

Woodard, Luke, *Sketches of a Life of 75,* Richmond, Indiana, 1907.

Woodward, Walter C., *Timothy Nicholson: Master Quaker,* Richmond, Indiana, 1927.

Wright, *Literary Life* — Wright, Luella Margaret, *The Literary Life of the Early Friends, 1650–1725,* New York, 1932.

Minutes of meetings, proceedings of conferences and of similar gatherings are not included in this bibliography.

PERIODICALS

American Friend, The, Philadelphia, 1894–1912. Richmond, Indiana, 1913–

British Friend, The, London, 1843–1913.

BFHA — *Bulletin of the Friends Historical Association,* Philadelphia, 1906–

Evangelical Friend, The, 1905–1914.

Friend, The, Philadelphia, 1827–

Friends Intelligencer, The, Philadelphia, 1844–

Friends Review, The, Philadelphia, 1847–1894.

Irish Friend, The, Belfast, 1837–1842.

JFHS — *Journal of the Friends Historical Society,* London, 1903–

Yorkshireman, The, Pontefract, 1833–1837.

The following American publications ran to more than two volumes:

The Friend or Advocate of Truth, Philadelphia, 1828–1830.

Friends Miscellany, edited by John and Isaac Comly, Philadelphia, 1831–1839.

Miscellaneous Repository, edited by Elisha Bates, Mt. Pleasant, Ohio, 1827–1836.

The Gospel Expositor, edited by Dougan Clark, Columbus, Ohio, 1883–1885.

A list of Quaker periodicals throughout the world is given in the *Handbook of the Religious Society of Friends,* 1941, pp. 100–102.

G

H

I

J

L

M

P

S

U